A BIBLIOGRAPHY
OF AFRICANA

CONTRIBUTIONS IN
LIBRARIANSHIP AND INFORMATION SCIENCE

Series Editor: *Paul Wasserman*

Urban Analysis for Branch Library System Planning
Robert E. Coughlin, François Taieb, and Benjamin H. Stevens

Frontiers in Librarianship: Proceedings of the Change Institute, 1969
School of Library and Information Services, University of Maryland

Subject Retrieval in the Seventies: New Directions. An International Symposium
Hans (Hanan) Wellisch and *Thomas D. Wilson*, Editors

Quantitative Methods in Librarianship: Standards, Research, Management
Irene Braden Hoadley and *Alice S. Clark*, Editors

Public Relations for Libraries: Essays in Communications Techniques
Allan Angoff, Editor

Human Memory and Knowledge: A Systems Approach
Glynn Harmon

Libraries in the Political Scene: Georg Leyh and German Librarianship, 1933-1953
Marta L. Dosa

Information Retrieval and Documentation in Chemistry
Charles H. Davis and *James E. Rush*

Integrative Mechanisms in Literature Growth
Manfred Kochen

A BIBLIOGRAPHY OF AFRICANA

HANS E. PANOFSKY

Contributions in Librarianship and

Information Science, Number 11

Greenwood Press

Westport, Connecticut ● *London, England*

Library of Congress Cataloging in Publication Data

Panofsky, Hans E
  A bibliography of Africana.

  (Contributions in librarianship and information science; no. 11)
  Includes index.
  1. Africa—Bibliography.   I. Title.   II. Series.
  Z3501.P15   016.96   72-823
  ISBN 0-8371-6391-9

Library of Congress Catalog Card Number: 72-823
ISBN: 0-8371-6391-9

First published in 1975

Greenwood Press, a division of Williamhouse-Regency Inc.
51 Riverside Avenue, Westport, Connecticut 06880

Manufactured in the United States of America

To Gianna

When all is said and done, a bibliography is not a bible. It pretends to no authority, either explicit or implied. At best it may serve men as a storehouse and a chest of tools from which each must select for himself those items best suited to his work.

From Karl W. Deutsch and Richard L. Merritt,
Nationalism and National Development.
An Interdisciplinary Bibliography

Contents

PART FIVE
Guide to Resources in African Nations

PART SIX
On Collecting and Disseminating Africana

Acknowledgments

To friends and colleagues at Northwestern University, Northwestern University Library, the Melville J. Herskovits Library of African Studies in the Northwestern University Library, and the Program of African Studies at Northwestern University.

To friends and colleagues elsewhere in the United States, particularly at the Center for Research Libraries, Yale, Indiana, Michigan State, Stanford, Columbia, Roosevelt, and the University of Chicago.

To students and institutions of Africa and in Africa, especially in Britain and Ghana.

To the former assistant in Africana at Northwestern University Library, Beverly Freeman, who typed the manuscript.

To Anne Potter who typed the final draft and to the Program of African Studies at Northwestern who paid for her work.

They all have my sincere thanks.

A BIBLIOGRAPHY
OF AFRICANA

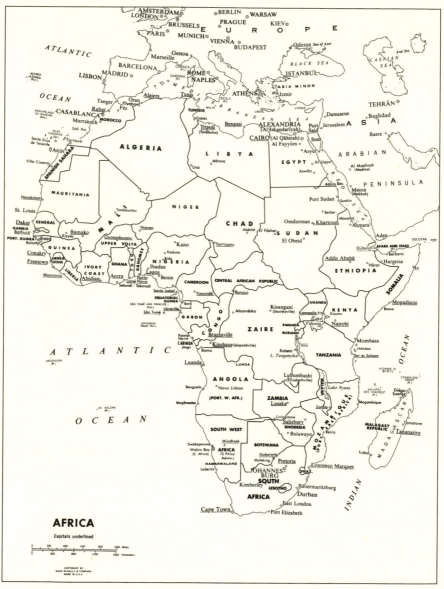

AFRICA

Capitals underlined

Introduction

What is Africana? To some, particularly those in South Africa and England, the word connotes a rare collector's item, usually dealing with European travel and exploration in Africa, one of the many types of publications of interest to antiquarian booksellers. To the present writer, it means any type of publication dealing with Africa and including possibly anything and everything published in Africa. Africana consists of trade publications, scholarly books, government publications, all of which are designed to facilitate the working of governments both directly and indirectly. A statistical publication, for example, should help the work of a planning agency. A comic strip aimed at encouraging citizens to toil harder may, from some points of view, be an even more important piece of ephemera than a statistical publication.[1]

Africana is not limited to the printed and written media, which may be stored and preserved on microform or one of the electronic computer storage devices.[2] It can be motion-picture film, a sound recording on tape, videotape, or any old or new storage device of the audiovisual array of equipment. Data which we can assimilate through touch or smell can, for the foreseeable future, be ignored in a discussion of Africana. It is unfortunate for both current and future scholarship that most university libraries are still restricting their acquisitions to written sources and their various derivatives.

There is in the minds of many as great a confusion about the nature of Africana as there is about African studies. Is it undertaken exclusively in Africa or outside that continent? Is the field of study appropriate just for Africans or blacks? Is it the sole

3

preserve of the social scientist, or does it grudgingly admit scholars in the humanities as well? The growing scholarly strength of indigenous Africans and those in the diaspora elsewhere in the world may change the essence and purport of the field once more. There are also many problems of delimitation. Even from the single point of view of bibliographic organization, when one attempts to organize the literature that has proliferated over the last century or so, one is faced with a severe dilemma of subject versus area. This overview of Africana does not intend to be complete; it is designed to discuss and list worthwhile sources for those who desire to go beyond a summary statement.[3]

The author has attempted to compile a handbook for students of Africa (particularly those with bibliographic needs beyond their own discipline or geographic area of specialization), librarians other than those fully specialized in African bibliography, and, not least, laymen who want to gain more depth on some aspects of Africa.

Increasingly it will become necessary to apologize for one's lack of African ethnicity in one's attempt to deal with African matters. In fact, there is an increasing number of bibliographers and scholars of Africa in Africa. All of them are to some extent area specialists, Africana librarians, or scholars concerned with the production of research tools.

In this guide, I will trace the history and development of African studies throughout the world, particularly in the former colonial countries and in the United States; second, offer a guide to the principal bibliographies and bibliographic sources of Africana; third, describe various types of publications available; and, finally and most importantly, present an extensive inventory of significant (as judged by present demand) and recent publications arranged by discipline and geographic area.

Notes

[1]Valerie Bloomfield, "African Ephemera," in James D. Pearson, and Ruth Jones, eds. *The Bibliography of Africa* (New York: Africana Publishing Corp., 1970), p. 223-239.

[2]For a no longer entirely up-to-date statement, see my "Role of

Microform in the Acquisition and Bibliographical Control of Africana," in Pearson and Jones, eds., *The Bibliography of Africa*, p. 286-309. Very useful is Allen B. Veaner, *Evaluation of Micropublication: A Handbook for Librarians* (Chicago: American Library Association, 1971), and the chapter "Microform Technology" in *Annual Review of Information Service and Technology*, ed. Carlos A. Cuadra (Chicago: Encyclopedia Britannica, 1966-).

   ³This is not even attempted by Peter Duignan, ed., *Guide to Research and Reference Works on Sub-Sahara Africa* (Stanford: Hoover Institution Press [1972], Hoover Institution Bibliographical Series No. 46), 1102 p.

PART ONE

The Study of Africa

If one looks at the twists and turns that the study of Africa has taken through the centuries, one becomes aware of certain patterns that connect scholarly interests with the main economic and ideological preoccupations dominant in the areas from which the studies emanated. One becomes aware of the obvious but underrated fact that the scholarly activity was unilateral and tended to be centered around the organization of knowledge devised by the culture and value system of the scholars rather than around facts and realities of the African continent. It was —and to a great extent still is—a one-way traffic. The ever-changing image of Africa, therefore, is a mirror reflecting the obscure and unconscious motivations of the enquirers.

Among the Greeks, black Africans aroused great respect and were esteemed to be close to the gods. Throughout Greco-Roman antiquity, color was explained by environmental theories, and no stigma was attached to pigmentation. Africa was a natural aggregate of the Mediterranean life-style. On this fascinating subject, which has understandably captured the interest of the African scholars, the following are recommended: Alain Bourgeois, *La Grèce antique devant la Négritude* (Paris: Présence Africaine, 1971), 135 p., and Frank M. Snowden, Jr., *Blacks in Antiquity: Ethiopians in the Greco-Roman Experience* (Cambridge, Mass.: The Belknap Press of Harvard University Press, 1970), 364 p.

During the deep European slumber, the Arab civilization spread through Africa from the sixth century on. The immense amount of scholarly activity conducted by Arabs about and in Africa is only now becoming available to non-Arabic readers.[1] The proselytizing and trading character of the Arab influence was very pervasive. The greatest of Arab historians of Africa was Ibn Batutah (1304-1368), who crossed much of Africa. His reports of his travels have been translated into English by H.A.R. Gibb: Ibn Batutah, *Travels in Asia and Africa, 1325-1354* (London: Routledge and Kegan Paul, 1929), 398 p.

Not until the Renaissance, with its voyaging, pillaging, and colonial activities, did the racial debasement of Africans begin.[2] In order to justify to themselves the trade of human beings as chattel

9

and the appalling acts of savagery that this entailed, the Christian nations of Portugal, Spain, England, and Holland had to convince themselves and others that blacks and Orientals were inferior and bad and had to be rescued from themselves. Combining greed, godliness, and a keen spirit of observation, the Renaissance man, on the verge of mastering scientific enquiry but still susceptible to the obscure fears and beliefs of the Middle Ages, had no trouble in relieving his guilt by projecting on the Africans the evil and savagery he was perpetuating. With the Enlightenment, the Age of Reason, and the loss of religious fervor, Europeans began to look at the "savages" with different eyes, and the image of Africa began a brief reversal. See: Henri Gregoire, *An Enquiry Concerning the Intellectual and Moral Faculties and Literature of Negroes*, trans. D. B. Warden (College Park, Md.: McGrath Publishing, 1967), 253 p. (This is a reprint of the 1810 edition printed by Thomas Kirk in Brooklyn, N.Y.), and Marie Condorcet, Jean Antoine Nicolas, Marquis de Caritat, *Esquisse de tableau historique des progrès de l'esprit humain, suivie de réflexions sur l'esclavage des Nègres* (Paris: Masson, 1822), 440 p. Europeans saw civilization as the corruptor. Only a return to nature, to the primitive state of life, they thought, could guarantee happiness and salvation—and so it was that the myth of the "bon sauvage" was born.

The return of an imperial Europe after the French Revolution and the restoration of the legitimacy of power versus justice inaugurated the colonial period and the scramble for Africa. Again, there is a fundamental ambiguity in the vast literature of this period. On one side, the solitary heroic explorer, scientist, military man, or missionary is bound to Africa emotionally and scientifically embraces the myth of the gift of progress and "civilization"; on the other, he is covering for greed, domination, exploitation, and genocide. (For references to the colonial period, see the section on colonial times below.)

The academic study of Africa in Europe and elsewhere, typically in Germany, used to be a part of Oriental studies. Thus within the reports of the various Oriental congresses will be found papers dealing with Africa.

In this sense African studies today are an offspring of Oriental studies, and the birth of their international academic respectability dates from the twenty-fifth Orientalist congress in Moscow in 1960, where it was felt that African studies should stand on their own.[3] Their great international academic development is linked to area studies, a post World War II nomenclature, although Oriental studies go back to the early nineteenth century.[4]

Anthropology, which was the handmaiden of colonial administration, was that discipline to which most of the early Africanists—a term that received common usage only in the early 1960s—belonged. Gradually, an interest in Africa spread into the other social sciences and then into the humanities.

AREA STUDIES

The underlying rationale for area studies is twofold. The more obvious side is the need for accumulation of information, whether for scholarly or strategic purposes. Second, there is a growing feeling of the scientific inadequacies of the traditional and social disciplines and of their inability to explain current behavior, let alone predict it in the future. There is some hope that an interdisciplinary approach may lead to a greater understanding of the behavior of people, both overseas and at home. Anthropologists in particular hope that those who gain a better understanding of some other culture will comprehend their own civilization, or at least themselves, better.

Those who wish to refer to the military origin of area study programs should consult the experience of at least one midwestern university (Brady, *Foreign Area and Language Study Program at the University of Missouri*)[5] or review a more general statement (Fenton, *Area Studies in American Universities*).[6] Neither publication refers to Africa, but Fenton does mention libraries as being the locus of the seminar and of use to the instructors for information.

One of the best statements concerning area studies is that of Robert B. Hall: "Funds must be available so that library resources can be built up for the area, without regard to disciplinary boundaries."[7]

An interdisciplinary approach underlies area study. This can occur either when scholars of different disciplines (or of different schools within the same discipline) focus on the same geographical area or when the interdisciplinary approach occurs in the mind of the same individual. Just before his death in 1963, Melville J. Herskovits wrote:

It has been said that the research value of an area lies in the fact that it affords a *locus* for the study of problems . . . it is to be thought of as a place that provides those in the behavioral and historical sciences with a laboratory in which they can test their hypotheses. But more than this, it encourages focus on a problem, and there is no problem in the context of area studies that does not impel the student to stray outside the bounds of his discipline.[8]

The notion of Africa or any other developing continent as a laboratory is rightly resented. Some claim that the only justification for being outside one's own geographical area is to do some good there as defined by the people of the host country. This can be what the late Allan Holmberg called "participant intervention." (In Peru, Holmberg and his colleagues from Cornell University had control of a large *hacienda* and brought about improvements; for example, they introduced a better potato seed, thus causing an improvement in levels of nutrition. The ramifications of these effects were studied fully.)[9]

Area studies, certainly in its origins, was less a byproduct of wanting to improve the lot of a people than a tool of social control. It originated ways and means of trying to understand better and hence to govern more effectively persons in distant lands:

An accurate acquaintance with the nature, habits and customs of alien populations is necessary to all who have to live and work among them in any official capacity, whether administrative, executive officers, missionaries or merchants, because in order to deal effectively with any group of mankind it is essential to have the cultural knowledge.[10]

The climax to the area-study approach toward Africa within a colonial environment was the publication of Lord Hailey's *African Survey* (London: Oxford University Press, 1938), probably inspired by a Rhodes Memorial Lecture delivered in Oxford by Jan Christiaan Smuts in 1929.[11] This is not to suggest that the 1956 and 1957 revisions of it, which are still in print, are not of considerable use today for an understanding of Africa's colonial heritage. It is probably the first, and likely the last, attempt to place the diverse aspects of Africa within one volume.

African studies in the United States, if we ignore some wartime activities during World War II at the University of Pennsylvania, dates from the founding of the Program of African Studies at Northwestern University in 1948.[12] Another measuring rod could be the Department of State's *Language and Area Study Programs in American Universities* (1964), which lists sixteen programs. The 1973 issue of *Directory of African Studies in the United States,* issued by the Research Liaison Committee of the African Studies Association (located at Brandeis University), enumerates no fewer than 238 universities and colleges offering courses on Africa.

These many African studies centers have had a large impact on the development of library collections. The increased volume of publications pertaining to Africa has obviously led to the growth of the volume of materials that libraries collect about Africa. Moreover, the existence of African studies centers usually means the offering of courses of instruction and the undertaking of research where books, journals, and other library materials are needed.

The growth of the African ingredient of college and university libraries does not just reflect the existence of formal African studies programs. In addition, it certainly has strengthened the demand for locally available Africana and bibliographical access to the Africana universe. Perhaps a dozen libraries in the United States have special staff members assigned to the acquisition, bibliographical organization, and service to users of Africana.

Many more, of course, perform activities pertaining to Africa as part of their general duties.

The need for a special treatment of Africana has been avoided in most libraries in much the same way as has been the case for Latin Americana. This state of affairs may be expected to endure for the foreseeable future, or for as long as writings on Africa are in European languages.

The integrated handling of Africana with the rest of the collection may be desirable to a considerable degree; yet there is a need for African library specialists (one or more, depending on the size of the institution and the stress it places on Africana). Many institutions will need at least a part-time Africana acquisitions librarian, perhaps one working also on some other part of the Third World. This librarian must know the field of current interest and trend in teaching and research and how these needs can best be satisfied within particular budgetary limitations. The African acquisitions librarian must know about the particular book trade that may be able to satisfy his demands, as well as alternate acquisition channels.

Few institutions can afford a cataloger of Africana; however, specialization in this area is necessary if there is to be intelligent and original cataloging. While an increasing proportion of current imprints in English and, soon, other European languages will be available from the Library of Congress through MARC (Machine-Readable Cataloging), there is always a great deal of antiquarian and current ephemeral material that will be made more easily accessible through the work of a specialist cataloger.

Some public-service librarians should be especially equipped to give reference service for Africana, although all librarians with access to Winchell and/or Walford can give fairly good service.[13] Africanists without access to a special librarian would greatly benefit not only from consulting these guides but from perusing the sources to which the individual references may ultimately lead.

This should not bring anyone to the conclusion that there is no need for area specialist librarians. One needs excellent, competent, and imaginative specialists who, in addition to being able to perform effectively within their profession, are acquainted with the particular problems inherent to collecting and disseminating Africana. They may work as Africana acquisitions librarians, catalogers, reference librarians, curators, or any combination of these functions.

The North American literature of librarianship contains little beyond infrequent journal articles on how Africana is managed in one institution or another.[14] There are, of course, a few exceptions. For example, the October 1959 issue of *Library Trends*, edited by Wilfred J. Plumbe, was devoted entirely to current trends in newly developing countries; it included Helen Conover's "Bibliography of Newly Developing Areas." More than ten years ago (in June 1962), the American Library Association met in Miami; under the chairmanship of David Kaser, the acquisition section of the Resources and Technical Services Division presented a symposium of specialists on acquiring library materials from newly developing areas in the world. These talks were reprinted in *Library Resources and Technical Services*, no. 1 (Winter 1963) and covered almost the entire world. The final example—and no doubt the most profound consideration for area librarianship to date—is the Graduate Library School of the University of Chicago's thirteenth annual conference held from May 20-22, 1965, entitled "Area Studies and the Library."[15]

Area librarianship is one of the branches of special librarianship which has been splendidly analyzed by Eldred Smith in the study sponsored by the Council on Library Resources.[16] The growing volume and complexity of publishing call for a growing number of specialists within libraries to organize and service this material. Cooperation and products of automation free an increasing number of librarians to become library specialists in one or more disciplines or some area of the globe, or, best of all, a combination of discipline and area. The Africana bibliographer must be a librarian who knows something about Africa. This something may have been acquired in the one institution in the United States that offers formal instruction, Indiana University; in Britain at the University of London School of Librarianship or the University of Wales; or, best of all in Africa.[17]

AFRICAN STUDIES PROGRAM

A rapid survey of African studies as it is practiced at present beyond the United States may be helpful to an understanding of African bibliography.

GREAT BRITAIN

In Great Britain, African studies in universities is a more recent development than in the United States. Not surprisingly, a great number of universities offering African studies are in London and Oxford. Three other universities offer specialization within Africa: the University of Birmingham (West Africa), University of Sussex (East Africa), and the University of York (Southern Africa). Significant also is the Centre of African Studies at Edinburgh University.[18] The International African Institute in London is most important for its compilation and analysis of African bibliography. Membership dues, which are $10.00 for individuals and $12.50 for institutions, provide the quarterly *Africa*, published since January 1928. Through 1970, this journal included a "Bibliography of Current Publications" classified into eleven broad categories in the social sciences and humanities; references to monographs and journal articles were included.[19] Since January 1971, a separate *International African Bibliography* has been issued quarterly ($6.40 per annum). Continuing the review of *Africa* it contains well-informed and constructively critical book appraisals and a most useful "Notes and News" section reporting on research activities and publications from all parts of the world. The main part of the journal contains scholarly articles, usually written by anthropologists, often in French. The institute has also issued two African bibliography series: Series A is a regional one and B a subject one. Between 1950 and the end of 1972 the International African Institute also published quarterly *African Abstracts*.[20]

The Royal African Society has issued the quarterly *African Affairs* since 1901. Its content is oriented more toward the political, economic, and popular than that of *Africa*. It contains a useful, short bibliographic section, which is now compiled by D. H. Simpson, the librarian of the Royal Commonwealth Society.

The African Studies Association of the United Kingdom had issued a bulletin three times a year. Now it publishes *African Research and Documentation*.

Students of Africa in Britain and others interested in past accumulations of material have access to some valuable guides. Most significant is *A Guide to Manuscripts and Documents in the British Isles Relating to Africa* (London: Oxford University Press, 1971), compiled by Noel Matthews and M. Doreen Wainright and edited by James D. Pearson. This basic guide, compiled in response to the request of the International Technical Committee for the Guide to the Sources of the History of Africa of the International Council of Archives, directs the student to Africana located in the British Isles.

Academic British institutions concerned with Africa are listed in Merran Fraenkel's compilation, the *International Register of Organisations undertaking Africanist Research in the Social Sciences and Humanities*.

The basic cumulation of the work done at British academic institutions is by the Standing Conference on Library Materials on Africa, *Theses on Africa Accepted by Universities in the United Kingdom and Ireland* (Cambridge: Heffer. 1964), 74 p. This is updated by the annual *United Kingdom Publications and Theses on Africa*, which was started with the volumes for 1963 and 1964 published in 1966.

SCOLMA, the Standing Conference on Library Materials on Africa, appears to maximize the rather limited (by United States standards) financial resources of British institutions concerned with Africa. It is a sharing of responsibilities and a dissemination of information. In fact, British University and other libraries, following the example of the former Farmington Plan in the United States, have agreed to specialize geographically and by subject. For example, Exeter University concentrates on collecting on Ghana. Scholars in Britain, having exhausted their local library resources, may prefer to go to Exeter or borrow from there rather than locate the publication in London or Ghana.

Two journals issued by Cambridge University Press deserve special mention for excellence. *The Journal of African History*, published since 1960 and now issued quarterly, first edited by Roland Oliver and John Fage and currently also by J. R. Gray and Shula Marks, is the scholarly journal of African history. The articles and book reviews, almost always in English, are of a high standard. Frequently, the reviews are frankly critical. The other is *The Journal of Modern African Studies*, a quarterly which began publication in March 1963 and has been edited throughout by David Kimble. It is a little less authoritative and punctual in appearance than *The Journal of African History*. The subtitle is "A Quarterly Survey of Politics, Economics and Related Topics in Contemporary Africa." Included in each issue is a section entitled "Africana" and reviews. Occasional review articles are included. There is a real need for more review articles. Their place has not yet been found in the social sciences.[21]

FRANCE

We turn now to the other major colonizer of Africa: France —where African studies is probably less of a special field than in the Anglo-Saxon world. The Societé des Africanistes has issued its *Journal* since 1931; this publication contains many significant articles by anthropologists. The bibliographical section, which now appears only annually, has become less significant because of the multitude of other sources.

An important journal on Africa published in France is the quarterly *Cahiers d'études africaines*, starting in January 1960 and published by Mouton. Just as *Africa* has an occasional article in French, so the *Cahier d'études africaines* publishes an occasional one in English. Its quality is comparable to the *Journal of Modern African Studies*, though it has a somewhat more scholarly slant.

The main bibliographical work pertaining to Africa performed in France is done by the Centre d'Analyse et de Recherche Documentaires pour l'Afrique Noire, better known by its acronym CARDAN.[22] The early work of CARDAN presented itself as the hope for a breakthrough in the application of modern techniques to bibliographical and data retrieval not only in the social sciences but specifically pertaining to Africana. A lot of good work went on under the sponsorship of the Centre National de la Recherche Scientifique (CNRS), in particular the Section d'Automatique Documentaire.[23] This work rested in part on the pioneering efforts of the late Barbara Kyle[24] and UNESCO's International Committee on Social Science Documentation. Unfortunately, the computerized bibliographic data never were generated beyond a trial period. CARDAN has continued to produce innumerable sheets of bibliographical entries, most of which are kept in the Paris office to enable it to answer the research questions of Francophonic Africanists. The *Fiches analytiques* (analytic cards) and *Fiches signaletiques* (descriptive cards) are issued three times a year with an annual index.

CARDAN also collaborated with the International African Institute in issuing *African Abstracts*, French abstracts or, rather, a complete French edition, *Analyses africanistes*, which began publication in January 1967. This publication ceased with the October 1972 issue.

Other relevant French index cards are those issued by the Fondation Nationale des Sciences Politiques (FNSP), which, since 1959, has issued *Fiches de documentation africaine.*[25]

The *List of French Doctoral Dissertations on Africa, 1884-1961* (Boston: G. K. Hall, 1966, 334 p.) has been compiled by Marion Dinstel, former librarian of the African Documents Center at Boston University Libraries. Theses are arranged by country and/or area and then alphabetically by author; 2,918 titles are entered. There is an author index and a subject index confined to topics considered to be of informational interest. Unfortunately, no attempt has been made to determine in which North American library these theses can be found. The largest collection of foreign doctoral dissertations is probably that of the Center for Research Libraries in Chicago, but it is restricted, unless specifically requested by one of its members, to printed dissertations. These are arranged in one constantly updated alphabet.

Sources for more recent French dissertations follow. The Universités de Paris I et Paris II, Centre de Documentation Africaine, published *Thèses et mémoires africanistes: Departement de droit et économie des pays d'Afrique* (September 1972). With a minor change in title, this publication annually lists theses and dissertations pertaining to Africa produced at the Université de Paris. It includes finished research and research in progress. Most of these research papers are only typed or mimeographed. They are listed by faculty.

Between June 1964 and September 1965, the Société des Africanistes, Centre de Documentation et d'Information, published six issues of *Bulletin d'information*. It listed names of research workers and theses of different types completed and in progress. This bulletin was superseded in 1969 by CARDAN's "Recherche, enseignement documentation africanistes francophones," *Bulletin d'information et de liaison*. The first volume includes the "Inventaire des resources documentaires africanistes à Paris," which lists 129 agencies alphabetically (printed on one side only), giving addresses, names of officials, nature of libraries, titles, and frequency of publications. Each year has: "Bibliographie française sur l'Afrique au sud du Sahara," établie par le Comité Interbibliothèques de Documentation Africaine (CIDA), arranged by country and with author and subject indexes; "Inventaire de thèses et mémoires africanistes de langue française soutenus," a listing of finished research with author and subject index; and "Inventaire de thèses africanistes de langue française en cours," a listing of research in progress, also with author and subject indexes.

BELGIUM

CIDESA, the Centre International de Documentation Economique et Sociale Africaine, has issued since 1963 what is now called "Bulletin d'information sur les recherches dans les sciences humaines concernant l'Afrique" [Bulletin of information on current research on human sciences concerning Africa]. The bulletin lists theses and other research work when they are first announced and later when they are completed. The entries consist of brief abstracts in both English and French and are arranged alphabetically by author. It also includes an index. Since there were merely 156 entries for 1971, this work is obviously highly selective. It appears particularly incomplete with regard to research in progress in the United States.

The other series published by CIDESA is really issued by CEDESA,* the Centre de Documentation Economique et Sociale Africaine, Enquêtes Bibliographique. Seventeen have been issued between 1959 and 1970 on very different topics indeed.

On the whole, there is a low level of mutual awareness between Anglophonic and Francophonic Africanists. UNESCO's International Committee on Social Science Documentation has certainly helped to reduce the gap, and so did the all-too-rare articles in the U.S. *African Studies Bulletin* on Africanists' research in France.[26] Belgium's long relationship with Zaïre has resulted in a great and continuing volume of publications being generated in the former metropolitan country. One of the most significant institutions is the Académie Royale des Sciences d'Outre-mer with its many series of scientific publications in the social and natural sciences, many of which are concerned with Zaïre.

A lot of good work went on in particular in the Musée Royal d'Outre-mer in Tervuren just outside Brussels, a magnificent museum which issues numerous important series of scientific publications, including the annual *Bibliographie ethnographique de l'Afrique sud-saharienne.* This publication started in 1932 (covering the years 1925–1930) and until 1960 was concerned only with the Congo. Olga Boone, the conservateur, was responsible for this publication until 1967.

The giant in Zaïrien bibliography is Theodore Heyse.[27] Very significant work has and is being done by Marcel Walreat.

Another set of fiches that deserves mention is that issued by J. B. Cuyvers, secretaire general of CIDESA. About 1,500 slips a year are issued, intended to be filed according to the Universal Decimal Classification.

Useful to anyone really desiring to understand the numerous cards or fiches that are being issued is René Bureau, "Les services des fiches bibliographiques," in J. D. Pearson and Ruth Jones,

*There is no substantive difference between CIDESA and CEDESA. They may be considered as different imprints of the same publisher.

eds., *The Bibliography of Africa* (New York: African Publishing Corp., 1970).

A great contribution to fiche organization has been the Library of Congress's *Africa South of the Sahara: Index to Periodical Literature, 1900-1970* (Boston: G. K. Hall, 1971).[28] Supplement I, published in 1974, covers the years 1971 and 1972.

SWITZERLAND

Switzerland's connections with Africa should not be underestimated. (This is not the place to discuss the role of Swiss banking and medical facilities as a resource for the leaders of Africa, nor to stress the importance of the Economic Commission for Europe and specialized agencies of the United Nations, such as the International Labour Office and the World Health Organization in Geneva, for African development.) African studies are largely centered in Geneva at the Institut Africain de Genève. Since 1962, a semiannual journal of high quality has been published: *Genève-Afrique [Geneva-Africa]*. Its emphasis is on contemporary social sciences and history. The journal is most hospitable to bibliographical articles; for example, F. Hanspeter Strauch's "La contribution des auteurs suisses à la connaissance de l'Afrique" (vol. 7, 1968), and Bernard Clere and Madeleine Hann's "La croix rouge et l'Afrique: Essai bibliographique" (vol. 9, 1970).

AFRICAN STUDIES IN MODERN AFRICA

Formal education in Africa initially followed a foreign model, particularly in the areas colonized by the French and the British. Francophonic universities in such places as Dakar still follow a curriculum designed in Paris for the French. In the English-speaking universities, many of which initially had a special relationship with the University of London, more was taught about the history and geography of the mother country than about the African homeland of the university. This was in part because the expatriate faculty had studied in Europe and usually knew little about the country where they were teaching, let alone its neighbors.

Since 1960, institutes and programs of African studies have been established in most African countries. There are institutes of African studies at the following African universities: Cameroun, Ghana, Kenya, Ibadan, Ife and Nsukka in Nigeria, Sierra Leone, and Zambia. In Senegal at the Université de Dakar, the Institut Français d'Afrique Noire, founded in 1939, became the Institut Fondamental d'Afrique Noire (IFAN). Similar bodies function on smaller scales in other Francophonic universities of Africa.

Unlike comparable centers and programs in the United States, the institutes—not the departments—appoint their own faculty members. The discipline that is most strongly represented in the institutes of African studies is probably history. An extensive writing and rewriting of African history, done largely by African historians, is taking place. Their work is gradually filtering down into the secondary and primary schools. The major task of the rewriting and publishing of history and other textbooks has been underway for some years in Tanzania, Liberia, and elsewhere.

The Association of African Universities in Accra, Ghana, acts as a clearinghouse for information of mutual interest between African universities. This, of course, covers more than just the field of African studies.

One of the most important cultural events within this field of studies is the International Congress of African Studies. It is hosted in Africa and brings world attention to the continent. The first took place in December 1962 in Accra, the second in Dakar in December 1967, and the third in Addis Ababa in December 1973.[29]

Too recent for consideration in the present volume is: Richard D. Lambert, *Language and Area Studies Review* (Philadelphia: American Academy of Political and Social Science, 1973), 490 p.

Notes

[1]For references on Arabic ties to Africa, see section on North Africa.
[2]C. R. Boxer, *The Portuguese Seaborne Empire, 1415-1825* (London: Hutchinson, 1969) 426 p.; A. Adu Boahen, "The Coming of the Europeans," in *The Horizon History of Africa* (New York: American Heritage Publishing, 1971), p. 305-351.

[3]Melville J. Herskovits, "The Development in Africanist Studies in Europe and America," in Bown Lalage and Michael Crowder, eds., *Proceedings of the First International Congress of Africanists, Accra 1962* (Evanston, Ill.: Northwestern University Press, 1964), p. 29-45.

[4]Usually the origins of area studies are not placed further back than World War II; two writers refer to courses being offered for the study of Latin America at the University of Texas in 1915: Joseph Axelrod and Donald N. Bigelow, *Resources for Language and Area Studies: A Report on an Inventory of the Language and Area Centers Supported by the National Defense Education Act of 1958* (Washington, D.C., American Council on Education, 1962), p. 3.

[5]Thomas A. Brady, *Foreign Area and Language Study Program at the University of Missouri,* University of Missouri Bulletin 46, no. 21, Arts and Science Series No. 2 (Columbia, Mo., 1945), 160 p.

[6]William Nelson Fenton, *Area Studies in American Universities* (Washington, D.C.: American Council of Education, 1947), 89 p.

[7]*Area Studies: With Special Reference to Their Implications for Research in the Social Sciences,* Pamphlet No. 3 (New York: Social Science Research Council, May 1947), p. 45.

[8]Melville J. Herskovits, "Africa and the Problem of Economic Growth," in Melville J. Herskovits and Mitchell Harwitz, eds., *Economic Transition in Africa,* Northwestern University African Studies No. 12 (Evanston, Ill.: Northwestern University Press, 1964), p. 11-12.

[9]This work has not yet and may never be fully written up. See John and Mary Collier, "An Experiment in Applied Anthropology," *Scientific American* 196 (January 1957): 37-45.

[10]Royal Commission on University Education, 1913, cited in Robert Sutherland Rattray, *Ashanti* (London: Oxford University Press, 1923), p. 5.

[11]For a brief statement about the three editions, see Helen F. Conover, *Africa South of the Sahara, A Selected Annotated List of Writings* (Library of Congress, 1963), Item no. 13, p. 4.

[12]*The First Twenty Years, 1948-1968* (Northwestern University Program of African Studies), 1968, 62 p.

¹³Constance M. Winchell, *Guide to Reference Books,* 8th ed. (Chicago: American Library Association, 1967), 741 p. and three supplements; and Arthur John Walford, *Guide to Reference Material,* 2nd. ed., vol. 2: *Philosophy, Psychology Religion, Social Sciences, Geography, Biography and History;* vol. 3: *Generalities, Languages, the Arts and Literature* (London: The Library Association, 1968-1970).

¹⁴An example is Glenn L. Sitzman, "Uganda's University Library," *College and Research Libraries* 29, no. 3, (May 1968): 200-209, 212.

¹⁵ *The Library Quarterly,* vol. 35, no. 4, October 1965; also published as a separate work , edited by Tsuen-Hsuin Tsien and Howard W. Winger, *Area Studies and the Library* (Chicago: The University of Chicago Press, 1966). This author's "African studies and American libraries," p. 96-105, was also issued as Reprint no. 2 by Northwestern University. Program of African Studies.

¹⁶Eldred Smith, "The Specialist Librarian in the Academic Research Library" (May 1971), 52 leaves (typescript). Also note Richard H. Dillon, "The Phantom of the Library: The Creative Subject Specialist," in Caroline Wire, ed., *Library Lectures* 9-16 (Baton Rouge. La.: Louisiana State University Library, 1971), p. 100-115. Rather disappointing is Robert A. Stueart, *The Area Specialist Bibliographer: An Inquiry into His Role* (Metuchen, N.J.: Scarecrow Press, 1972), 152 p.

¹⁷Alan Taylor, "Introduction to the Bibliography of Sub-Saharan Africana at Indiana University," *African Studies Bulletin* 8, no. 2 (September 1965): 97-99.

¹⁸For more detail, consult Standing Conference on Library Materials on Africa (SCOLMA). *The SCOLMA Directory of Libraries and special Collections,* 3d. ed. (London: Crosby Lockwood, 1973) 118 p.

¹⁹Ruth Jones, "Forty-one Years of African Bibliography," *Africa,* 41, no. 1 (January 1971): 54-56.

²⁰*Africa* and *African Abstracts* have been reprinted by Dawson, Cannon House, Folkstone, Kent, England.

²¹Compare Julie A. Virgo, "The Review Article: Its Characteristics and Problems," *The Library Quarterly* (University of Chicago) 41, no. 4 (October 1971): 275-291.

²²It is described by its first two directors Françoise Izard et René Bureau in *Cahier d'études africaines* 6, 1, no. 21 (1966): 130-139. There is an updated translation by John B. Webster in *African Studies Bulletin* 10, 3 (December 1967): 66-81. See also Britta Rupp, "Quelques notes sur la situation de la bibliographie africaniste en France," *Library Materials on Africa* (London), 8, 1 (July 1970): 37-71.

²³Jean Claude Gardin, "A European Research Program in Document

Retrieval," *The American Behavior Scientist* 7, no. 10 (June 1964): 12-16.

[24]See, for example, her "Some Further Consideration in the Application to Social Science Material of Up-to-Date Methods of Bibliographical Control and Information Retrieval," *The Journal of Documentation* 14, no. 4 (December 1958): 190-196, and as incorporated in an excellent textbook, D. L. Foskett, *Classification and Indexing in the Social Sciences* (London: Butterworth, 1963), especially p. 120-128.

[25]J. D. Pearson and Ruth Jones, eds., *The Bibliography of Africa* (London: Frank Cass; New York: Africana Publishing Corporation, 1970), pp. 314-315.

[26]Note especially James S. Coleman, "Research on Africa in European Centers," 2, no. 3 (August 1959): 6-9, obviously now largely outdated, and Joanne Coyle Dauphin, "French Provincial Centers of Documentation and Research on Africa," 9, no. 3 (December 1966): 48-65.

[27]See his "Le travail bibliographique Colonial Belge de 1876 jusqu'en 1933," *Zaire* (June 1948): 1-20.

[28]For a useful review of Hall's publications concerning Africa, see Jean E. Meeh, a member of the African section of the Library of Congress, "The Publications of G.K. Hall," *Africana Library Journal* 2 (Autumn 1971): 18-21.

[29]Lalage Bown and Michael Crowder, eds., *Proceedings of the First International Congress of Africanists* (Evanston,: Ill. Northwestern University Press; London: Longman, 1964), 369 p., and *Congrès International des Africanistes* (Paris: Présence Africaine, 1972), 583 p.

PART TWO

Bibliographies and Serials

BIOBIBLIOGRAPHIES

Strictly interpreted, there are probably only three African bibliographies of bibliographies. The first is the South African Public Library in Cape Town's *Bibliography of African Bibliographies South of the Sahara*, 4th ed. (1961), 79 p. It is perhaps overly weighted in favor of southern Africana and the arrangement according to the Universal Decimal Classification seems to favor use by a special European in-group. (The fifth edition is forthcoming.) Next comes Joseph Bogaert's *Sciences humaines en Afrique: Guide bibliographique, 1945-1965* (Brussels: Centre de Documentation Économique et Sociale Africaine, 1966), 226 p. It consists of 1,494 numbered entries presented in a classified manner. One part consists of general works of reference and information, the other of specialized bibliographies by subject matter. There are author, geographic, and subject indexes.

The other biobibliography is that compiled by Anthea Garling; *Bibliography of African Bibliographies* (Cambridge, England: African Studies Centre, 1967), which is now out of print, appeared in a mimeographed form and consisted largely of entries taken from Theodore A. Besterman's *A World Bibliography of Bibliographies*, 4th ed. (Lausanne: Societas Bibliographica, 1965-1966). Volume 1, columns 166-190, in Besterman's five-volume work is concerned with Africa.

Much shorter is the seven-page *Africa South of the Sahara*, an introductory list of bibliographies compiled by Helen F. Conover in 1961.[1] Although it is now dated, this list remains a fine one of twenty-nine basic sources; it is annotated and designed to serve the general reader. No comparable list is available, although it can perhaps be extracted from this work.

Very useful too are the still unpublished teaching notes by Alan Robert Taylor, "Bibliographical and Archival Resources for African Studies."[2] The manuscript, divided into thirteen geographical and seven subject sections for a total of forty-six pages, was probably prepared in 1972. A copy should be available at Indiana University Library in Bloomington, Indiana.

RETROSPECTIVE, SYSTEMATIC BIBLIOGRAPHY OF AFRICA

There are a considerable number of these works, some exclusively concerned with Africa, others with Asia as well; some focus on the black world while others have narrower political bounds. Perhaps the most rational approach is to trace the most significant of these works chronologically, leaning on the work of Alan Taylor.

Among the three general bibliographies on Africa that Helen Conover has prepared and published, only *Africa South of the Sahara* (1957) has a general section on bibliographies, listing nineteen of them.[3]

The long-awaited *Guide to Africa Research and Reference Works*, edited by Peter Duignan and compiled by Helen Conover and Peter Duignan, published by the Hoover Institution Press, is a recent book. It contains "Bibliographies for Africa in General."[4]

GENERAL RETROSPECTIVE BIBLIOGRAPHIES OF AFRICA

For general retrospective bibliographies, Alan Taylor's work is outstanding. The first general retrospective bibliography concerned with Africa is that compiled in 1841 by Henri Ternaux-Compans: *Bibliothèque asiatique et africaine, ou catalogue des ouvrages relatifs a l'Asie et l'Afrique qui ont paru depuis la découverte de l'imprimerie jusqu'à 1700 Paris, 1841.*[5] It contains 3,184 numbered entries of works published between 1473 and 1700 in chronological order and with author and geographical indexes.

Ternaux-Compans' work is brought forward almost two centuries by Jean Gay's *Bibliographie des ouvrages relatifs à l'Afrique et à l'Arabie: Catalogue methodique de tous les ouvrages français et des principaux en langues étrangères, traitant de la géographie, de l'historie, du commerce, des lettres et des arts de l'Afrique et de l'Arabie* (1875; reprint ed., Amsterdam: Meridian Publishing Co., 1961). Gay provided a classified bibliography with short biographical notes on the authors represented. There are two indexes—one to places, the other to names of authors.

The third retrospective bibliography is that compiled by Philip Viktor Paulitschke, *Die Afrika-Literatur in der Zeit von 1500 bis 1750 n. ch., ein Beitrag zur geographischen Quellenkunde* (1882; reprint ed., in Amsterdam: Meridian Publishing Company, 1964), 122 p. In 1887 the following work was published: Gabriel Kayser, *Bibliographie d'ouvrages ayant trait à l'Afrique en général dans ses rapports avec l'exploration et la civilisation de ces contrées depuis le commencement de l'imprimerie jusqu'à nos jours* . . . (Brussels, 1887), 176 p.

E. A. Petherick's *Catalogue of an Exclusive Collection of Books, Pamphlets, Views, Maps and Transactions of Societies Relating to Africa* (1902; reprint ed., Octagon Books, 1965), is a priced, classified catalog of 3,048 items for Africa and 406 for Madagascar and other African islands.

The Bibliography of the Negro in Africa and America, compiled by Monroe N. Work (New York: H. W. Wilson Co.; reprint ed., Octogon books, 1965), appeared in 1928. Part one, "The Negro in Africa," is divided into nineteen chapters according to subject. It lists a number of periodicals from which references are taken and includes an author index. The preface by Anson Phelps Stokes includes the following:

> He gives everyone the feeling that his feet are squarely planted on the ground and that he knows how to be entirely impartial and objective. . . .
>
> I for one, am extremely glad that an American Negro, with only a trace of white blood, had the imagination to conceive of the work on broad lines, the scholarly mind to follow the best bibliographical standards in its preparation, and the persistence to carry it through effectively in spite of the enormous labor and difficulties involved. . . . It is a monument of which any man or race may well feel proud. (p. XIII.)

In 1930, the library of the Royal Commonwealth Society in London produced a *Subject Catalogue of the Library of the Royal Empire Society.* Volume I is devoted to the British Empire generally and Africa.

In 1956 appeared the International African Institute's *Select Annotated Bibliography of Tropical Africa* compiled under the direction of Darryll Forde.[6] It is divided into sections on geography, ethnography, sociology and linguistics, administration and government, economics, education, missions, and health. Within these sections, material is first classified into major geographical areas and then according to subject. This work was a byproduct of the Twentieth Century Fund Study of Africa.[7]

In 1958, the International African Institute published the *Africa Bibliography Series: Ethnography, Sociology, Linguistics and Related Subjects.* Compiled by Ruth Jones, it was issued in parts: *West Africa* (1958), 116 leaves; *North-East Africa* (1959), 51 leaves (Sudan, Ethiopia, and Somalia); *East Africa* (1960), 62 leaves (Ruanda-Urundi, Kenya, Uganda, Tanganyika, and Zanzibar) and *South-East Central Africa and Madagascar* (1961), 53 leaves (The Rhodesias, Nyasaland, Mozambique, and Madagascar). The volumes are divided first by territory (now mainly sovereign states) and then into general, ethnographic, and linguistic categories. Monographs, journal articles, and government publications are included. Authors' names are not always given in full, and the abbreviations to some of the journals are sometimes difficult for the uninitiated to interpret. There is an ethnic and linguistic index, and an author index, based on the bibliographical card index of the International African Institute.

Dorothy B. Porter is the editor of the *Catalogue of the African Collection in the Moorland Foundation* (Washington, D.C.: Howard University, 1958), 398 p. It contains fifteen general sections, the first of which includes eighty-six bibliographies. It is followed by a regional arrangement; within regions, the work is further broken down by countries. There is an index. The work is supplemented by Helen Parker Alexander, "A Supplement to the Catalogue of the African Collection in the Moorland Foundation of the Howard University Library" (Master's thesis, Catholic University of America, 1963), 106 p. It has the same arrangement as the main catalog, but it considers only western Africa.

The section on Africa in the American Universities Field Staff's *A Select Bibliography: Asia, Africa, Eastern Europe, Latin America* (New York: American Universities Field Staff, 1960), 534 p., is fifty-four pages long. The items are arranged according to country and then by subject. There are indexes to authors and titles. Many of the entries are lightly annotated. Recently, the American Universities Field Staff issued a *Select Bibliography, Asia, Africa, Eastern Europe, Latin America. Cumulative Supplement, 1961-1971* (New York: American Universities Field Staff, 1973), 357 p.

Tenri Central Library, Tenri, Japan, *Africana, Catalogue of Books Relating to Africa in the Tenri Central Library* (1960), 431 p. (Tenri Central Library Series No. 24), is a catalog of about 3,200 items, most of which comprised the library of the late Viscount Takesada Tokugawa, a professor at Tokyo University and director of the Naval Institute of Technology. The material is arranged first by country and then by subject. Full collation is given for the entries, and there is an index. A *Supplement* (1964), 282 p. (Tenri Central Library Series No. 27), has been issued.

Another work is the *Dictionary Catalog of the Schomburg Collection of Negro Literature and History, The New York Public Library* (Boston: G. K. Hall, 1962), 9 vols.; supplement, 2 vols., 1967, Jean Blackwell Hutson, long-time curator of what was the private library of Arthur A. Schomburg, has written a preface to the catalog.[8]

The *Library Catalogue* of the School of Oriental and African Studies at the University of London (Boston: G. K. Hall, 1963), contains twenty-eight volumes divided into author, title, and subject catalogs. A supplement was issued in 1968.

The fifteen-volume *Catalogue of the Colonial Office* in London (Boston: G. K. Hall, 1964) is divided into author, subject, and classified sections. A supplement was issued in 1967, and a second one in 1973.

Another handy volume is Harvard University Library, *Africa: Classification, Schedule, Classified Listing by Call Number, Alphabe-*

tical Listing by Author or Title, Chronological Listing (Cambridge, Mass., 1965), 786 p. (Widener Library Shelflist No. 2).⁹ It has since been replaced by *African History and Literature: Classification, Schedule, Classified Listing by Call Number, Chronological Listing, Author and Title Listing and African Documents Listing by Call Number* (Cambridge, Mass.: Harvard University Press, 1971), 600 p. (Widener Library Shelflist No. 34).

African Bibliographic Center, *African Affairs for the General Reader: A Selected and Introductory Bibliographical Guide, 1960-1967* (Westport, Conn.: Greenwood Publishing Company, 1967), 209 p. (Special Bibliographic Series 5, No. 4), edited by Daniel Matthews, is arranged by subject and then geographic area. It contains three separate indexes: title, author, and a special one for elementary and secondary schools. Many of the 1,737 items indicate the age level for which the work is suitable.

John Paden and Edward Soja, comps. and eds., *The African Experience*, Vol. IIIA: *Bibliography* (Evanston, Ill.: Northwestern University Press, 1970), 1103 p., is divided into three parts. The first contains references arranged to follow the topic summaries or modules of the *Syllabus*, which is volume 2 of *The African Experience*. Part 2 consists of references arranged for the forty-two independent countries and surrounding islands of Africa, followed by Rhodesia and the other colonial territories. Part 3 is an author index to the previous two parts. This ponderous work consists of over 4,000 references selected from a reference reservoir of over 100,000 items. The creation of this work is discussed in detail in the introduction, and the more technical aspects in the companion volume (IIIB), *The African Experience, Guide to Resources.* Paden's and Soja's selection of the references is good.

The main part of the bibliography is certainly the first one. Entries often contain a few lines of abstract. In the section by country, references are arranged according to the five broad sections of the *Syllabus*: "African Society and Culture," "Perspectives on the Past," "Social Change," "Consolidation of Nation-States," and "Africa and the Modern World." Less than justice is done to a final section labeled "General Materials" and "Bibliographies." Many bibliographies are not included.

Alan Robert Taylor, "Bibliographical and Archival Resources for African Studies," 45 leaves, xerographically reproduced, has been prepared for students of Indiana University's graduate library school. This excellent guide should certainly be published.

BRIEF GUIDES TO AFRICANA

There are two compilations by Kenneth M. Glazier, formerly assistant curator of Africana at Hoover and now chief librarian at the University of Calgary, Alberta, Canada. In *Africa, South of the Sahara, A Select and Annotated Bibliography, 1958-1963* (Hoover Institution, 1964), 65 p. (Hoover Bibliographical Series No. 16), the compiler has included the most important 150 works in English issued or reissued during the period. Entries, alphabetically by author, are annotated from standard, generally available sources. Dr. Glazier has attempted with considerable success to obtain a geographical and subject balance. The short volume includes indexes to titles and subjects. This work is complemented by Glazier's *Africa South of the Sahara, A Select and Annotated Bibliography, 1964-1968* (Hoover Institution Press, 1969), 139 p. (Hoover Institution Bibliographical Series 42), which is similar to the earlier volume.

A somewhat larger selection is one compiled by John Cudd Brown and Kraig A. Schwartz with the help of Murray S. Martin: *Africa: A Selective Working Bibliography*, (University Park, Pennsylvania, Pennsylvania State University Library, 1970), 140 leaves.

One other compilation of this type is Peter Duignan et al., comps., *Africa South of the Sahara: A Bibliography for Undergraduate Libraries* (Williamsport, Penn.: Bro-Dart, 1971), 105 p. (Foreign Area Materials Center, Occasional Publication No. 12).

A useful pamphlet edited by Charles A. Geoffrion is *Africa: A Study Guide to Better Understanding* (Bloomington, Ind.: Bureau of

Public Discussion and African Studies Program, Indiana University, 1970), 33 p.

One useful compilation no longer available in an up-to-date edition is the *Checklist of Paperbound Books on Africa*, compiled under the auspices of the Foreign Area Materials Center of the University of the State of New York, State Education Department and the National Council for Foreign Area Materials and distributed by the African Studies Association (1967), 59 p. This work, based on the June 1967 edition of *Paperbound Books in Print*, is arranged alphabetically by author within broad subjects. The present demand for extracting Africana from *Paperbound Books in Print* is not large enough to warrant the needed funds for a revised edition.

GUIDES TO SOURCES

The *Joint Acquisitions List of Africana (JALA)* is the most comprehensive listing of newly published or reprinted monographs, monographic serials, government documents, new journal titles—in fact anything issued in the current and five preceding years, excluding journal articles and chapters of anthologies.[10] Anything published in or about Africa is included on the basis of a card received from the first contributing library. A bimonthly, *JALA* first appeared in January 1962; its present annual cost is fifteen dollars. No cumulations have been attempted so far. Through 1971, contributions to *JALA* appeared in the new catalog of the Melville J. Herskovits Library of African Studies at Northwestern University Library in Evanston, Illinois, published by G. K. Hall Company in 1972. The number of entries in each issue varies widely, although it is usually between five hundred and nine hundred. The 3-1/2" x 5" catalog cards are reduced in size so that eighteen cards will fit on a page.

JALA has been widely used in Africa, North America, and Europe as an acquisitions aid, and less often as an aid in cataloging. With increased standardization and growing tolerance for minor variations in cataloging form, as well as an improved cataloger's photographic camera, the images of *JALA* should also serve as either a guide or actual catalog card. Libraries that contribute to *JALA* are listed here in alphabetical order, as these are by and large the most important U.S. collections of Africana:

CLU University of California, Los Angeles
CSt Stanford University Libraries, Stanford, California
CSt-FRI -Food Research Institute
CSt-H -Hoover Institution on War, Revolution and Peace
CtY Yale University Library, New Haven, Connecticut
CtY-E -Economic Growth Center
DHU Howard University, Washington, D.C.
DLC Library of Congress, Washington, D.C.
ICRL Center for Research Libraries, Chicago, Illinois
ICRL-CAMP -Cooperative Africana Microform Project
IEN Northwestern University, Evanston, Illinois
IEN-L -School of Law
MBU Boston University, Boston, Massachusetts
MBU-A -African Documents Center
MiEM Michigan State University, East Lansing
NjP Princeton University, Princeton, New Jersey
NN New York Public Library
NN-Sc -Schomburg Collection
NNUN United Nations, New York
PPDU Duquesne University, Pittsburgh, Pennsylvania
WvU West Virginia University, Morgantown

JALA lists entries in one alphabetical order, according to what librarians call the main entry, which for some means name of author, be it personal or corporate. For a classified list not restricted like *JALA* to complete bibliographical units we turn to the International African Institute's *Africa*, which, through 1970, contained a bibliography of current publications. Since January 1971, this section has been issued as a separate quarterly publication, *International African Bibliography (IAB)*. Entries are arranged alphabetically by author within eleven broad subject headings, and an annual index of authors is issued. This is certainly the most useful current bibliography for scholars of Africa in the social sciences and humanities and for librarians who can take the necessary time to search through a number of issues.

If a more restricted choice is wanted with some annotations and useful bibliographical essays, reviews, and notices of forthcoming publications, the reader is referred to the African Bibliographic Center's *Current Bibliography on African Affairs,* which appears bimonthly.

Between 1950 and the end of 1972, the International African Institute, with the aid of UNESCO, issued *African Abstracts,* a review of abstracts appearing in current periodicals; it was especially strong in ethnological, social, and linguistic studies.

A newcomer to the field is the *Africana Library Journal (ALJ),* a quarterly bibliography and news bulletin that began in 1970. The annual subscription rate for individuals is fifteen dollars; that for libraries and institutions is twenty-five dollars. Issues consist of articles on special collections, acquisition trips, new periodicals, reviews of reference works, reports of meetings, and the like. The major part of the journal is devoted to bibliography—first a subject section, then a geographical one, and finally a subject and keyword index.

While the *ALJ* contains more material than *Library Materials on Africa* issued in Britain three times a year from 1962 to 1972, the quality of articles and reviews in the latter compares very favorably with that of *ALJ.*

As a result of the Leverhulme Conference on Libraries in Tropical Africa, held in Salisbury, Rhodesia, the Standing Committee on African University Libraries (SCAUL) was formed and now issues a newsletter. Six issues have appeared since 1965.[11] SCAUL and its newsletter are concerned with all aspects of libraries and librarianship in Africa, not merely with Africana.

Between October 1962 and the end of 1964, six issues of the *Africana Newsletter,* edited by Peter Duignan and published by the Hoover Institution, appeared. The first four issues were bilingual. Even with the end of this extravagance, it was impossible to maintain this journal. In 1965, it merged with the *African Studies Bulletin,* which, particularly after the merger, was hospitable to bibliographical matter. Inclusion of this matter ceased with the title change to *African Studies Review* in 1970. Some bibliographic notes are published in the *African Studies Newsletter* that has appeared since 1967, currently six times a year.

Two publications, one in London, the other in Stanford, California, lead a precarious existence because of their small circulation. *United Kingdom Publications and Theses on Africa* has been issued by the Standing Conference on Library Materials on Africa since 1963. The North American equivalent is the *United States and Canadian Publications on Africa*. The first issue of that annual volume was published in 1960 by the U.S. Government Printing Office for the Library of Congress. It contains 477 general works arranged according to broad categories (articles separated from books), and 633 arranged according to individual countries or groups of countries. There is an author index.

The most recent volume is for 1966; like the volumes for 1961 on, it was published by the Hoover Institution. The arrangement is still the same as that for the 1961 volume, although it contains more than twice as many entries. This venture will cease or perhaps be continued by the African Bibliographic Center.

The continuation of the British list is also most uncertain. Nothing, unfortunately, became of the discussion begun at the International Conference on African Bibliography in 1967 in Nairobi on a merger between the British and North American lists, which would have provided a single source for the bulk of the English-language publications published on Africa, outside the continent.

Another source for current journal articles is *African Affairs*, the journal of the Royal African Society, which started in 1901. Since July 1968, it has included a section entitled "Articles on Africa in Non-Africanist Journals." An increasing volume of scholarly journals, entirely or partially concerned with Africa, is found in the immense volume of general journals and those with a disciplinary focus.

For the many unfamiliar with foreign languages, *Translations on Africa*, issued by the United States Joint Publications Research Service of the Department of Commerce, will be useful. These translations, drawn mainly from articles published in the Soviet

Union and the People's Republic of China, also include many from French and other sources. From 1962 through 1971, 1,096 issues of *Translations on Africa*, occupying some twenty feet of shelf space, were published.

TYPES OF PUBLICATIONS

NEWSPAPERS

The importance of newspapers, especially those published in Africa, can hardly be exaggerated. They are one of the prime sources of data for historians and other social scientists as well as for the humanist and linguist.

For the most rapid review of African newspapers, Colin Legum's brief section in the general article on newspapers in volume 16 of the *Encyclopedia Britannica* (1971) can be recommended. Legum gives the total number of daily newspapers for the African continent as 231.

There are several fairly useful listings of African newspapers; in some instances, they indicate where they may be consulted.

The Library of Congress has prepared, and the Superintendent of Documents has issued, three editions of *African Newspapers in Selected American Libraries*. This union list was last issued in 1965 and is available from GPO. It reports that 708 newspaper titles are held in thirty-three libraries.

Newspapers, particularly those printed on poor paper stock, as are most of those in Africa, must be microfilmed as soon as a reasonable volume has accumulated. A complete—or as complete as possible—file should be microfilmed and an archival negative generated. That archival negative, by definition, should be used only as a source for additional copies; it should never be used in a microfilm reader. Important African newspaper titles are listed in Hans Panofsky and Robert Koester, "African Journals and Newspapers," in John N. Paden and Edward W. Soja, *The African Experience*, Vol. IIIB, *Guide to Resources*, p. 52-53.

Some significant African newspapers are:

Abidjan Matin, Abidjan, Ivory Coast, 1954(?)-
Afrique nouvelle, Dakar, Senegal, 1949-
Cape Times, Cape Town, South Africa, 1876-
Daily Graphic, Accra, Ghana, 1950-
Daily Mail, Freetown, Sierra Leone, 1931-
Daily Nation, Nairobi, Kenya, 1960-
Daily Times, Lagos, Nigeria, 1925-
East African Standard, Nairobi, Kenya, 1902-
Egyptian Gazette, Cairo, U.A.R., 1880(?)-
Elima, Kinshasa, Zaïre, 1972-
L'Essor, Bamako, Mali, 1963(?)-
Ethiopian Herald, Addis Ababa, Ethiopia, 1943- (weekly)
Fraternité matin, Abidjan, Ivory Coast, 1959-
Gambia Echo, Bathurst, Gambia, 1934- (weekly)
Ghanaian Times, Accra, Ghana, 1958-
Daily News, Dar es Salaam, Tanzania, 1973-
New Nigerian, Kaduna,tn .9h-
Rand Daily Mail, Johannesburg, South Africa, 1902-
Rhodesia Herald, Salisbury, Rhodesia, 1891-
Le Temps du Niger, Niamey, Niger, 1960(?)- (weekly)
The Times of Swaziland, Mbabane, Swaziland, 1896- (weekly)
Uganda Argus, Kampala, Uganda, 1912-
West African Pilot, Lagos, Nigeria, 1937-
Windhoek Advertiser, Windhoek, South-West Africa, 1919-
    (semiweekly)

It is obviously not feasible for most libraries, let alone other institutions or individuals, to subscribe to more than a few titles. Newspapers in newsprint format are usually not available on interlibrary loan; microfilm, however, frequently is. *Newspapers in Microform, Foreign countries* 1948-1972, published by the Library of Congress (7th ed., 1973), provides information on location and holdings, including negatives. It provides names of overseas libraries that hold materials not available in the United States. Malcolm McKee's guide, "African Newspapers on Microfilm," distributed by the Standing Conference on Library Materials on Africa, is a very useful tool. One can also profitably consult with J.M.D. Crossey, curator of the African Collections at Yale University Library, who has a vast knowledge and some records pertaining to African newspapers.

Northwestern University and a number of other institutions probably subscribe to a larger number of newspapers (including those in microfilm from the Library of Congress) than is justified in view of the high price of subscriptions. Ideally, an institution's needs may well be satisfied through rapid interlibrary loan. There is also some risk that the Library of Congress may cease to microfilm African newspaper titles due to a lack of demand; hence the necessity of cost-sharing with institutions outside of the Library of Congress.

Another batch of titles is available to members of the Association of Research Libraries (ARL) Foreign Newspaper Microfilm Project administered by the Center for Research Libraries (CRL). Institutions that are not members of ARL or CRL can belong to the project for annual dues of $785. The following African titles are currently received and microfilmed:

Congo (Brazzaville), *La Semaine*, 1966-
Ethiopia, *Ethiopian Herald*, 1956-
Ghana, *Daily Graphic*, 1956-
Kenya, *Daily Nation*, 1962-
Liberia, *The Liberian Age*, 1956-
Morocco, *La Vigie Marocaine*, 1957-
Mozambique, *O Noticias*, 1956-
Nigeria, *Daily Times*, 1956-
Republic of South Africa, *The Cape Times*, 1938-, and *Die Transvaler*, 1956-
Southern Rhodesia, *Rhodesia Herald*, 1956-
United Arab Republic, *Al Ahram*, 1956-
Zaïre, *Elima*, 1973-

There are several sources for subscription and other information about African newspapers. The only guide available for many years was Helen Kitchen, ed., *The Press in Africa* (Washington, D.C.; Ruth Sloan Associates, 1956), 96 p. More recently Fritz Feuereisen and Ernst Schmacke, *Die Presse in*

Afrika, ein Handbuch für Wirtschaft und Werbung (Munich: Verlag Dokumentation, 1968), 251 p., appeared. This work is arranged alphabetically by country and then by title. It gives information about the nature of the newspaper and advertising details.

Advertising and Press Annual of Africa (Cape Town: National Publishing Co.) has appeared since 1949. A growing proportion of it over the years has been devoted to southern Africa. Nevertheless, it is still useful for titles, addresses, and subscription rates for many newspapers throughout Africa.

GAZETTES

Virtually every sovereign state issues a government gazette as do some subnational units. In the smaller and Francophonic countries of Africa, the gazette may be the only official vehicle for announcing government action, from the awarding of patents and trademarks to the promulgation of martial law. Unlike newspapers and the reports of legislative debates, gazettes do not contain opinions and discussions; they indicate what the law is.

In the United Nations Library in New York City, the New York Public Library, and some of the larger law libraries, official government gazettes are collected with the eagerness they deserve. Some libraries acquire gazettes merely as an acquisition tool. Many gazettes report regularly on the issue of government publications. For example, in the case of Malawi, these are not announced in any other way. Gazettes, however, have a disadvantage in that, per linear foot, they contain less information for most students than other types of publications. Countries with a large volume of governmental activity may issue a gazette daily of fifty or one hundred pages. The New York Public Library has microfilmed most of its gazettes, which are available for sale from the Kraus Periodicals Company.

Another important source is the Foreign Official Gazette Project (FOG), sponsored by the ARL and administered by the CRL; annual dues are one hundred dollars. In 1959, FOG began receiving positive microfilm copies of the 1958 official gazettes of thirteen Latin American countries. In 1961, the membership voted to expand the project, beginning with the 1960 gazettes of approximately eighty-seven more countries. FOG differs from the Foreign Newspaper Microfilm Project in that only loan copies are available. The gazette project does no filming; it merely purchases positive copies for loan. FOG offers twenty-two African national gazettes through interlibrary loan to member institutions, while Kraus Periodicals offers some forty-six African national gazettes for sale and has a good many more for former national, regional, and subnational units. FOG has been criticized less for incomplete coverage (for among its gazettes are some of the more important ones) than for its slowness in acquiring the most recent reels or for too many gaps. These omissions are hardly likely to be random ones. The greatest drawback is that the FOG gazette holdings usually start with those for 1960, while those held by the New York Public Library usually only go back to the mid-1950s.

A considerable number of the Francophonic gazettes or "journaux officiels" has been microfilmed for earlier years by the Association pour la Conservation et la Reproduction Photographic de la Presse (ACRPP). The Cooperative Africana Microform Project has been buying the entire African output of ACRPP.

JOURNALS

The best sources for African journals are the guides issued by the Library of Congress. The first one, *Research and Information on Africa, Continuing Sources*, compiled by Helen Conover and introduced by Harry J. Krould, special assistant for European and African affairs (the order is significant), was published in 1954. It includes 520 entries, many of them annotated. Not all entries correspond to publications but to institutions that may have publications of their own. This seventy-page pamphlet is an interesting historical document, which is still of some practical use today. Its main use is to find journals on Africa listed that, perhaps with a different title or focus, have existed for at least twenty years.

In 1961 *Serials for African Studies* appeared, also compiled by Helen Conover. Its 2,082 entries, many annotated, are drawn from all parts of the world. The arrangement is alphabetical by title. There is a general index and one to organizations. This list excludes virtually all official publications, as well as geological and meteorological ones. For most serials listed, a location in a U.S. library is indicated.

Sub-Saharan Africa, a guide to serials, appeared in 1970. According to the LC's information office:

> *Sub-Saharan Africa: A Guide to Serials* is for sale at $5.25 a copy from the Superintendent of Documents, U.S. Government Printing Office, Washington, D.C. 20402. Compiled by the African Section of the Library's General Reference and Bibliography Division, the 409 page guide contains 4,670 entries recording a selection of serials published before 1969 in western languages and in African languages using the Roman alphabet. It includes many of the titles appearing in *Serials for African Studies*, issued by the Library in 1961, except that publications specifically on North Africa (Algeria, Libya, Morocco, Tunisia and the United Arab Republic) have been excluded. Most of the titles are held by the Library of Congress and other American Libraries represented in the National Union Catalog. In selecting the entries, the compilers have included monographic series, yearbooks, directories, and annual reports of learned institutions. Several categories of publications have been excluded, however, such as annual reports of African government departments, serials of most territorial, provincial, and municipal administrations, publishers' lists, daily press releases, missionary journals devoted primarily to religious material rather than African affairs, and telephone directories.
>
> Notes to several hundred entires include information as to where the serials are abstracted or indexed. A list of the abstracting and indexing services cited in such notes is supplied, and there are indexes to subjects and organizations.

One need only add that this is an attractive, hardcover volume. It has been favorably reviewed by Douglas Varley, now university librarian in Liverpool, who has had extensive experience in southern Africa, in *Library Materials on Africa* (March 1971): 207-210. J.M.D. Crossey also reviewed this work favorably in the *Africana Library Journal* 2 (Spring 1971): 19, 21, reminding readers that "it has been suggested at a meeting of the African Studies Association Archives-Libraries Committee that a supplementary publication be compiled and published: this would show holdings in other libraries—including microfilms—of the scarcer or rare titles and other rare titles omitted altogether due to incomplete information."

How does a potential reader get at the vast volume of information embedded in the serial literature? Bibliographies on different subjects or disciplines will be discussed below, as will national bibliographies that may occasionally help. Conventional indexes such as those published by the H. W. Wilson Company and, through 1972, *African Abstracts* are useful, as are UNESCO's annual volumes to International Social Science Documentation. Also available is *Africa South of the Sahara: Index to Periodical Literature, 1910-1970* (Boston: G. K. Hall, 1971), 4 vols. and Supplement I.

For those readers who would like a brief selection of journals from which they might make their choice for possible subscription or loan in a library, two references are cited. (1) Hans E. Panofsky and Robert Koester, "African Newspapers and Periodicals," in John N. Paden and Edward Soja, eds., *The African Experience*, vol. IIIB: *Guide to Resources* (Evanston, Ill.: Northwestern University Press, 1970), p. 33-53, is primarily a classified list of journals according to the 100 modules of the Paden/Soja Syllabus. (2) For the politically enlightened, one can recommend Sanford Berman, "African Magazines for American Libraries," *Library Journal* (April 1, 1970): 1289-1293.

Two obstacles preventing one from benefiting fully from the periodical literature are the inability to cope with the language in which the publication is written and, even if one knows the language, the unintelligibility of the abbreviations.

A mass of usually periodical articles appears in *Translations on Africa* issued by the Joint Publications Research Service (JPRS) of the U.S. Department of Commerce. For the period 1957-1962, that is, from the beginning of JPRS translations, there is a useful geographical index compiled by Julian W. Witherell, now head of the African section of the Library of Congress, in *African Studies Bulletin* 6, no. 1 (March 1963): 22-37.

For a continuation of an index one must turn to: *Bibliography*—index to U.S. JPRS research translations: International developments (Africa, Latin America, Near East, international communist developments), v. 1-6, July/September 1962-June 1968, Washington D.C., Research and Microfilm Publications, v. 7-8, July 1968-June 1970. New York, COM Information Corporation; and *Transdex*: bibliography and index to the United States Joint Publications Research Service (JPRS) translations, New York, COM Information Corporation, v. 9-1971. Continues monthly bibliography index to current publications. *Transdex* is both an index to the JPRS as well as a source for the actual documents in microform or hard copy.

USEFUL ACRONYMS

Once a text of an article has been found in the English language, a decoding of acronyms or abbreviations may be necessary. The best guide is the one issued by the Deutsche Afrika-Gesellschaft (DAG) [German Africa Society]: *Abbreviations in Africa* (Bonn, 1969), 250 p. Also available is *Abbreviations in the African Press* (New York: CCM Information Corporation, 1972), 108 p. These abbreviations were compiled by the Joint Publications Research Service (JPRS). For the abbreviations, frequently an acronym, the full name is given in the original language and also in English translation if this differs from the original. The country of common use is also indicated. This book contains about two thousand abbreviations commonly found in the African press.

Notes

[1]"The following bibliography of bibliographies has been compiled in response to a request from the Joint Committee on African Resources of the Association of Research Libraries and the African Studies Associa-

tion. Its immediate purpose is to offer a guide to libraries and study groups which are beginning to assemble collections on Africa. For this reason the bibliographical sources selected are limited largely to those which emphasize readily available material, adapted to the use of the general reader." Helen F. Conover, *Africa South of the Sahara*, p. 1.

²For an early, generally available statement, see Alan R. Taylor, "Introduction to the Bibliography of Sub-Saharan Africa at Indiana University," *African Studies Bulletin* 8, no. 2 (September 1965): 97-99.

³The three are: *Introduction to Africa, A Selective Guide to Background Reading, Prepared by the Library of Congress, European Affairs Division, [sic]* (The University Press of Washington, 1952), 237 p; *Africa South of the Sahara, A Selected Annotated List of Writings, 1951-1956* (Washington: The Library of Congress, Reference Department, General Reference and Bibliography Division, 1957), 269 p., 616 entries, for the most part annotated; *Africa South of the Sahara, A Selected Annotated List of Writings*, (Washington, D.C.: Bibliography Division, Reference Department, Africa Section, 1963), 354 p.; 2,172 items are included, many of them annotated. Available from the Superintendent of Documents, U.S. Government Printing Office. These first two bibliographies are out of print. They are available from the Library of Congress Photoduplication Service.

NOTE: "Library of Congress Publications on Africa South of the Sahara" *The Quarterly Journal of the Library of Congress 27*, 3 (July 1970): 194-196. This issue of the journal is a tribute to the tenth anniversary of the African Section of the Library of Congress.

⁴An early reference is: Peter Duignan, "Guide to African Research Projected Outline," *Library Materials on Africa 2*, no. 1 (June 1964): 15-16. See this author's review in *The Library Quarterly* (Chicago) 43, no. 1 (January 1973): 92-94. Robert Koester reviewed it in *Library Journal* (November 15, 1972): 3696.

⁵It was reprinted by B. H. Gruner of Amsterdam in 1963 and sold in the United States by Argonaut of Chicago (1967).

⁶Reprinted by Kraus Reprint Co., 1969.

⁷George Herbert Tinley Kimble, *Tropical Africa* (New York: Twentieth Century Fund, 1960), 2 vols.

⁸Arna Bontemps, "Special Collections of Negroana," *Library Quarterly* 14, no. 3 (July 1944): 187-193.

⁹Reviewed by this author in *Library Quarterly*, 37, no. 1 (January 1967): 131-132.

¹⁰Published by the Melville J. Herskovits Library of African Studies, Northwestern University, Evanston, Illinois.

"The first six issues have been microfilmed by the Cooperative Africana Microform Project (CAMP) in Chicago, Center for Research Libraries. CAMP holds an archival negative and a loan positive.

PART THREE

Guide to Resources, by
Subject and Discipline

In turning to a disciplinary approach to Africana, we have ordered the material in blocks of aggregates covering today's conventional academic compartmentalizations. A less academic and more Africa-centered sequence, although desirable, would more likely have disoriented the readers than enlightened them.

MISCELLANEOUS SUBJECTS

AFRICA GENERAL

We shall once more remind the reader that African studies is not a discipline. Africanists draw from many of the traditional disciplines which are brought to bear on the study of this continent.

Before turning to the large handbooks, the following pamphlet may be recommended strongly: Charles A. Geoffrion, ed., *Africa: A Study Guide to Better Understanding* (Bloomington, Ind.: Bureau of Public Discussion and African Studies Program, 1970), 33 p.[1] It is useful for home study and extension activities.

For a larger tool, which is intended for classroom use but no doubt is also helpful without a teacher, *The African Experience*, edited by John N. Paden and Edward W. Soja, is recommended. It was published in three volumes in 1970 by Northwestern University Press. Volume 1, *Essays*, contains the most recent synthesis of current research and delineates the important themes within particular areas of study. By integrating these specialized approaches into a broader conceptual framework, the authors and editors demonstrate significant linkages among the different disciplines and build collectively toward a balanced understanding of Africa. The other volumes are *Syllabus* (vol. 2), *Bibliography* (vol. 3A), and *Guide to Resources* (vol. 3B).[2]

A means of keeping up to date with ongoing research in the social sciences and humanities concerning Africa is to follow the work of Merran Fraenkel of the Research Information Liaison Unit of the International African Institute (IAI) in London, who in 1971 published *International Register of Organisations Undertak* ing Africanist Research in the Social Sciences and Humanities (1970), 65 p.[3] This register is updated by Current Africanist Research: International Bulletin No. 1, published by the IAI in November 1971.[4] It contains references to nearly fifteen hundred projects.

While Francophonic research is included in the IAI volumes, it also is likely to be well covered in the following work: Marcel Walreat, Les études africaines dans le monde: Hier, aujourd'hui, demain (Brussels: Centre de documentation economique et sociale, 1971), 104 p.

For basic information not contained in the Information Almanac or even the Statesman's Yearbook, the following works may be of help. Europa Publications in London first published Africa South of the Sahara in 1971, revised it lightly the following year.[5] A 1973 edition (1163 p.) has also appeared.

The researcher who is looking for pictures and desires a more popular format should consult: Louis Barron, ed. Africa, 4th ed. (New York: Harper and Row, 1971), 360 p. The information is arranged alphabetically under fifty headings with a bibliography for each one.

It is debatable whether this is the right place for the next entry. This work is so good, however, that it deserves mention on numerous occasions. It is Colin Legum's Africa Contemporary Record. To date, five volumes have been issued—those for 1968-1969, 1969-1970, 1970-1971, 1971-1972, and 1972-1973.[6] The books are published in London by Rex Collings and distributed by the Africana Publishing Corporation in New York City. Each volume includes a country-by-country review and reproduces many documents that are virtually unobtainable directly.

PAN-AFRICANISM

Two important histories of Pan-Africanism were written in German; another less scholarly and historical work is in French. They are: Imanuel Geiss, Panafrikanismus: zur Geschichte der Dekolonisation (Frankfurt: Europäische Verlagsanstalt, 1968), 489 p.; Hanspeter F. Strauch, Panafrika, kontinentale Weltmacht im Werden. Anfänge, Wachstum and Zukunft der afrikanischen Einigungsbestrebungen (Zurich: Atlantis, 1964), 416 p.; and Philip

Decraene, *Le Panafricanisme*, 4th ed. (Paris: Presses Universitaires de France, 1970), 128 p.

The classic on this topic in English by George Padmore has been reissued with a new introduction: *Pan-Africanism or Communism* (New York: Doubleday, 1970), 439 p. This is a reprint of the 1957 edition, the only other one, in fact, with a new introduction by Azinna Nwafor.[7] Another useful, though not too widely noted, study is: Vincent Bakpetu Thompson, *Africa and Unity: The Evolution of Pan-Africanism* (London: Longman; New York: Humanities, 1969), 412 p.[8]

Full bibliographical studies of all the leaders of pan-Africanism are still needed, in particular those of W.E.B. DuBois, George Padmore, and Marcus Garvey. In fact, only Edward Blyden has found his biographer—Hollis R. Lynch.[9] Work on DuBois continues to be done by Herbert Aptheker, but thus far only the bibliographical volume has been published. It contains 626 p. Sooner or later University Microfilms in Ann Arbor, Michigan, should be able to provide copies of Thomas Tames Heiting's doctoral dissertation, "W.E.B. DuBois and the Development of Pan-Africanism, 1900-1930," written at the Texas Technological University at Lubbock, 1970. Clarence G. Contee of Howard University has published some interesting work on DuBois, and no doubt more will be forthcoming.[10]

Pan-African congresses took place in continental Europe and England during the first half of the twentieth century. A retrospective look at the movement was provided at the Third Annual Conference of the American Society of African Culture in 1960.[11] A future perspective is provided by Imamur Imiri Baraka (LeRoi Jones), ed., *African Congress, A Documentary of the First Modern Pan-African Congress* (New York: Morrow, 1972), 493 p.

Further useful leads in the vast literature on Pan-Africanism will be found in the January 1972 issue of *A Current Bibliography on African Affairs* (series 2, vol. 4, no. 1).[12]

Pan-Africanism has been and remains a rallying point for black people everywhere. A recent manifestation of this fact was the choice of *The Pan-Africanist* as the title for the journal published by the students in the Program of African studies at Northwestern University. Many of the articles are significant reflections of Pan-Africanism, particularly the article by Elone Nwabuzor, "Pan-Africanism: The Last and Inevitable Stage of Black Power," *The Pan-Africanist*, no. 3 (December 1971); 33-36.

ORGANIZATION OF AFRICAN UNITY AND ECONOMIC COMMISSION FOR AFRICA

There are at least two Pan-African societies: the Organisation of African Unity (OAU) and the Economic Commission for Africa (ECA), both headquartered in Addis Ababa. Numerous reference works reprint the OAU's charter and occasionally some resolutions of the organization. At the organization's beginning in 1963, access to documents was freely available; now this has become very difficult indeed. The OAU unfortunately issues next to nothing for the benefit of scholars, either free of charge or for payment. All that can be offered here are two accounts and some additional references: Zdenek Červenka, *The Organisation of African Unity and its Charter* (London: Hurst, 1968; New York: Praeger, 1969), and Jon Woronoff, *Organizing African Unity* (Metuchen, n.g.: Scarecrow Press, 1970), 703 p.[13] See also Ronald K. Nagel, "Documentary Resources on the Organisation of African Unity on Its First Quintade," *A Current Bibliography on African Affairs*, n.s. 3 (November-December 1970), p. 19-24. Of particular interest is Dorothy Nelkin, "Socialist Sources of Pan-African Ideology," in William H. Friedland and Carl G. Rosberg, eds., *African Socialism* (Stanford, Calif.: Hoover Institution, 1964). p. 63-79, 288-290. This is also issued as reprint no. 157, New York State School of Industrial and Labor Relations at Cornell University, Ithaca, New York.

The ECA is one of several regional organizations of the United Nations. It was established in 1958 and since then has released some thirty linear feet of documents. These documents can be found through the United Nations *Documents Index*, which is divided into two series: Series A is a subject index and Series B a country index. Both are issued ten times a year. It must be stressed that not all ECA documents available for distribution are sent to recipients of depository sets. Most material does come more or less automatically, but to receive even more it is necessary to make special arrangements with the ECA library.

The following books contain valuable documents not easily located elsewhere. First is Louis B. Sohn, ed., *Basic Documents of African Regional Organisations* (Dobbs Ferry, N.Y.: Oceana, 1971)[14] (Inter-American Institute of International Legal Studies). It is divided into four volumes: "Documents Relating to the Organization of African Unity, the African Development Bank and Some of the Organizations of French-speaking Africa," "The Remainder of Documents of French-speaking Africa," "Documents of Regional Organizations in West, North and East Africa," and "Documents Relating to the Association of Various Groups of African States with the European Economic Community." Also useful, especially if revised regularly, is United Nations Economic Commission for Africa, *Directory of Intergovernmental Cooperation Organisation in Africa* (1972), 94 p. (E/CN. 14/1).

A view of the ECA is found in James S. Magee's article, "What Role for E.C.A. or Pan-Africanism Revisited," *Journal of Modern African Studies* 7, no. 2 (July 1969): 330-334.

Some hints on trying to understand the Afro-Asian group in the United Nations is contained in an article by Mohamed A. El-Khawas, "The Afro-Asian group in the United Nations," in *A Current Bibliography on African Affairs*, n.s. 3 (November-December 1970): 5-18.

LIBERATION MOVEMENTS

It may well be a small step from Pan-Africanism, the OAU, and the ECA to African liberation movements, or Freedom Fighters. There is a committee of the OAU on National Liberation (NLC) "of twelve members charged with responsibility for assisting by all means possible the struggle of the national liberation movements in those parts of Africa which are not considered to be free from colonialism. The NLC's headquarters and staff are in Dar es Salaam."[15] Nothing is released by the NLC for the benefit of the world community of scholars and other interested parties. While obviously much of their work has to remain confidential, something might well be issued, if only to counter the well-funded propaganda services of the Republic of South Africa and Portugal in North America and Europe.

One recently published volume, when it was first announced, seemed helpful for gaining a better understanding of the many organizations struggling mainly in southern Africa, but also in Guinea Bissau and the other areas of Africa that are still more or less under Portuguese control: Richard Gibson, *African Liberation Movements: Contemporary Struggles against the White Minority Rule* (London: Oxford University Press, 1972), 384 p. However, the book does not seem to measure up to the difficult task of unraveling the aims and methods of the host of organizations trying to set Africa free. This book has already received two extremely poor reviews and one passable one.[16]

Somewhat better is Kenneth W. Grundy, *Guerrilla Struggle in Africa: An Analysis and Preview* (New York: Grossman, 1971), 204 p. essentially a scholarly analysis. The book concludes with a forecast of a possible sequence of events in Rhodesia and Portuguese Africa from 1983 to 1991. It also contains a review of the major guerrilla organizations currently operating in Africa. The author's analysis is based mainly on then-published journal and newspaper accounts, including the publications of the Freedom Fighters themselves.

The winter 1972 issue of *Africa Today* (Denver) 19, is entitled "Guerrilla Warfare" and contains the following articles: "The Azores over Africa," Gil Fernandes; "The Future of Guerrilla-Revolution in Southern Africa," J. Bowyer Bell; "Guerrilla Warfare in Southern Africa: Myth and Prognosis," Henry B. Masauko Chipembere; "The Reality of Guerrilla Warfare," Davis M'gabe; "Guerrilla Warfare: Then, Now and Tomorrow," Edward A. Hawley; "Angola: History, Insurgency and Social Change," Gerald J. Bender; "American Military Aid to Ethiopia and Eritrean Insurgency," Robert A. Diamond and David Fouquet; and "The British-Rhodesian Agreement and United States Policy," Michael F. Lofchie.

The late Kwame Nkrumah's *Handbook of Revolutionary Warfare* (New York: International Publishers, 1969), 122 p., is a pamphlet intended for wide distribution. It is designed to form part of the equipment of a Freedom Fighter and is divided into two parts: "Know the Enemy" and "Strategy, Tactics and Techniques." A potential fighter, a fighter, and their supporters are given the necessary historical background of the struggle, and organizational structure is outlined for ultimate success as are details for effective fighting.

At least three recent bibliographies for students of liberation movements have been issued. Sanford Berman, comp., "African Liberation Movements: A Preliminary Bibliography," *Ufahamu* (Los Angeles: African Studies Center, UCLA), 3 (Spring 1972): 107-128, has also been issued in mimeographed form by the Institute of Social Research at Makerere University in Kampala where Berman was librarian. Francis A. Kornegoy has compiled "Resistance, Liberation and Guerrilla Warfare: A Selected Survey," *African Bibliographic Center: Current Reading List* 8 (August 1971), 12 p. Also useful is Anirudha Gupta, "African Liberation Movements: A Bibliographical Survey," *Africa Quarterly* (New Delhi) 10 (April-June 1970): 56-62. Finally, S. Ansari, *Liberation Struggle in Southern Africa* (Gurgaon, India: Harzana Documentation Service, 1972), 118 p., is a bibliography with many references to United Nations documents. In the United States it is available from South Asian Books, Box 502, Columbia, Missouri, for six dollars.

THE MILITARY

The transition from the liberation movements to the military is a natural one. The military both facilitates the work of the liberation movements in some parts of Africa and prevents their success elsewhere.

The publications of the Institute for Strategic Studies in London are highly informative and are often updated. A good summary is Richard Booth, *The Armed Forces of African States, 1970* (London: Institute of Strategic Studies, 1970), 27 p. (Adelphi Paper No. 67). This pamphlet gives basic economic and demographic information as well as figures about the nature of each country's military force. A much fuller volume is Ernest W. Lefever, *Spear and Scepter: Army, Police and Politics in Tropical*

Africa (Washington, D.C.: The Brookings Institution, 1970) 251 p.[17]

Ruth First, a South African political refugee now living in England, is the author of the excellent *The Barrel of a Gun: Political Power in Africa and the Coup d'Etat* (Baltimore: Penguin, 1972), 513 p. The introduction states that "this book is about army intervention in politics, but more about politics than armies." The role of the military is discussed in general for Africa and in detail for the Sudan, Nigeria, and Ghana. The work is well documented with many references to the daily press.

Claude E. Welch, Jr., ed., *Soldier and State: A Comparative Analysis of Military Intervention and Political Change* (Evanston, Ill.: Northwestern University Press, 1970), 320 p., "analyzes two major areas: the factors leading to military involvement in politics, and the impact of military-based rule upon individual African states." While examples are drawn mainly from Francophonic Africa—Dahomey, Upper Volta, Zaïre, and Algeria—there is a chapter dealing with Ghana and a great deal of general analysis, which is well documented in many footnotes, a chronology, and a bibliography through 1968.

For references to earlier and more recent publications three bibliographies may be recommended: "Militär in Afrika, aus gewählte neuere literatur zum Militär in Afrika," *Afrika Spectrum* (January 1971): 78-88; Marion E. Doro, "Bibliographic Essay on the Role of the Military in African Affairs," *Current Bibliography on African Affairs* 4, no. 3 (May 1971): 190-197; and Joseph P. Smaldone, "Materials for the Study of African Military History," *Current Bibliography on African Affairs* 4, no. 3 (May 1971).

GEOGRAPHY

A basic reference is *A Dictionary of Geography*, comp. Francis John Monkhouse, 2d ed. (London: Edward Arnold, 1970), 378 p.

For a literature search, use of the fifteen-volume *Research Catalogue of the American Geographical Society* (Boston: G. K. Hall, 1962) is often productive. Separate volumes are available, and volume eleven is concerned with Africa. The way to update one's information is to consult *Current Geographical*

Publications issued monthly by the same society. The student with high academic ambitions may want to examine: Clyde Eugene Browning, *A Bibliography of Dissertations in Geography: 1901 to 1969* (Chapel Hill: University of North Carolina Press, 1970), 96 p.

Confining ourselves now to the geography of Africa or African geography (there is a difference), a handbook and two surveys come to mind. Professor Sanford Harold Bederman of the department of geography at Georgia State University has compiled *A Bibliographic Aid to the Study of the Geography of Africa* (Atlanta, Ga.: Bureau of Business and Economic Research, Georgia State University, 1970), 212 p. This work contains 1,900 numbered citations preceded by a guide to periodicals, and is arranged by regions and countries; each region is followed by a subject index. There is an author index at the end of the volume. The two surveys are Benjamin E. Thomas, "Geography," in Robert A. Lystad, ed., *The African World: A Survey of Social Research* (New York: Praeger, 1965), p. 527-534, and Peter Gould, "Geography, Spatial Planning and Africa: The Responsibilities for the Next Twenty Years," in Gwendolen M. Carter and Ann Paden, eds., *Expanding Horizons in African Studies* (Evanston, Ill.: Northwestern University Press, 1969), p. 181-203. Gould uses the new concepts of quantitative geography.

The African Experience (referred to earlier) is edited by political scientist John N. Paden and geographer Edward W. Soja. Soja and Paden are the authors of the second chapter of the prologue, "The African Setting." It contains five color maps.

While several textbooks on the geography of Africa are available, none is entirely satisfactory.

Among recent one-volume works on Africa is: Alfred Thomas Grove, *Africa South of the Sahara*, 2d ed. (London: Oxford University Press, 1970), 280 p. It may be symptomatic of the volume of demand and the high cost of illustrated book production that the three more or less standard works were issued in 1964. Much of the information in them is likely to be at least ten years old.

Harm J. DeBley, *A Geography of Sub-Saharan Africa* (Chicago: Rand McNally, 1964), 435 p., is likely to be stronger on the physical aspects of geography than R. J. Harrison Church, *Africa and the Island* (New York: John Wiley, 1964), 494 p., which is probably better in the realm of economic geography. (Rumor has it that the Library of Congress delayed cataloging DeBley's work because of some uncertainty about the treatment of part of the author's name. Searchers for this volume in libraries should look in the card catalog under both "D" and "B.") The Church volume is an excellent textbook aimed at seniors in high school as well as college students. A third textbook is William A. Hance, *The Geography of Modern Africa* (New York: Columbia University Press, 1964), 653 p. (Hance is one of the "father figures" of African studies in the United States.)

Another volume is R. Mansell Prothero, ed., *People and Land in Africa South of the Sahara: Readings in Social Geography* (New York: Oxford University Press, 1972), 344 p.

MAPS

With regard to atlases, the situation is poor. There is no recent atlas of Africa—nothing in fact that has taken the place of the *Times Atlas of the World*, vol. IV: *Southern Africa and Europe* (1956). It contains ninety-six colored plates and an index. *Philip's Modern College Atlas of Africa*, 1971, is merely a general world atlas with somewhat increased emphasis on the African continent. As we go to press the following has become available: *The Atlas of Africa* (Paris: Jeune Afrique, 1973), 335 p.

Of still considerable interest today are the slight volumes produced by James Francis Horrabin, *An Atlas of Africa*, 2d ed. (New York: Praeger, 1961), 126 p. According to the author:

This book is not intended for the specialist. Its aim is to provide for the intelligent newspaper reader a summary of some of the key facts about one of the great "burning problems" of today. Nor does it pretend to be objective. It has been drawn and written in the fixed conviction that Europeans and Americans owe Africans a big debt; and that the doctrine of *apartheid* and the "color mentality" are un-civilized, un-Christian and altogether damnable. It emphasizes the historical background because that background is helping to shape the point of view of educated Africans today; and it is important that we should understand their point of view.

Mr. Horrabin is no longer alive, and no one presently publishing seems to have his ability to draw and comment on fundamental issues in his enlightened manner.

For historical maps, there is a useful exhibition catalog but it is now difficult to obtain: City of Johannesburg, *Public Library and Africana Museum. Exhibition of Decorative Maps of Africa up to 1800*, 4-16 August 1952, 177 p. (mimeo.) This descriptive catalog is arranged chronologically. It describes the 170 maps exhibited in some detail, and contains an index to personal names.

Much more easily available is Ronald Vere Tooley, *Collectors' Guide to Maps of the African Continent and Southern Africa* (London: Carter Press, 1969), 132 p. It contains a hundred plates.

Helpful also is F. Adetowun Ogunsheye, "Maps of Africa, 1500-1800: A Bibliographical Survey," *Nigerian Geographical Journal* 7, no. 1 (1964): 34-42.

Berlin, Deutsche Staatsbibliothek, *Afrika auf Karten des 12 bis 18 Jahrhundert* (Leipzig, Edition Leipzig, 1968), is a lavish volume consisting of seventy-seven maps, all of which have been faithfully reproduced. A book describing the maps is included in a pocket of the atlas of maps first issued from the twelfth to the eighteenth centuries.

Gasoline companies issue road maps for Africa just as for other continents. They are quite scarce in Africa, however, generally disappearing very quickly after they have been issued. Useful not merely to the motorist are the Michelin maps that are issued in three large sheets: one for North and West Africa, one for East Africa, and one for Central and South Africa.

Rand-McNally in Chicago issues wall maps of Africa; their latest revision was in 1967. The National Geographic Society in Washington, D.C., also issues maps to accompany its journal *National Geographic*, its latest appearing in 1971. One side of the sheet is labeled "The Peoples of Africa," indicating contemporary political borders and main roads; the other, "Heritage of Africa," shows African groupings prior to European contact as well as the continent's topography. There is also a Bartholomew map of 1970 covering the whole continent.

HISTORY

Since Duignan's *Guide* has treated history very well indeed, this section will refer to some of the recent work not included by Duignan.

Perhaps at the start we should stress that virtually all writing of the past may be of some interest to a historian, and a growing volume of current publications is concerned with former events. Professional historians are a fairly recent breed, and their output constitutes only a small proportion of a historian's data. There is a growing number of African historical journals both in Africa and elsewhere. (We must stress that historical journals published in Africa are not exclusively concerned with African history just as American historical research does not exclusively focus on the Americas.)

While the volume of historical articles concerned with Africa is still small, the number is increasing. The *American Historical Review* includes a number of book reviews of works concerned with Africa. Each issue also includes a listing of recently published articles. The African section, which started in October 1964, has been well compiled since its beginning by David E. Gardinier of Marquette University in Milwaukee. There are some twenty serials listed under the general topic "history" in the 1970 *Sub-Sahara Africa Guide* issued by the Library of Congress. The most important is without a doubt the *Journal of African History*. To date it occupies, unbound, some eighteen inches of shelf space, growing by about two inches in recent years. It is still available from the Cambridge University Press from the beginning of 1960. The other important African historical journal published in this country is *African Historical Studies*, now the *International Journal of African Historical Studies*, which started in 1968 and has consisted of two issues through 1971. In 1972, it became a quarterly and from then on was published for the Boston University African Studies Center by the Africana Publishing Corporation.

For persons interested in a slightly less elevated level of historical analysis, even comprehensible and interesting to high school students, we recommend *Tarikh*, which since 1965 has been published twice a year for the Historical Society of Nigeria by Longmans of Nigeria. It is available in the United States from the Humanities Press.

Two recently published bibliographies are of particular significance to students of history. One is *African History and Literature: Classification Schedule, Classified List of Call Numbers, Chronological Listing, Author and Title Listing and African Documents Listing by Call Number* (Cambridge, Mass.: Harvard University Press, 1971), 600 p. Widener Shelflist, No. 36. This volume is without doubt the most inclusive listing to be found in a single volume of interest to historians and others. Harvard's Widener Library has, by and large, not believed in employing Africana specialists, at least in an identifiable position. This is partly due to Harvard's general strength in just about everything and the proximity of Boston University, which is very strong in Africana, particularly government publications and ephemera. The other quite different bibliography, produced without the aid of a computer, is Daniel Matthews, *Current Themes in African Historical Studies: A Selected Bibliographical Guide to Resources for Research in African History*, Special Bibliographic Series, vol. 7, no. 2 (Westport, Conn.: Negro Universities Press, 1970), 289 p. Part I by Samir M. Zoghby is titled "A Bibliography of Medieval Africa"; Part II is "Current Themes in African Historical Studies, Classified by Subject and by Area"; and Part III is "Topics of the African Diaspora." This volume was favorably reviewed by Malcolm D. McKee, *Journal of African History* 12, no. 4 (1971): 678-679.

Before turning to chronologically specialized studies, those geographically limited to a country or group of countries will be discussed below. Paradoxically, a fairly recent trend is for studies of African history to be concerned with Africans rather than with their European colonizers. One such work is by Naomi Mitchison, *The Africans* (London: Blond, 1970), 232 p. Another is Robert W. July, *History of African People*, 2d ed. (New York: Scribner's,

1974), 731 p., which emphasizes the modern history of black African states. July's work was favorably reviewed by Robert Smith in *Africa* 41, no. 1 (January 1971): 71-72.

For the French reader, there is Hubert Deschamps, ed., *Histoire generale de l'Afrique noire et de Madagascar et des Archipels,* Tome I: *Des Origine à 1800* (Paris: Presses Universitaires de France, 1970), 576 p. In *Journal of African History* 12, no. 3 (1971): 487-489, John D. Hargreaves reviewed this work favorably in his article "Africa Encompassed." He is critical of the bibliography.

Persons in search of a textbook for a survey course in African history should consider using Robert O. Collins, ed., *African History: Text and Readings* (New York: Random House, 1970), 594 p. The ninety-four readings, arranged in five broad regions of sub-Saharan Africa, are taken from the whole range of written documentation. Unfortunately, this book lacks a bibliography.

Finally, a volume that deserves serious consideration (even though it could be considered a "coffee table" book, especially since it was published for the 1971 Christmas trade) is *The Horizon History of Africa* (New York: American Heritage, 1971), 528 p. E. Jefferson Murphy gave this book a generally favorable review in *Africa Report* 17, no. 1 (January 1972): 33-34. This handsome volume contains some of the best writings of historians—African, European, and American—of Africa.

The International Scientific Committee under the chairmanship of Dr. Aklilu Habte, president of the Haile Selassie I University, has appointed editors for the UNESCO *General History of Africa,* an eight-volume work scheduled to be completed by 1978. The editors are all Africans; no doubt, most of the assistant editors and collaborators will be African, too. The history will be concerned with the entire African continent from prehistoric Africa to the "march toward independence."[18]

PREHISTORY

We turn now to the prehistory of Africa, an immense field of study in which rapid progress is hampered by the high cost of archeological work. Yet progress was fast enough to compel Desmond Clark to revise his *World Prehistory: A New Outline*, which first appeared in 1961, in 1967. The second edition, published by Cambridge University Press, appeared in 1969.[19]

The best overview, as far as Africa is concerned, is probably J. Desmond Clark, *The Prehistory of Africa* (New York: Praeger, 1970), 302 p.[20]

Those who like references to the best articles on African prehistory that have appeared in the *Journal of African History* should consult John D. Fage and Roland Oliver, eds., *Papers in Africa Prehistory* (Cambridge University Press, 1970), 331 p.[21]

For just the Iron Age notes, see Peter Lewis Shinnie, ed., *The African Iron Age* (Oxford: Clarendon Press, 1971), 281 p. Two articles that survey recent radiocarbon dates are J.E.G. Sutton, "New Radiocarbon Dates for Eastern and Southern Africa," *Journal of African History* 13, no. 1 (1972): 1-24, and Frank Willett, "A Survey of Recent Results in the Radiocarbon Chronology of Western and Northern Africa," *Journal of African History* 12, no. 3 (1971): 339-370. The editors of *Journal of African History* plan to publish once every two years articles on radiocarbon dating for one-half of the continent. Other articles on prehistory include D. W. Phillipson's "Note on the Later Prehistoric Radiocarbon Chronology of Eastern and Southern Africa," *Journal of African History* 11, no. 1 (1970): 1-15 and a series of six survey articles, "Radiocarbon dates for Sub-Saharan Africa," compiled by Brian Fagan.[22]

PRECOLONIAL AFRICA

One volume on precolonial times is particularly significant: Richard Gray and David Birmingham, eds., *Pre-colonial Trade: Essays on Trade in Central and Eastern Africa before 1900* (London: Oxford University Press, 1970), 308 p. Jan Vansina, in his brilliant review in *Journal of African History* 11, no. 4 (1970), notes that in the future the various essays collected in this volume will have to be expanded into books to do justice to topics for which data are becoming available.

COLONIAL TIMES

Some of the most important sources for colonial history and, indirectly, the history of Africa and Africans are British parliamentary papers. These have been available in the original in some of the world's larger research libraries, as well as in a microcard edition. Recently, the Irish University Press has rearranged by subject and photographically reproduced the nineteenth-century papers. Of particular relevance to students of Africa are the seventy volumes so labeled and the ninety-five concerned with the slave trade. These two sets cost $5,577 and $6,820, respectively. To date, no adequate index has been provided, although the publisher hopes to provide one in the future.[23] Meanwhile, available free of charge from the press is an eighty-page pamphlet, *Africa*, that summarizes the contents of each volume and cites references to the original documents. A fifty-five-page pamphlet on the slave trade volumes is also a-vailable.

For a better understanding of Africans and black men every-where the work of the European (including American) dis-coverers or explorers should be viewed from a less Eurocentric perspective. That is, one should try to understand their relation-ship to Africans and the roles Africans played not only in carrying the white men's load but also in showing him the way so that he could inform the wider world, particularly his oppressor, what it was like in Africa. A good anthology edited by Robert I. Rotberg is *Africa and Its Explorers: Natives, Methods and Impact* (Cambridge, Mass.: Harvard University Press; London: Oxford University Press, 1970), 351 p.[24]

MODERN HISTORY

An excellent text stressing more recent times is Robin Hallett, *Africa to 1875: A Modern History* (Ann Arbor: The University of Michigan Press, 1970), 483 p. (The University of Michigan History of the Modern World), a well-written synthesis with a good bibliography.[25]

Newly available is Peter C. Hogg, *The African Slave Trade and Its Suppression: A Classified Bibliography* (London: Cass, 1973), 409 p., which contains classified material on the slave trade in and from Africa and its eradication but not slavery as such, either inside or outside Africa. This bibliography contains some 2,500 items, some of which are annotated.

Robert L. Hess and Dalvan M. Coger have compiled: *Semper ex Africa; A Bibliography of Primary Sources from Nineteenth Century Tropical Africa, as Recorded by Explorers, Missionaries, Traders, Travelers, Administrators, Military Men, Adventurers and Others* (Stanford University, Hoover Institution Press, 1972), 800 p. (Bibliographical series no. 47). This book, containing more than 7,700 entries, is the reproduction of an unedited manuscript. At its high price (thirty-five dollars), an edited and generally better product could have been expected. However, if used with circumspection, this volume will be of service to some specialists.[26]

There was a useful symposium at the thirteenth annual meeting of the African Studies Association held in Boston in 1970, entitled "Contributions of History to African Research in the Last Five Years," chaired by G. Wesley Johnson. The papers, as is the unfortunate custom, were published considerably later in the *African Studies Review*. The five articles are useful both for their texts and bibliographies: Ralph A. Austen, "Economic History," 14, no. 3 (December 1971): 425-438; Martin A. Klein, "African Social History," 15, no. 1 (April 1972): 97-112; Leo Spitzer, "Interpretative African Intellectual History: A Review of the Past Decade, 1960-1970," 15, no. 1 (April 1972): 113-118; John Ralph Willis, "The Historiography of Islam in Africa: The Last Decade (1960-1970)," 14, no. 3 (December 1971): 403-424; and Marcia Wright, "African History in the 1960's: Religion," 14, no. 3 (December 1971): 439-445.

THE SCIENCES AND APPLIED SCIENCES

Many of the publications of African scientists—and it is as yet a small group—usually appear in the learned journals of Europe and America, and are retrievable through the abstract or index that carries the publications of the particular science. Here we will confine ourselves to the natural sciences and medicine and will not repeat the useful references given in Duignan's *Guide*.

UNESCO's *Survey on the Scientific and Technical Potential of the Countries of Africa* (1970), 296 p., is an inventory of scientific and technical research institutions in Africa by country and by discipline. Forty countries are included and 722 institutions analyzed.

UNESCO issued in September 1972 its *List of Scientific and Technical Periodicals Published in Thirty-two Countries of Africa from 1960 to 1970*, 69 p. This list is arranged alphabetically by country. Particulars, not always complete, of 725 periodicals are given. There is a title index. Some ceased publication within the decade. The thirty-two countries listed are independent ones, excluding those of North Africa, to which the UNESCO Field Science Office for Africa (Nairobi) is accredited.

FAUNA

Before turning to the science of man, one should note: Reginald Ernest Moreau, *The Bird Faunas of Africa and Its Islands* (New York: Academic Press, 1966), 424 p. The author says about his book: "If I were allowed an eighteenth century latitude of subtitle for this book it would be 'an eco-geographical discussion with its roots in the past.' "

Of immense significance for man and beast is Hugh Waddell Mulligan, *The African Trypanosomiases* (London: Allen and Unwin, 1970), 950 p. This authoritative and comprehensive reference work by twenty-seven contributors deals with a group of closely allied diseases of man and animals caused by infection with the species of the genus *Trypanosoma*.

MEDICINE

The quarterly *African Journal of Medical Sciences* began publication in 1970. It is edited by A. Olufemi Williams of the Department of Pathology, University College Hospital, Ibadan, and published in Oxford by Blackwell Scientific Publications.

NUTRITION

In the field of nutrition two publications may be useful. University of Ibadan, Food Science and Applied Nutrition Unit, *Bibliography of Nutrition Books for Training Centers in Tropical Countries* (Ibadan, 1971), 45 p., is arranged according to fourteen subjects. It includes no index. References are largely confined to monographs. See also Marshall H. Segall, *Cross-cultural Research in Nutrition: A Synopsis and Guide to Research with Emphasis on Eastern Africa* (Syracuse: Program of Eastern African Studies, 1970), 34 p.

PSYCHIATRY

With regard to psychiatry, the proceedings of the first Pan-African Psychiatric Conference in Abeokuta, Nigeria, 1961, and the second conference held in Dakar in 1968, are available.

Since 1965, *Psychopathologie africaine* has been published by the Societé de psychopathologie et d'hygiène mentale de Dakar (B.P. 5097). Further references may be extracted from J. N. van Luijk, *Selected Bibliography of Sociological and Anthropological Literature Relating to Modern and Traditional Medicine in Africa* (Leiden: Afrika-Studiecentrum, 1969). The 933 items are arranged alphabetically. Also available is Charles Tettey, "Medicine in Africa: A Bibliographical Essay," in *A Current Bibliography on African Affairs*, n.s. 3, no. 1 (January 1970): 5-18.

One of the world's greatest centers for the study of tropical medicine is the University of London's School of Hygiene and Tropical Medicine. G. K. Hall Company published the school's *Dictionary Catalogue* in 1965 and has now issued the first supplement.

AGRICULTURE

Agriculture is one of many disciplines that refuses to be neatly classified among either the natural sciences or the social ones.

Our first concern is with the scientific aspects of agriculture, which, in the 1971 printing of the *Encyclopedia Britannica*, has been treated purely under the entries "Agriculture, Primitive" and "Tropical Agriculture." The monthly *Tropical Abstracts*, published by the Royal Tropical Institute in Amsterdam, abstracts a large proportion of the relevant periodical literature.[27] Some specialized journals relevant to tropical agriculture will be found in *Biological Abstracts*. Almost a decade ago, this institute issued a duplicated list of some four hundred current periodicals on Africa. Probably a quarter of these journals are predominantly concerned with African agriculture.[28]

For a historical treatment of animals, there is Hellmut Epstein's *Origin of the Domestic Animals in Africa* (New York: Africana Publishing Corp., 1971), 2 vols.

Perhaps agricultural economics deserves to be placed both in the "agriculture" as well as the "economics" section of this work. A classic in this area is Colin Clark and Margaret R. Hasswell, *The Economics of Subsistence Agriculture*, 4th ed. (London: MacMillan; New York: St. Martin's, 1970), 267 p.

In 1971 the Commonwealth Bureau of Agricultural Economics in Oxford, England, issued: *Aspects of Agricultural Policy and Rural Development in Africa (1964-1970): An Annotated Bibliography*, ed. Margaret A. Bellam, 5 vols. (Annotated Bibliographies Series B., Africa.)

There is still an occasional need to refer to the bibliography compiled by Ruth S. Freitag, which is rightly considered a model for subject bibliography: *Agricultural Development Schemes in Sub-Saharan Africa* (Library of Congress, 1963), 189 p.

Systems of land tenure are the most significant factors determining agricultural and urban economic patterns. In 1970, the Food and Agricultural Organization of the United Nations (FAO) issued *Bibliography on Land Tenure in Africa* (Rome) 57 p. This bibliography is arranged first by country and then alphabetically by author. It includes an author index.

The following work is an example of the successful interrelationship accompanying the holding of a conference and the publication of the result: Abidjan, *Conference on Agricultural Research Priorities for Economic Development in Africa, April 5-12, 1968. I Reports II-III Papers* (Washington, D.C.: National Academy of Sciences, 1969), 3 vols. This conference was organized in cooperation with FAO and the Ivory Coast government, with financial support from the U.S. Agency for International Development (AID).

Two other FAO items are Bernard Dulfer, *Training Facilities for Cooperative Personnel in African Countries* (Rome, 1971), 158 p., which considers institutions both in and out of Africa, and Vaptistis-Titos Patrikies, *Development—A Bibliography* (Rome, 1969), 136 p.[29] The 469 entries, all annotated, particularly related to food and agriculture, are largely limited to post-1960 publication.

African agricultural school students, especially in the Francophonic areas, will benefit from D. Parrot, *Bibliographie de base pour les écoles d'agriculture d'Afrique tropicale et de Madagascar* (Paris: Bureau de developpement de la production agricole, 1968), 24 p.

THE SOCIAL SCIENCES

ANTHROPOLOGY, SOCIOLOGY, AND RELATED TOPICS

This writer has never found it easy to differentiate between these two sciences concerned with the study of man. Surely it is an oversimplification to consider anthropology as the study of man in culture, the single individual, and sociology as the study of man as a member of a group. Anthropologists have traditionally worked in the developing world, and sociologists in the developed one. In the classification of library material, anthropology belongs, at least in the Universal Decimal Classification, in the 500 category with biology, while sociology is placed in the 300 category along with the other social sciences.

Anthropology—and this discipline has long had a special relationship with Africa—is now largely in disfavor, being wrongly accused of "wanting to keep us primitive." In fact, there probably are no departments of anthropology in Africa's universities, at least in name; they prefer the name "sociology" or even "rural sociology."

Gordon D. Gibson of the Smithsonian Institution and others in the December 1969 issue of *Current Anthropology* published "A Bibliography of Anthropological Bibliographies: Africa."[30] This has also been issued separately and, for persons who order their publications outside the United States, is available from Robert Machelose and Company Ltd. in Glasgow, Scotland. This compilation is almost an essential starting point for serious anthropological research on Africa. The work is probably not known to those who are not regular readers of *Current Anthropology*.

Reference has already been made to *African Abstracts* above. It ceased to be published with the completion of the twenty-third volume covering 1972. An insufficient volume of subscribers, fewer than two thousand globally, have covered too small a proportion of rising costs that not even the assistance of UNESCO and the Ford Foundation were willing to bridge. *African Abstracts* will be particularly missed by some of the personal and institutional subscribers who do not receive a large proportion of the journals abstracted. The G. K. Hall Company of Boston reproduced the card catalog of the International African Institute, which includes a cumulative index to *African Abstracts.*

There is likely to be some continuing interest in Harold K. Schneider's *Concordance of words in the titles of African Abstracts* (Bloomington, Ind.: Indiana University, Department of Anthropology, 1971), 515 p., covering vols. 1-17 (1950-1966) minus the linguistic abstracts. This machine printout has had a small distribution, probably just within the United States. It has not yet been analyzed in the computer literature. Rightly, there has been considerable doubt about the effectiveness of titles as a means of labeling the products of social scientists. The low cost of keypunching and programming costs, and probably the comparatively low computer costs for obtaining the printout compared to the considerable benefits derived from this kind of work, may well justify its continuation. At least it will lead to a supply of more descriptive titles.[31]

Returning to substance, we will try to review a few of the better recent works of anthropologists concerned with Africa. The best and certainly the most readable is Paul James Bohannan and

Philip Curtin, *Africa and the Africans*, rev. ed. (New York: National History Press of Doubleday, 1971), 391 p. This volume is a heavily revised, improved, and updated version of the 1964 volume.

For a great insight, Melville J. Herskovits' last major work is recommended: *The Human Factor in Changing Africa* (New York: Alfred Knopf, 1962; London: Routledge Kegan Paul, 1963), 500 p. Surprisingly, there has been little discussion of this summary work of some forty years of study. This work, on the whole, succeeds in seeing Africa on its own terms and is an attempt to crowd virtually all aspects of African life into fourteen chapters.[32] Significantly, Herskovits rarely uses the term "tribalism" and then usually with quotation marks. The use of this term is the hallmark of much Eurocentric thinking and writing on this and related topics.

There are, unfortunately, very few African sociologists or anthropologists publishing. One who comes to mind immediately is Ghana's former Prime Minister, Kofi Abrefa Busia.[33] Another, who has not been in the limelight of international politics, is Arche Mafeje, head of the department of sociology at the University of Dar es Salaam.[34] Victor Uchendu, *The Igbo of Southeast Nigeria* (New York: Holt, Rineholt and Winston, 1965), 111 p., is particularly interesting since the author discusses his own people. This is also done by Jomo Kenyatta, *Facing Mount Kenya: The Tribal Life of the Gikuyu* (1938, reprint ed., New York: Random House, 1962), 339 p.

Four other recent general works on Africa by anthropologists deserve mention: Jacques Maquet, *Power and Society in Africa* (New York, Toronto: World University Library, 1971), 256 p.;[35] John Middleton, *Black Africa: Its Peoples and Their Cultures Today* (New York: Macmillan, 1970), 457 p., reprints of some of the author's previously published papers with new introductory notes; Ronald Cohen and John Middleton, eds., *From Tribe to Nation: Studies in Incorporative Process* (Scranton, Pa.: Chandler, 1970), 276 p.;[36] and Leo Kuper and M. G. Smith, *Pluralism in Africa* (Berkeley and London: University of California Press, 1971), 546 p., edited by a sociologist and an anthropologist, respectively.

Elliot P. Skinner, ed., *Peoples and Cultures of Africa, an Anthropological Reader* (Garden City, N.Y.: Doubleday/Natural History Press, 1973), 756 p., is an anthology consisting of thirty-six articles, some in translation. The arrangement is by broad subject.

Those who desire more particularly sociological references should refer to Peter C. W. Gutkind and John B. Webster, *A Select Bibliography on Traditional and Modern Africa* (New York: Syracuse University, 1968), 323 p. (Program of African Studies, Occasional Bibliography No. 8), and Dieter von Schrotter and Jungen H. Wolff, "Bibliographie der neueren sozialwissenschaftlichen Literatur über Schwarz-Afrika," *Kölner Zeitschrift der Sozial und Sozial psychologie,* Sonderheft 13 (December 1969): 717-766. The latter consists of 1,186 alphabetically arranged references with an index of broad subject headings, subdivided by countries.

DEMOGRAPHY AND POPULATION STUDIES

The terms *demography* and *population studies* are not interchangeable. The former is "the formal analysis of the components of population dynamics while the latter is concerned with a broader field covering demography plus distribution and interrelationships with nondemographic variables." This definition is from D. I. Pool, "Perspective on Tropical African Demography," *Africa* 39, no. 2 (April 1969): 167-176,[37] which provides not only useful definitions but analyzes the three important volumes published in 1968. Also published in 1968 were: the article by William A. Hance, "The Race between Population and Resources: A Challenge to the Prevailing View That Africa Need Not Worry about Population Pressure," *Africa Report* 13, no. 1 (January 1968): 6-12; William Brass, et al., *The Demography of Tropical Africa* (Princeton, N.J.: Princeton University Press), 539 p.; Robert F. Stevenson, *Population and Political Systems in Tropical Africa* (New York: Columbia University Press), 306 p.; and John Caldwell and Chukuka Okonjo, eds., *The Population of Tropical Africa* (New York: Columbia University Press; London:

Longman Green), 457 p. Parts of two volumes of Princeton University, Office of Population Research, *Population Index Bibliography, Cumulated by Authors and Geographical Areas* (Boston: G. K. Hall, 1971), 9 vols., contain references to Africa and countries therein. More recent information can be found in the supplements that G. K. Hall will publish, or in the quarterly *Population Index*. Useful too is David and Ingeborg Rodel, "Population in Sub-Saharan Africa, 1965-1971: A Bibliography," *Rural Africana* 14 (Spring 1971): 137-179. About six hundred references, taken mainly from the *Population Index*, are arranged topically.

To raise standards and to strive toward some uniformity of census material, the Economic Commission for Africa of the United Nations has published *Demographic Handbook for Africa* (Addis Ababa: ECA, 1971), 127 p.

Returning again to the wider scene, the following articles can be recommended: D. I. Pool, "The Development of Population Policies," *Journal of Modern African Studies* 9, no. 1 (May 1971): 91-105, and Apia E. Okorafor, "Africa's Population Problems," *Africa Report* 15, no. 6 (June 1970): 22-23.

Specifically on fertility, note Thomas E. Dow, Jr., "Fertility and Family Planning," *Journal of Modern African Studies* 8, no. 3 (October 1970): 445-457, and Pierre Pradervand, *Family Planning Programmes in Africa* (Paris: Organization for Economic Cooperation and Development, 1970), 77 p.

URBANIZATION

A link with the previous section may be Ian D. Park, "Urbanization and Fertility Control in Tropical Africa," *African Urban Notes* 6, no. 1 (Spring 1971): 25-43. One recent textbook attempts to codify what is known about urbanization in Africa and its relationship to population and migration. It is William A. Hance, *Population, Migration and Urbanization in Africa* (New York: Columbia University Press, 1970), 450 p.[38]

Particularly useful is William John Hanna and Judith Lynne Hanna, *Urban Dynamics in Black Africa: An Interdisciplinary*

Approach (Chicago: Aldine-Atherton, 1971), 390 p. This volume "is an important first step towards developing systematic generalisation about African city life."[39] It includes an unusually full bibliography.

In 1965, the International African Institute published a reading list, *African Urbanization.* Seven years later a bibliography with essentially the same title and focus, compiled by Hyacinth I. Ajaegbu, appeared. It includes 2,874 references—about three times the number contained in the 1965 volume. The 1972 edition has an index to towns cited, useful to the few who will not be able to place their town of study into the correct country, and an author index. What is needed now are some bibliographic essays to evaluate this vast literature, to indicate strength and weaknesses to aid future research. No doubt many of these publications and nonpublications (such as conference papers) must have been replaced by later offerings.

The following warrants citation: *Seminar on social problems and Consequences of Urbanization,* Nairobi, 1967, "Urbanization: Its Social Problems and Consequences; Report of the Seminar on Social Problems and Consequences of Urbanization," held in Nairobi, 26 November-6 December 1967 (Nairobi, East African Literature Bureau, 1969), 340 p.[40]

Two German bibliographies contain some entries not found among the almost three thousand entries compiled by H. I. Ajaegbu. "Ausegwählte neure Literatur zur Urbanisierung in Tropisch Afrika," *Afrika Spectrum* (February 1971): 84-92, emphasizes the post-1967 literature. The whole issue of this journal is devoted to urbanization. Also of note is Alex J. Halbach, *Tropisch-Afrika. Eine Kommentierte Aufsatz-Bibliographie* (Munich: Weltforum, 1971), 299 p., which is arranged according to seven subject sections and chapters, chronologically within chapters.

Probably the best current way to keep up with research and publications on urbanization is to refer to and read regularly (as regularly as this struggling journal appears) *African Urban Notes,* which is produced largely through the efforts of Ruth Simms Hamilton at Michigan State University.

MASS COMMUNICATIONS

For information about the press in Africa, still the best work is Fritz Feuereisen and Ernst Schmacke, eds., *Die Presse in Afrika, ein Handbuch für Wirtschaft und Werburg* (Munich: Verlag Dokumentation, 1968), 251 p. Newspapers are arranged alphabetically by country and then by title. For each paper, there is a statement about its nature and language and other information needed by a potential advertiser.

A recent summary is found in "Africa: Overview," which appears in John C. Merrill, *The Foreign Press* (Baton Rouge: Louisiana State University Press, 1970), p. 273-303.

The world of radio is covered well in German Africa Society, *Commercial Radio in Africa* (Munich: German Africa Society, 1970), 307 p.

A full text on mass communication is now available, and, as a byproduct, we have a most useful bibliography which is being distributed free of charge. These are: William A. Hachten, *Muffled Drums: The News Media In Africa* (Ames, Iowa: Iowa State University Press, 1971), 314 p.,[41] and his *Mass Communications in Africa: An Annotated Bibliography* (Madison, Wis.: University of Wisconsin, Center for International Communications Studies, 1971), 121 p. The 536-1/2 references are arranged by types of communication, then alphabetically by author. There are many cross-references and country and author indexes.

One important book that appeared after Hachten's bibliography is the collection of papers published by the Scandinavian Institute of African Studies. This collection resulted from a seminar held in 1970 in Helsinki on the following problems: how do the mass media, notably the press, function in Africa and how is Africa reported abroad? Olav, Stokke, ed., *Reporting Africa in the African and International Mass Media* (Uppsala: Scandinavian Institute of African Studies, 1971), 250 p.[42]

POLITICAL SCIENCE

This section will be divided into a bibliographic and a substantive part. Among the first, the place of honor belongs to Patrick J. McGowan for his *African Politics: A Guide to Research, Methods, and Literature* (Syracuse, 1970), 85 p., (Syracuse University, Program of Eastern African Studies, Occasional Paper No. 5) 45 p.[43] All students of African politics should own a personal copy. The first part of the work contains references to research method (interpreted very broadly); the second refers to studies of specific countries, comparative work, and special topics such as "Bureaucracy and Civil Service."

McGowan has a reference to Karl Deutsch and Richard L. Merritt, *Nationalism and National Development: An Interdisciplinary Bibliography* (Cambridge, Mass.: MIT Press, 1970), 519 p., which covers the literature published between 1935 and 1966, some five thousand titles in all. One section, composed of 314 references, refers specifically to Africa. A useful keyword-in-context (KWIC) index constitutes the second half of the volume.

For socialism, we now have the following useful bibliography: A.H.K. Jumba-Masagazi, comp., *African Socialism: A Bibliography and a Short Summary* (Nairobi: East African Academy, Research Information Center, 1970), 68 p. (Information Circular 4).

Turning once again to the nation-state and legislative bodies, we recommend Miriam Alman, *Debates of African Legislatures* (Cambridge, England: Heffer for the Standing Conference on Library Materials on Africa, 1972), 79 p.

For basic information and bibliographical references on local government, see Samuel Humes and Eileen Martin, *The Structure of Local Government: A Comparative Survey of 81 Countries* (The Hague: International Union of Local Authorities), 1969. Of the eighty-one countries considered, nineteen are in Africa. For each, there is a brief description and bibliography: the bibliography is short, with sometimes incomplete references.

The basic source for all governmental operations is the government gazette, which may be the only publication that governments issue. Gazettes can be issued by a government several times a day in hundreds of pages; more commonly, the amount is less. Nevertheless, when a lot of paper is issued in many series, it provides a major housekeeping problem for large academic libraries, particularly legal ones. The following publication—now outdated—covers only Anglophonic Africa: Richard Christophers, "African Official Gazettes, Part I," *Library Material on Africa* (London) 6, no. 2 (November 1968): 49-57. Christophers identifies the first issue for 1968, frequency, price, and contents. No one seems to have published comparable information for non-English-speaking Africa. See p. 43 above.

In the realm of international relations, we refer once again to Colin Legum, *Africa Contemporary Record*, and also cite Jeune Afrique's annual *Africa 1971* and succeeding volumes.[44] About half of the 440-page volume covers general topics, labeled "Insights" and "Big Projects"; the other half is arranged alphabetically by country, with basic information, maps, and illustrations.

Mohamed A. El-Khawas of Federal City College in Washington, D.C., in a commentary in *A Current Bibliography on African Affairs*, n.s. 3 (November-December 1970): 5-18, discusses "the Afro-Asian group in the United Nations." His page and a half of references, like his article, concentrates on voting records.

Legislatures generally produce some orderly records. There is, however, a larger portion of material which can be very disorderly indeed. Political parties and other groupings are the main producers of what can be described as ephemera.[45]

The year 1973 saw the publication of Robert Shaw and Richard L. Sklar, *Bibliography for the Study of African Politics* (University of California at Los Angeles: African Studies Center), 206 p. (Occasional Publication Series No. 9). The choice of entries is a good one. The arrangement of the almost four thousand entries is in seventy-one sections. There are several indexes, including an author index.

Turning now to substantive material in the area of political science or government, the following are examples of recent publications not listed in the Duignan *Guide*.

Most important is Donald George Morrison, Robert Cameron Mitchell, John Naber Paden, Hugh Michael Stevenson with Lynn F. Fischer, Joseph Kaufert, Kenneth E. Larimore, and C. William Schweers, Jr., *Black Africa: A Comparative Handbook* (New York: The Free Press, 1972), 483 p. Comparative data are presented on thirty-two independent black African countries. This work is a result of a study of national integration and political stability in black Africa begun at Northwestern University in 1967. The first part of the book presents data on 172 variables for the countries of study. The second part consists of country profiles complete with map and selected references. The third part is entitled "Cross-national Research on Africa: Issues and Context." Appendix 1 presents the African national integration project data bank. The authors of this work are eager to make available much of the data (of which only a small proportion has been published to date), particularly to African institutions. Inquiries should be directed to the Institute of Behavioural Research, York University, Downsview, Canada, and soon also to Vogelback Computing Center, Northwestern University, Evanston, Illinois, and the Inter-University Consortium for Political Research, the University of Michigan at Ann Arbor.

An important new quarterly journal, *African Review*, a journal of African politics, began publication in 1971. It emanates from the department of political science of the University of Dar es Salaam in Tanzania for $7.50 annually.

In the all-important field of public administration, up-to-date information is lacking. We may, however, refer to the review article by A.H.M. Kirk-Greene, "The New African Administrator," *Journal of Modern African Studies* 10, no. 1 (May 1972): 93-107. A composite volume of the Inter-African Public Administration seminars (IAPA), edited by David Anderson, will be forthcoming.

There are at least two collections of readings that lend themselves to use in a college course on African politics. The first is Marion E. Doro and Newell M. Stultz, eds., *Readings in African Politics* (Englewood Cliffs, N.J.: Prentice Hall, 1970) 362 p. T.V. Sathyamurthy, who reviews this volume and the following one in *Journal of Modern African Studies* 11, no. 2 (July 1972): 317-319, considers the editors' selection to be narrowly behavioristic and to rely too heavily on American contributors. Irving L. Markwitz, ed., *African Politics and Society: Basic Issues and Problems of Government and Development* (New York: The Free Press; London: Collier Macmillan, 1970), 485 p., was reviewed more favorably as it drew on a wider range of contributors, not all of whom were political scientists.

For many purposes, the following two books may be more useful, as they reproduce actual documents, than the preceding two: *Africa, Independent: A Study of Political Developments* (New York: Clark Scribner, 1972), 317 p. (Keesing Research Report No. 6) and Ian Brownlie, ed., *Basic Documents on African Affairs* (London: Oxford University Press, 1971), 556 p.

The following are rather awkward and potentially troublesome areas of concern for political scientists in most parts of the world, including Africa. They have been the focus of two anthologies: Arnold J. Heidenkeimer, ed., *Political Corruption: Readings in Comparative Analysis* (New York: Holt Rinehart, 1970), 582 p. (seven of the papers are concerned with Africa), and Hugh C. Brooks and Yassin El-Ayouty, eds., *Refugees South of the Sahara: An African Dilemma* (Westport, Conn.: Negro Universities Press, 1970), 307 p. While many of the contributors are not political scientists, the work appears to be mainly one of academic persuasion.

THE LAW

Duignan's *Guide* provides such rich information on this subject that we shall refer only to recent publications or editions.

One earlier general survey is a good summary: A. Arthur Schiller, "Law," in Robert A. Lystad, ed., *The African World, Survey of Social Research* (New York: Praeger, 1965). Useful for law students and others is Eugene Cotran and Neville N. Rubin, eds., *Readings in African Law* (New York: Africana Publishing Corp., 1970), 2 vols.[46] These volumes constitute the most thorough introduction to customary law yet published. The material is drawn from about seventy sources; it is, however, limited to Anglophonic Africa and materials in English. Much of this work was done by anthropologists rather than lawyers. The originals from which these volumes were prepared are usually found only in the largest research libraries.

Cotran and Rubin are also the editors of the *Annual Survey of African Law*, which began publication in 1967 (London, Cass).

There are chapters for virtually every country's main legal decisions and other matters of juridical interest that occurred during the year. These volumes are not limited to coverage of Commonwealth African countries but contain, albeit more briefly, information on Francophonic and other African countries. South Africa is, of course, excluded since the *Annual Survey of South African Law*, published by Juta and Co., has been published since 1948.

For some new and revised work by Anthony N. Allott, who is responsible for so much of African legal research in England, see *Judicial and Legal Systems in Africa*, 2d ed. (London: Butterworth), 314 p. (Butterworth's African Law Series 4), and *New Essays in African Law* (London: Butterworth, 1970), 348 p. (Butterworth's African Law Series 13).

Particularly good on Zaïre and other countries of Francophonic Africa is Université Libre de Bruxelles, *L'organisation judicaire en Afrique noire* (Brussels: Editions de l'Institut de Sociologie, 1969), 292 p.

Turning now to bibliography, for just a span of a few years there is Charles Szladits, *A Bibliography on Foreign and Comparative Law: Books and Articles* (Dobbs Ferry, N.Y.: Oceana, 1955). Three volumes and three supplements have been issued to date. It includes some 2,000 items on Africa. For a very important though specialized aspect of African law, there is "Acquisition and Use of State Lands in Africa: A Bibliography," *African Law Studies* 3 (February 1970): 23-52, which was prepared by the African Law Center at Columbia for the second meeting of a conference of representatives of several West African law faculties.

The largest collection for students of African law in the United States is no doubt at the Library of Congress. Zuhair E. Jwaideh, chief of the Near Eastern and African law division at LC, in his "African Law Collections in the Library of Congress," *The Quarterly Journal of the Library of Congress* 27, no. 3 (July 1970): 213-221, discusses the main sources for information on African law—government gazettes and official journals—all, or almost all, available at LC.

In Africa, Addis Ababa has become one of the main centers for the study of law. The following mimeographed volume was recently published: Thierry G. Verhelst, ed., *Legal Process and the Individual. African Source Material* (Addis Ababa: Haile Selassie I University, Faculty of Law, The Center for African Legal Development, 1972), 381 p. This volume includes background papers, a bibliography and selected legislation on exceptional tribunals, arrest and detention legal aid and the Ombudsman, as well as the report and resolutions of the ECA Conference of African Jurists, Addis Ababa, 1971.

ECONOMICS

The International Monetary Fund in Washington, D.C., publishes the very useful *Surveys of African Economies*. Each volume is concerned with documenting regional aspects in the particular group of countries. Above all, these volumes contain summaries of the economic condition of individual countries. The following volumes have been issued to date:

Vol. 1: Cameroon, Central African Republic, Chad, Congo (Brazzaville) and Gabon (1968), 365 p.
Vol. 2: Kenya, Tanzania, Uganda, Somalia (1969), 448 p.
Vol. 3: Dahomey, Ivory Coast, Mauritania, Niger, Senegal, Togo and Upper Volta (1970), 786 p.
Vol. 4: Democratic Republic of Congo (Zaïre), Malagasy Republic, Malawi, Mauritius and Zambia (1971), 477 p.

Following are some of the more useful books on African economic development. Andrew M. Kamarck, *The Economics of African Development*, rev. ed. (New York: Praeger, 1971), 352 p., examines the various sectors of the economy. To each of the chapters is appended a selected bibliography. Numerous statistical tables are included in the text and appendixes. Another useful text is Peter Robson and D. Lury, eds., *The Economies of Africa* (Evanston, Ill.: Northwestern University Press; London: Allen and Unwin, 1969), 528 p.[47] The nine chapters on individual countries review their economic plans and achievement. This volume brings together a great deal of material which previously could be located only in scattered journal articles and reports.

Of the many relevant documents of the ECA, only one will be mentioned here because of its inclusiveness: United Nations, Economic Commission for Africa, *A Survey of Economic Conditions in Africa, 1967* (New York: United Nations, 1969), 175 p. (United Nations publications sales no. E68.11.k.4 E/CN14/409/Rev. 1). Newer versions of these succinct reports are published regularly.

An important book which argues that development results from the spread of new technology rather than the flow of capital is Thomas DeGregory, *Technology and the Economic Development of the Tropical African Frontier* (Cleveland: Case Western Reserve Press, 1969), 531 p.[48] This work, like others written in English, usually is concerned with what was British Africa. Hence, the following references: Achille Elisha, *Les institutions internationales et le développement économique en Afrique, Recherches bibliographiques,* (Thèse de doctorat, Paris, 1969), 1968, 120 p., and *Industrie africaine par pays et par secteur,* annual supplement to *Afrique,* Paris (1972), 448 p. The latter contains useful advertisements to and about foreign firms operating in Africa together with other information needed by businessmen. A similar work is United States, Department of Commerce, *Digest of African Countries' Economic Development Plans* (Washington, D.C.: U.S. Government Printing Office, 1970).

Three recent works pertaining to taxation are worth noting. The first, not confined in its treatment to Africa, is John F. Due, *Indirect Taxation in Developing Economies* (Baltimore: Johns Hopkins University Press, 1970), 201 p.[49] This work provides ready access to what economists have to say about customs, duties, excises, and sales taxes. Milton C. Taylor, ed., *Taxation for African Economic Development* (New York: Africana Publishing Corp., 1970), 556 p.,[50] is an anthology. Its numerous contributions are already dated and are likely to be judged as colonialist. Third is Robert C. Hammond and Marc J. van dan Abeelen, *African Tax Systems* (Amsterdam: International Bureau of Fiscal Documentation, 1970-). This work is looseleaf in two volumes. The sheets are arranged alphabetically by country and date. Special outlines, according to which the data are presented, have been worked out for the Anglophonic and Francophonic countries. The sole division in both outlines is between direct and indirect taxes.

For teachers of African economics, three references may be cited: Helen Kimble, "On the Teaching of Economics in Africa," *Journal of Modern African Studies* 7, no. 4 (December 1969): 713-741; Ann Seidman, *An Economics Textbook for Africa*, 2d ed. (London: Methuen, 1972), 333 p.; and Edith H. Whetham and Jean I. Currie, *The Economics of African Countries* (Cambridge, England: Cambridge University Press, 1972), 288 p.[51] The Seidman volume, as the title implies, is a general economics textbook suitable for use in African colleges rather than a work from which foreigners can learn about African economies.

Among bibliographies dealing with African economics, the following may be useful: J. Dirck Stryker, *Economic Problems of Africa: Selected Bibliography* (New Haven: Yale University, Economic Growth Center, 1971), 26 p. This short bibliography, confined to recent publications, is arranged in broad categories. The Economic Growth Center Library has one of the largest collections in the United States pertaining to African economies. The catalog of the Melville J. Herskovits Library of African Studies at Northwestern University (G. K. Hall Company) includes cards from the center based on its shelflist and after January 1969 as a contributor to the *Joint Acquisitions List of Africana.*

The following work, while restricted to the Commonwealth, is not limited to Africa: Ian F. E. Hamilton, *Regional Economic Analysis in Britain and the Commonwealth* (New York: Schocken Books, 1969). References are arranged geographically by broad groupings or countries and then chronologically.

Among more specialized bibliographies are the following: L. Olu Akinwale, comp., *Marxism and African Economic Development, 1952-1968: A Bibliography* (Ibadan: Nigerian Institute of Social and Economic Research, 1968), 72 p., and Marvin P. Miracle, "The Literature on the Economics of Marketing," *African Urban Notes* 5, no. 2 (Summer 1970): 3-28.

LABOR

A focus on labor cuts across many of the traditional academic disciplines. There are scholars and practitioners concerned exclusively with African labor or labor in Africa; some are economists, others sociologists, and so forth.

The most important general study, at least for a large part of Anglophonic Africa and beyond, is B. C. Roberts, *Labour in the Tropical Territories of the Commonwealth* (London: Bell, 1964), 426 p. While this large work was written some ten years ago, it does provide the needed background.

To update this subject, two articles by V. L. Allen in the *Journal of Modern African Studies* are recommended. The first is a review article, the second largely methodological: "The Study of African Trade Unionism," 7, no. 2 (July 1969): 289-307 and "The Meaning of the Working Class in Africa," 10, no. 2 (July 1972): 169-189.

Significant too is Willie Smith, "Industrial Sociology in Africa: Foundation and Prospects," *Journal of Modern African Studies* 6, no. 1 (May 1968): 81-95. Smith recommends that industrial sociology be a focus of a research center, which should be a part of an African university.

Migrant labor has been an area of research and publication for many years. One of the early volumes that continues to influence the writing on migratory labor is Isaac Schapera, *Migrant Labour and Tribal Life: A Study of Conditions in the Bechuanaland Protectorate* (London: Oxford University Press, 1947), 248 p. A recent article on this topic is Sara S. Berry, "The Marketing of Migrant Labor Services in Africa: A Relatively Unexplored Topic," *African Urban Notes* 5, no. 3 (Fall 1970): 144-153. In a related field, there is Guy Hunter, "Employment Policy in Tropical Africa: The Need for Radical Revision," *International Labour Review* 105, no. 1 (January 1972): 35-57.

The spring 1972 issue of *Africa Today* 19, no. 2, had labor and development as its theme. Some of the articles in it were: "Namibia's General Strike," Barbara Rogers; "Trade Unions in Botswana," Seretse Khama; "The Contemporary Role of African Trade Unions," William F. Friedland; "The Transnational

Relations of African Trade Unions," Gary K. Busch; "American Labor and Africa," UAW-AFL-CIO; "Polaroid's Experiment in South Africa: Enlightened Engagement and the Structure of Apartheid," Erik P. Eckholm.

With regard to bibliographies on labor in Africa, there is nothing even close to up to date. William H. Friedland, *Unions, Labor and Industrial Relations in Africa, An Annotated Bibliography* (Ithaca, N.Y.: Cornell University, Center for International Studies, 1965), 159 p. (Cornell Research Paper in International Studies No. 4), is a model bibliography that may still be available for two dollars. It contains 683 references that are arranged alphabetically and preceded by subject and geographical indexes. A slightly earlier bibliography is Michigan State University, *Bibliography on Labor Problems in Africa with Special Reference to West Africa* (1964). This work is divided into ten subject sections that are subdivided into two to four sections each. Somewhat more recent is George P. Martens, "African Labor Unions, An Annotated Bibliography" (Northwestern University, Vogelback Computing Center, 1969), which, unfortunately, has never been published or even widely distributed. Useful also is: G. E. and Colin W. Newbury, *Annotated Bibliography of Commonwealth Migrations: The Tropical Territories in Africa, Former British Dependencies and Independent States* (Oxford: Institute of Commonwealth Studies, 1969). Arrangement is by regions and then by countries.

Those interested in the British-based sources on labor in Africa should consult the short paper by C. H. Allen, "Africa Trade Union Material," in Valerie Bloomfield, comp., *Conference on the Acquisition of Material from Africa* (London: Inter Documentation Co., 1969), p. 144-146.

Those concerned with United States, or specifically the AFL-CIO, involvements and their derivations in Africa should subscribe to the *AALC Reporter*, a monthly publication of the African-American Labor Center.

Further bibliographical references to labor in Africa can be extracted from the card catalog of Cornell University, New York State School of Industrial and Labor Relations (Boston: G. K. Hall, 1967), and International Labour Office (Geneva) Central

Library, International Labour Documentation, *Cumulative Edition*, 1965-1969 (Boston: G. K. Hall, 1970), 8 vols., and its *Subject Index to International Labour Documentation*, 1957-1964 (Boston: G. K. Hall, 1967), 2 vols.

STATISTICS

In this section, bibliographies precede the other references. First mention should be made of the one contained in Duignan's *Guide* United Nations, Economic Commission for Africa *Bibliography of African Statistical Publications, 1950-1965* (Addis Ababa, December 1966), 256 p. (E/CN. 14/Lib/SerC/2.). Not surprisingly, this work is arranged geographically. We may add its *Bibliography of African Statistical Publications* (Addis Ababa, August 1971), 19 p. (E/CN.14/Lib/SerC/2/Addl), an addendum prepared for the seventh session of the conference of African statisticians held in Dakar, October 13-22, 1971.

Turning now to substantive titles, if this be a suitable way of differentiating between bibliographical and nonbibliographical items, pride of first place belongs to Joan M. Harvey, *Statistics Africa: Sources for Market Research* (Beckenham, England: CBD Research, Ltd., 1970), 175 p. "Arranged alphabetically by country, . . . Each country section contains the address of the central statistical office and other organizations which produce statistics with a description of each organization and also of the libraries housing statistical information. The principal bibliographies of statistics and the major statistical publications are arranged under the following topics: general, production, external trade, internal distribution, population, standard of living. Each statistical publication cited is annotated." Duignan *Guide*, p. 266.

For a recent, convenient listing of the location of foreign trade publications in libraries in the United States, one should consult: Jan Wepsiec, *Serial Publications on the Foreign Trade of the Countries of Africa South of the Sahara* (Waltham, Mass.: Brandeis University, African Studies Association, 1971), 40 p. The 250 titles listed are arranged under the current name of the country. The usual symbols of the National Union Catalog are used. The acknowledgments on pages three and four list virtually all of the more-or-less full-time African bibliographers in the United States.

Fortunately, even a scanty knowledge of German will suffice to make use of Fritz Betz, ed., *Entwicklungshilfe in Afrika: ein statistisches Kompendium* . . . (Munich: Weltforum for IFO-Institut für Wirtschaftsforschung, 1970), 120 p.

PSYCHOLOGY

Psychology did not receive any separate attention in the Duignan *Guide,* although some references were included in the chapter on medicine and health. Particularly noteworthy are E. L. Klingelhofer, *A Bibliography of Psychological Research and Writing on Africa* (Dar es Salaam: University College, 1967), 31 p. (mimeo.) and Leonard Doob, "Psychology," in Robert A. Lystad, ed., *The African World,* 373-415.

Four more recent references are: S. H. Irvine, et al., "A Bibliography of Psychological and Related Writings," *A Current Bibliography on African Affairs,* n.s. 4, no. 4 (July 1971): 261-264; H. C. Hoorweg, *Psychology in Africa, A Bibliography* (Leyden: Afrika Studiecentrum, 1969), 139 p; Nova Toupet, "Bibliographie commentée de psychologie africaine (s'arretant fin 1967)," *Bulletin de l'IFAN* (Dakar) B 31, no. 4 (October 1969): 1039-1214; and Claudine Descloites, *La psychologie appliqué en Afrique, bibliographie* (Aix-en-Provence: Centre africain des sciences humaines appliquées, 1968), 34 p. (Collection des travaux du C.A.S.H.A. No. 4). The 1,045 references in Toupet, some annotated, are arranged into fifteen sections. There is an author index. The first section of this bibliography lists some nine other ones.

As many of the writings on psychology and Africa are in French, we are fortunate to have the following: Frederic R. Wickert, ed., *Readings in African Psychology: From French Language Sources* (East Lansing: Michigan State University, African Studies Center, 1967), 381 p.

Child psychology is a particularly significant sub-field of the discipline. The following work is useful: Judith L. Evans, *Children in Africa: A Review of Psychological Research* (New York: Teachers College Press, 1970), 115 p. (Publication of the Center for Education in Africa).

LINGUISTICS

This section, as many previous ones, will merely amplify and update Duignan's *Guide.*

John D. Murphy and Harry Goff, comps., *A Bibliography of African Languages and Linguistics* (Washington, D.C.: The Catholic University of America Press, 1969), 147 p., is a bibliography confined to monographs according to the International African Institute's *Handbook of African Languages* classification. An index to authors and languages is included.

Much of what is contained in the various volumes of the *Handbook* has been discredited by Joseph H. Greenberg's reclassification of African languages on the basis of their genetic interrelations. The degree of acceptance of Greenberg's theories can be construed by the fact that he is partly the author of the short article on African languages in the *Encyclopedia Britannica 1*, p. 312-314, 1971 and his map showing the classification of African languages is also reproduced in *Collier's Encyclopedia, 1.*

A good essay, "Linguistics," by Joseph H. Greenberg is chapter 15 in Robert A. Lystad, *The African World*, a survey of social research, 1965, 416-441, 549-554. Greenberg, *The Languages of Africa*, (Bloomington Indiana University, 1966), 180 (Research Center in Anthropology, Folklore and Linguistics) is the key work in African linguistics.[52]

A bibliography that illustrates the interrelationship of many aspects of the social sciences and the humanities (and, incidentally, serves as an example of a useful yet hardly accessible bibliography) is the following compiled by John N. Paden: "A Working Bibliography on Language Pluralism and National Integration with Special Reference to Africa. An Appendix to the Paper, Language Ethnicity, Religion and Race: Units or Variables in the Study of National Integration," paper presented at Northwestern University, May 13-15, 1969, 23 p.[53]

Among good recent collections are: Guy Atkins, ed., *African Language Studies* (London: University of London School of Oriental and African Studies, distributed by Luzac, 1970), 435 p., and David Dalby, ed., *Language and History in Africa: A Volume of Collected Papers Presented to the London Seminar on Languages and History in Africa* (London: Frank Cass, 1970; New York: Africana Publishing Corp., 1971), 159 p.[54] Dalby recommends in "A Note on African Language Bibliography" that a generic classification for African language should be attempted only where there is no disagreement (for example "Bantu"); otherwise, the classification should be geographic (for example "West Africa").[55]

There is one fairly new bibliography of Bantu languages that supplements references in the *Handbook*: André Jacquot, *Elements de bibliographie linguistique bantoue* (Brazzaville: Office de la récherche scientifique et technique outre-mer, 1968), 22 p. The 197 items are listed alphabetically. There is an index. One other G. K. Hall catalog is the *Catalogue of the C. M. Doke Collection of African Languages, The University of Rhodesia Library* (1972), 546 p., which has about 8,390 entries. It is particularly strong in works on Bantu philology. The catalog also contains a complete bibliography of Doke's writings, most of which, surprisingly, are not in the collection.

A recent book is Thomas A. Sebeok, ed., *Current Trends in Linguistics*, Vol. 7: *Linguistics in Sub-Saharan Africa* (The Hague: Mouton, 1971), 972 p. Jack Berry and Joseph H. Greenberg are the associate editors, David W. Crabb and Paul Schachter the assistant editors. This is a large state-of-the-art report by twenty-eight different contributors. Particularly useful is the checklist of language and dialect names prepared by William Welmers. The introductory paper in this volume is Desmond Cole's "The History of African Linguistics to 1945."

A good introduction for the layman to the complexities of African languages and linguistics is Pierre Alexandre, *Languages and Language in Black Africa*, trans. Frances A. Leary (Evanston, Ill.: Northwestern University Press, 1972), 132 p.[56] An even briefer introduction that facilitates the transition to literature is Jack Berry, "Language Systems and Literature," in John N.

Paden and Edward W. Soja, eds., *The African Experience* (Evanston, Ill.: Northwestern University Press, 1970). This article is clear and well documented.

THE HUMANITIES

RELIGION AND MISSIONS

This section will largely supplement the useful selection contained in Duignan's *Guide.*

The literature is large and consists of the writings of practitioners who may or may not also be academics.

A good overview is provided by Noel Q. King, *Christian and Muslim in Africa* (New York: Harper and Row, 1971), 153.[57] It includes notes, sources, and a reading list. See also his *Religion in Africa: A Pilgrimage into Traditional Religions* (New York: Harper and Row, 1970), 116 p.,[58] John S. Mbiti, *African Religions and Philosophy* (New York: Praeger, 1969), 200 p., and his *Concepts of God in Africa* (New York: Praeger, 1970), 348 p. Both of Mbiti's volumes contain sizable bibliographies. See also Okot p' Bitek, *African Religions in Western Scholarship* (Kampala: East African Literature Bureau, 1971), 140 p.; Thomas A. Beetham, *Christianity and the New Africa* (London: Pall Mall, 1967), 206 p.; Vincent Monteil, *Islam noir* (Paris: Editions du Seuil, 1971), 420 p. (Coll. Esprit. Ser. Frontière ouverte); and Tarence O. Ranger, and I. N. Kimambo, *The Historical Study of African Religion* (Berkeley: University of California Press, 1972), 307 p., which reproduces some of the papers of a conference held in Dar es Salaam in 1970. The volume is restricted to religious history of East and Central Africa. Another outcome of that conference was probably the newsletter *African Religious Research,* African Studies Center, University of California, Los Angeles, No. 1, April 1971, which is issued twice a year.

A rather complex suggestion of how research on African religions might be analyzed is James W. Fernandez, "Contemporary African Religion: Confluents of Inquiry," in Gwendolen M. Carter and Ann Paden, eds., *Expanding Horizons in African Studies* (Evanston, Ill.: Northwestern University Press, 1969). Note also Marcia Wright, "African History in the 1960's: Religion," *African Studies Review* 14, no. 3 (December 1971): 439-445. This short article discusses some of the most significant publications of the past decade.

For persons needing to supplement Robert Cameron Mitchell, et al., *A Comprehensive Bibliography of Modern African Religious Movements* (Evanston, Ill.: Northwestern University Press, 1966), 132 p., there are H. W. Turner, "Bibliography of Modern African Religious Movements. Supplement I number 1340-1601," *Journal of Religion in Africa* 1, no. 3 (1968): 173-211, and his "Bibliography of Modern African Religious Movements. Supplement II nos. 1602-1917," *Journal of Religion in Africa* 3, no. 2 (1970): 161-208. Dr. Turner is working on a third supplement and a cumulative edition.

There are numerous journals devoted to religion in Africa in addition to the title just mentioned: *African Ecclesiastical Review* (1959-), Musaka, Uganda, quarterly; *Ministry* (1960-), P.O. Box 12, Morija, Lesotho, quarterly; *Flambeau* (1964-), Centre de Littérature Evangelique, B.P. 1133, Yaounde, Cameroun; *Bulletin of the Society for African Church History* (1963-), Department of Religious Studies, University of Aberdeen, King's College, Aberdeen Scotland, annual; *African Theological Journal* (1968-), Lutheran Theological College, P. O. Box 55, Usa River, Tanzania, annual; *Orita* (1967-), Department of Religious Studies, Ibadan University, Ibadan, Nigeria, semiannual; *Cahiers des religions Africaines* (1967-1971), Centre d'Etudes des religions Africaines, Université Kinshasa, B. P. 867, Kinshasa, semiannual.

EDUCATION

Duignan's *Guide* contains references to just about all bibliographies on education worthy of consultation. Particularly helpful is John W. Hanson and Geoffrey W. Gibson, *African Education and Development Since 1960: A Select and Annotated Bibliography* (East Lansing, Mich.: State University, Institute of International Studies in Education and African Studies Center, 1966), 327 p. It is arranged topically, divided into nine parts and one of appendixes. Within parts, the arrangement is by country and then alphabetically by author. There are cross-references and an overall author index.

For a larger and more up-to-date volume of references, one should consult University of London, Institute of Education, *Catalogue of the Comparative Education Library* (Boston: G. K. Hall, 1971), 6 vols. Two volumes each are by author, subject, and region. In 1969 the Institute's Collection of Education in Tropical Africa (Boston: G. K. Hall, 1964), was merged with the collection of the Institute's Department of Comparative Education. Some 114,000 cards are inthe combined catalog; supplements will probably be issued.

Some additional bibliographies follow. See, for example, Johannes Christian Coetzee, *Annotated Bibliography of Research in Education* (Pretoria: Human Sciences Research Council, 1970), 181 p.

France, Secretariat d'Etat aux affairs étrangères chargé de la cooperation, Bureau pour le developpement de la production agricole (BDPA), *Bibliographie de base pour les écoles d'agriculture d'Afrique tropicale et de Madagascar* (Paris: Le Bureau, n.d.), 24 p. is of course particularly pertinent for schools of tropical agriculture.

United Nations, Economic Commission for Africa, *Selected Bibliography: Manpower and Training Problems in Economic and Social Development* (July 1967), (E/CN.14/Lib/SerC/3), 45 p., is arranged by broad subjects, within which books, articles, and documents are separated.

See Centre africain de formation et de récherche administratives pour le developpement, *General bibliography on training in public administration* (Tangier, Morocco, 1971), 60 p. (mimeo.). The African Training and Research Center in Administration for Development (CAFRAD) has published *Cahiers africaines d'administration publique* twice a year since 1967.

Finally, a very specialized bibliography is John H. Case, *Annotated Bibliography on Science and Mathematics Education in Sub-Saharan Africa* (Paris: UNESCO, 1970), 234 p. This work is restricted to countries where English is the medium of instruction, South Africa excluded. The bibliography separates science from mathematics and is then arranged by region. There are author and subject indexes.

Contemporary educational policy (excluding university education) was the theme of the 1968 biannual conference of the African Studies Association of the United Kingdom. Nineteen papers focusing on contemporary issues of educational policy are included in Richard Jolly, ed., *Education in Africa: Research and Action* (Nairobi: East African Publishing House, 1969), 313 p.

Information about African universities is not easy to obtain. The sources in the annually revised *World of Learning* are usually accurate. Fuller information can be found in African American Institute, *African Colleges and Universities* (New York: AAI, 1970), 123 p. The arrangement is by sovereign state, excluding Rhodesia and South Africa. The information presented is essentially extracted from college and university catalogs rather than from special questionnaires. An attempt is made to present basic information that an American, and possibly an African, student may want to know.

As an outcome of the 1962 conference on the future of higher education in Africa, organized by UNESCO and held at Tananarive, and some succeeding meetings, the Association of African Universities was formed. Its headquarters are in Accra. It has held a series of conferences, the most significant of which was one held in Accra in 1972: Tijani M. Yesufu, ed., *Creating the African University: Emerging Issues of the 1970s* (Ibadan: Oxford University Press, 1973), 294 p. The book contains a discussion of general questions and case studies. The association administers the Inter-Africa Universities Scholarship Program. By means of its Documentation Centre, information is disseminated to member universities and other interested parties.

LITERATURE

African literature is the topic of an article in the *Encyclopedia Britannica* included for the first time in the 1971 printing.

The bibliography of African literature is extensive as is the discussion of what is African literature. Is it anything written and possibly also published in Africa? Does the writer have to be black? May he be black and writing outside of Africa? Is African literature restricted to the literature in African languages? What about oral African literature? This section will once again be largely restricted to references either not found in Duignan's *Guide* or an earlier edition.

The pride of place among these bibliographies belongs to the late Janheinz Jahn. Jahn restricted his second edition to black Africa, but not so in: Janheinz Jahn, *A Bibliography of Neo-African Literature from Africa, America and the Caribbean* (New York: Praeger, 1965), 359 p. The new edition is: Janheinz Jahn and Claus Peter Dressler, *Bibliography of Creative African Writing* (Nendeln, Liechtenstein: Kraus-Thomson, 1971), 446 p.[59] Within Jahn's self-imposed restriction, this volume is as comprehensive as anyone could make it. It is worth reading the introductory pages as they explain the arrangement of the countries.

A much more selective volume is: John A. Ramsaran, *New Approaches to African Literature, A Guide to Negro-African Writing and Related Studies*, 2d ed. (Ibadan: Ibadan University Press, 1970), 168 p. Also selective is Hans Zell and Helene Silver, with contributions by Barbara Abrash and Gideon-Cyrus M. Mutiso, *A Reader's Guide to African Literature* (New York: Africana Publishing Corp.; London: Heinemann Educational Books, 1971), 232 p.[60] This is an unusual reference work indeed, for it is frequently entertaining as well as scholarly. It begins with a scholarly introduction. The first 122 annotated references are concerned with bibliographies, criticism, and anthologies. Part I consists of writings in English, arranged geographically, and Part II is concerned with French and English translations. Gideon-Cyrus M. Mutiso's section contains references to "politically committed literature in English." Other sections are devoted to "children's books," "some articles on African literature," and "periodicals and magazines." Another part of this admirable volume consists of biographies, each about two pages or so in length, and illustrated with photographs and footnotes. "Essential addresses" include those of publishers and booksellers.

Janheinz Jahn, et al., *Who Is Who in African Literature, Biographies, Works, Commentaries* (Tübingen: Erdmann, 1972), 407 p., includes sketches of a wide range of African authors. Pal

Páricsy, comp., *A New Bibliography of African Literature* (Budapest: Center for Afro-Asian Research of the Hungarian Academy of Sciences, 1969), 105 p. (Studies on Developing Countries, No. 24), is largely concerned with updating the first edition of Jahn's bibliography and is of little use to those with access to Jahn's volume published in Liechtenstein.

Specialists should note: Nancy I. Schmidt, "A Bibliography of American Doctoral Dissertations on African Literature," *Research in African Literature* 1, no. 1 (1970): 62-65.[61] Her thorough search revealed only thirty-seven dissertations.

A "literary index" is included in the Library of Congress, *Africa South of the Sahara: Index to Periodical Literature* (Boston: G. K. Hall, 1971), vol. 4, p. 643-744. These large one hundred pages are divided into sections on poetry, novels, plays, and short stories, and the works of authors are arranged alphabetically within sections. It does not, however, contain references not found elsewhere. The arrangement by literary genre and then author has some merit. See also National Book League, *Creative Writings from Black Africa (Sub-Saharan): Checklist* (London: National Book League, 1971) 30 p.

While it is not easy to learn about future publications in the field of African literature, the following sources may help. For scholarly material, one should make a thorough scrutiny of *Research in African Literature* and the annual MLA (Modern Language Association) *International Bibliography*. A section on African literature has been included since June 1968. The appearance of actual publications, rather than scholarly criticism, is reported in many African literary journals, the most important of which is *Cultural Events in Africa*, a monthly published in London since 1965; as its title implies, it is concerned with all the arts. Many literary works are also included in the bimonthly *Joint Acquisitions List of Africana*, published by the Melville J. Herskovits Library of African Studies at Northwestern University. For the many readers who do not care to spend time searching in bibliographies before they can enjoy their literature, we can recommend a subscription to the African Writers Series that has been issued by Heinemann Educational Books in London since 1962 and by the Humanities Press in New York. A 1972 checklist includes 106 volumes. Also note *The Conch Review of Books,* a quarterly literary supplement on Africa that began publication in March 1973. It is available from Conch Magazine, Department of African Studies, State University of New York, New Paltz, N.Y.

While all the references cited above are also concerned with Francophonic African literature, the following three references deal with it exclusively: Thérèse Baratte-Eno Belinga, *Bibliographie auteurs africains et malgaches de langue française. 3e édition revue et mise à jour avec la collaboration du Service "Etudes et Documentation,"* ORTF/DAEC (Paris: Office de Radiodiffusion Télévision Française, 1972), 124 p.;[62] Thomas Cassirer, "Periodicals and Other Recently Published Source Material Useful for the Study of African Literature in French," *Research in African Literature* 1, no. 1 (Spring 1970): 66-69; and Macalister C. Cairus, "The African Colonial Society in French Colonial Novels," *Cahier d'études africaines* 9, no. 2 (1969): 175-193. This last article includes a list of fifty-two novels published from 1912 to 1965.

Biobibliographical articles are published in the *Africana Library Journal.* To date, the following have appeared: Helene Silver, "Chinue Achebe," vol. 1, no. 1 (Spring 1970): 18-22; Barbara Abrash, "Fanz Fanon, Bio-bibliography," vol. 2, no. 3 (Autumn 1971): 9-12; and James M. Gibbs, "Wole Soyinka Bio-bibliography," vol. 3, no. 1 (Spring 1972): 15-22. Soyinka has also been the subject of a literary biography: Gerald Moore, *Wole Soyinka* (New York: Africana Publishing Corp.; London: Evans Bros., 1972), 114 p. References to earlier studies of African writers, including the three on Achebe, can be found in Zell's *A Reader's Guide to African Literature.*

There are numerous anthologies of African literature. Fifty-seven are listed and annotated in the Zell volume mentioned above, and Jahn lists 118 anthologies.

Ulli Beier, comp. and ed., *African Poetry, an Anthology of Traditional African Poems* (Cambridge: Cambridge University Press, 1966), 80 p., is a slim and attractive volume intended for school use in Africa and elsewhere. The poems are arranged by theme and are drawn from many parts of Africa. There are explanations and sources, many of them in German.

Jack Berry, Robert Plant Armstrong, and John Povey, "Proceedings of a Conference on African Languages and Literature," held at Northwestern University, April 28-30, 1966," 140 p. (mimeo.), contains "pilot papers of a conference . . . together with the edited transcripts and discussion arising out of the papers." It is regrettable that this volume was never formally published. (It is available on loan or for purchase from CAMP/CRL in Chicago.) The preliminary version contains far too much administrative detail and too little literary analysis. Nevertheless, parts of many of the papers are valuable.

The bulk of the contents of Charles Angolf and John Povey, *African Writing Today* (Woodhaven, N.Y.: Maryland Books, 1969), 304 p., appeared in *The Literary Review*. After an essay by John Povey, the volume continues with stories, poetry, and a novella by some of Africa's lesser known authors from Ethiopia, Ghana, Nigeria, Sierra Leone, Uganda, and Zambia.

Oscar Ronald Dathorne and Willfried Feuser, eds., *Africa in Prose* (Hammondsworth, Middlesex: Penguin Books, 1969), 384 p., is a collection of forty-four extracts taken from the entire continent, dating from the beginning of the twentieth century to the present. The editors provide an introduction, biographical notes, and a brief introduction to each extract.

James E. Miller, Jr., et al., *Black African Voices* (Glenview, Ill.: Scott Foresman, 1970), 431 p., is an anthology of verse and prose arranged alphabetically by author. It is evidently a text intended for school use, with "Discussion Questions" appended and the usual brief biographical lines. The choice of authors and their material is a good one. This book is intended to be used as a resource volume, preferably with the aid of a good teacher. It obviously is not intended to be read in the order in which the works appear.

Wilfred Cartey and Martin Kilson, *The African Reader*, Vol. 1, *Colonial Africa* (New York: Random House, 1970), 266 p., is an anthology arranged by the following themes: reaction to conquest, methods of and adaptations to colonial rule, emergence of the masses and elite-mass-nexus, formation of national institutions. Vol. 2, *Independent Africa* (429 p.), is also arranged by themes: African institutions, the foundations for self-rule, movement for independence, the role of the intellectual in independent Africa, repression and resistance, and militarism in Africa.

As for Albert S. Gérard, *Four African Literatures: Xosa, Sotho, Zulu and Amharic* (Berkeley: University of California Press, 1971), 458 p., it is hard to see what themes hold this anthology together. The first three are the largest ethnic groups of South Africa, the fourth the largest Ethiopian group.

Contributors to Christopher Heywood, ed., *Perspectives on African Literature: Selections from the Proceedings of the Conference on African Literature Held at the University of Ife, 1968* (London: Heinemann Educational Books, 1971), 175 p., are James Ngugi, Eldred Jones, Abiola Irele, David Cook, David Rubadiri, E. Ofori Akeyea, Ime Ikiddeh, Oyin Ogunba, Brenda ackman, A. Afoloyan, A. Izerbaye, and Lalage Bown. Pal Páricsy, ed., *Studies on Modern Black African Literature* (Budapest: Center for Afro-Asian Research of the Hungarian Academy of Sciences, 1971), 121 p. (Studies on Developing Countries, No. 43), is a translation which "appeared originally in Hungarian in the Black African Literature special issue of *Helikon!*" There are eight essays altogether, including those by Páricsy, Lindfors, Ravenscroft, Brutus, and another Hungarian, Tibor Keszthelui. "The essays are followed by a bibliography of translations and critical studies published in Hungary between 1942 and 1969."[63]

Dennis Duerden and Cosmo Pieterse, eds., *African Writers Talking: A Collection of Interviews* (London: Heinemann Educational Books; New York: Africana Publishing Corp., 1972), 195 p., contains interviews with eighteen of Africa's best known Anglophonic authors.[64] The interviews, fully introduced and documented, can be highly recommended for those wishing to learn about Africa and its literature. Excellent full-page photographs of the authors add to the full bio- and bibliographic treatment of the authors. The actual tapes on which the work is based are available in London and in several libraries in the United States, including the one at Northwestern University and the Schomberg Collection of The New York Public Library.

Finally, there is Eustace Palmer, *An Introduction to the African Novel: A Critical Study of Twelve Books by Chinua Achebe, James*

Ngugi, Camara Laye, Elechi Amadi, Ayi Kwei Armah, Mongo Beti, and Gabriel Okara (New York: African Publishing Corp., 1972), 176 p. (Studies in African Literature).[65]

Oral Literature

Moving from a transcript of interviews of African writers, we turn to oral literature. First comes Harold Scheub, *Bibliography of African Oral Narratives* (Madison, Wis.: University of Wisconsin Press, 1971), 160 p. (African Studies Program, Occasional Paper No. 3).

Veronika Görög, "Bibliographie analytique selective sur la littérature orale de l'Afrique noire," *Cahier d'études africaines* 8, no. 3 (1968), no. 31, 453-501, contains 385 entries and includes an ethnolinguistic index. This bibliography is continued in the same journal: vol. 9, no. 4 (1969), no. 36, 641-666, and vol. 10, no. 4 (1970), no. 40, 583-631.

The following is included in Zell's "Stop Press Addendum": Ruth H. Finnegan, *Oral Literature in Africa* (Oxford: Clarendon Press, 1970), 558 p. (Oxford Library of African Literature). This is already supplemented by: Greta M. K. Avery, "A Bibliography of Oral Literature (Addition to That of R. Finnegan)," *Africana Research Bulletin* (Sierra Leone) 1, no. 2 (January 1971): 27-29.

Finally, one may note: "Major Collections at the Center for African Oral Data," Archives of Traditional Music, Indiana University, Bloomington, Indiana, *African Studies Newsletter* 5, no. 3 (June 1972): 37-41. Its tabular presentation is arranged by collector, year of collection, area/group, accession number, and number of tapes. It includes a list of phonotape collections of African oral data probably ready for processing in 1972-1973.

Children's Literature

This section introduces a few references to publications suitable for readers of precollege age. Best of all are the titles read by their contemporaries in Africa that reflect not their colonial heritage but their traditions (in part of precolonial origin) and their current striving. They include the African Junior Library and the African Reader Library series published by the African Universities Press in Lagos. They are available in the United States through the Africana Publishing Corporation in New York City and in Great Britain through Ginn and Company. The East African Publishing House (EAPH) in Nairobi has published the East African Readers Library and the East African Junior Library. Since Northwestern University Press no longer distributes EAPH, it is uncertain where these small volumes are available in the United States. Heinemann Educational Books distributes them from London.

The following two volumes were written especially for American youth: Edward R. Kolergon, *Africa, South of the Sahara* (Boston: Allyn and Bacon, 1970), 106 p. (Afro-Asian Regional Studies), a well-illustrated study unit for the high school level, and Mary Penick Motley, *Africa, Its Empires, Nations and People, A Reader for Young Adults* (Detroit: Wayne State University Press, 1969), 164 p.

Good titles from Africa will be found in the "children's books" section in Zell and Silver, *A Readers Guide to African Literature*. More are cited in Lalage Bown, "Children's Books from Africa," *Interracial Books for Children* 2, no. 4 (Spring 1970), available from the Council on Interracial Books for Children in New York City, and Maureen Beatrice Sewitz, comp., "Children's Books in English in an African Setting, 1914-1964," Johannesburg, University of Witwatersrand, Department of Bibliography, Librarianship and Typology, 1965, 89 p. (mimeo.), which is arranged geographically with an author index. This latter work is based on the holdings of libraries of Johannesburg and the H. W. Wilson's *Children's Catalog*.

We now turn to references by a scholar—an anthropologist and librarian—who has had a long-time interest in African children's literature, Dr. Nancy J. Schmidt, who is the *Africana Library Journal (ALJ)* editor for children's and young people's literature. Her articles in chronological order (in part predating the *ALJ*) follow. "Children's Literature about Africa," *African Studies Bulletin* 8, no. 3 (December 1965): 61-70, is followed by a bibliography of children's books about the people of Africa listing sixty-seven titles of books on the people of Africa suitable for children. Books recommended for lower elementary grades and junior high and older pupils are so marked. See also "Children's Literature about Africa: A Reassessment," *African Studies Review* 13, no. 3 (December 1970): 469-488; "Children's Books About Africa by African Authors," *ALJ* 2, no. 3 (Autumn 1971): 5-6; "Books by African Authors for Non-African Children," *ALJ* 2, no. 4 (Winter 1971): 11-13; and "Children's Books about Africa in Series: Picture Books," *ALJ* 3, no. 1 (Spring 1972): 3-5.

A recent full bibliography is James P. Johnson, *Africana for Children and Young People, A Current Guide for Teachers and Librarians* (Westport, Conn.: Greenwood Press, 1971), 172 p. (Special Bibliographic Series, Vol. 8, No. 1). This bibliography is not restricted to books. It is arranged geographically by large regions—Central, East, West and South. Nonfiction is separated from fiction as are books from audiovisual materials. Useful directory information is also included.

THEATER

The conventional division between literary genres and music, drama, and the graphic arts is largely a Euro-American one. In Africa, the arts are more closely related; they form a normal part of life and are not necessarily the work of specialists. It is only for the convenience of users of this volume that the arrangement of the various arts follows a non-African pattern.

There is as yet no general text in English on the theater in Africa. In French and for Francophonic Africa, one can recommend: Robert Cornevin, *Le Théâtre en Afrique noire et à Madagascar* (Paris: Le Livre Africain, 1970), 335 p. This book looks like a popularization but it is really a scholarly work with numerous footnotes and a useful classified bibliography.

For another bibliography, consult: N. B. East, ed., *African Theatre, A Checklist of Critical Materials* (New York: Africana Publishing Corp., 1970), 47 p.[66] This list is divided into seven parts: bibliography, general, North, South, East, West, and film. It was previously published in part in the *Afro-Asian Theatre Bulletin* 4, no. 2 (Spring 1969).

Some specialists will be interested in: E. N. Hussein, "An Annotated Bibliography of Swahili Theater," *Swahili* 39, no. 1/2 (1969): 49-60.

MUSIC

There are at least three fairly recent essays with bibliographical appendixes that survey African music: Alan P. Merriam, "Music and the Dance," in Robert A. Lystad, ed., *The African World* (1965), 452-468, "Bibliography and Literature Cited," 556-558; Klaus Wachsmann, "Ethnomusicology in African Studies: The Next Twenty Years," in Gwendolen M. Carter and Ann Paden, eds., *Expanding Horizons in African Studies* (1969), 131-142; and Klaus Wachsmann, "Ethnomusicology in Africa," in John N. Paden and Edward W. Soja, *The African Experience* (1970), pp. 128-151.

The major bibliography is the one compiled by Lionel John Palmer Gaskin under the direction of Klaus Wachsmann: *A Select Bibliography of Music in Africa* (London: International African Institute, 1965), 83 p. (African Bibliography Series B). This bibliography of almost 3,500 items was reprinted in 1971 with corrections. There is no need for those who already have the 1965 edition to purchase this new printing. The corrigenda are reproduced in *Africa* 41, no. 4 (October 1971): 324-325. This includes the references to Klaus P. Wachsmann, ed., *Essays on Music and History in Africa* (Evanston, Ill.: Northwestern University Press, 1971), 268 p., which was already referred to in the 1965 bibliography.

An annotated bibliography was compiled by: Douglas Varley, *African Native Music: An Annotated Bibliography* (London: Royal Empire Society, 1963), 116 p. It has been reprinted by Dawsons of Pall Mall (London) 1970, and by International Publications Service (New York), 1971.

Useful too and most inexpensive is Darius L. Thieme, *African Music: A Briefly Annotated Bibliography* (Washington, D.C.: Library of Congress, Reference Department, Music Division, 1964), 55 p. It was reprinted in 1970 and is available from the

Superintendent of Documents, U.S. Government Printing Office, for seventy-five cents.

Another even briefer listing is: Richard Colving, "Black Music, A Bibliographic Survey, *Choice* 6, no. 9 (November 1969): 1169-1179.

Turning now to special aspects of music, we may start with Alan P. Merriam, *African Music on LP: An Annotated Discography* (Evanston, Ill.: Northwestern University Press, 1970), 200 p. The publication of this discography is the climax of many years of labor. The arrangement is by recording company and then in the order in which the records were released. Merriam supplies each record with a bold number, reaching a total of 389. There are no less than eighteen indexes. All information is taken from the record label and any notes that accompanied the record. Note also Alan Merriam's plea for further African discography in James Pearson and Ruth Jones, eds., *The Bibliography of Africa* (1970).

With regard to musical instruments there is: Margaret M. DeLange, comp., *Catalogue of the Musical Instruments in the Collection of Professor Percival R. Kirby* (Johannesburg: Africana Museum, 1967), 155 p. This collection is on loan to the museum. The first section of the catalog relates to those instruments which formed the basis of Percival Robson Kirby, *The Musical Instruments of the Native Races of South Africa* (Witwatersrand University Press, 1953). The arrangement is according to a classification scheme recommended by Erich M. von Hornbostel in "The Ethnology of African Sound Instruments," *Africa* 6, no. 2 (April 1933): 129-157, no. 3 (July): 277-311.

Returning to more current times, one should note: International Folk Music Council, London, *Films on Traditional Music and Dance; a First International Catalogue*, ed. Peter Kennedy (Paris: UNESCO, 1970), 261 p. It lists 381 films according to country. Thirty-four of these are African. The information presented was gathered by means of questionnaires. The questions pertain to location, type, duration, characteristics (that is, technical ones), production, distribution, and synopsis.

There is no easy way of keeping up to date with the issue of new phonograph records on anything, let alone from Africa. In 1969 Alan Merriam ceased to be music editor of *Africa Report.* There are occasional references to "Music and Dance" in *A Current Bibliography on African Affairs* (Washington, D.C.).

THE PLASTIC ARTS

As in music, there is an outstanding bibliography about African art compiled by John Lionel Palmer Gaskin and published by the International African Institute in 1965. It is still available at a modest price; there are almost five thousand references. After some introductory sections, the bulk of the work is arranged by region and then country with the following subdivisions: figures and masks, buildings and furniture, clothing and adornment, rock art, techniques, utensils, tools, weapons, miscellaneous, African art today. There is a 169-item section of "Bibliographies of Africana Likely to Be of Use to the Student." Catalogs and guides to museums, exhibitions, and collections are arranged by the following categories: general, Africa, and then by country, mainly European and the United States. Page 94 lists special numbers of periodicals, a total of forty-seven. An index to periodicals is included, along with separate author, geographical and ethnic, and subject indexes.

Only one field of African art—dress—has been bibliographically supplemented: Joanne Bubolz Eicher, *African Dress, A Selected and Annotated Bibliography of Sub-Saharan Countries* (Michigan State University, African Studies Center and Department of Textiles, Clothing and Related Arts, 1969), 134 p. The 1,025 references are arranged by broad regions and then by countries. There is an author index. The references are limited to works in English. References are to journal articles and the relevant sections in monographs. "Dress" is interpreted broadly; it includes related industries, body decoration, and mutilation. Unfortunately, it contains many errors and inaccuracies.[67]

Turning now to substantive volumes on African art, the most significant book is Frank Willett, *African Art: An Introduction* (New York: Praeger; London: Thames and Hudson, 1971), 288 p.[68] This excellent book is not in large format. It is above all the work of a university professor, an anthropologist and an archaeologist, who has spent many years in Nigeria and for some years has been professor of African art. The volume is concerned with plastic arts and architecture and treats its subject matter largely historically. This book is no mere text, for it contains 249 plates, 61 of which are in color.

Another fine volume is: Dennis Duerden, *African Art* (London: Paul Hamlyn, 1969), 80 p. The text is accurate and concise, but it is mainly the fifty-one superb plates, all of them in color, that give the book its appeal.

A much larger book is: Michael Leiris and Jacqueline Delange, *African Art*, trans. Michael Ross (London: Thames and Hudson, 1968), 454 p. The authors consider this a provisional study. Its text, however, is sound and the 444 plates, some in color, are excellent. The bibliography contains 504 items. Notes on the illustrations identify the pieces and relate them to similar ones.

One recent book places art into a wider perspective: Douglas Fraser and Herbert M. Cole, eds., *African Art and Leadership* (Madison, Wis.: University of Wisconsin Press, 1972), 332 p.[69] Five of the eleven essays were first presented in a 1965 symposium, "The Aristocratic Tradition in African Art," at Columbia University. The essays, by seven art historians, four anthropologists, a historian, and a physician have been turned by the editors into a readable volume throwing light on the meaning behind Africa's great sculptural tradition. The book contains 124 illustrations.

A recent work, which is likely to gain in significance, is: Robert Plant Armstrong, *The Affecting Presence: An Essay in Humanistic Anthropology* (Urbana, Ill.: University of Illinois Press, 1971), 206 p.[70]

The following volume is concerned with African architecture: Paul Oliver, ed., *Shelter in Africa* (New York: Praeger, 1971), 240 p. This well-integrated text consists of sixteen contributions by architects, anthropologists, a sociologist, a town-planner, and a political scientist, all with extended experience in Africa. There are bibliographies at the end of each chapter.

The following excellent work has now been published: Labelle Prussin and David Lee, "Architecture in Africa: An Annotated

Bibliography," *Africana Library Journal* 4, no. 3 (Autumn 1973), 2-32. The interpretation of architecture is a broad one. The arrangement is alphabetical.

The following is a rather specialized reference, which also serves to illustrate how scattered and in what unsuspected journals one may find relevant information: Rames Jauva, "African Art Collections in Budapest," *Africa Quarterly* (New Delhi) 8, no. 4 (January-March 1969): 383-386.

There are many handbooks to museums in Europe and America. There is now a good one for Africa: Gundolf Seidenspinner, comp., *Museums in Africa, A Directory* (Munich: German African Society; New York: Africana Publishing Corp., 1970), 594 p. As is customary for such works, it was compiled by means of questionnaires. The one used for this volume had sixteen questions. The resulting answers are arranged by country and city. An appendix groups museums by type. A brief keyword index is also included.

Art and ethnographic collections of Africana are described in Peter Duignan, *Handbook of American Sources for African Studies* (1966), p. 177-193. The chapter on art includes a list with addresses of twenty-six private collectors in the United States, with geographic emphasis on their collections and number of pieces held. By now this is, of course, rather incomplete and dated information. Fortunately, there is a current periodical on the subject: *African Arts*, a quarterly that began publication in autumn 1967 and is published by the African Studies Center of the University of California at Los Angeles at twelve dollars per year.[71] While *African Arts* has been edited by John Povey, whose field is African literature, the journal has concentrated on the plastic arts with a relatively smaller coverage of literature, music, and the dance. The journal contains a regular section on current and continuing exhibitions. Not surprisingly, many art dealers advertise in *African Arts*. This, and much more importantly, a subsidy from the Kress Foundation enables the journal to print many beautiful colored plates. Hopefully, more Africans will contribute in the future so that the journal will be less of a house organ for Euro-American collectors.

An excellent paper by Frank Willett is "Sources for Teaching

about African Visual Art in American Schools and Colleges,"
Africana Library Journal 3, no. 2 (Summer 1972): 15-19. Purchase
and rental information is given for plaster casts, lantern slides,
filmstrips, phonographs, teaching kits, and films. The final section consists of books in the English language on African art.

COOKING

One other art form is cooking. The literature is considerable
and not treated with sufficient respect and attention in most
bibliographical guides. Four recent works follow.

Harva Hachten, *Kitchen Safari: A Gourmet's Tour of Africa* (New
York: Atheneum, 1970), 274 p., is an attractive book concerned
with the entire African continent (excluding the islands). It is
arranged according to five large regions. It includes a glossary of
African terms, a list of substitutions, and a list of stores carrying
recipe ingredients, which is arranged by U.S. states; stores that
will fill mail orders are starred.

See also Helen Mendes, *Soul Food: An African Legacy* (New
York: Macmillan, 1970), 256 p., and Bea Sandler, *The African
Cook Book* (New York: World Publishing, 1970), 232 p., which
includes menus and recipes from Ethiopia, the Sudan, Morocco,
Senegal, Kenya, Tanzania, Mozambique, Zanzibar, Malagasy,
South Africa, Liberia, and Ghana. The book features recipes for
an African buffet, additional recipes arranged by type, and
appendixes, including one on food sources.

For her *Black Academy Cookbook: A Collection of Authentic
African Recipes* (Buffalo, N.Y.: Black Academy Press, 1972), 188
p., Odinchezo Oka gathered recipes from African students in the
United States, particularly for Euro-American cooks.

Notes

[1] Favorably reviewed by Barbara Abrash in *Africana Library Journal* 1,
no. 4 (Winter 1970): 28.

[2] Note the review of Paden and Soja, *The African Experience* by Brian M.
Fagan in *Africa Report* 16, no. 1 (January 1971): 40 (Fagan laments the

absence of a chapter on the origin of man, a chapter he was to have written himself.)

[3]Reviewed constructively by James D. Pearson in *Africana Library Journal*, 2, no. 2 (Summer 1971): 14-15.

[4]Briefly reviewed in *UNESCO Bulletin for Libraries* 26, no. 3 (May-June 1972): 167.

[5]The revision was critically reviewed in *Times Literary Supplement* (March 10, 1972): 268.

[6]Vol. 1 was favorably reviewed by Richard Rathbone in the *Journal of African History* 11, no. 2 (1970): 294-295. All three volumes have been reviewed by Patrick J. McGowan, a political scientist on the faculty of Syracuse University and a member of its Program of Eastern African Studies. McGowan was enthusiastic about vols. 1 and 2 in the *Africana Library Journal* 2, no. 1 (Spring 1971): 17-18, and favorable in the same journal 3, no. 1 (Spring 1972): 24.

[7]Interesting review by Martin Kilson, "Blacks of the World Unite—If Possible," *The New York Times Book Review* (March 12, 1972): 27-28, 30.

[8]Reviewed by A.H.M. Kirk-Greene in *Africa* 42, no. 1 (January 1972): 64-65.

[9]*Edward Wilmot Blyden: Pan-Negro Patriot, 1832-1912* (London: Oxford University Press, 1970), 272 p., and Hollis R. Lynch, ed., *Black Spokesman: Selected Published Writings of Edward Wilmot Blyden* (London: Cass, 1971), 354 p. (Africa Modern Library, 14).

[10]Clarence Contee, "W.E.B. DuBois and African Nationalism: Notes on Some Primary Sources," *A Current Bibliography on African Affairs*, n.s. 3, no. 2 (February 1970): 21-26, and "The Encyclopedia Africana Project of W.E.B. DuBois," *African Historical Studies* 4, no. 1 (1971): 77-91. See also Irene Diggs, "DuBois—Revolutionary Journalist Then and Now," *A Current Bibliography on African Affairs*, n.s. 4, no. 2 (March 1971): 95-117, and Rayford Logan, *W.E.B. DuBois: A Profile* (New York: Hill and Wang, 1971), 324 p.

[11]*Pan-Africanism Reconsidered* (Berkeley and Los Angeles: University of California Press. 1962), 377 p.

[12]See Alice Hoover, "Pan-Africanism, A Selective Bibliography," 10-24, Francis A. Kornegay, Jr., "The Pan-African Legacy: Some Historical and Contemporary Perspectives," 24-31, and "Periodicals for Pan-African Studies," 32-36, which gives addresses and full subscription information on twenty-four journals, some of interest in African studies, others also to African-American ones.

[13]Reviewed by A.H.M. Kirk-Greene in *Africa* 42, no. 1 (January 1972): 64-65.

[14]Favorably reviewed in *Choice* 9, no. 3 (May 1972): 353.

[15]Colin Legum, "Organisation of African Unity," *Encyclopedia Britannica* (1971) 16: 1089.

[16]*Times Literary Supplement* (May 26, 1972): 598; Basil Davidson, "Who Are the Liberators," *West Africa* (May 26, 1972): 657-658; and Alan Baldwin, *African Digest* 19, no. 4 (August 1972): 89-90.

[17]Favorably reviewed by Frank Ralph Galino, *Journal of Modern African Studies* 10, no. 2 (1972): 319-320.

[18]See *Africa* 41, no. 4 (October 1971): 322, for the names of the editors (indicating institutional affiliation) and the title of volumes.

[19]See the review artticle by Thurston Shaw, "Africa in Prehistory: Leader or Legend," *Journal of African History* 12, no. 1 (1971): 143-153.

[20]Favorably reviewed by Jan Vansina, *American Historical Review* 77, no. 3 (June 1972): 812-813.

[21]Briefly reviewed by Colin Flint in *Journal of African History* 12, no. 3 (1971): 507.

[22]The articles appeared in the following issues of *Journal of African History:* vol. 2, no. 1 (1961), vol. 4, no. 1 (1963), vol. 5, no. 1 (1965), vol. 7, no. 3 (1966), vol. 8, no. 3 (1967), and vol. 10, no. 1 (1969).

[23]Note Susan K. Rishworth of the Africa Section of the Library of Congress, "The Publications of the Irish University Press: The British Parliamentary Papers on Africa," *Africana Library Journal* 3, no. 1 (Spring 1972): 26-29.

[24]Note the interesting review by Lenwood G. Davies, *Journal of Modern African Studies* 9, no. 4 (1971): 649-650.

[25]Favorably reviewed by John D. Hargreaves, *Journal of African History* 11, no. 4 (1970): 605-606.

[26]An adverse review by J.M.D. Crossey, *African Library Journal* 3, no. 3 (Autumn 1972): 24.

[27]For a scientific investigation of this and related topics, see S. M. Dawani, the librarian of the Institute of Tropical Agriculture in Ibadan, "Periodical Literature of Tropical And Subtropical Agriculture," *UNESCO Bulletin for Libraries* 26, no. 2 (March-April 1972): 88-93.

[28]*A Guide to Serials* (1970), 98 p.

[29]Favorably reviewed by Philip J. Thiuri in *Africana Library Journal* 2, no. 2 (Summer 1971): 15.

[30]Briefly described in *Africana Library Journal* 1, no. 3 (Fall 1970): 9.

[31]Compare to the index of the *American Political Science Review* compiled by Kenneth Janda and discussed in his *Data Processing: Application to Political Research,* 2d ed. (Evanston, Ill.: Northwestern University Press, 1969).

[32]George H. T. Kimble, "How to Explain the Continuing Popularity of Witch Burning," *The New York Times Book Review* (October 28, 1962): 3, 36. Note also the review by John Hatch, the *Journal of Modern African Studies* 1, no. 4 (December 1963): 555-557, and the very perceptive one by Harold K. Schneider, *Africa Report* 8, no. 3 (March 1963): 27.

[33]Mainly known for the following books: *Report on a Social Survey of Sekondi-Takoradi* (London: Crown Agent for the Colonies, 1950), 164 p.; *The Position of the Chief in the Modern Political System of Ashanti* (London: Oxford University Press for the International African Institute, 1951), 233 p.; *The Challenge of Africa* (New York: Praeger, 1962), 150 p.

[34]"The Ideology of 'Tribalism,'" *Journal of Modern African Studies* 9, no. 2 (1971): 253-261.

[35]Well reviewed by Smart A. Ekpo, *Journal of Modern African Studies* 10, no. 2 (1972): 314-315.

[36]A brief and hostile review by Lucy Mair, *Africa* 41, no. 3 (July 1971): 253.

[37]Note also, although this is somewhat dated: Frank Lorimer, et al., "Demography," in Robert A. Lystad, *The African World* (1965), pp. 271-303.

[38]Not too favorably reviewed by Joel W. Gregory, *Africa* 42, no. 1 (January 1972): 70-71, and Robert A. Obudho, *Journal of Modern African Studies* 10, no. 2 (July 1972): 315-317.

[39]Review by Marc Howard Ross, *Journal of Modern African Studies* 11, no. 3 (September 1973): 498-501.

[40]This is entry no. 258 in *Africana Library Journal* 2, no. 2 (Summer 1971): 25.

[41]Favorably reviewed, as is the bibliography by James F. Scotton for the Institute of Mass Communications, University of Lagos in *Journal of Modern African Studies* 10, no. 1 (May 1972): 154-156.

[42]Appreciatively reviewed by Lise Heiken, Department of Political Science, University of Ife, in *Journal of Modern African Studies* 10, no. 2 (July 1972): 322-323.

[43]Reviewed by J.M.D. Crossey, "A Resources Guide to African Politics," *Library Materials on Africa* 8, no. 1 (July 1970): 79-80.

[44]Favorably reviewed by *Times Literary Supplement* (March 31, 1972): 378.

[45]Note particularly, among the rare literature on this topic, Valerie Bloomfield, "African Ephemera," in Pearson and Jones, eds., *The Bibliography of Africa*, 223-239, including thirty-three references.

[46]Favorably reviewed by Jeswald W. Salacuse, The Ford Foundation,

Beirut, Lebanon, *Journal of Modern African Studies,* 10, no. 1 (May 1972): 152-154.

[47]Favorably reviewed by F. Akin Olaloku, Department of Economics, Dalhousie University, Halifax, Nova Scotia, *Journal of Modern African Studies* 9, no. 4 (December 1971): 653-654.

[48]Favorably reviewed by Alan Rufus Waters in *Journal of Modern African Studies* 9, no. 3 (October 1971): 479-486.

[49]Favorably reviewed by Jacob P. Meerman, *Journal of Modern African Studies* 10, no. 1 (May 1972): 164-168.

[50]Much more adversely reviewed in 49 above.

[51]This book was unfavorably reviewed as "a textbook with some wrong definitions" in an important article, "The Spectre of Precision in the Third World," *Times Literary Supplement* (September 15, 1972): 1066-1067.

[52]Among significant reactions is the one by Fodor Istvan, "Le classification des langues Negro-Africaines et la théorie de J. H. Greenberg," *Cahier d'Etudes Africaines* (Paris) 8, no. 32 (1968): 617-631.

[53]Library of African Studies, Northwestern University.

[54]Reviewed favorably by Jan Vansina, *Journal of African History* 12, no. 3 (1971): 493-496.

[55]In James Pearson and Ruth Jones, eds. *The Bibliography of Africa* (1970): 193.

[56]This work first appeared as *Langues et langages en Afrique Noir* (Paris: Payot 1967) 171 p. It was favorably reviewed by W. H. Whiteley, *Africa* 38, no. 4 (October 1968): 491-492.

[57]Favorably reviewed by Humphrey J. Fisher, *Journal of African History* 13, no. 1 (1972): 155-157.

[58]Critically reviewed by Gabriel M. Setiloane, *Journal of African History* 12, no. 2 (1971): 335-337.

[59]Favorably reviewed by Cyril Columbus Treister who refers to Jahn as the "dean of European Africanists," in *Africana Library Journal* 2, no. 4 (Winter 1971): 26-27, and briefly by Mary Ann Miller, "Selected Reference Books in 1971-72," *College and Research Libraries* 33, no. 4 (July 1972): 323.

[60]Favorably reviewed by Leon E. Clark, "Bibliography with a Difference," *Africa Report* 17, no. 3 (March 1972): 35, and Cyril Columbus Treister, *Africana Library Journal* 2, no. 4 (Winter 1971): 26-27. Briefly noted by Rita Keckeissen, "Selected Reference Books of 1971-72," *College and Research Libraries* 33, no. 4 (July 1972): 325.

[61]*Research in African Literature* is available from the African and Afro-

American Research Institute, University of Texas. The first issue is out of print and was reprinted by the African Studies Association.

[62]"Lists anthologies and critical works of African and Madagascan literature in French. It also lists by country the works of three hundred authors." *Library Materials on Africa* 7, no. 2 (November 1969): 59.

[63]Cyril Columbus Treister review in *Africana Library Journal* 2, no. 4 (Winter 1971): 26-27.

[64]Reviewed far too negatively in *Choice* 10, no. 4 (June 1973): 630.

[65]Favorably reviewed in *Choice* 9, no. 8 (October 1972): 976.

[66]A brief favorable review by Barbara Abrash in *Africana Library Journal* 1, no. 3 (Fall 1970).

[67]*Choice* 8, no. 5-6 (July-August 1971): 659.

[68]Reviewed favorably and with scholarly depth by Robert Plant Armstrong, *African Arts* 4, no. 4 (Summer 1971): 72-74. Also favorably reviewed by G. I. Jones in *Africa* 42, no. 1 (Januray 1972): 75-78.

[69]Favorably reviewed by Robert Plant Armstrong, *African Arts* 5, no. 4 (Summer 1972): 84-85 and *Choice* 9, no. 7 (September 1972): 800.

[70]Favorably reviewed by John Povey in *African Arts* 4, no. 3 (Spring 1971): 63-64. Very favorably reviewed by Austin J. Shelton in *The Conch Review of Books* 1, no. 1 (March 1973): 22.

[71]This journal appeared bilingually through spring 1970 as *African Arts/Arts d'Afrique.*

PART FOUR

Guide to Resources in
Non-African Areas

COLONIAL POWERS

We shall first approach the discussion of sources for African studies located within the former colonial powers. Here we shall include the few residual territories that remain under colonial control, and of course the only real remaining colonial power, Portugal.

David P. Henige, *Colonial Governors from the Fifteenth Century to the Present* (Madison, Wis.: University of Wisconsin Press, 1970), 461 p., includes the dates of office of colonial governors over 412 territorial units owned at some time by twelve present or former colonial powers. Sources are given in addition to useful introductory information. There is a bibliography for each colonial power and a consolidated index to governors' names.

FRANCE

France (and probably Belgium) continues to be the intellectual home and main trading partner of her former colonies. The literature about French colonization in Africa is vast. Fortunately, we now have a reliable guide in: David Gardinier, "French Colonial Rule in Africa: A Bibliographical Essay," in Gifford Prosser and William Rogers Louis, eds., *France and Britain in Africa: Imperial Rivalry and Colonial Rule* (New Haven: Yale University Press, 1971), p. 787-950. This work discusses the most important literature published between 1914 and 1960.

The bibliographical situation of Africana in France is discussed in: Britta Rupp, "Quelques notes sur la situation de la bibliographie africaniste en France," *Library Materials on Africa* 8, no. 1 (July 1970): 37-71. On a more limited scale, there is Paule Brasseur, "The Written Sources for the History of Africa: French Periodicals of the Nineteenth Century," *Africana Library Journal* 2, no. 4 (Winter 1971): 20-22. There is also a model of a bibliography that grew out of James Pearson's desire to publish a guide to African bibliographies. It is a bibliography of bibliographies: Paule Brasseur and Jean François Maurel, *Les*

119

sources bibliographiques de l'Afrique de l'Ouest et de l'Afrique Equatoriale d'expression française (Dakar: Bibliothèque de l'Université, 1970), 88 p. This work covers former French West and former French Equatorial Africa but does not include Burundi, Rwanda, or Zaïre. The introductory sections are concerned with multidisciplinary research institutes, learned societies, universities, archives, manuscripts, official publications, including gazettes, periodicals, and general and special bibliographies. The remainder of this small volume is arranged alphabetically by name of country. Within the section for each country, the arrangement is according to subject. The book concludes with an index.

Another source is International Council on Archives, *Sources de l'histoire de l'Afrique au sud du Sahara, dans les archives et bibliothèques françaises I Archives* (Zug, Switzerland: Inter-Documentation A.G., 1971), 959 p. (Guide to the sources of the history of Africa, vol. 3).[1] The index to the preceding volume will be a separate publication and presumably volume 4. These volumes will be two of eight published by Inter Doc. All are published with the support of UNESCO, constituting a guide to the sources of the history of Africa found in Europe and the United States. The volume deals mainly with archives but also contains information on manuscripts, maps, and plans. The pattern of arrangement for archives listed depends on whether they are public or private agencies. Printed archives constituted by official publications (e.g., gazettes) are also considered. References are given to the Bibliothèque Nationale, the overseas section of the National Archives, and archives from French overseas territories housed in Aix-en-Provence. The French West African archives are in Dakar, but microfilm may be consulted in Paris.

Some ideas about the holdings of libraries in Paris pertaining to Africa and their difficulties can be gathered from: Britta Rupp, "Problèmes relatifs à l'acquitision des materiaux en provenance de l'Afrique," in Valerie Bloomfield, ed., *Conference on the Acquisition of Material from Africa* (Zug, Switzerland: Inter-Documentation, 1969), p. 19-47.

One important French agency concerned with overseas

documentation in the French sphere is discussed in: "Centre d'étude et de documentation sur l'Afrique et l'Outre-Mer, Paris," *Library Materials on Africa* 7, no. 3 (March 1970): 78-84. CEDOM, a division of the Direction de la Documentation, assists with the publication of Law Documentation française and publishes *Afrique contemporaine.* CEDOM maintains a large photographic file.

As a part of France, we shall also consider the few remaining African colonial or overseas territories of France: Comoro Islands, French Territory of the Afars and Issas, and Réunion. These three small areas constitute a sub-section in Duignan's *Guide.* Frequently, books on Madagascar refer to these territories, particularly the groups of Indian Ocean islands.

The Comoro Islands

There are four small islands and some even smaller ones in the Mozambique Channel between north of the northern tip of Madagascar and the coast of Mozambique—that is, between 11 degrees and 13 degrees south and 43 degrees and 45 degrees east.

Barbara Dubins has contributed two bibliographical essays to the September 1969, vol. 12, no. 2, issue of the *African Studies Bulletin*: "The Comoro Islands: A Bibliographical Essay," p. 131-137, and "Nineteenth-century Travel Literature," p. 138-146. In the first article she cites: Bureau pour le Developpement de la Production Agricole, *Territoire des Comores bibliographie* (Paris: BDPA, 1964), 75 p. There is no evidence of this volume being available in a United States library.

The literature on the Comoro Islands is sparse, particularly that written in English. In 1962, the Information Service of the French Embassy in New York City issued an attractive, illustrated fifteen-page pamphlet with basic information in English. The main four islands are: Mayotte, Anjouan, Mohéli, and Grand Comore (the largest). There is a 1966 census: France, Institut National de la statistique et des études économiques, *Resultats statistiques du recensement général de la population des Comores effectué en juillet-septembre 1966* (Paris, 1968), 106 p. The grand total was 259,235 persons. This figure is based on a one-fifth sample census.

The following are references not cited by Duignan or in the Dubins article: Claude Robineau, *Société et économie d'Anjouan* (Paris: Office de la Récherche Scientifique et téchnique d'Outre-Mer [ORSTOM], 1966), 260 p., and H. J. Ottenheimer, "Culture Contact and Musical Style: Ethnomusicology in the Comoro Islands," *Ethnomusicology* (Middletown, Conn.) 14, no. 3 (September 1970): 458-462.

A reference cited incompletely by Dubins and the *Encyclopedia Britannica* is: Hildebert Isnard, "L'archipel des Comores," *Cahiers d'Outre Mer* (Paris) 6, no. 21 (January-March 1953): 5-22.

There was in Dar es Salaam a national liberation movement of Comoro that in 1969 and 1970 issued statements that were mimeographed; the 1970 statement was addressed to the United Nations.

Réunion

Réunion is located at 21 degrees north and 55 degrees east; it is the largest of the Mascarene Islands. It has an area of 969 square miles and had, according to the 1967 census, a population of 416,525 persons; see French Embassy, Service de Presse et d'Information, New York, *The Island of Réunion* (New York, 1971), 12 p.

This island has been of interest for many years not just to historians but also to stamp collectors. Surprisingly, no bibliography could be located by the present writer. Some recent references, arranged chronologically, follow. See France, Institut national de la statistique et des études économique, *Annuaire statistique de la Réunion*, 1952-1955 (Paris, 1956), 106 p. There are also volumes for 1955-1958 and 1958-1960.

Most of Roger Vailland, *La Réunion* (Lausanne: Editions Rencontre, 1964), 192 p., consists of photographs. In André Scherer, *Histoire de la Réunion* (Paris: Presses Universitaires de

France, 1965), 128 p. (Que sais—je no. 1164), includes a twenty-three entry bibliography. Two of the essays in *Etudes réunionaises, histoire, droit économie de la Réunion par F. Borella, B. Parisot, M. Parodi [and] G. Weill* (Paris: Editions Cujas, 1965), (Annales de la Fraculté de droit et de sciences économiques Aix-en-Provence) are historical, the other two economic. Eliard Ranjit Cercle, *Réunion, 1969, une colonie française* (Paris: F. Maspero, 1969), 127 p. (Dossier partisans), is an analysis of a colonial economy with a plea for true development.

Réunion has magnificent archival resources, and a number of valuable guides have been published. The following volumes have all been compiled by Albert Longman, the archivist of Réunion, and published by the Archives Departmentales de la Réunion. *Documents concernant les Iles de Bourbon et de France pendant la regie de la Compagnie des Indes* (1953), 202 p., is an inventory of material in archival depositories in Paris. *Classement et inventaire du fonds de la Compagnie des Indes (Serie C) 1665-1767* (1956), 392 p., is an inventory with indexes of material in the archives of Réunion. Between 1932 and 1949 appeared the first series of a journal based on the Réunion archives. A second series started to appear in 1954: *Requeil de documents et de travaux inédits pour servir a l'histoire de la Réunion*, Nouvelle series no. 1 (1954), 112 p., no. 2 (1957), 261 p., no. 3 (1959), 329 p., no. 4 (1960), 205 p.

The Afars and Issas (Formerly French Somaliland)

This small colony consisting of Djibouti and hinterland, an Ethiopian enclave, used to be known as French Somaliland. The literature about this area is skimpy. About the only recent publication available in English is: Virginia Thompson and Richard Adloff, *Djibouti and the Horn of Africa* (Stanford: Stanford University Press, 1968), 246 p.[2] The book contains a useful bibliography.

One publication not cited by Thompson and Adloff is: Abdul Hafiz Mahmassani, comp., *Djibouti, French Somaliland* (Beirut, Lebanon: "Dar Al-Assima," 1965), 48 p. This is an illustrated volume with numerous advertisements; there is a translation from the French in English and Arabic.

Revue Française, "Survey of Political, Economic and Social Affairs in French Territory of Afars and Issas" (Washington, D.C.: Joint Publications Research Service, *Translations on Africa* no. 922 (JPRS 51004, 22 July 1970), is a series of ten short articles. See also James S. Waggener, *The Future of French Somaliland; A Research Report Submitted to the Faculty* (Maxwell Air Force Base, Ala.: Air University, 1969), 134 p.[3]

One scholarly journal is published in Djibouti. Between 1966 and 1972 ten issues of *Pount: Bulletin de la societé d'études de l'Afrique orientale* have been issued. This journal is occasionally concerned with the area in which it is published.

Fortunately, the Library of Congress' Accessions list, *Eastern Africa*, issued by its Nairobi office, reports occasionally the receipt of publications from the French territory of the Afars and Issas. These publications are sent to Washington where they are added to the collection of the Library of Congress.

GERMANY

This short section is concerned with German colonial Africa as well as the postcolonial era of German interest in Africa. It is amazing that during such a short number of years (1884-1919) when Germany actually held colonies, the Germans produced such an immense amount of official, quasi-official, and nonofficial writing about their possessions.

A useful guide that rightly stresses the difficulty of separating German colonial from foreign policy is: Andrew R. Carlson, *German Foreign Policy, 1890-1914, and Colonial Policy to 1914: A Handbook and Annotated Bibliography* (Metuchen, N.J.: The Scarecrow Press, 1970), 333 p. Useful is chapter 4, "German Colonial Policy" (with maps) and the bibliographic section on general colonial policy, specifically German Africa.

One of the largest collections on German Africa in this country is at the Hoover Institution, which has published: Jon Bridgeman and David E. Clarke, *German Africa, A Select Annotated Bibliography* (Stanford University, The Hoover Institution on

War, Revolution and Peace, 1965), 120 p. (Hoover Institution Bibliographical Series 19).[4] It includes a good note on German official and semi-official publications, geographically classified sections, some pages by Duignan, "British Confidential Prints, Microfilmed British Documents Dealing with German Africa," and appropriate German serials and newspapers. It contains no indexes.

The following can be strongly recommended: Hartmut Pogge von Strandmann and Alison Smith, "The German Empire in Africa and British Perspective: A Historiographical Essay," in Gifford Prosser and William Roger Louis, eds. *Britain and Germany in Africa* (New Haven: Yale University Press, 1967), p. 709-795. Ralph A. Austen also contributed to the work on the bibliographical essay. Note also: Hartmut Pogge von Strandmann, "The German Role in Africa and German Imperialism: A Review Article," *African Affairs* 69, no. 277 (October 1970): 381-389.

German specialists or those proficient in German can consult: International Council of Archives, *Quellen zur Geschichte Afrikas nördlich der Sahara in den Archiven der Bundesrepublik Deutschland* (Zug, Switzerland: Inter-Documentation Co., 1970), 126 p. (Guide to the Sources of the History of Africa 1).[5] The guide is concerned with sources in Germany for the history of Africa from Mauritania and Sudan to the Cape of Good Hope, Madagascar, and other islands. Sources are described by repository and, within each repository, by group or series. The guide is devoted primarily to public and private archives. It takes into account collections of historical significance in libraries and museums.

We turn now to German Africanist research, which is active in both West and East Germany. The main agency that reports on activities is the Deutsche Afrika Gesellschaft in Bonn; it has issued a volume compiled by Jochen Köhler, *Deutsche Dissertationen über Afrika, 1918-1959* (Bonn, 1962). This information is extracted from the *Jahresverzeichnis der an den deutschen Universitäten und Hochschulen erschienen Schriften.* The 795 dissertations are arranged by country and larger geographical divisions in alphabetical order, with a special section for Africa as a whole and colonies. There is a Stichwort Verzeichnis, and an author index.[6]

126   A BIBLIOGRAPHY OF AFRICANA

This has been supplemented by *Afrika Bibliographie*, also published by Schroeder for the Deutsche Afrika-Gesellschaft. The first volume covers 1960-1961; subsequent volumes are yearly. The last one available is that for 1967.

Two recent surveys of German Africanist research are: Michael Koll, "Organisations formen sozialwissenschaftlicher Afrikaforschung in der Bundesrepublik, ein Uberblick," *Internationales Europaforum* 3 (1969): 227-233, and "Vergleichende Daten und Fakten (a) Uberblick über die interdisciplinare Afrikaforschung in der Bundesrepublik Deutschland (b) Afrikakundliche Lehranstaltungen an den Universitäten und Hochschulen der Bundesrepublik Deutschland," *Afrika Spectrum* (Hamburg) 2 (October 1969): 81-115.[7]

ITALY

Italy's long colonial ties with the Horn of Africa and parts of North Africa have perhaps been less fully documented than the colonial history of other countries.

One classic among bibliographies is: Douglas H. Varley, *A Bibliography of Italian Colonisation in Africa with a Section on Abyssinnia* (London: Dawson of Pall Mall, 1970), 92 p. This is a reprint of the 1936 work with a brief new introduction. (Mr. Varley is one of a small group of distinguished English librarians who have worked in different parts of Africa. Currently, he is librarian at the University of Liverpool.)

A much more recent bibliography is: Sunil Kumar Sahu, "Bibliography of Italy's Colonial Policy in Africa," *Africa Quarterly* (New Delhi) 9, no. 4 (January-March 1970): 402-413. The same issue has a summary article by perhaps the most distinguished of Italy's contemporary Africanists teaching at the University of Naples: Teobaldo Filesi, "Twenty Centuries of Italy's Relationship with Africa," p. 316-330.

See also Roberto Aliboni, "Africanists Studies in Italy," *African Affairs* (London) 69, no. 275 (April 1970): 163-169, and Giuseppe A. Costanzo, "Italian Studies in Africa," *Journal of Modern African Studies* 7. no. 2 (July 1969): 309-317. The Italian African Studies Association has issued quarterly, since 1968, semiannually now, *Bollettino della Associazione degli Africanisti Italiani.* This bulletin compares favorably with similar bulletins issued elsewhere. The Italian scholarly writing which appears in different journals has been indexed in the *Bollettino* in a bibliographical section at the end of each issue, starting with the 1969 volume.

Africa is the official journal of the Istituto Italiano per l'Africa. It has been published monthly in Rome since 1946.

Carlo Giglio and Elio Lodolini, *Guida delle Fonti per la Storia dell' Africa a Sud del Sahara esistenti in Italia, I* (Zug, Switzerland: Inter-Documentation, 1973), 449 p., is volume 5 of the International Council of Archives, *Guide to the Sources of the History of Africa.* A scholarly introduction, with numerous citations by Giglio, occupies the first seventy-seven pages of the volume. The bulk of the volume lists official state archives by proveniences, first the central archives and then the various state archives.

PORTUGAL

This section is concerned with Portugal and Africa as well as with what the Portuguese claim as their overseas territories: Guinea-Bissau, Angola, and Mozambique. Next to South Africa, these are the parts of the African continent which stir the most profound feelings within those who believe in the full liberation of Africa and others who think that these sizable remnants of colonialism will remain forever. Not surprisingly, the bulk of the literature in support of the colonial view is written in Portuguese and most of the publications of liberation movements and their supporters are in English and French. However, one must remember that Portuguese is the official language of all the nationalist movements of Guinea-Bissau, Mozambique, and Angola.

Sources for Portuguese colonial history are voluminous. They are held in depth in libraries of former or present metropolitan powers and in the United States in the libraries that are traditionally strong on Africa, especially Northwestern University and the University of California at Los Angeles. The availability of Portuguese material has been aided by the seemingly haphazard gifts of certain Portuguese serial publications by the Gulbenkian Foundation.

There are two G. K. Hall catalogs not confined to Portuguese Africa or even Portugal itself. The focus of the *Catalogue of the Greenlee Collection, Newberry Library (Chicago* 1971), 2 vols., is Portuguese literature and history, including overseas areas. The *Catalog of the Oliveira Lima Library (Catholic University of America)*, Washington, D.C. (1970), 2 vols., is from one of the most important repositories in the United States for books dealing with the history, literature, ethnology, and culture of Portuguese-speaking people.

A guide which this writer has found difficult to use is Mary Jane Gibson, comp., *Portuguese Africa: A Guide to Official Publications* (Washington, D.C.: Superintendent of Documents, U.S. Government Printing Office, 1967), 217 p. The 2,831 entries are arranged according to their place of publication in Africa. Those published in Portugal have unfortunately been excluded. Partly because of the inadequacies of the index and more because of the complexities of Portuguese names, this guide is more difficult to use than others issued by the Library of Congress.

Useful, particularly for those in southern California, is: George Bender, Tamera J. Bender, Donna S. Hill, and Cesar T. Rosario, *Portugal in Africa: A Bibliography of the UCLA Collection* (Los Angeles: University of California, African Studies Center, August 1972), 315 p. (Occasional Paper No. 12) (mimeo). The entries in this bibliography are based on the UCLA shelflist, which presumably contains cards from the six UCLA university libraries that hold this material. The arrangement follows that of the Library of Congress classification; books, however, are separated from periodicals and government publications that are both arranged geographically. Hopefully, other institutions will follow Gerald Bender's suggestion and prepare lists or even catalogs of their Portuguese holdings concerned with Africa. Under the former Farmington Plan (now called the Foreign Acquisition Plan), Northwestern University collects from and on the Portuguese territories. A larger proportion of Portuguese publications remains to be cataloged, however.

Portuguese colonial history has occupied many writers, both

native and foreigner. Highly recommended is the work of James Duffy, especially his *Portugal in Africa* (Penguin Books, 1962), 240 p.

For greater depth, two review articles in the *Journal of African History* should be noted. C. R. Boxer, "S. R. Welch and His History of the Portuguese in Africa, 1495-1806," 1, no. 1, (1960): 55-63 in which Boxer tears Welch apart unmercifully. B. Jewsiewicki, "Africa and the Portuguese Empire: L'économie de l'empire portugais aux XVe et XVIe siècles. Par V. Magalhães Godinho, Paris. S.E.V.P.E.N., 1969, 852 p., 12, no. 3 (1971): 481-485, gives a fairly favorable appraisal, although Godinho is criticized for not taking into consideration some recent writers and for omissions in his bibliography.

Turning to the current scene, one may refer to: William Minter, *Portuguese Africa and the West* (Baltimore: Penguin Books, 1972), 176 p. This is a study by a young American sociology student with considerable experience in Africa, including teaching at the FRELIMO (Frente de Libertação de Mosambique), the Mozambique Liberation Movement's secondary school in Dar es Salaam, from 1966 to 1969. It is unlikely that this tract, committed to the liberation of southern Africa, has had the wide impact it deserves. See too David Abshire and Michael A. Samuels, eds., *Portuguese Africa: A Handbook* (New York: Published in cooperation with the Center for Strategic and International Studies, Georgetown University, by Praeger, 1969), 480 p. (Handbooks to the Modern World). This is a comprehensive and well-documented review by scholars from various disciplines and with various points of view.[8]

We now turn to some works with a particularly pro-African point of view. First is a bibliography by Ronald H. Chilcote, *Emerging Nationalism in Portuguese Africa; A Bibliography of Documentary Ephemera through 1965* (Stanford University, Hoover Institution, 1969), 114 p. (Hoover Institution Bibliography series, No. 39). This bibliography is based in part on the compiler's own collection. He lists articles, books, and documents. He has also written *Emerging Nationalism in Portuguese Africa, Documents* (Stanford, Calif.: Hoover Institution Press, 1972), 646 p. (Hoover Institution Publication 97).

In Paul M. Whitaker, "The Revolution of 'Portuguese Africa,' "
Journal of Modern African Studies 8, no. 1 (April 1970): 15-35, the
author traces historically the struggle of the liberation
movements both in their internal complexities and their struggle
against the Portuguese. The situation is confusing in both cause
and effect due to contradictory sources of information.

Africa Today (Denver) devoted its July-August 1970 issue, 17,
no. 4, to the theme "Allies in Enpire: The U.S. and Portugal in
Africa." Thirty-four pages are divided into three parts: "U.S.
Economic Involvement," "U.S. Military Involvement," and
"American Foreign Policy and Portuguese Colonialism."

Much of the anti-Portuguese struggle finds a literary expres-
sion almost entirely in Portuguese. Two bibliographies that were
compiled virtually simultaneously must be cited: Gerald M.
Moser, *A Tentative Portuguese-African Bibliography: Portuguese
Literature in Africa and African Literature in the Portuguese
Language* (University Park, Pa.: Pennsylvania State University
Libraries, 1970), 148 p. (Pennsylvania State University Libraries,
Bibliographical Series No. 3), and Amandio Cesar and Mario
Antonio, *Elementos para umba bibliográfia da literatura e cultura:
Portuguese ultramarina contemporanee* (Lisbon: Agencia-Geral do
Ultramar, 1968), 177 p.

Guinea-Bissau

There is a bibliographical scarcity on Guinea-Bissau, particularly in English. There is, however, one most useful volume: Basil
Davidson, *The Liberation of Guiné: Aspects of an African Revolution*,
with a foreword by Amilcar Cabral (Baltimore: Penguin Books,
1969), 169 p. (Penguin African Series AP27). This book is based
on both documentary study and first-hand observation as a guest
of PAIGC, the Partido Africano da Independencia da Guiné e
Cabo Verde. See Amilcar Cabral, *Revolution in Guinea: An
African's People Struggle, Selected Texts*, rev. ed. (London: Stage 1,
1971), 142 p.

Another study based on first-hand experience by a fine French
journalist, available in translation, is: Gerard Chaliand, *Armed*

Struggle in Africa: With the Guerillas in "Portuguese" Guinea (New York: Monthly Review Press, 1969), 142 p.

The following is an example of U.S. congressional documents which are rarely cited in bibliographies: U.S. Congress House Committee on Foreign Affairs, Subcommittee on Africa, *Report on Portuguese Guinea and the Liberation Movement. Hearing,* 91st Cong. 2nd sess., February 16, 1970 (Washington, D.C.: U.S. Government Printing Office, 1970), 25 p.

A well-documented, recent journal article by a Swedish political scientist who enjoyed PAIGC hospitality is: Lars Rudebeck, "Political Mobilisation for Development in Guinea-Bissau," *Journal of Modern African Studies* 10, no. 1 (May 1972): 1-18.

Angola

Angola is not too well provided with bibliographies. Among the few that Duignan lists is Margaret Joan Greenwood, *Angola: A Bibliography* (Cape Town: Cape Town University School of Librarianship, 1967), 52 p.

There is a wealth of recent material available in English and French on Angola, most of it focusing on the anticolonial struggle. This work will be presented chronologically, starting with 1969. John A. Marcum, *The Angolan Revolution: An Anatomy of an Explosion, 1950-1962* (Cambridge, Mass: MIT Press, 1969), 380 p., is a scholarly book which has not received the attention in reviews it deserves. The first part discusses three sources of Angolan nationalism: the Luanda Mbundu in the northeast, the Bankongo in the northwest, and the Ovimbundu in the central-west. Part two discusses the events of 1961, and the third part those of 1962 and 1963. The work is fully referenced.

Douglas L. Wheeler, "The Portuguese Army in Angola," *Journal of Modern African Studies* 7, no. 3 (October 1969): 425-439, is largely concerned with post-1961 history.

In Mario de Andrade and Marc Ollivier, *La guerre en Angola. Etude socio-économique* (Paris: Maspero, 1971), 160 p. (Cahiers libres 209-210), the first part outlines the socioeconomic situation of Angola until 1960, including the geographical and historical background. The second part relates the effect of the war. The brief third part is concerned with Angola in the imperialist strategy.

The first part of Douglas L. Wheeler and René Pelissier, *Angola* (New York: Praeger, 1971), 296 p., is historical (it is written by Wheeler); the second part (by Pelissier) for the 1961-1970 period is political. There is a fair amount of documentation.[9]

See, too, Basil Davidson, "Angola in the Tenth Year: A Report and an Analysis, May-July 1971," *African Affairs* 70, no. 278 (January 1972): 37-49; and Don Barnett and Roy Harvey, *The Revolution in Angola: MPLA Life Histories and Documents* (Indianapolis and New York: Bobbs-Merrill. 1972), 312 p.

A sympathetic popular account is Basil Davidson, *In the Eye of the Storm: Angola's People* (New York: Doubleday, 1972), 367 p. Davidson explains that the MPLA (Movemento Popular de Libertação de Angola) is not merely fighting the Portuguese; they are at the same time fighting for a socialist revolution.[10]

Mozambique

Duignan's *Guide* lists a number of useful bibliographies of Mozambique. Let us start with Filipe Gastão de Moura Coutinho de Almeida de Eca, who has written the very useful *Subsidios para uma bibliografia missionária mocambicana (católica)* (Lisbon: published by the author, 1969), 157 p.[11]

From the sizable liberation literature, a few examples will be given. The most important work is: Eduardo Mondlane, *The Struggle for Mozambique* (Baltimore: Penguin, 1969), 222 p. This volume was published after the assassination of Dr. Mondlane in Dar es Salaam on February 3, 1969. The author hopes that "the purpose of this book [will] show what Portuguese colonization has really meant for the African, to trace the true origins of the war, and to try to indicate what the struggle means to the participants and what is emerging from it in terms of new social structures which may help to mould the Africa of the future." This was accomplished by the author. Probably the best way to keep up with FRELIMO is to subscribe to *Mozambique Revolution*, which has been published since 1965.[12]

An interesting pamphlet published by the Committee of Returned Peace Corps Volunteers (CRV), New York Chapter, Africa Committee, is: *Mozambique Will Be Free* (New York: The Committee, 1969), 45 p.

Students and librarians who would like a brief but good overview of the most important serial publications concerned with Portuguese Africa should refer to: R. W. Pound, "Portuguese Speaking Africa," in Valerie Bloomfield, ed., *Standing Conference on Library Materials on Africa. Conference on the acquisition of material from Africa. University of Birmingham, 25 April 1969* (Zug, Switzerland: Inter-Documentation, 1969), p. 65-72.

SPAIN

Spain's colonial possessions are limited to the Spanish Sahara and some islands, including the Canary Islands.

The following article gives an excellent and well-documented overview of Spanish-African studies and African studies in Spain; Marcel Walraet, "L'africanisme et les études africaines en Espagne," (Brussels) Academie royale des sciences d'outre-mer, *Bulletin des séances*, n.s. 2 (1970): 224-252.

For Spanish Sahara, one recent publication, in Spanish and Arabic, is: Instituto de Estudios Africanos, *La accion de España en Sahara* (Madrid: Consejo Superior de Investigaciones Cientificas, 1971), 30 p., 90 p.

Students of geography, history, and, most of all, cartography will benefit from U.S., Board of Geographic Names, *Spanish Sahara*, Gazeteer No. 108 (June 1969). These volumes have been issued or reissued for most countries of the world.

Travelers, usually not students of Africa, who visit the Canary Islands (which at their nearest point are only sixty-seven miles from the northwest African mainland)[13] should note: A. Gordon-Brown and John Norton, eds., *The Canary Islands: A Choice Guide for the Visitor* (London: Robert Hale, 1971), 150 p.

A useful note on the most significant publication of Spanish Africa is that by D. H. Varley, university librarian at the University of Liverpool, the institution in Great Britain that has taken responsibility for collecting on and from Spanish-speaking Africa, in: Valerie Bloomfield, ed., *Conference on the Acquisitions of Material from Africa* (1969), 73-76. Finally, see Susan Knoke Rishworth, comp., *Spanish-speaking Africa, A Guide to Official Publications* (Washington, D.C.: Superintendent of Documents, U.S. Government Printing Office, 1973), 66 p. This publication by the African Section is concerned with publications at the Library of Congress and some other large libraries in the United States. Publications of Equatorial Guinea, prior to independence in 1968, are included, as are Spanish Sahara, Morocco (Spanish Zone), 1913 to 1957, and relevant ones from Spain. There is an index to subjects, authors, and titles.

GREAT BRITAIN

We now turn to a country with large sources of information about former colonies. The main and only remaining African territory for which Great Britain retains responsibility is Southern Rhodesia (Zimbabwe), which is more conveniently discussed in the section on southern Africa. In this section we will mention only the Seychelles. These islands are about 600 miles northeast of the Malagasy Republic and, considering that their 1967 population was estimated to have been only 48,730, they have been described at great length in many works, both official and unofficial.[14] One recent book is: R. Burton Benedict, *People of the Seychelles*, 3d ed. (London: Ministry of Overseas Development, 1970), 74 p. The best collection for publications of the Seychelles is no doubt found in London, probably at the Foreign and Commonwealth Library.

BELGIUM

An excellent guide to the many Africana centers in Belgium is: Joanne Coyle Dauphin, "Belgian Documentation Centers on Africa," *African Studies Bulletin* 8, no. 3 (December 1965): 21-39. This can be updated by the International African Institute's *Current Africanist Research*, November 1971-.

There are, above all, the series published by the Académie royale des sciences d'outre mer and those by the museum in

Tervuren, a suburb of Brussels.[15] While much of the scholarly and other work focuses on Zaïre, this may well be increasingly less the case.

NON-COLONIAL POWERS

SCANDINAVIA

The Scandinavian Institute of African Studies (Nordiska Afrika Institutet) in Uppsala, Sweden, circulates information about Africa in the Scandinavian countries, stimulates and supports research of Scandinavia in Africa, and publishes mainly on practical socioeconomic questions. The institute focuses particularly on eastern Africa.

Knud Larsen, a Danish librarian who was head of the East African School of Librarianship at Makerere, is author of "Scandinavian Libraries and Africa," *Library Materials on Africa* 7, no. 1 (July 1969): 17-21.[16]

The guide to archives located in Scandinavia for the history of Africa is: International Council of Archives, *Scandinavian Sources in Denmark, Norway and Sweden* (Zug, Switzerland: Inter-Documentation, 1971), 101 p. (Guide to the Sources of African History, no. 8).

SWITZERLAND

The most important Swiss scholarly contribution to African studies is the semiannual *Genève-Afrique (Geneva-Africa)*, which the Institut africain de Genève began publishing in 1962. Its emphasis is on the history, culture, and current economic, political, and social problems of sub-Saharan Africa. The journal contains good book reviews and bibliographical articles, including: Hans-Peter F. Strauch, "La contribution des auteurs suisses à la connaissance de l'Afrique," 7, no. 2 (1968): 91-107, and his "La contribution suisse à la connaissance de l'Afrique. Etude de la fin de la première guerre mondiale jusqu' à nos jours," 8, no. 1 (1969): 60-87.

Because the International Red Cross is largely a Swiss organization, we may include here: Bernard Clerc and Madeleine Hann, "La Croix Rouge et l'Afrique: essai bibliographique," 9, no. 1 (1970): 94-101.

INDIA

Since 1961 the Indian Council for Africa in New Delhi has published the useful *Africa Quarterly*, whose emphasis is on political, social, economic, and historical matters. Its library issues a monthly *Documentation List: Africa*, which started in 1964. This is a good index to periodicals held in the library.

There is little available source material to document Indian policy toward Africa. One of the few articles is Anirudha Gupta, "A Note on Indian Attitudes to Africa," *African Affairs* (London) 69, no. 275 (April 1970): 170-178.

ISRAEL

Israeli-African relations are an interesting topic which has not yet been fully documented. Studies such as: Jehudi J. Kamarek, *Israeli Technical Assistance to African Countries* (Geneva: Institut Africain de Genève, 1969), 115 p., make a useful beginning, as does the following report reproduced for restricted circulation: Z. Y. Herschlag, ed., *Israel-Africa Cooperation. Research Project, Progress Report* (Tel Aviv: Research Project on Israel-Africa Cooperation, Department of Developing Countries, Tel-Aviv University, 1970), 618 p. The latter is an in-depth study of technical aid by Israel in Cameroon, Dahomey, Ghana, the Ivory Coast, and Upper Volta. The final section of this report gives an annotated list of projects.

Abel Jacob, "Israel's Military Aid to Africa," *Journal of Modern African Studies* 9, no. 2 (August 1971): 165-187, contains a good deal of documentation, more fully provided in the author's "The Political Outcomes of Foreign Aid: Israel's Foreign Aid Program to Africa" (PhD. dissertation, University of California, Los Angeles, 1969).

Israel is regarded as an evil imperial power, particularly among liberation groups far from the scene of military action. One pamphlet that strives to document this attitude is: Madison Area Committee on Southern Africa, *South Africa and Israel*, 2d. ed. (Madison: The Committee, 1971), 42 p.

COMMUNIST POWERS

The following work gives a good overview: Ursula Paolozzi, *Communism in Sub-Saharan Africa: An Essay with Bibliographic Supplement* (Washington, D.C.: American University, Center for Research in Social Systems, 1969), 44 p. Marthe Engelborghs-Bertels, according to Duignan's *Guide* a specialist in Chinese studies at the Centre d'Etude de Pays de l'Est in Brussels, has written the following: "Articles publiés par les pays à regime communiste, Academie Royale des Sciences d'Outre-Mer (ARSOM) Brussels," *Bulletin des séances* n.s. 8, no. 4, 600-606; "Afrique et les pays communiste," ARSOM, *Bulletin des séances*, n.s. 9, no. 4 (1963): 662-690, 10, no. 2 (1964): 263-291, and "Les pays de l'est et la decolonisation particulièrement en Afrique" (bibliographie) ARSOM, *Memoires in 8*, n.s. 28, 2, (1963), 62 p. 218 titles mostly for 1960 and 1961.[17]

CZECHOSLOVAKIA

A scholarly article is: Zbynek Malý, "Africana in Czechoslovakia," *Library Materials on Africa* 9, no. 2 (November 1971): 50-97.

The following two brief reviews overlap only in part: Michael Koll, "Notizen über die tschechoslovakische Afrikaforschung," *Internationales Afrika Forum* 5, no. 6 (June 1969): 524-526, and Peter Skalnik, "African Studies in Czechoslovakia: Achievements and Perspectives," *African Studies Bulletin* 12, no. 2 (September 1969): 213-222. Skalnik's article reviews the eight centers in Czechoslovakia where Africanist research has been carried out. Seven of the eight centers are in Prague, the other in Bratislava. Detailed bibliographical references, citing for the most part publications from 1965 on, are included at the end of the article.

POLAND

The useful *Africana Bulletin* (Warsaw) includes "Polish Anthropological Studies in Africa," 15 (1971): 129-136 by Tadeusz Dzierzykray-Rogalski, with fourteen references to the work of this scholar and other Poles.

Those desiring to pursue this topic should note Polski Instytut Spraw Miedzynarodowych, Warsaw, Zaklest Kajow Afryki, *Bibliografia polskich publikacji na femat Afryki*, comp. Maciej Kozmiński and Jan Milewski (Warsaw, 1965), 2 vols.

Scholars may have access to institutions that can request through interlibrary loan: T. Dzierzykray-Rogalski, "Polish Africanist Studies in the Field of Anthropology in the Past Twenty-five Years," *Przegled anthropologiczny* 35, no. 1 (1969): 225-234.

HUNGARY

The Center for Afro-Asian Research of the Hungarian Academy of Sciences in Budapest is the center for research on Africa in Hungary. It issues a numbered series.

UNION OF SOVIET SOCIALIST REPUBLICS

A bibliographer who documents relations of the Soviet Union and China with Africa is: Max Liniger-Goumaz, "L'U.R.S.S., la Chine populaire et l'Afrique; essai bibliographique," *Genève Afrique* 8, no. 2 (1969): 69-78.

No authoritative study has yet been written on Soviet policy toward Africa. Meanwhile, we have to rely on: Helen Des Fosses Cohen, *Soviet Policy toward Black Africa: The Focus on National Integration* (New York: Praeger, 1972), 240 p. (Praeger Special Study Series), and a more specialized study, Arthur Jay Klingelhoffer, *Soviet Perspectives on African Socialism* (Rutherford, N.J.: Fairleigh Dickinson University Press, 1969), 276 p.

Among the better and more specialized studies, there is:

Robert Legvold, *Soviet Policy in West Africa* (Cambridge, Mass.: Harvard University Press, 1970), 371 p.[18]

Soviet writing on Africa has been reviewed by Mary Holdsworth in her *Soviet African Studies, 1918-1959: An Annotated Bibliography* (Oxford: Oxford University Press, 1961), 80 p. (Chatham House Memorandum). Some five hundred items are arranged in classified bibliographical form. This has been supplemented by Central Asian Research Centre, London, *Soviet Writing on Africa, 1959-1961: An Annotated Bibliography* (London: Oxford University Press, 1963), 93 p. The 433 references are less fully annotated than in Holdsworth's bibliography.

The most comprehensive recent survey of Soviet African studies is: U.S.S.R., Academy of Sciences, Institute of Africa, *Survey of African Studies in the Soviet Union* (Moscow, 1969), 445 p. Much briefer surveys are: S. Kuznetzova, "Current Bibliography on African Studies in the U.S.S.R.," *Library Materials on Africa* 6, no. 2 (November 1968): 47-48, and V. Abramiv, "The Current State of African Studies in the Soviet Union," *Research Review* (Institute of African Studies, Legon, University of Ghana) 6, no. 2 (1970): 15-26.

We have a useful article on I. I. Potekhin, who was the Soviet Union's most prominent Africanist: Luba A. Holowat, "Selected Bibliography of the Works of I. I. Potekhin 1947-1964," *African Studies Bulletin* 12, no. 3 (December 1969): 315-322. Potekhin's most important scholarly publication was the one edited and written jointly with D. A. Olderogge, *Narody Afriki* [Nations of Africa] (Moscow: Acadia Nauk Institut etnografii, 1954), 731 p. A revised and updated edition appeared in German as: *Die Völker Afrikas, ihre Vergangenheit und Gegenwart* (Berlin: VEB Deutscher Verlag der Wissenschaften, 1961), 2 vols.[19]

Returning to bibliography, we note the work of an advanced Czechoslovak graduate student from Charles University of Prague who spent 1966-1968 at Syracuse University. Ladislav Venys, comp., "A select Bibliography of Soviet Publications on Africa in General, and Eastern Africa in particular 1962-1966" (Syracuse, N. Y., 1968), 125 p. (mimeo.) (Maxwell Graduate

School of Citizenship and Public Affairs. Program of Eastern African Studies. Occasional Bibliography No. 11). Three supplements have appeared so far.

CHINA

No bibliographies or bibliographic essays on China and Africa appear to have been published as yet. Extant, however, are one good general volume, two journal articles, and special reports. First is Bruce D. Larkin, *China and Africa, 1949-1970: The Foreign Policy of the Peoples Republic of China* (Berkeley: University of California Press, 1971), 268 p.[20]

Another author of a forthcoming book on China and Africa is Tarey Y. Ismael. He has already published "The People's Republic of China and Africa," *Journal of Modern African Studies* 9, no. 4 (December 1971): 507-529. Ismael's sources for his article are largely journal and newspaper reports and some volumes of the international relations literature. Most sources are drawn from Western Europe and North America.

Two research reports referring to East Africa follow: George B. Keller, *Communist Chinese influence in East Africa. A Research Report Submitted to the Faculty* (Maxwell Air Force Base, Ala.: Air University, 1969), 119 p. (Air Command and Staff Research Study, Air University. Report No. 69-0675); and George T. Yu, *China and Tanzania: A Study of Cooperative Interaction* (Berkeley, Calif.: University of California, 1970), 100 p. (Chinese Research Monographs 5).

Notes

[1] *UNESCO Bulletin for Libraries* 26, no. 2 (May-June 1972), p. 166.

[2] Reviewed as colonialist-sounding by Norman Bennett in *Annals of the American Academy* no. 384 (July 1969): 169.

[3] A negative microfilm copy has been made by the Stanford University Photographic Department for the Hoover Institution (Microfilm DT411w131).

[4] See review in *Libarary Materials on Africa* 3, no. 1 (May 1965): 12.

[5]Skimpily reviewed in *UNESCO Bulletin for Libraries* 25, no. 4 (July-August 1971): 234.

[6]*Library Materials on Africa,* 1, no. 1 (December 1962): 13-14.

[7]This journal is published by the Deutsche Institut fur Afrika-Forschung, 2 Hamburg, 36, Schleausenbruck 1, German (U.S. distributor, Africana Publishing Corporation, New York City).

[8]Mary Darrah Herrick, *Library Journal* (April 1, 1970); *Choice* 7, no. 5 (May 1970): 442.

[9]A favorable review is by David Birmingham, "Past and Present in Angola," *Journal of African History* 12, no. 4 (1971): 662-663.

[10]See the truly favorable review by Richard Gott, "A War for All People," *New Statesman* 84, no. 2171 (October 27, 1972): 602; also *Times Literary Supplement* (December 1, 1972): 1451.

[11]See the favorable shorter notice in *Africa* 41, no. 4 (October 1971): 353.

[12]It is reprinted and distributed by the Liberation Support Movement, Richmond, British Columbia, Canada.

[13]Robert Percy Beckinsale, "Canary Islands" *Encyclopedia Britannica* (1971), 4, 765-767, including bibliography. A more satisfactory article than for many other African areas.

[14]Great Britain, Government Publications, Sectional list no. 69 "Overseas Affairs," revised December 1971 (London: Her Majesty's Stationary Office), p. 74. In the United States British government publications are available from Pendragon House, Redwood City, California.

[15]These are conveniently and authoritatively listed in *Sub-Saharan Africa, A Guide to Serials* (1970), no. 40-46, 4077-4097.

[16]See his "Libraries and Library Training in East Africa," in Anna-Britta Wallenius, ed., *Library Work in Africa* (Uppsala: Scandinavian Institute of African Studies, 1966), p. 28-38.

[17]*Library Materials on Africa* 1, no. 3 (1963): 22.

[18]Reviewed by William Gutteridge, *Journal of African History* 12, no. 4 (1971): 670-671.

[19]Reviewed by Igor Kopytoff, *American Anthropologist,* n.s. 65, no. 1 (February 1963): 162-166, who compared the original Russian and German editions.

[20]Favorably reviewed by editor David Williams in *West Africa* (December 10, 1971): 1449-1450; Julian R. Friedman, *Africana Library Journal* 2, no. 4 (Winter 1971): 27-28; Robert W. Hannah, "Chinese Interests in Africa," *African Studies Review* 15, no. 1 (April 1972): 13-131.

PART FIVE

Guide to Resources in
African Nations

This part concerns itself with the literature of the countries of Africa, arranged by broad region, starting with the North, then East, followed by the West, Center, and South Africa.

NORTH AFRICA AND THE MAGHREB

The inclusion of references to North Africa, though unusual, is more desirable than its omission. There is little justification for separating the countries bordering the Mediterranean, let alone the Arabic-speaking states, from the rest of Africa. It is undesirable to divide Africa in two; this is disliked by vocal elements in North and sub-Saharan Africa. It is one continent, and the drawing of cultural borders between North Africa and the rest is difficult. Where, for example, does the Sudan fit? Neither Islam nor the spread of Arabs or Arabic is confined to the north of Africa. Nevertheless, there has been a tendency for many organizations and books to restrict their attention to sub-Saharan Africa. The main argument seems to be that countries where Arabic is the predominant and usually the national language belong to the Middle East. Some observers compromise and include the countries of the Maghreb in a discussion of Africa but omit the United Arab Republic (Egypt). Nevertheless, in this work, the entire African continent has been included.[1]

Before discussing some publications pertaining to the various states of North Africa, there will be some mention of books concerned with North Africa as a whole, even including other parts of the Middle East or Arabic-speaking countries. (The practice of dealing with parts of the continent before turning to individual countries will be followed below.)

A learned work for a start is: Jean Sauvaget, *Introduction to the History of the Muslim East, A Bibliographical Guide* (Berkeley and Los Angeles: University of California Press, 1965), 252 p. Unfortunately, this volume concentrates almost exclusively on the eastern part of the Muslim world, that is, east of Cairo.

A small, practical guide is: Florence Ljungren and Mohammed Hamdy, *Annotated Guide to Journals Dealing with the Middle East and North Africa* (Cairo: American University in Cairo Press, 1964), 105 p., which was based on a questionnaire reproduced in the book. The guide refers to 281 non-Arabic journals and 73 Arabic journals in Roman script. There is also a listing of Arabic journals in Arabic script and separate subject indexes for Arabic and non-Arabic journals.

A handbook which the publisher of the *World of Learning* has issued since 1948 is *Middle East and North Africa*, 19th ed. (London: Europa Publications, 1972), 931 p. Its original title was *Middle East*. This reference book was favorably reviewed for being so up to date.[2]

A less statistical work, which probably will be outdated rather quickly and is unlikely to be revised, is Michael Adams, ed., *The Middle East: A Handbook* (New York: Praeger, 1971), 633 p. Forty-two authors contributed to it. Among the essays particularly relevant to Africa are one by Norman Daniel on the Sudan and one by Tom Little on the United Arab Republic. There are references to African countries in the sections on political affairs, economic affairs, social patterns, and the arts and mass media.

Specialists may wish to join the Middle East Studies Association, headquartered at New York University, which issues a bulletin and a roster of fellows. The roster was last published in October 1970. The scholarly journal of the association is: *International Journal of Middle East Studies* (Cambridge University Press, 1970-).

Turning now to specifically political sources, let us mention first a rather old reference, which has not been updated. It is Ibrahim Abu-Lughod, "Politics of the Middle East and North Africa: the Literature of the 1960's," *Choice* 4, no. 1 (March 1967): 17-21. This is a short bibliographical essay by a professor of political science at Northwestern University. It is supplemented by Evan I. Farber, librarian of Earlham College.

A more up-to-date and longer unannotated list of titles is contained in the following, which is updated more or less annually: U.S., Foreign Service Institute, Center for Area and Country Service, *A Select Functional and Country Bibliography for Near East and North Africa* (Washington, D.C.: Department of State, 1971),

42 p. The entries, unnumbered, are arranged in twenty-five sections, the majority being geographic ones.

Note also: Ali Mohammad Fatemi, et al., *Political Economy of the Middle East: A Computerized Guide to the Literature* (Akron, Ohio: Department of Economics, University of Akron, 1970), 346 p., 326 p., 49 p. The Fatemi volume is part of a project called International Development Awareness System (IDEAS).

The first five volumes of Menahem Mansoor, *Political and Diplomatic History of the Arab World, 1900-1967: A Chronological Study* (Washington, D.C.: NCR/Microcard Editions, 1972), consist of a chronological account of internationally significant events about the Arab world. The last two volumes contain a keyword index to the previous five. The two index volumes contain thirty-three separate indexes covering various periods.

Of particular interest to librarians is the August 1972 issue of *Leads*, a fact sheet put out by the International Relations Round Table (IRRT) of the American Library Association. This issue is titled "Library Development in the Middle East and North Africa." A mere thirteen pages long, it contains reports on five countries, and is the work of the Ford Foundation, the Library of Congress, and UNESCO.

THE ARAB WORLD

The few references obviously cannot do justice to an immense civilization. They may only throw some light on the complexity of the problem of documenting the history and contemporary life of the Arab world. Let us start with Samir M. Zoghby, "Blacks and Arabs: Past and Present," *Current Bibliography on African Affairs* (Washington, D.C.) n.s. 3, no. 5 (May 1970): 5-22, and George Dimitri Selim, *American Doctoral Dissertations on the Arab World, 1883-1968* (Washington, D.C.: U.S. Government Printing Office, 1970), 103 p.

Probably difficult to procure is: Rolf Reichert, *A Historical and Regional Atlas of the Arab World* (Salvador, Brazil: Central de Estudos Afro-Orientas, Univers federal de Bahia, 1969), 204 p.

A recent work is Wagdy Rizk Ghali, comp., *Arab Dictionaries:*

An Annotated Comprehensive Bibliography (Cairo: The author, 1971). It lists general and special dictionaries, and is mono-, bi-, tri, or multilingual. It also includes a list of conversation and phrase books and a special list of terms. Author, title, subject, language, and chronological indexes are provided.

The following book shows the vast volume and range of journals in Arabic: Abdelghani Ahmed-Bioud, comp., *3,200 revues et journaux arabes 1800-1965* (Paris: Bibliothèque nationale, 1969), 252 p. This work was supported by the Maison des Sciences de l'Homme, and publication was made possible by a grant from the French commission to UNESCO. The Bibliothèque nationale worked with nineteen other libraries in Europe and the Middle East. Entries are arranged by title in Arabic, followed by a transliteration, place of publication and dates, one or two words characterizing the contents of the journal, and the name of libraries where it can be found. Microfilm for journals in the Bibliothèque nationale can be obtained from ACRPP in Paris.

One of the few generally available surveys is: Mohammed M. Aman, "Bibliographic Services in the Arab Countries," *College and Research Libraries* 31, no. 4 (July 1970): 249-259. The article is arranged by type of publication: national bibliographies, government documents, theses, subject bibliography, and general recommendations.[3]

North Africa differs from the Maghreb; it also includes Libya and the United Arab Republic (Egypt). The outstanding historian is Charles-André Julien, whose most recent work is *L'Afrique du Nord en marche* (Paris: Julliard, 1972), 439 p. Julien is one of the few French academics who has been critical of the French colonial administration.[4] Most of his works contain valuable bibliographies. One of his earlier works has recently become available in translation: *History of North Africa: Tunisia, Algeria, Morocco from the Arab Conquest to 1830,* trans. John Petrie, ed. C. C. Steward, ed. and rev. R. Le Tourneau (London: Routledge and Kegan Paul, 1970), 446 p.[5]

Another recent and much reviewed work is Jamil M. Abun-Nasr, *A History of the Maghreb* (Cambridge University Press, 1971), 416 p.[6] Note also: Jacques Berque, *Le Maghreb entre deux guerres,* rev. ed. (Paris: Seuil, 1970), 496 p.

Annuaire de l'Afrique du Nord is prepared by the Centre de Recherches et d'Etudes sur les Sociétés Mediterranéennes (CRESM) in Aix-en-Provence, France, and published in Paris by Editions du Centre National de la Recherche Scientifique. The *Annuaire* began publication in 1962. The 1970 issue contained signed essays covering the entire Maghreb and items of particular importance on the four countries of focus: Algeria, Libya, Morocco, and Tunisia. It included political, sociocultural, and economic chronologies for the four countries, a section of documents and academic studies, and finally a 225-page bibliographic section. In the bibliography are signed book reviews, a classified bibliography in European languages stressing sociopolitical and economic topics, and a classified bibliography in Arabic, which is broader in scope. There are separate author and subject indexes and a list of acronyms. It is a scholarly handbook, indeed, and indispensable for the social scientist concerned with North Africa.

See Samir Amin, *The Maghreb in the Modern World: Algeria, Tunisia Morocco*, trans. Michael Perl (Baltimore: Penguin Books; Harmondsworth, Middlesex, 1970), 256 p.[7] The author is an Egyptian economist who studied in France and has worked as a teacher and consultant in various parts of Francophonic Africa.

A good college text is Clement Henry Moore, *Politics in North Africa: Algeria, Morocco and Tunisia* (Boston: Little, Brown, 1970), 360 p. (Little, Brown Series in Comparative Politics, Country Studies).

Noteworthy also is: Keith Sutton, "Political Association and Maghreb Economic Development," *Journal of Modern African Studies* 10, no. 2 (July 1972): 191-202.

BIBLIOGRAPHY

The scholarly journal *Libyca*, published annually since 1953 and now issued by the Conseil de la Recherche Scientifique, Centre de Recherches Anthropologiques, Préhistoriques et Ethnographiques, in Algiers, includes a section entitled "Bibliographie-Maghreb-Sahara, Anthropologie, Préhistorie, Ethnographie."

These references can be supplemented by: J. Desanges and S. Lancel, "Bibliographie analytique de l'Afrique antique (1960-1962)," *Bulletin d'archeologie Algérienne* 1 (1967): 277-304; J. Desanges and S. Lancel, "Bibliographie analytique de l'Afrique antique II (1963-1964)," *Bulletin d'archeologie Algérienne* 2 (1967): 315-341; and Tadeuze Katula, "Note bibliographique complémentaire sur l'Afrique du Nord aux IVe et Ve siècle," 343-349 in the same journal. The main division of these bibliographies is between protohistory, the Roman period, and the Christian period. The note by Katula is a review of German Germanovich Diligenski, *Sevenniia Afrika v. IV-V vekakh* (Moscow, 1961), 302 p.

Most interesting are the Playfair bibliographies: Robert Lambert Playfair, *Bibliography of the Barbary States*, Pt. 1: *Tripoli and Cyrenaica*, Pt. 2: Henry Spencer, *Bibliography of Tunisia from the Earliest Time to the End of 1891* (1888-1893; reprint ed., Farnborough Hants: Gregg International Publishers, 1971). They are, surprisingly, not noted in the standard guides. They are indispensable for references to works of the nineteenth century and earlier.

Jumping to the middle of the twentieth century, there is: Helen Conover, *North and Northeast Africa, A Selected Annotated List of Writings, 1951-1957* (Washington, D.C.: Library of Congress, 1957), 182 p. It included 349 numbered items; more than 200 additional works are referred to in notes. The arrangement is by country and then by two to five broad subjects. Nothing since has been published to update this volume fully.

Useful are the bibliographical articles in the *Revue française de l'histoire d'outre-mer* (Paris) headed "Chronique de l'histoire d'outre-mer." The following fairly recent ones pertain to North Africa and the Maghreb: Jean Ganiage and André Mantel, "L'Afrique du Nord," 52, no. 186 (November 1965): 127-133, André Martel, "Le Maghreb," 55, no. 199, (1968), 231-259, and his 57, no. 206 (1970), 91-132 with same title.

Most useful is Peter Walzinger, "Bibliographie der sozialwissenschaftlichen Literatur über Nordafrika," *Kölner Zeitschrift der Sozial und Sozialpsychologie* 13 (December 1969):

767-787. This article contains 584 alphabetically arranged references with a subject index.

An article covering a much more limited area, both geographically and in time span, is: George N. Atiyeh, "Recent American Works on Northwest Africa," *The Quarterly Journal of the Library of Congress* 27, no. 3 (July 1970): 277-282. Atiyeh, head of the Near East Section of the Orientalia Division of the Library of Congress, provides a useful bibliographical essay of works about the Maghreb published in the last two decades.

Since January-February 1964, the periodical *Maghreb* has been published every other month. Its subtitle is: *Etudes et documents Algérie, Libya, Maroc, Tunisie.* It is available from La Documentation Française in Paris. Each issue reviews the events of the previous two months and gives a chronology for the Maghreb and the four countries of concern. Parts of studies and documents are reproduced, as are sections of laws. In the final section, "Notice bibliographique," books and journal articles are reviewed.

Acquisitions for a library in North Africa are discussed (at least for the benefit of German readers) in Emil Kummerer, "Bericht über eine Beschaffungsreise nach Nordafrika," *Zeitschrift für Bibliothekswesen und Bibliographie* 18, no. 3 (1971): 174-178.

Scholars visiting Great Britain in search of material on North Africa will benefit from consulting: Robert Lewis Collison, *Directory of Libraries and Special Collections on Asia and North Africa* (London: Crosly Lockwood; Hamden, Conn.: Archon, 1970), 123 p.

MOROCCO

Morocco's population, estimated to be 15.5 million in mid-1970, is growing rapidly. Over the years, a large volume of writings has appeared about Morocco. A useful start can be made with Norman Robert Bennett, *A Study Guide for Morocco* (Boston: Boston University, African Studies Center, Development Program, 1968), 72 p. The guide is divided into eight subject sections, which are introduced briefly, followed by a bibliography. The references are mainly to works in English: monographs, journal articles, and even official reports. As stated in the introduction, material is cited that is viewed "as being relevant to the needs of A.I.D. [U.S. Agency for International Development] personnel."

Many people, particularly Americans, think of Morocco as a land for tourists who benefit from relatively uncrowded beaches and the work of local craftsmen in silver and leather. Among the guidebooks, the best is probably Christopher Kininmonk, *Guide to Morocco* (London: Jonathan Cape, 1972), 384 p. Another, although now partly out of date, is Harold Dennis-Jones, *Your Guide to Morocco* (London: Redman, 1965), 278 p.

A book of considerably more substance is Neville Barbour, *Morocco with 91 Illustrations and 5 maps* (London: Thames and Hudson, 1965), 239 p.

There is no good general history of Morocco available in English. The best French one is probably Henri Terrasse's *Histoire du Maroc* (Casablanca: Editions Atlantides, 1949-1950), 2 vols., which has a full bibliography. It is partially superseded by: Jean Louis Miège, *Le Maroc et l'Europe 1830-1894* (Paris: Presses universitaires de France, 1961-1963), 4 vols. This is the fundamental work on the socioeconomic impact of the West on Morocco, challenging the traditional view of Morocco's isolation. Also note: Edmund Burke III, "Pan-Islam and the Moroccan Resistance to French Colonial Penetration, 1900-1912," *Journal of African History* 13, no. 1 (1972): 97-118, and John P. Halstead, *Rebirth of a Nation: The Origin of the Rise of Moroccan Nationalism 1912-1944* (Cambridge, Mass.: Harvard University Press, 1967), 323 p. (Harvard Middle East Monograph 18).

A fascinating account of one of the ruling families is Gavin Maxwell, *Lords of the Atlas: The Rise and Fall of the House of Glavua, 1893-1956* (New York: Dutton, 1966), 318 p. This book surpasses most fiction in holding the reader's attention. It is also very attractively produced, with numerous photographs and other illustrations.

In a more conventional format is Stephane Bernard, *The Franco-Moroccan Conflict, 1943-1956* (New Haven: Yale University Press, 1968), 680 p., a study commissioned by the Carnegie Endowment.

A frequently cited work is Douglas E. Ashford, *Political Change in Morocco* (Princeton: Princeton University Press, 1961), 432 p. (Princeton Oriental Studies, Social Science, No. 3).

The following account no doubt desired to justify its dedication to Mohammed V, King of Morocco, "great statesman of our age": Leonard Borden Blair, *Western Window on the Arab World* (Austin: University of Texas, 1970), 328 p.

More highly recommended, although not too easily obtainable, is an unidentified translation from the French: Barakah al-Mahdi Bin, *The Political Thought of Ben Barka* (Havana, Cuba: Tricontinental, 1968), 186 p. Part 1 is entitled "Revolutionary Option in Morocco"; part 2 is "Political Articles, 1960-1965."

For an economic overview, the Bank report is still strongly recommended: International Bank for Reconstruction and Development, *Economic Development of Morocco* (Baltimore: Johns Hopkins University Press, 1966), 356 p.

Students of U.S.-Moroccan relations should consult: Luella J. Hall, *The United States and Morocco, 1776-1956* (Metuchen, N.J.: Scarecrow Press, 1971), 1,114 p.

BIBLIOGRAPHY

A good recent bibliographic survey is: Wanda Auerbach, "The National Bibliography of Morocco," *Africana Library Journal* 3, no. 1 (Spring 1972): 7-13. The few who want to pursue Moroccan documentation further should consult M. J. Menon, *Maroc, l'indexation de la documentation scientifique, technique et économique adaptée au développement du Maroc* (Paris: UNESCO, 1971), 121 p. (No. 2497/RMO. RD/DBA).

Map makers, explorers, and other seekers of names need what is available for most countries of the world: U.S., Board of Geographic Names, *Morocco, Official Standard Names Approved by the U.S. Board of Geographic Names* (Washington, D.C.: U.S. Government Printing Office, 1970), 923 p.

Returning to sources of wider appeal, see Ahmad Muhammad al-Miknasi, *Sources et bibliographies d'histoire Marocaine (du XVIe à la première moitié du XXe siècle). Etude bio-bibliographique* (par) A. Meknassi (Tétouan, 1963), 164 p.

For students and practitioners of government and administration, there is good reason to consult: Tangier, African Training and Research Centre in Administration for Development, Library, *Bibliography on Morocco (Books and Articles of Reviews, Classified in the Library of C.A.F.R.A.D.)*, Tangier, CAFRAD, Centre de Documentation, 1970).

Scholars considering working in Morocco and others who want to familiarize themselves with that country should consult: Kenneth Brown, Wilfried J. Rollman and John Waterbury, "Research Facilities in Morocco," *Middle East Studies Association Bulletin* (New York) 4, no. 3 (October 1970): 55-67. It is concerned with the very practical questions a potential research worker needs to know from cost of living, to housing, to research clearance to library facilities and bibliographical sources.

The retrospective bibliography of Morocco first appeared as partial reprints from *Hesperis: Bibliographie marocaine, 1923-1933* (Paris: Larose, 1937), 606 p. The further references from *Hesperis* are: 1934-1935 *26*, p. 605-673, 1939. A classified list of numbered items:

1936-1939 *30*, p. 3-122, 1943. (Reprint Kraus 1967)
1940-1943 *34*, p. 797-928, 1947.
1944-1947 *38*, p. 929-1161, 1951.
1948-1951 *42*, p. 1163-1580, 1955.
1952-1953 *Hesperis-Tamuda 3* 1962.

The gap between 1954 and 1961 has not yet been bridged. For 1962, 1968, and 1969 there is the *Bibliographie nationale marocaine*, a mimeographed publication. The arrangement is according to the Universal Decimal Classification (UDC). There is a subject but no title index.

A small volume (thirty-seven leaves) of the *Bibliographie Nationale Marocaine* for 1968 has been issued by the Bibliothèque Génerale et Archives du Maroc in Rabat. The arrangement is by UDC. There is a brief subject index and an Arabic section of ten leaves and an index.

ARCHIVES

The archival resources of Morocco, in Arabic as well as in

French and Spanish, are large and have barely been charted. There is a catalog to the Arabic manuscripts in Rabat; the two volumes were compiled by I. S. Allouche and A. Regragui, Rabat, Morocco, al-Khizanah al-Ammah lil-Kutub wa-al Mustanadat, *Fihris al-makhtutat al-Arabiyah al-mahfuzah fi al-Khizanah al-Ammah bi-Rabat al Fath, 1921-1953* (Paris: Librerie orientale et américaine, 1954-58). See also Rabat, Morocco, al-Khizanah al-Ammah lil-Kutab wa-al-Mustanadat, *Liste de manuscrits arabes, selectionnés parmi ceux qui sont conservés à la Bibliothèque génerale et archives du Maroc, reproduits par l'Unité mobile de microfilm de l'UNESCO* (Rabat, 1962), 112 p. This catalog is the outcome of the work of UNESCO's mobile microfilm unit. During the unit's six-month stay, 1,200 volumes were filmed. The negative is in Morocco, and a positive print went to the Arab League in Cairo.

ALGERIA

Algeria, a vast country of almost 920,000 square miles, had an estimated population of 14.77 million in 1971. It has been independent since 1962.

There is neither a satisfactory general history of Algeria available in English nor a good study of contemporary Algeria. Most writings about Algeria have been in French, and the few good English studies concern themselves with North Africa as a whole or some special aspect of Algeria. In this section, a few studies and bibliographies concerned with Algeria or some aspect thereof will be cited. Let us start with David C. Gordon, *The Passing of French Algeria* (New York: Oxford University Press, 1966),* and Pierre Bourdieu, *Sociologie de l'Algérie*, 3d ed. (Paris: Presses Universitaires de France, 1970), 128 p. (Que-sais-je? no. 802).

Of particular interest is H. G. Barnby, *The Prisoner of Algiers: An Account of the Forgotten American-Algerian War, 1785-1797* (London: Oxford University Press, 1966), 343 p.

The struggle for Algeria's independence—an unusually long and violent one for Africa—is well portrayed in the motion picture "The Battle of Algiers," a film classic.

One may refer also to the work of Frantz Fanon who worked as a psychiatrist in Algiers between 1952 and 1956 and the next four years as editor of the FLN's newspaper, *El Moudjahid,* in Tunis.[9] His most important and only full-length works in English translation are: *Black Skin, White Masks—The Experiences of a Black Man in a White World* (New York: Grove, 1968); *Studies in a Dying Colonialism* (New York: Grove, 1967); *The Wretched of the Earth* (New York: Grove, 1968); and *Toward the African Revolution* (New York: Grove, 1969). The last volume contains political essays, articles, letters, and notes about Africa and the problems of colonialism. The material covers the most active period in Fanon's life, from the publication of *Black Skin, White Masks* (1952) to that of *The Wretched of the Earth* in 1961, the year he died.

An American historian of France who became an active supporter of the Algerian cause is Richard Brace. See Richard and Joan Brace, *Ordeal in Algeria* (Princeton, N.J.: Van Nostrand, 1960), 453 p.

A more topical account, now perhaps forgotten by most and probably hard to procure, is: Edward Behr, *The Algerian Problem* (Harmondsworth: Penguin Books, 1961; New York: Norton, 1962), 260 p. Noteworthy also are: Edgar O'Ballance, *The Algerian Insurrection, 1954-1962* (Hamden, Conn.: Archon; London: Faber, 1967), 231 p.; and, covering much of the same period, William Quandt, *Revolution and Political Leadership: Algeria, 1954-1968* (Cambridge, Mass.: MIT Press, 1969), 313 p.

To learn about the unique and, hence, innovative aspects of the Algerian revolution, one should consult: Thomas L. Blair, *The Land and Those Who Work It; Algeria's Experiment in Workers' Management* (Garden City, N.Y.: Doubleday, 1969), 312 p., and David and Mavina Ottaway, *Algeria, The Politics of a Socialist Revolution* (Berkeley: University of California Press, 1970), 322 p.

A study by a scholar is Alf Andrew Heggoy, *Insurgency and Counter-Insurgency in Algeria* (Bloomington, Ind.: Indiana University Press, 1972), 327 p. (Indiana University International Studies).[10]

Finally, a good article is Edward R. F. Sheehan, "The Algerians

Tend to Go It Alone, Raise Hell, Hold Out and Grow," *The New York Times Magazine*, (April 23, 1972): 18 ff.

BIBLIOGRAPHY

The classic bibliography of Algeria is: Sir Robert Lambert Playfair, *A Bibliography of Algeria from the Expedition of Charles V in 1541 to 1887* (London: Murry, 1888), 304 p., and the *Supplement to the Bibliography of Algeria from the Earliest Time to 1895* (London: Murry, 1898). The two parts of this bibliography are frequently found bound together. They were reprinted in 1971 by Gregg.

No specific bibliography seems to cover the first half of this century, and one must rely on general French bibliographies. A recent publication, however, is: R. I. Lawless, comp., *A Bibliography of Works on Algeria Published in English since 1954* (Durham, England: University of Durham, Centre for Middle Eastern and Islamic Studies, 1972). This bibliography is classified and contains more than five hundred items drawn from periodical articles and monographs. Another work covering essentially the war period is: J. C. Tomlinson, "Algeria, 1954-1962: A Select Bibliography with Annotations" (Submitted in partial requirement for the University of London diploma in librarianship, August 1964). A mere 151 works, excluding periodical articles and United Nations material, are covered. The bibliography is arranged in sixteen sections. There is an author index.[11]

Useful in spite of its brief coverage and likely to be more easily available is: African Bibliographic Center (Washington, D.C.) "Algeria Panorama, A Selected Bibliographic Survey, 1965-1966," *Special Bibliographic Series* 5, no. 2, (1967), 17 p.

Two more scholarly works are Alf Andrew Hoggoy, "The Sources for Nineteenth Century Algerian History: A Critical Essay," *Muslim World* (Hartford, Conn.) 54 (1964): 292-299, and his "Books on the Algerian Revolution in English: Translations and Anglo-American Contributions," *African Historical Studies* (Boston) 3, no. 1 (1970): 163-168.

The current bibliography, *Bibliographie de l'Algérie*, issued twice a year, began publication in October 1963. The slim (under one-hundred pages) publication is based on the deposit of French and Arabic books and periodicals in the national library. The arrangement is according to ten broad classes and then alphabetical. There are author, title, and other indexes.

The following two bibliographies are specialized ones: Camille Lacoste, *Bibliographie ethnologique de Grand Kabylie* (Paris: Mouton, 1962), 104 p., 732 entries—many of them annotated, about a Berber people living along the Mediterranean coast to the east of Algiers[12]—and Centre des sciences humaines appliquées, *Bibliographie sur le département de Batna* (Aix-en-Provence: CASHA, 1969), 37 p.

Potential field workers in Algeria and others should read carefully: I. William Zartman, "Research Facilities in Algeria," *Middle East Studies Association Bulletin* (New York) 4, no. 1 (February 1970): 42-50. The article stresses the climate of research, particularly for Americans, rather than citing references to publications.

Among the few available guides to archives in Algeria is E. Esquer, *Les archives algériennes et les sources de l'histoire de la conquête* (Algiers: Imprimerie de l'Université, 1912), 63 p.

Librarians and documentalists in particular may be interested in J. Founu Tchnigoua, "Documentation and Development, Experience in Algeria," *UNESCO Bulletin for Libraries* 26, no. 2 (March-April, 1972): 73-79.

TUNISIA

Tunisia has an area of 63,378 square miles with a population estimated at 5.1 million in 1971. Tunis, including its suburbs, had a population of 666,724 in 1966. One of the residential suburbs is Carthage, founded by the Phoenicians in 814 B.C.

Tunisia is located between the western and eastern Mediterranean and between Europe and the Sahara. It was a Barbary state under the suzerainty of Turkey and under French protection between 1881 and 1955 when the French recognized Tunisia's independence.

The literature about Tunisia is very large indeed, even without considering Turkish and Arabic resources. A good start can be made with: Howard C. Reese, et al., *Area Handbook for the Republic of Tunisia* (Washington, D.C.: U.S. Government Printing Office, 1970), 415 p. This handbook was prepared under the auspices of Foreign Area Studies (FAS) of American University in Washington, D.C., by the System Research Corporation. This volume has everything that a handbook should have, including a bibliography.

A more informal and illustrated introductory text is William Spencer, *The Land and People of Tunisia* (Philadelphia: Lippincott, 1967), 160 p. (Portraits of the Nation Series). Note also Wilfred Knapp, *Tunisia* (New York: Walker, 1970), 224 p. (Nations and Peoples Series).

Tunisia has attracted the interest of political scientists and other academics who have found it a hospitable and congenial place for study. A few of the more recent works will be listed chronologically. See Charles F. Gallagher, "Tunisia," in Gwendolen M. Carter, *African One-Party States* (Ithaca: Cornell University Press, 1962), p. 11-86, 503-506. This chapter follows the same outline as the other essays in the volume: historical background, land and people, the political process, contemporary issues, external relations, and bibliography.

Nicola A. Ziadeh, *Origins of Nationalism in Tunisia* (Beirut: American University of Beirut, 1962), 167 p. (Faculty of Arts and Sciences, Oriental Series No. 37), is a much more specialized study concentrating on Tunisian nationalism through the 1920s. It is particularly valuable since it is based in part on sources in Arabic that are cited in notes and bibliography. The author is professor of modern Arab history at the American University of Beirut.

Several other works are: Charles A. Micaud, et al., *Tunisia: The Politics of Modernization* (New York: Praeger, 1964), 204 p.; Clement H. Moore, *Tunisia Since Independence: The Dynamics of One-Party Government* (Berkeley: University of California Press, 1965), 230 p.; and Lars Rudebeck, *Party and People: A Study of Political Change in Tunisia* (London: Hurst, 1969), 285 p. This last book was first published in 1967 as no. 48 of the publications of the Political Science Association, Uppsala, Sweden. It is based on a thorough study of printed and mimeographed sources in French and extensive interviewing of politicians, officials, students, and journalists in Tunisia. Charles A. Micaud in "Politics in North Africa," *Africa Today* (Denver) 18, no. 4 (October 1971): 60-64, reviewed the books by Moore and Rudeback.

The following book is particularly good in evaluating the French impact on Tunisia: Dwight L. Ling, *Tunisia: From Protectorate to Republic* (Bloomington, Ind.: Indiana University Press, 1967), 273 p.

A psychologically and sociologically oriented study by a political scientist is: Mark Arnold Tessler, "The Nature of Modernity in a Transitional Society: The Case of Tunisia" (Ph.D. dissertation, Northwestern University, 1969), 425 p.

Finally, there is a contribution on current affairs: Lorna Hahn, "Tunisia Moves Toward a New World Role," *Africa Report* (New York) 17, no. 7 (July-August 1972): 27-29.

ECONOMIC DEVELOPMENT

A general study, in spite of its rather specific title, is: Ghazi Duwaji, *Economic Development in Tunisia: The Impact and Course of Government Planning* (New York: Praeger, 1967), 222 p. (Praeger Special Studies on International Economic Development). This work includes a discussion of all sections of the economy, frequently in historical perspective. It contains eighty-nine tables and four maps.

Labor is discussed in more detail in: Willard W. Beling, *Modernization and African Labor: A Tunisia Case Study* (New York: Praeger, 1965), 259 p. (Praeger Special Studies in International Economics and Development).[13]. This study examines the relative roles that ideology and nationalism play in the international relations of African labor. The author, now at the University of Southern California, used to edit the now defunct *Maghreb Digest.*

Returning to the management or, rather, governmental sector of the economy, one can recommend *The Economic Yearbook of Tunisia, 1966-67,* issued by the Tunisian Union for Industry,

Commerce and Handicraft under the patronage of the Secretariat of State for the Plan and National Economy (1967), 302 p. This is a sumptuous promotion volume with a full-page colored portrait and introduction by President Habib Bourguibar.[14] The enterprises listed include governmental ones. While this volume was no doubt prepared to attract foreign investors, it will also be of interest to scholars of the economy and politics of Tunisia, as well as less scholarly minded tourists.

BIBLIOGRAPHY

Norman Robert Bennett, *A Study Guide for Tunisia* (Boston: Boston University, African Studies Center, Development Program, 1968), 50 p., is a most useful guide arranged into eight broad sections. A brief introductory section is, in each case, followed by an alphabetical listing of bibliographical entries.

Michelle Roccagni, with an introduction by John Simmons, "Research Facilities in Tunisia," *Middle East Studies Association Bulletin* (New York) 6, no. 1 (February 1972): 30-36, is concerned with the problems facing a scholar about to visit Tunisia; it covers accommodation and library and archival resources.

There is the great retrospective bibliography compiled by Sir Robert Lambert Playfair, *The Bibliography of the Barbary States* (see p. 150). Part 2 covers Tunisia.

For more current publications one must refer to Roger Le Tourneau, "L'Afrique du Nord: Etat des travaux," *Revue française de science politique* (June 1959): 411-453.

For publications since 1962, the best source is: *Annuaire de l'Afrique du Nord*. See "Bibliographie sur la Tunisie, 1970-71," *Tunisie-Actualités* 7 (1972): 49, 59. The first section lists titles of journals and newspapers published in Tunisia in French. The bulk of the work is classified bibliography of mainly journal articles. About half of this work is in Arabic. *Tunisie-Actualités* has carried bibliographical sections previously.

A rather specialized bibliographical essay is: Joel Montague, "Disease and Public Health in Tunisia: 1882-1970: An Overview of the Literature and Its Sources: Part 1," *A Current Bibliography on African Affairs*, n.s. 4, no. 4 (July 1971): 25-260.

Tafeb Baccouche, "Bibliographie critique des études linguistiques concernant la Tunisie," *Revue Tunisienne des sciences sociales* 7, no. 20 (March 1970): 239-286, is a classified list of 247 items, most of them annotated. This journal is issued by the Centre d'Etude et de Recherches Economique et Sociales in Tunis.

LIBYA

Libya has an area of 679,358 square miles. Its population was estimated at 2.01 million in 1971. After domination by Carthage, Rome, the Vandals, the Ottoman Empire, and Italy, Libya became independent in 1952 as a monarchy and in 1969 as the Arab Republic of Libya. The really important recent fact about Libya is the discovery and exploitation of oil after 1957; in 1972, the Libyan government received $2 billion from taxes on oil companies.

The differences between Tunisia and Libya as countries are hard to exaggerate, yet with Libya's much greater wealth these differences will decrease.

A good start for gaining an overview of the country is Stanford Research Institute, *Area Handbook for Libya, Prepared for the American University* (Washington, D.C.: U.S. Government Printing Office, 1969), 307 p. The volume includes separate bibliographies for the four sections: social, political, economic, and national security.

None of the following books is particularly satisfactory. Among them the most important *general* works will be listed chronologically.

Henry Serrano Villard, *Libya: The New Arab Kingdom of North Africa* (Ithaca, N.Y.: Cornell University Press, 1956), 165 p., deals essentially with "prepetroleum" Libya.[15] The author, a Foreign Service officer since 1928, was chief of the Department of State's Division of African Affairs during World War II and first United States minister to independent Libya.

Paul W. Copeland, *The Land and People of Libya* (Philadelphia: Lippincott, 1967), 158 p. (Portraits of the Nations Series), is an attractive, well-illustrated handbook that gives a good feeling for the diversity of the country. Somewhat similar is Terence Blunsum, *Libya: The Country and Its People* (London: Queen Anne Press, 1968), 117 p. It includes a preface by the press counselor of the Libyan embassy in London and is thus not completely objective about Libya and its former king.

John Wright, *Libya* (London: Benn, 1969), 304 p. (Nations of the Modern World), is a history from the earliest times through 1968. Particular stress is placed on the 1911-1951 period.

Anthony Thwaite, *The Deserts of Hesperides: An Experience of Libya* (London: Secker and Warburg, 1969), 180 p., is an attractive, rather personal record of a young Englishman who was drafted to serve as a sergeant of the Royal Army Education Corps in Tripolitania from 1950 to 1951 and as a university teacher in Cyrenaica from 1965 to 1967.

Our next section will consider more specialized works on ethnography, history, geography, politics, and economics. It will conclude with bibliographies. Edward Evan Evans-Pritchard, *The Sanusi of Cyrenaica* (Oxford: Clarendon Press, 1949), 240 p., is a study of the origin and history of the dominant Arab group in Cyrenaica, the Sanusiya order (1843-1942), with special attention to political development and wars with Italy and relation to the Italian colonizers from 1932 to 1939.[16]

For a scholarly study of particular interest to anthropologists and others concerned with conflict, see E. L. Peters, "Some Structural Aspects of the Feud among the Camel Herding Bedouin of Cyrenaica," *Africa* (London) 37, no. 3 (July 1967): 261-282. It was based on the author's field work from 1948 through 1950.

The geographical works on Libya are of a widely differing nature. The first is Gamal E. E. Danasouri, *Studies in the Geography of the Arab World in Africa* (Cairo: Anglo-Egyptian Bookshop [165, Mohamed Faird St.], 1968), 345 p. In spite of the broad title, this book, except for its last chapter, is concerned only with Libya. The stress is on physical geography, with one chapter on recent development, current trends, and prospects of industry in Libya.

An interesting book is Helmuth Kanter, *Libyen-Libya*, trans. J. A. Hellen and I. F. Hellen (Berlin, 1967), 163 p. The author, a geographer and a physician, visited Libya seven times between

1933 and 1965, spending nearly three years there altogether. He usually traveled with small camel caravans. There is a fine analytical index dividing this work of true scholarship into the following parts: physical geography, man and his way of life, health services and environmental sanitation, and diseases. It contains a supplement of illustrations and seventeen folding maps in color. It is a bilingual work in German and English.

The following three works are all by Philip Ward and published in London by Faber and Faber: *Touring Libya, The Western Provinces* (1967), 102 p.; *Touring Libya, The Southern Provinces* (1968), 103 p.; and *Touring Libya, The Eastern Provinces* (1969), 102 p. They are attractive, intelligent guidebooks with maps, photographs, and some historical information as well.

An engaging little book by Welsh author and poet Gwyn Williams is *Green Mountain: An Informal Guide to Cyrenaica and Its Jebel Akhdar* (London: Faber, 1963), 136 p. It includes a note on Celts in Libya.

Agnes Newton Keith, *Children of Allah* (Boston: Little, Brown, 1966), 467 p., is the work of a professional writer who lived and worked in Libya from 1955 to about 1964. It is not recommended to anyone in search of hard data quickly but will appeal to those who have the interest and time to absorb local atmosphere.

Adrian Pelt, *Libyan Independency and the United Nations: A Case Study of Planned Decolonization* (New Haven: Yale University Press, 1970), 1,016 p., is a detailed account by the former United Nations commissioner in Libya from 1950 to 1952. The work in large parts rests on United Nations documents only partially open to the public. The complexities of United Nations documentation are eased by an appendix.

Majid Khadduri, *Modern Libya: A Study in Political Development* (Baltimore: Johns Hopkins University Press, 1963), 404 p., concentrates on the 1950-1960 period. It contains no bibliography but has a useful sprinkling of notes. The author has written many other works concerned with the political and legal aspects of Middle Eastern countries.

John Norman, *Labor and Politics in Libya and Arab Africa* (New York: Bookman Associates, 1965), 219 p., deals largely with the development of the Libyan General Labor Unions (LGLU) in different parts of the country. Notes refer mostly to United States and Libyan newspapers and United Nations documents.

There is little scholarly publishing on recent events in Libya—nothing solid, in fact, since the 1969 coup that ended the monarchy. Of some interest is *Modern Libya*, the spring 1965 supplement to *Afro-Mideast Economic Bulletin*. This issue of some forty pages was published in cooperation with The Permanent Mission of Libya to the United Nations and aimed at potential investors and tourists.

Walt Wandell, *Rivers to the Sea: A Profile of Modern Libya* (Wiesbaden, Germany: You and Europe Publications, 1966), 136 p., is concerned with the former royal family. The author of this journalistic impression used to be stationed at the former United States Wheelus Air Base.

BIBLIOGRAPHY

Part 1 of Sir Robert Lambert Playfair's *The Barbary States* (see p. 150) deals with Tripoli and Cyrenaica.

Roy Wells Hill, *A Bibliography of Libya* (Durham, England: University of Durham, Department of Geography, 1959), 100 p. (Research Papers, Series No. 1, 1959), is a classified bibliography dealing primarily with the geography and economy of Libya. There is no index.

Mohammed Murabet, *A Bibliography of Libya with Particular Reference to Sources Available in Libraries and Public Archives in Tripoli* (Valetta, Malta: Progress Press, 1959), 86 p., is a classified bibliography containing 710 entries. In Philip Ward, *A Survey of Libyan Bibliographical Resources*, 2d ed. (Tripoli: Libyan Publishing House, 1965), 44 p., 43 p.[17] Both English and Arabic language material is surveyed.

Gerald S. Savitz, *The Libyan Library Development Plan: A Special Report for Ministry of Education and Guidance* (Tripoli, 1970), 13 leaves, may update and expand on the sparse information on bibliographic services in Libya supplied by Abdul Hamid Zoubi, secretary of the Libyan National Commission for UNESCO.[18]

Of note among special publications is: John Anthony Allen, *A Select Map and Air-photo Bibliography in Libya with Special Reference* to Coastal Libya (London: Published with the assistance of the University of Libya, the School of Oriental and African Studies and the Bristol Petroleum Co. Ltd. by Luzac, 1970), 117 p. (Libya University of London University Joint Research Project, General Report, Vol. 4).

Hans Schlüter, comp., *Bibliography of Libya, 1957-1969 with Supplementary Material, 1915-1956* (Boston: G. K. Hall, 1973), 305 p., is a short title catalog of about 3,600 entries. It is an extensive listing, covering such topics as religion, education, history, geography, travel, cartography, communications, medicine, and public health. The fields of archaeology, geology, economics, and politics have been indexed selectively because of the vast number of works published on these subjects since 1957.

EGYPT

Egypt has an area of 386,100 square miles and, according to a 1971 United Nations estimate, a population of 34.13 million.

The literature about Egypt is vast, even when excluding Egyptology and works in Arabic. Only some of the more significant works about modern Egypt will be mentioned below.

First, a few general guides will be considered, then historical, political, and socioeconomically relevant volumes paying particular attention to the late President Nasser and Islam.

Harvey Henry Smith, et al., *Area Handbook for the United Arab Republic* (Egypt), 2d ed. (Washington, D.C.: U.S. Government Printing Office, 1970), 554 p. (The American University Foreign Area Studies), is a revision of the *U.S. Army Area Handbook for the United Arab Republic (Egypt)* published in December 1964, which in turn was the revision of a study published in 1957. The 1970 handbook begins with a brief summary about the country. It includes sections on Egypt's society, politics, economies, and national security. The bibliographies are similarly arranged. Each section recommends sources.

Donald Newton Wilbar, *United Arab Republic, Egypt* (New Haven: Human Relations Area Files (HRAF) Press, 1969), 461 p., represents a very extensive revision of *Egypt,* published by HRAF in 1957. The arrangement is not unlike that of the previous volume. Sociological aspects are stressed, but attention is also paid to political and economic matters. The bibliography is divided into these sections.

A rather different type of handbook is *Egypt: A New Nagel Encyclopedia Guide* (London: Barrie and Jenkins, 1972), 816 p. A more tourist-oriented handbook, this guide is exactly what a traveler visiting Egypt for the first time needs. It contains numerous maps, plans, and illustrations, most of which are in black and white.

For those who prefer smaller handbooks, the following two are good: Robert Owen and Terence Blunsum, *Egypt, The Country and Its People* (London: Queen Anne Press, 1966), 116 p., and U.S., Department of State, Bureau of Public Affairs, Office of Media Service, *Arab Republic of Egypt,* rev. ed. (Washington, D.C.: U.S. Government Printing Office, 1972), 8 p. (Publication 81250, Background Notes).

HISTORY AND POLITICS

Gabriel Baer, *Studies in the Social History of Modern Egypt* (Chicago: University of Chicago Press, 1969), 259 p. (Publications of the Center for Middle Eastern Studies No. 4), is concerned with the 1800-1950 period. It is a good, well-documented scholarly volume.

Robert O. Collins and Robert L. Tignor, *Egypt and the Sudan* (Englewood Cliffs, N.J.: Prentice-Hall, 1967), 180 p. (The Modern Nations in Historical Perspective), is aimed at the college market. It contains a list of suggested readings.

Mahmud Yusuf Zayid, *Egypt's Struggle for Independence* (Beirut: Khayats, 1965), 258 p., is a rather specialized history focusing on the background of the Anglo-Egyptian Treaty of 1936.

Gregory Blaxland, *Objective Egypt* (London: Frederick, Muller, 1966), 319 p., looks at military and diplomatic affairs from the point of view of the British establishment.

An attractive, readable volume with seventy-one illustrations, two maps, a truly select bibliography, and a few pages of "who's who" with dates is Gordon Waterfield, *Egypt* (London: Thames and Hudson, 1967), 230 p.

Modern Egypt (London: Ernest Benn, 1967), 281 p. (Nations of the Modern World), is written by Tom Little, an experienced British correspondent who had concentrated a quarter of a century on reporting from the Middle East. More up to date by the same author is "The United Arab Republic," in Michael Adams, ed., *The Middle East: A Handbook* (New York: Praeger, 1971), p. 317-334.

The following two volumes, both historical and political, are truly scholarly. Peter Malcolm Holt, ed., *Political and Social Change in Modern Egypt: Historical Studies from the Ottoman Conquest to the United Arab Republic* (London: Oxford University Press, 1968), 400 p., is written by a professor of Arab history at the School of Oriental and African Studies (SOAS), University of London. The essays, revised papers of a 1965 conference, cover source materials, the period 1517 to 1798, and shorter chronological periods. The second volume, Peter J. Vatikiotis, *Egypt since the Revolution* (New York: Praeger, 1968), 195 p., includes papers based on a small working conference held at SOAS in September 1966. The editor is professor of politics with reference to the Near and Middle East in the University of London and chairman of the Centre for Middle Eastern Studies, SOAS.[19] The papers lack the scholarly sweep of the Holt volume. Most interesting is the final paper by Derek Hopwood, "Some Western Views of the Egyptian Revolution"; it covers post-1952 publications in English.

The all-important topic of Anglo-Egyptian relations is discussed by John Marlowe under that title (London: Frank Cass, 1965) 468 p. Documentation and bibliography are skimpy. In sharp contrast is: Lenoir Chambers Wright, *United States Policy toward Egypt, 1830-1914* (New York: Exposition Press, 1969), 270 p. This comprehensive work, originally a doctoral dissertation at Columbia University in 1953, rests on the U.S. Department of State files found in the National Archives. A selected bibliography is included.

GAMAL ABDEL NASSER

Nasser was a charismatic leader and has been the subject of much writing. Few of his own works are easily available in English. One is: Gamal Abdel Nasser, *Egypt's Liberation: The Philosophy of the Revolution* (Washington, D.C.: Public Affairs Press, 1955), 119 p. This is unusually honest and frank writing.

The first full biography on Nasser is: Robert St. John, *The Boss, The Story of Gamal Abdel Nasser* (New York: McGraw-Hill, 1960; London: Arthur Barker, 1961), 325 p. The author, a radio commentator and foreign correspondent, has written this book in an interesting and breezy style more usually associated with novels.

Peter H. Mansfield, *Nasser's Egypt* (Harmondsworth, Middlesex: Penguin Books, 1965), 222 p. (Penguin African Library AP16), and *Nasser* (London: Methuen, 1969), 217 p. (Makers of the Modern World No. 1), are written by a British Middle East correspondent. Mansfield is a former member of the British Foreign Service who can both speak and read Arabic fluently.

Robert Stephens, *Nasser, A Political Biography* (London: Alan Lane the Penguin Press, 1971), 635 p., is a good book, supported by bibliographical references and a select bibliography.

R. Hrair Dekmejian, *Egypt under Nasir, A Study in Political Dynamics* (Albany: State University of New York Press, 1971), 368 p., traces the evolution of the Egyptian political system from the 1952 revolution through the 1967 war. It is based to some degree on sources in Arabic and contains a bibliography.

Anouar Abdel-Malek is author of *Egypt: Military Society: The Army Regime, the Left and Social Change under Nasser*, trans. Charles Lam Markmann (New York: Random House, 1968), 459 p.[20] Abdel-Malek is a Copt and hence a descendant of ancient Egyptians; he is also a sociologist, former left-wing political activist, and a research scholar under the sponsorship of the Centre National de la Recherche Scientifique (CNRS). The preface of the volume summarizes Egypt's 1952-1967 political history. The book deals with Egyptian society before the 1952 coup, the social character of the military regime, and the search for a national ideology. The book is unusually well and fully documented with source notes and a brief bibliography.

An interesting volume and one that can help justify the inclusion of Egypt in a discussion on Africa is: Taraq Y. Ismael, *The U.A.R. in Africa: Egypt's Policy under Nasser* (Evanston, Ill.: Northwestern University Press, 1971), 258 p. The author examines the evolution and substance of Egypt's Africa policy in detail in case studies pertaining to the Sudan and Zaïre. Footnotes are liberally scattered throughout the work, many giving sources in Arabic.

A recent book is Mohamed Hassanein Heikal, *The Cairo Documents: The Inside Story of Nasser and His Relationship with World Leaders, Rebels and Statesmen* (New York: Doubleday, 1973), 360 p. According to the Library of Congress' transliteration, the author is Muhammad Hasanayn Haykal. It was prominently reviewed in the *New York Times Book Review* (January 21, 1973) by Eric Pace, who has reported for the *Times* (London) from Cairo and Beirut. Pace considered this book, written by a most knowledgeable, though partial, friend of the late leader most important for an understanding of Nasser. Nevertheless, he cites instances of conflicting evidence the author ignored. The book has no index.

As a means of updating scholarly information on post-Nasser Egypt and also to demonstrate the quantity of the periodical literature, see: P. J. Vatikiotis, "Egypt's Politics of Conspiracy (Events following Death of President Nasser in 1970)," *Survey* (London) 18 (Spring 1972): 83-99; Georgi Mirsky, "The Path of the Egyptian Revolution (Comments on Economic and Social Events since 1952)," *New Times* (Moscow) 30 (July 1972): 21-24; Alvin Z. Rubinstein, "Egypt since Nasser," *Current History* 62 (January 1972): 6-13; "Contribution of the Arab Republic of Egypt," *Middle East Journal* (Washington, D.C.) 26 (Winter 1972): 55-68; J. P. O. O'Kane, "Islam in the New Egyptian Constitution: Some Discussion in al-Ahram," *Middle East Journal* 26 (Spring 1972): 134-148; and, finally, see the discussion by Anwar el-Sadat, "Where Egypt Stands," *Foreign Affairs* 51 no. 1 (October 1972): 114-123.

ISLAM

Once again, the choice of volumes included here is merely suggestive of the scope of this vast field—a field that has barely been explored by scholars writing in English and French.

Let's begin with Walter J. Fischel, *Ibn Khaldun in Egypt: His Public Function and His Historical Research (1382-1406): A Study in Islamic Historiography* (Berkeley: University of California Press, 1967), 217 p. Ibn Khaldun was born in Tunis, May 27, 1332, arrived in Alexandria on December 8, 1382, and died in Cairo on March 17, 1406. Khaldun, one of the greatest historians of all times, was not only a student of Islam but of Judaism and Christianity as well. Fischel's small volume is the summation of many years of research on Ibn Khaldun. Both biographical and historiographic, it is restricted to the last twenty-three years of his life. "Ibn Khalduniana, a bibliography of writing on and pertaining to Ibn Khaldun," p. 171-212, a section in the above mentioned Fischel volume, is concerned with the entire life of Ibn Khaldun.

Moving once again into the present, there are Morroe Berger, *Islam in Egypt Today: Social and Political Aspects of Popular Religion* (Cambridge University Press, 1970), 138 p., and two volumes on the Muslim Brotherhood: Richard P. Mitchell, *The Society of the Muslim Brothers* (London: Oxford University Press, 1969), 349 p., and Christina Phelps Harris, *Nationalism and Revolution in Egypt: The Role of the Muslim Brotherhood* (The Hague: Mouton for the Hoover Institution, 1964), 276 p. The first book concerns the early Brotherhood (1928-1954).[21] The second is an attempt by a political scientist to place the Muslim Brotherhood into perspective. It includes a full bibliography of sources in Western languages and in Arabic.

SOCIOLOGY

James B. Mayfield, *Rural Politics in Nasser's Egypt: A Quest for Legitimacy* (Austin: University of Texas Press, 1971), 288 p., is based on pre-1967 field work by a faculty member of the Middle East Center of the University of Utah. It contains a bibliography. A related work is: Hanaa A. Kheir-El-Dine, "Some Aspects of

Regional Differences in the U.A.R. (Variations in Consumer Spending, the Pattern of Income Distribution and Degree of Population Internal Mobility and Its Determinants in Governates of the U.A.R.)," *L'Egypte contemporaine* (Cairo) 62 (January 1971): 61-82.

Returning to the city, we have: Janet L. Abu-Lughod, *Cairo: 1001 Years of the City Victorious* (Princeton: Princeton University Press, 1971), 283 p. (Princeton Studies on the Near East). It is an attractive volume, indeed, with its 156 illustrations and large format. It includes a methodological note hidden in a methodological appendix and a truly classified bibliography. At least one important article has appeared since: K. Peterson, "Villagers in Cairo: Hypotheses versus Data," *American Journal of Sociology* 77 (November 1971): 566-573.

ECONOMICS

The following analysis was written by economists for economists: Bent Hansen and Girgis M. Marzouk, *Development and Economic Policy in the U.A.R. (Egypt)* (Amsterdam: North Holland Publishing Corp., 1965), 333 p.

Patrick O'Brian, *The Revolution in Egypt's Economic System, from Private Enterprise to Socialism, 1952-1965* (Issued under the auspices of the Royal Institute of International Affairs, London: Oxford University Press, 1966), 354 p., traces, explains, and evaluates the dangers in Egypt's economic organization. It has a bibliography.

Mostafa H. Nagi, *Labor Force and Employment in Egypt: A Demographic and Socioeconomic Analysis* (New York: Praeger, 1971), 286 p. (Praeger Special Studies in International Economics and Development), includes seventy-five tables and many notes. Like most of the other books in the Praeger Special Studies series, it has no index.

Finally, a popular volume, illustrated and with just an occasional footnote and a slight indication of sources in the brief preface, is: Tom Little, *High Dam at Aswan: The Subjugation of the Nile* (London: Methuen, 1965), 242 p.

BIBLIOGRAPHY

We can begin with H. L. Maple, *A Bibliography of Egypt Consisting of Works Printed before A.D. 1801* (Pietermaritzburg, 1952), 84 p. It lists the works of 750 authors who published material before the appearance of *Description de l'Egypte* in 1809. The *Description* was a monumental work of twenty-four volumes, which was published as a result of Napoleon's Egyptian expedition of 1798. It was a complete investigation of the country by French scientists and included detailed studies of Egyptian antiquities, natural history, and politics.

An important work is: Heimann Jolowicz, *Bibliotheca aegyptiaca. Reportium über die bis zum jahre 1857 in bezug auf Agypten, seine Geographie, Landeskunde Naturgeschichte, Denkmäler, Sprache, Schrift, Religion, Mythologie, Geschichte, Kunst, Wissenschaft etc. erschienenen schriften akademischer Abhandlungen und Aufsätze in wissenschaftlichen und anderer Zeitschriften* (Leipzig: Englemann, 1858), 244 p., and its seventy-five-page supplement (1861). Roughly translated the title is: "A repertory of publications until the year 1857 concerning Egypt, its geography, natural sciences, monuments, language, script, religion, mythology, science, etc. that have appeared in publications, the papers of learned societies and essays in scientific and other periodicals."

Another classic is Prince Ibrahim-Hilmy, *The Literature of Egypt and the Sudan from the Earliest Times to the Year 1885 (i.e. 1887) Inclusive. A Bibliography Comprising Printed Books, Periodical Writings, and Papers of Learned Societies; Maps and Charts; Ancient Papyri, Manuscripts, Drawing.* (1886-1888, reprint ed., Liechtenstein: Kraus Reprint, 1966). It is an author list, including about twenty thousand titles, with some subject and form headings by an Egyptian political exile.[22]

René Maunier, *Bibliographie économique, juridique et sociale de l'Egypte moderne (1798-1916)* (1918, reprint ed., New York: Burt Franklin, 1972), 372 p., is a classified bibliography of almost 6,700 titles of books and periodical articles primarily in French. It contains author and subject indexes.

See, too, Henri Lorin, *Bibliographie géographique de l'Egypte*

(Cairo: Institut français d'archeologie de l'Egypte, 1928, 1929), 2 vols. Henri Lorin directed the work of Henriette Agrel and others for the 1928 volume, which is concerned with physical and human geography. There are 6,158 numbered entries, classified, with an author index. The 1929 volume, compiled by Henri Munier, is concerned with historical geography and contains 2,683 classified entries with an author index.

Ida A. Pratt, comp., "Modern Egypt, a List of References to Material in the New York Public Library," appeared monthly in the *Bulletin of the New York Public Library* from September 1928 through April 1929. Prepared under the direction of Richard Gottheil, this bibliography was reprinted as a separate 320-page volume.

The annotated entries in Helen Conover's *Egypt and the Anglo-Egyptian Sudan: A Selective Guide to Background Reading* (Washington, D.C., 1952), 26 p., one of her first attempts in the African field, are the same as those found in her *Introduction to Africa* (1952). The entries, all to publications in English, are largely of monographs and journal articles of what was contemporary material; no bibliographies are included.

Gamal-Eddire Heyworth-Dunne, *Select Bibliography on Modern Egypt* (Cairo: The Renaissance Bookshop, 1952), 41 p., includes 167 numbered items in all languages, many annotated, some at length. Lyman H. Coult (with K. Durzi), *An Annotated Research Bibliography of Studies in Arabic, English and French of the Fellah of the Egyptian Nile, 1798-1955* (Miami: University of Miami Press, 1958), 144 p. The bibliographical sources are indicated, including journals. These are author and subject indexes. The bulk of this work consists of 831 numbered items presented in a classified order.

Arabic and non-Arabic sources are cited in Abdel Rahman Zaki, *A Bibliography of the Literature of the City of Cairo* (Cairo: Société de géographie de l'Egypte, 1964). See also Janet Abu-Lughod's volume on Cairo referred to above.

Since 1956, the National Library and Archives of the Arab Republic of Egypt have issued a monthly bulletin recording the receipts of the previous month: Cairo, *Dar al-Kutab al-Misriyah*

[Legal deposit monthly bulletin]. Each issue is divided into European languages and much larger Arabic parts and then government publications and school books, all arranged by Universal Decimal Classification. This is followed by separate author, subject, publisher, and printing press indexes. The monthly issues are cumulated annually in a similar arrangement. The formal entry for the annual volumes is much the same as for the monthly one: Cairo, *Dar al-Kutab al-Misriyah al-Nashrah a-Misriyah lil-matbu'at.*

Also noteworthy are the following three references: John A. Williams, "Research Facilities in the U.A.R.," *Middle East Studies Association Bulletin* 4, no. 2 (1970); George Chandler, "Egypt," in *Libraries in the East: An International and Comparative Study* (London: Seminar Press, 1971), 28-38; and Seoud M. Matta, "In Search of the Nile: The Challenge to Libraries in Egypt," *Wilson Library Bulletin* 44, no. 10 (June 1970): 1040-1045.

THE SUDAN

"Sudan" (meaning "black" in Arabic) is the vast area just to the south of the Sahara from the east coast to the west. This section will be concerned with the eastern Sudan, the former Anglo-Egyptian Sudan.[23] We will eventually deal with the western Sudan of which the French Sudan, later to become Mali, was a part.

The area of the Sudan is 967,500 square miles—about equal to that of Texas, Alaska, and New Mexico combined. The 1971 population estimate was 16 million. It is Africa's largest country in area and fourth largest in population.

The Sudan has been covered admirably bibliographically. The best available bibliographic guides are found in Helen Conover's *Africa South of the Sahara: A Selected Annotated List of Writings* (1963), p. 227-235, items 1450-1502. This is repeated in part and supplemented in Duignan's *Guide to Research and Reference Works on Africa South of the Sahara* (1973), p. 815-826, items 2664-2710.

Noteworthy, too, are the unannotated entries of the following two compendia: John Paden and Edward Soja, ed., *The African Experience* (Evanston, Ill.: Northwestern University Press, 1970),

3A: section 134, p. 625-630; and Donald George Morrison, Robert Cameron Mitchell, John Naber Paden, and Hugh Michael Stevenson, *Black Africa: A Comparative Handbook*, (New York: Free Press, 1972), p. 343-352.

For a brief overview, the articles on the Sudan in the *Encyclopedia Britannica* (1971), vol. 21, are useful. Good introductory texts are: Kenneth D. D. Henderson, *Sudan Republic* (London: E. Benn, 1965; New York: Praeger, 1966), 256 p. (Nations of the Modern World); and Peter M. Holt, *A Modern History of the Sudan, from the Funj Sultinate to the Present Day* (London: Weidenfeld and Nicolson; New York: Grove, 1961), 242 p.

Note also the following, one of the all-too-few review articles: G. N. Sanderson, "The Modern Sudan, 1820-1956: The Present Position of Historical Studies," *Journal of African History* 4, no. 3 (1963): 435-461.

A fine volume on Meroe is Peter L. Shinnie, *Meroe, A Civilization of the Sudan* (London: Thames and Hudson; New York: Praeger, 1967), 229 p. (Ancient People and Places, Vol. 55). While this is a small book, it contains eighty-four plates and sixty-three figures.

Remaining works on the Sudan will be arranged in the following nonexclusive categories: general, Islam, and the Southern Sudan.

GENERAL

Ian Cunnison, *Baggara Arabs* (Oxford: Clarendon Press, 1966), 224 p., is written by an anthropologist who did his field work between 1952 and 1954.

Babikr Bedri, *The Memoires of Babikr Bedri*, trans. Yousef Bedri and George Scott (London: Oxford University Press, 1969), 250 p., is a translation of the first of three volumes which the elder Bedri wrote between 1944, when he was nearly eighty-five, and 1953, the year before he died. Four thousand copies of the three volumes were published in Arabic in 1961. The translation covers the years 1861 to 1891. The volumes include several maps and, more important, a historical introduction by P. M. Holt. Muddathir Abd-el-Rahim, *Imperialism and Nationalism in the Sudan: A Study in Constitutional and Political Development, 1899-1956* (Oxford: Clarendon Press, 1969), 275 p., covers the period of the Sudan's dependency after the Anglo-Egyptian agreement—incorrectly known as the "Condominium Agreement" —until the Sudan's independence.

An article covering more recent times is: Yusuf Fadl Hasan, "The Sudanese Revolution of October 1964," *Journal of Modern African Studies* 5, no. 4 (December 1967): 491-509. The author, director of the Sudan Research Unit, Faculty of Arts, University of Khartoum, bases his account in part on newspaper and ephemeral sources.

Two works on education are: Mohamed Omer Beshir, *Educational Development in the Sudan, 1898-1956* (Oxford: Clarendon Press, 1969), 276 p., and L. Sanderson, "A Survey of Material Available for the Study of Educational Development in the Modern Sudan, 1900-1963," *Sudan Notes and Records* 44 (1963): 69-81.

A classic in the still-small volume of studies of African trade unionism is: Saad Ed Din Fawzi, *The Labour Movement in the Sudan, 1946-1955* (London: Oxford University Press, 1957), 175 p. (Middle Eastern Monograph, No. 1).

Omar Osman and A. A. Suleiman, "The Economy of the Sudan," in Peter Robson and D. A. Lury, eds., *The Economies of Africa* (London: Allen and Unwin; Evanston, Ill.: Northwestern University Press, 1969), p. 436-470, is a handy, well-documented summary that includes twelve tables.

Richard Hill, author of *Sudan Transport: A History of Railway, Marine and River Services in the Republic of the Sudan* (London: Oxford University Press, 1965), 188 p., is a historian, a bibliographer, and a railway buff. He includes eighty-three half-page size plates in his work.

ISLAM

Peter M. Holt, *The Mahdist State of the Sudan, 1881-1898: A Study of Its Origins, Development and Overthrow*, 2d ed. (Oxford:

Clarendon Press, 1970), 285 p.,[24] is the work of a former archivist of the Sudan who uses original sources to get away from the Europeans' "romantic" reporting.[25]

One of the best of the many works (most of them far from scholarly) on the Mahdi is: Byron Farwell, *Prisoners of the Mahdi: The Story of the Mahdist Revolt from the Fall of Khartoum to the Reconquest of the Sudan by Kitchener Fourteen Years Later, and of the Daily Lives and Sufferings in Captivity of Three European Prisoners, a Soldier, a Merchant and a Priest* (London: Longman, 1967), 356 p. All three prisoners—Rudolf Slatin (the soldier), Father Ohrwalder, and Charles Newfeld—have published books on their experiences. The intriguing Slatin is the subject of a biography by Richard Leslie Hill: *Slatin Pasha* (London: Oxford University Press, 1965), 163 p. Hill has also translated *On the Frontiers of Islam: Two Manuscripts Concerning the Sudan under Turco-Egyptian Rule, 1822-1845* (Oxford: Clarendon Press, 1970), 234 p., from the Italian and French and added an introduction and notes. The writers of the two manuscripts were employed by Muhammed Ali-Pasha. Yusuf Fadl Fasan, "The Presentation of Islam in the Eastern Sudan," in I. M. Lewis, ed., *Islam in Tropical Africa: Studies Presented and Discussed at the Fifth International African Seminar, Ahmadu Bello University, Zaria, January 1964* (Oxford University Press for the International African Institute, 1966), p. 144-159, is restricted to the Nile Valley and the area east of it, known as Nubia.

Richard H. Dekmejian and Margaret J. Wyzomirski, "Charismatic Leadership in Islam: The Mahdi of the Sudan," *Comparative Studies in Society and History* 14 (March 1972): 193-214, is a scholarly article with forty-eight footnotes. It applies the thinking of Max Weber to a charismatic leader in the Sudan, the Mahdi.

An article about the Funj, who created the Sinnar Sultanate that dominated the northern Nilotic Sudan during the sixteenth through eighteenth centuries, is: Jay Spaulding, "The Funj: A Reconsideration," *Journal of African History* 13, no. 1 (1972): 39-53. The author examines widely printed evidence, some of it archaeological.

SOUTHERN SUDAN

The long and bitter civil war in Southern Sudan has been documented in part by the works below: Mohamed Omer Beshir, *The Southern Sudan: Background to the Conflict,* (London: C. Hurst, 1968), 192 p., containing nineteen memoranda and other documents for the period 1930 to 1965; Oliver Albino, *The Sudan: A Southern Viewpoint* (London: Oxford University Press for the Institute of Race Relations, 1970), 132 p.;[26] R. Gray, "The Southern Sudan," *Journal of Contemporary History* (London) 6, no. 1 (1971): 108-120;[27] David Roden, "Peace Brings New Hope and Massive Problems," *Africa Report* 17, no. 6 (June 1972): 14-17, and his "Sudan after the Conflict (Economic Conditions in the Three Southern Provinces)," *Geographical Magazine* 44, no. 9 (June 1972): 593-599; and Godfrey Morrison, *The Southern Sudan and Eritrea: Aspects of Wider African Problems,* rev. (London: Minority Right Group, 1971), 36 p. (Report ed. No. 5).

For an aspect of United States policy see: "U.S. Commits $4.45 Million to Assist Refugees in Southern Sudan; Statement, July 3, 1972," *Department of State Bulletin* (July 31, 1972): 145-146.

Well known among anthropologists was Sir Edward E. Evans-Pritchard. Here we shall refer only to his "Sources, with Particular Reference to the Southern Sudan," *Cahiers d'études africaines* (Paris) 11, no. 1 (1971): 129-179. His earlier works, those written between 1928 and 1961, are cited chronologically by one of his students: Conrad C. Reining, *The Zande Scheme: An Anthropological Case Study of Economic Development in Africa* (Evanston, Ill.: Northwestern University Press, 1966), 255 p. (Northwestern University African Studies, No. 17).

The state of the anthropological literature pertaining to the Southern Sudan as of 1965 is analyzed in: Andreas and Waltraud Kronenberg, "Der gegenwärtige Stand der Literatur über ethnische Gruppen im Süd Sudan," *Bulletin of the International Committee on Urgent Anthropological and Ethnological Research* (Vienna) 7 (1965): 107-123. It is "a comprehensive list of ethnic groups in the Southern Sudan. . . . The existing literature on these groups is also listed. It is shown that existing literature on this ethnologically relatively well investigated region is not adequate."[28] See also Yvan Van Garsse, *Ethnological and Anthropological Literature on the Three Southern Sudan Provinces: Upper Nile, Bahar el Ghazal, Equatoria (bibliography)* (St. Niklaas Waas Parklaan, Belgium: The author, 1972).

Three historical works, all published by Yale University Press, are: Robert O. Collins, *The Southern Sudan, 1883-1898* (1962), 212 p. (Yale Historical Publication, Miscellany 76); *King Leopold, England and the Upper Nile, 1899-1909* (1968), 346 p.; and *Land beyond the Rivers, The Southern Sudan, 1898-1918* (1971), 368 p. All three contain bibliographies.

For a relatively up to date view of the Sudan from the official Sudanese point of view, note: University Press of Africa, *Sudan Today* [Written, photographed, produced and published for the Ministry of Information, Khartoum] (Nairobi, 1971; London: Tavistock, 1971).

Important for historians, anthropologists, and other scholars of the Sudan are: Ian George Cunnison and Wendy Janes, eds., *Essays in Sudan Historiography* (New York: Humanities, 1972), 256 p., and Francis Mading Deng, *Tradition and Modernization: A Challenge for Law Among the Dinka of the Sudan* (New Haven: Yale University Press, 1971), 401 p. This last work is by a man studying his own culture. The Dinka, numbering some two million persons, live in the northwestern part of the Sudan.

BIBLIOGRAPHY

A number of bibliographies whose prime focus is Egypt are also concerned with the Sudan. The most important is the one compiled by Prince Ibrahim-Hilmy (see p. 173 above).

The prime bibliographies solely concerned with the Sudan are those compiled by Hill and El Nasri. Richard L. Hill, comp., *A Bibliography of the Anglo-Egyptian Sudan from the Earliest Times to 1937* (London: Oxford University Press, 1939), 213 p., "includes the Anglo-Egyptian Sudan and the other territories formerly under the pre-Mahdist Egyptian rule which were administered, however nominally from Khartoum. It does not include the former Egyptian possessions in Abyssinia or along the Eritrean and Somali coasts." As the author states, "Bibliographical niceties are ignored." No references to manuscript sources are made. The arrangement is by broad subject and their subdivisions. There are indexes to subjects and persons. Abdel Rahman El Nasri, comp., *A Bibliography of the Sudan, 1938-1958. Published on Behalf of the University of Khartoum* (London: Oxford University Press, 1962), 171 p., contains 2,763 entries. El Nasri is university librarian at the University of Khartoum. The entries are in the arrangement Hill used.

This bibliographic work is continued by two articles in *Sudan Notes and Records* (Khartoum): Asma Ibrahim and Abdel Rahman El Nasri, comps., "Sudan Bibliography, 1959-1963," 46 (1965): 130-166, and their "A Bibliography of the Sudan, 1964-1966," 49 (1968): 162-191. The first section of the earlier bibliography lists twenty-four new serials published since 1959. The other entries, for a total of 896, are divided into two broad sections. In the second bibliography the numbering of entries is continued from the earlier article, for a total of 1,893. The arrangement is by thirteen subjects.

References to more scholarly material can be found in: Daniel G. Matthews, "A Current Bibliography on Sudanese Affairs, A Select Bibliography from 1970-1964," *Special Bibliographic Series* 3, no. 4, July 1965, 28 p. (Reprinted, Westport, Conn.: Negro Universities Press, 1969).

The absence of works in Arabic in all these bibliographies (with the notable exception of that by Ibrahim-Hilmy) has now been remedied with the appearance of: Yusuf As'ad Daghier, *Sudanese Bibliography: Arabic Sources, 1875-1967* (Beirut: Beyrouth Librairie Orientale, 1968), 262 p. It is concerned with Arabic-language writings and translations by Sudanese writers. The arrangement is by subject; the final list is of 160 newspapers and periodicals giving editions and dates of publication. There is an author index. The resources listed are in the University of Khartoum, The National Library of Lebanon, The Université Saint Joseph in Egypt, National Library, Cairo, and the Jafet Library of American University of Beirut.

Maymouna Mirghani Hamza, comp., *Theses on the Sudan and by*

182   A BIBLIOGRAPHY OF AFRICANA

Sudanese Accepted for Higher Degrees (Khartoum: University of Khartoum and Sudan Research Unit, 1966), 63 p., includes institutions in Egypt, the United Kingdom, Germany, France, the Netherlands, and the United States. The arrangement is alphabetical; there are 263 numbered entries and a subject index. A second edition with the same title was issued by the University of Khartoum Library in 1971.

Viveca Halldin and Hakan Hermansson, *Sudan, en selektiv litteratur forteckning* (Uppsala: Nordiska afrikainstitutat, 1972), 21 p., is a classified bibliography. While the subject headings are in Swedish, virtually all the entries are for materials in English—references to monographs, journal articles, and government documents. Unfortunately, the citations to journal articles frequently exclude the date.

See also Peter F. M. McLoughlin, et al., *Research for Agricultural Development in Northern Sudan to 1967: A Classified Inventory and Analysis* (Frederickton, New Brunswick, Canada: P. M. McLoughlin Associates, 1971), 86 p. (Notes and Papers and Development). For the difficulties that will be experienced in obtaining Sudanese publications cited by McLoughlin and others, some help can be derived from the note of I.J.C. Foster of the University Library, Oriental Section, Durham, England, in Valerie Bloomfield, comp., *Conference on the Acquisition of Material from Africa* (Zug, Switzerland: Inter-Documentation, 1969), p. 128-131. Foster lists the newspaper titles from the Sudan and Libya acquired by Durham University and gives addresses for news agencies operating in the two countries. Durham has agreed to collect under the British Standing Conference on Library Materials on Africa (SCOLMA) scheme publications on and from the Sudan and Libya.

University of Khartoum Library, *The Classified Catalogue of the Sudan Collection in the University of Khartoum Library* (1971), is unpaged. The large volume contains 5,114 numbered items. It includes author and subject indexes in Roman and Arabic scripts.

ETHIOPIA

Ethiopia is Africa's sixth largest country in area, 457,256 square miles (about equal to Texas, Oklahoma, and New Mexico combined). With its 1971 estimate of 26 million people, it is the second largest country (after Nigeria) in population.

Ethiopia has an ancient written literature and, except for the short Italian occupation, was never a colony. Yet, we know relatively little about Ethiopia's past history or its present condition.

HISTORY AND POLITICS

A fine example of current Ethiopian scholarship is: Tadesse Tamrat, *Church and State in Ethiopia, 1270-1527* (Oxford: Clarendon Press, 1972), 327 p.[29]

A fairly satisfactory work is: Robert L. Hess, *Ethiopia, the Modernization of Autocracy* (Ithaca: Cornell University Press, 1970), 272 p.,[30] which is an expansion of an essay he contributed to Gwendolen Carter, ed., *National Unity and Regionalism in Eight African States* (1966). It has a fine bibliography. Hess tends to be biased in favor of the official order of things in Ethiopia. The opposite approach is taken by Richard Greenfield in his *Ethiopia, A New Political History*, rev. ed. (London: Pall Mall Press, 1967). He gives considerable attention to Girmame Neway who, with his brother, led the attempted 1960 coup.

A much less colorful, yet useful, publication is Peter Schwab, ed., *Ethiopia and Haile Selassie* (New York: Facts on File, 1972), 151 p. A volume in the series "Interim History, The Bridge Between News and Tomorrow's History," it is based on the records compiled by *Facts on File* and Schwab's doctoral dissertation, "An Analysis of Decision-making in the Political System of Ethiopia" (New School for Social Research, 1969).

The standard work according to Duignan's *Guide* is: Margery Perham, *The Government of Ethiopia*, 2d ed. (Evanston, Ill.: Northwestern University Press, 1969), 672 p. Another important work by a political scientist and student of Perham is: Christopher Clapham, *Haile Selassie's Government* (New York: Praeger, 1969),

218 p. It includes a bibliography. The treatment is historical and starts from the 1850s. A more interesting version is probably the author's doctoral dissertation, "The Institutions of the Central Ethiopian Government," which, according to the preface of the published volume, "is now buried in the inaccessible depths of the Bodleian Library (Oxford)."

Easily accessible and with a good summary of some of the conflicting evidence and its interpreation is Christopher Clapham, "The Ethiopian Coup d'état of December 1960," *Journal of Modern African Studies* 6, no. 4 (December 1968): 495-507.

A useful, well-illustrated volume, available only in French, is: André Davy, *Ethiopie d'hier et d'aujourd'hui* (Paris: Le livre africain, 1970), 254 p.

Of the many works by Richard Pankhurst, director of the Institute of Ethiopian studies, one deserves special mention: *Economic History of Ethiopia, 1800-1935* (Evanston, Ill.: Northwestern University Press, 1970), 772 p.[31]

ERITREA

Separatism has erupted in guerrilla warfare sporadically in the former Italian colony of Eritrea, whose integration with Ethiopia was arranged by the United Nations in 1952.

Documentation can be gathered from the indexes to newspapers, such as *The New York Times*, and from the Public Affairs Information Service (PAIS). There are references in Colin Legum, *Africa Contemporary Record* (1971-1972), to activities of 1971. The Legum volume also reproduces the Eritrean Liberation Front Anniversary Statement broadcast by Radio Damascus on September 20, 1971: "Voice of the Eritrean Revolution."

Other sources are: John Franklin Campbell, "Rumblings along the Red Sea: The Eritrean Question," *Foreign Affairs* 48, no. 3 (April 1970): 537-548, and Richard Lobban, "The Eritrean Liberation Front: A Close-Up View," *Munger Africana Library* (Pasadena, Calif.) no. 13 (1972), 20 p. Campbell, the former United States consul in Asmara from 1967 through 1969, also wrote "Background to the Eritrean Conflict: Deferred Results of

Colonial Map-making Geopolitics and Religion," *Africa Report* 16, no. 5 (May 1971): 19-20. This issue contains a number of other articles on Ethiopia.

SOCIOLOGY AND ANTHROPOLOGY

The most important works in these disciplines remain: Donald Nathan Levine, *Wax and Gold, Tradition and Innovation in Ethiopian Culture* (Chicago: Chicago University Press, 1965), 315 p.,[32] and William A. Shack, *The Gurage: A People of the Ensete Culture* (London: Oxford University Press, 1966), 470 p.

Other significant anthropological works are: Herbert S. Lewis, *A Galla Monarchy: Jimma Abba Jifar Ethiopia,* 1890-1932 (Madison, Wis.: University of Wisconsin Press, 1965), 148 p., and Asmaron Legesse, *Gada: Three Approaches to the Study of African Society* (New York: Free Press, 1973), 340 p.

From an earlier time, one should note the results of the German expeditions to Southern Ethiopia: Adolf Ellegard Jensen, *Im Lande des Gada Wanderungen zwischen Volkstrümmern Südabessiniens* (Stuttgart: Strecker und Schröder, 1936), 608 p. (Verlauf und Ergebnisse der XII. Deutschen Inner-Afrikanischen Forschungs-Expedition [DIAFE] 1934/35).[33] This is a lavish publication, as are the following three volumes issued by the Frobenius Institute in Frankfurt about the people of Southern Ethiopia and the results of the Frobenius expeditions (1950-1952 and 1954-1956) (all have English summaries): Adolf Ellegard Jensen, *Altvolker Süd-Athiopiens* (Stuttgart: Kohlhammer, 1959), 455 p.;[34] Eike Haberland, *Galla Süd-Athiopiens* (Stuttgart: Kohlhammer, 1963), 815 p.; and Helmut Straube, *Westkuschitsche Völker Süd-Athiopiens* (Stuttgart: Kohlhommer, 1963), 411 p.

An important recent study is C. R. Hallpike, *The Konso of Ethiopia: A Study of the Values of a Kushitic People* (Oxford: Clarendon Press, 1972), 342 p.[35]

Three recent scholarly journal articles—and there are few on Ethiopia—are R. H. Jackson, "Social Structure and Political Change in Ethiopia and Liberia," *Comparative Political Studies*

(Beverly Hills, Calif.) 3, no. 1 (April 1970): 36-62;[36] F. C. Gamst, "Peasantries and Elites without Urbanism: The Civilization of Ethiopia," *Comparative Studies in Society and History* (The Hague and Ann Arbor) 12, no. 4 (October 1970): 373-392; and R. Holloway, "Street Boys in Addis," *Community Development Journal* (Manchester) 5, no. 3 (July 1970): 139-144.

LINGUISTICS

In the tradition of Ethiopian semiticists, such as Wolf Leslau and Edward Ullendorff, is: Robert Hetzron, *Ethiopian Semitic* (Manchester: Manchester University Press, 1972), 145 p. (Journal of Semitic Studies, Monograph No. 2).

ECONOMICS AND DEVELOPMENT

David C. Korten, *Planned Change in a Traditional Society: Psychological Problems of Modernization in Ethiopia* (New York: Praeger, 1972), 387 p. (Praeger Special Studies in International Economics and Development), analyzes values and behavior in traditional roles in part as reflected in folk tales.[37] Student protest is analyzed in detail. A bibliography is included.

The following references deal with economic matters more concretely: Beguela Assefa, *A Profile of the Ethiopian Economy* (Addis Ababa: Oxford University Press, 1969), 127 p.; K. A. Cherian, *Ethiopia Today: An Up-to-Date Illustrated Review of Economic Conditions* (Addis Ababa: Central Printers Press, 1969), 172 p.; Peter Schwab, "Tax System in Ethiopia," *American Journal of Economics and Sociology* (New York) 29, no. 1 (January 1970): 77-88; D. Mohammed, "Private Foreign Investment in Ethiopia (1950-1968)," *Journal of Ethiopian Studies* 7, no. 2 (July 1969): 53-78; Commercial Bank of Ethiopia, Business Development Division, Market Research Section, *The Ethiopian Economy: Selected Topics* (Addis Ababa: The Bank, December 1970), p. 111; and Ethiopian Chamber of Commerce, *Trade Directory and Guide Book to Ethiopia, 1971-1972* (Addis Ababa: The Chamber, 1972), 331 p.

HAILE SELASSIE I

Although there are numerous excessively flattering accounts of the Emperor Haile Selassie, there is as yet no satisfactory biography.

The best available source is the emperor himself. Emperor Haile Selassie I, *Heywatenna ya-Ityopya ermejja* (Addis Ababa: Berhanenna Salem Press, 1973), 264 p.,[38] is his autobiography from 1892 to 1936 in Amharic. Contrary to his custom in all his other writings, the emperor here refers to himself in the first person singular rather than the royal "we." In *Selected Speeches of His Imperial Majesty Haile Selassie I, 1918-1967* (Addis Ababa: Imperial Ethiopian Ministry of Information, Publications and Foreign Languages Press Department, 1967), 693 p., the extracts are arranged by topics into eighteen chapters, with a concentration on education and international relations.

Turning now to biography proper, there is somewhat more than a column by Edward Ullendorff, in volume 10 of the 1971 edition of the *Encyclopedia Britannica*. Ullendorff is the author of *The Ethiopians*, 2d ed. (Oxford University Press, 1965), 235 p.

Dedicated to the emperor is: Christine Sandford (Lush), *The Lion of Judah Has Prevailed* (1955; reprint ed., Westport, Conn.: Greenwood Press, 1972), 192 p. This illustrated book concentrates on the early years of the emperor's reign, but does bring us to 1955.

Leonard Mosely, *Haile Selassie, the Conquering Lion* (London: Weidenfeld and Nicolson: Englewood Cliffs, N.J.: Prentice-Hall, 1964), 306 p., is a well-written, popular biography with important illustrations.

Charles Gorham, *The Lion of Judah: A Life of Haile Selassie I, Emperor of Ethiopia* (New York: Farrar, Straus and Giroux, 1966), 152 p., is a pleasant, easy-going volume concentrating on the early period of the emperor's life.

Fascinating not just for the light shed on the emperor is the article by Walter W. Ristoe, "The Haile Selassie Map of Ethiopia," *The Quarterly Journal of the Library of Congress* 27, no. 3 (July 1970): 257-266.

TOURISM

Duncan Forbes, *The Heart of Ethiopia* (London: Robert Hale, 1972), 224 p., is the kind of book that may help to make a trip to Ethiopia more meaningful.

Articles such as the following two can be found without difficulty: John Ravenson, "Ethiopia: Ancient Glories," *Africa Report* 17, no. 5 (May 1972): 29-30; and Judith Olmstead, "Ethiopia's Artful Weavers," *National Geographic* 143, no. 1 (January 1973): 125-141.

RETROSPECTIVE BIBLIOGRAPHIES

Giuseppe Fumagalli, *Bibliografia etiopica. Catalogo descrittivo e ragionato degli scritti pubblicati dalla invenzione della stampa sino a tutto il 1891. Intorno alla Etiopia e regioni limitrofe* (Milan: Hoepli, 1893), 288 p., is the most complete bibliography of early Ethiopia and Amharica. The 2,722 numbered items—all to materials in European languages—are arranged in a classified manner. There is an author index.

Silvio Zanutto, *Bibliografia Etiopica. Primo contributo: Bibliografia,* 2d ed. (Rome: Società anonima italiane arti grafiche, 1936), 54 p., was first published in 1929. In the 1936 edition of this bibliography of bibliographies, 141 bibliographies and related materials are arranged in a classified manner. Zanutto is also the author of *Secondo contributo: Manoscritti etiopici* (Rome: Sindacato Italiano arti grafiche, 1932), 178 p. The 319 manuscripts are carefully listed according to a geographical arrangement of the owning library; 242 are in European libraries and 29 in eighteen private and institutional collections in North America. Another Italian bibliography is Carlos Manetti, *Il Contributo Italiano alla esplorazione et allo studio dell' Etiopia* (Rome, 1936).

Stephen G. Wright, comp., *Ethiopian Incunabula from the Collections in the National Library of Ethiopia and the Haile Selassi I University* (Addis Ababa, 1967), 107 p., includes all books printed in the territory today called Ethiopia, before the Italian occupation of 1936-1941. Excluded are all books printed outside of

Ethiopia with an Addis imprint and all newspapers and periodicals. Two hundred twenty-three items are recorded according to author, printing press, and date between 1912 and 1936.

Renato Lefevre, *L'Ethiopia nella stampa del primo Cinquecento* (Como: Casa editore Pietro Cairoli, 1966), 79 p. (Publicazioni d'Istituto Italiano per l'Africa, Quaderni D'Africa serie I, No. 3) is a scholarly essay on sixteenth-century printing in Ethiopia. A briefer presentation by the same author with the same title is in *Africa* (Rome) 20 (1965): 345-369.

A very useful guide that concentrates on newer publications is John W. Sommer, *A Study Guide for Ethiopia and the Horn of Africa* (Boston University, African Studies Center, Development Program, 1969), 94 p. It is arranged in eight broad sections, which form an introduction to the classified bibliography. While the emphasis is on Ethiopia, Somalia and other parts of the Horn are also considered.

Ethiopia, Ministry of Foreign Affairs, *Bibliography of Ethiopia* (Addis Ababa, 1968), 46 p., is an alphabetical listing of the main publications, ancient and modern, on Ethiopia. The final page lists twelve current periodical publications on Ethiopia. It includes an introduction by Ato Ketema Yifru, then minister of foreign affairs.

Sellassie Sergew Hable, *Bibliography of Ancient and Medieval Ethiopian History* (Addis Ababa: Star Printing Press, 1969), 76 p., contains 918 numbered items classified into ten subject sections. There is an author index.

Harold G. Marcus, *The Modern History of Ethiopia and the Horn of Africa: A Select and Annotated Bibliography* (Hoover Institution Press, 1972), 641 p. (Hoover Institution Bibliographical Series No. 56), has 2,042 numbered entries, most of them annotated. These are drawn from 151 geographical journals published between 1800 and 1920. The arrangement is by language of the author's nation: English, French, Italian, German, Russian, and others. The listing of the 151 journals indicates which volumes were checked for the bibliography. A partial alphabetical list of books is mentioned in the bibliography. There are separate author, geographical, proper noun, and subject indexes.

George F. Black, comp., "Ethiopia and Amharica," *Bulletin of*

the New York Public Library 32, no. 7 (July 1928): 443-481, no. 8
(August 1928): 528-564, is a classified bibliography with an introductory essay.

Pierre Comba, *List of Books in Amharic in the Ethiopia Collection
of the University College of Addis Ababa April 1959* (Addis Ababa,
1961), 133 p.,[39] is an inventory of Amharic books collected up to
April 4, 1959. It makes no claim to be a complete bibliography. It
contains: Section Amharic auteurs items 1-386; section amharique, titres (auteurs anonymes) items 387-521; section amharique,
bibliographie items 522-529. A Ge'ez section is to be published
later. (Ge'ez is the classical language of Ethiopia which is related
to Amharic somewhat as Latin is to Italian.) An asterisk shows that
the work is also to be found in the National Library of Addis
Ababa. Authors' names are given in Amharic spelling with translations into Roman characters. Titles are in Amharic with French
translations. There are indexes to authors translated into
Amharic, authors of foreign origin, and publishers.

Robert L. Hess, "Library Shelflist: Ethiopia and the Horn of
Africa," 1973, 181 sheets (mimeo), is a listing of a personal collection.

The following periodically revised list, an unpaged machine
printout, was compiled by one of Hess's students: James Robert
Baylor, "Ethiopia: List of Works in English" (1970). The introduction describes it as "a computerized, un-annotated
bibliography of studies and travel accounts about the Empire of
Ethiopia. The works listed include monographs, journal articles,
magazine articles, theses, mimeographed works and typescript
manuscripts." The classified arrangement of this volume is un-
clear. Baylor's bibliography should be available from the
Department of History at the University of Illinois at Chicago
Circle.

Ethiopia, Ministry of Education and Fine Arts, Department of
Fine Arts and Culture, *Catalogue of Manuscripts Microfilmed by the
UNESCO Mobile Microfilm Unit in Addis Ababa and Gojjan
Province* (Addis Ababa, 1970), lists 369 manuscripts that have
been microfilmed.

Other useful works are: Christo Solomon Gebre, *A Decade of
Ethiopian Language Publication* (Addis Ababa: Haile Selassie I

University Library, 1970), and Christo Solomon Gebre, *List of Ethiopian Authors* (Haile Selassie I University Library, 1971).

By March 1971, the reference department of Haile Selassie I University library had indexed three thousand items in Ethiopian and selected foreign journals.[40]

Haile Gabriel Dogne, comp., "A Bibliography of Educational Publications on Ethiopia" (Addis Ababa: Haile Selassie I University, Faculty of Education, Research Centre, 1969), 100 p. (mimeo.), is classified into seven categories. Items in English and other European languages are listed first within each section, followed by entries in Amharic. As the compiler admits, it is difficult to locate many of the items enumerated.

Next are the first four bibliographies compiled at the Haile Selassie I University library; all are mimeographed. Pamela Bell, "Land Tenure in Ethiopia" (1968), 25 p., contains only entries in European languages. Gulilat Tage, "A Preliminary Bibliography on Ethiopian Economy" (1969), 113 p., is a classified list of English-language material, including books, periodical articles, and government documents. The emphasis is on the 1940-1967 period. Ursula Roberts and Solomon Amde, comps., "Medicine in Ethiopia" (1970), 152 p., contains 1,132 numbered entries. An addendum brings the total to 1,146. The compilers (from the Central Medical Library) hope to cover reasonably the 1942-1969 period. There are author and subject sections. The final bibliography is John M. Cohen, "A Select Bibliography on Rural Ethiopia" (1971), 32 p.

CURRENT BIBLIOGRAPHICAL SERVICES

The best vehicle for keeping abreast with new publications of Ethiopia in both Amharic and English is: The Library of Congress, National Program for Acquisitions and Cataloging, Accessions List, *Eastern Africa* (Nairobi, Kenya, The Library of Congress Field Office). This quarterly has been issued since 1968. Useful too are two irregular publications of the Institute of Ethiopian Studies, Haile Selassie I University: *Register of Current Research on Ethiopia and the Horn of Africa* (an annual issued since 1963), a classified arrangement of numbered entries and an index, and *List of Current Periodical Publications in Ethiopia* (first issued in 1964). The fourth compilation is dated July 1970. It is a classified list of 353 numbered entries with an index in Ethiopian languages.

The bibliographical situation and the state of libraries has been repeatedly reported by Rita Pankhurst, university librarian at Haile Selassie I University. Her most recent, easily available statement is: "Bibliographical Services throughout the World: Ethiopia," *Bibliography Documentation Terminology* (UNESCO) 12, no. 3 (May 1972): 111-112.

In March 1968 the Ethiopian Library Association issued a *Directory of Ethiopian Libraries,* compiled and edited by Geraldine Odester Amos of Haile Selassie I University. The directory is based on the 94 usable questionnaires of the 448 sent out. The institutions are listed alphabetically, with an index to the type of library, and by province.

LAW

The following three references presented chronologically should be useful: Jacques Vanderlinden, "A Supplement to the Bibliography of Ethiopian Law," *Journal of Ethiopian Law* 4, no. 2 (December 1967): 433-437; A. Arthur Schiller, "Customary Land Tenure among the Highland People of Northern Ethiopia: A Bibliography," *African Law Studies* 1 (June 1969): 1-22; and Marco Guadagni, *Ethiopian Labour Law Handbook* (Asmara: Il poligrafico,1972), 166 p.

SOMALIA

The Somali Democratic Republic covers an area of 246,201 square miles—about the size of Texas. According to a United Nations estimate for 1971, the population was 2.86 million. The country has been independent since 1960 when the former colony of British Somaliland was fused with the former Italian colony, which in 1950 had become a United Nations trusteeship. Information is relatively scarce on this interesting country.

Perhaps the most knowledgeable outsider is British social anthropologist Ioan Myrddin Lewis, who wrote the fine article in the *Encyclopedia Britannica* (1971) on the Sudan and many other works, some of which will be mentioned below.

For another brief, up to date, and generally available source, see United States, Department of State, Bureau of Public Affairs, Offices of Media Services, *Somali Democratic Republic*, rev. ed. (Washington, D.C.: U.S. Government Printing Office, 1972), 6 p. (Publication No. 7881). Another officially published and, of course, larger work is: Irving Kaplan, et al., *Area Handbook for Somalia: Prepared by the American University, Foreign Studies* (Washington, D.C.: U.S. Government Printing Office, 1969), 455 p.—a good summary indeed. It has the usual sections for an area handbook: social, political, economic, and national security, each with its separate bibliography.

For a more thorough historical background, one can recommend: I. M. Lewis, *A Modern History of Somaliland: From Nation to State* (London: Weidenfeld and Nicholson; New York: Praeger, 1965), 234 p.[41] Lewis tends to deal more extensively with modern times.

The best account of the English exploration of Somaliland is found in: Sir Richard Burton, *First Footsteps in East Africa,* ed. Gordon Waterfield (London: Routledge and Kegan Paul, 1966), 320 p. This work is as informative of the British and colonial mind about "the lower breed without the law" as it is about "foreign" lands. It demonstrates that accounts of travelers frequently teach us more about the explorer's home than about the lands which he has traversed.

The study in English of Italian colonialism in Somalia is by Robert L. Hess, *Italian Colonialism in Somalia* (Chicago: University of Chicago Press, 1966), 234 p. The work was based almost exclusively on Italian archival resources, which had not previously been made available to nonofficials, let alone foreigners.[42] This work contains a carefully annotated and detailed bibliography.

More recent is M. Pirone, "Questioni di storia somala," *Africa* (Rome) 24, no. 1 (March 1969): 19-32.

Turning to economics, see Giulio Querini, *Agricultura e sviluppo economico* (Rome: Edizioni "Richerche," 1969), 257 p.

(Université Catholique de Louvain, Faculté des sciences économiques, sociales et politiques, nouvelle serie No. 48). Querini worked for five years as an economic consultant to the government of Somalia. The first part of this work, written in Italian, is an analysis of theories of economic development; the second is specifically concerned with Somalia. More accessible is: Thadis W. Box, "Nomadism and Land Use in Somalia," *Economic Development and Cultural Change* 19, no. 2 (1971): 222-228.

Giuseppe Vedovato, "La strategia internazionale dello sviluppo e significato dell'opera della S.A.I.S," *Africa* (Rome) 25 (December 1970): 479-486, deals with the Italo-Somalia agricultural society. English readers will prefer: Azaz Mehmet, "Effectiveness of Foreign Aid: The Case of Somalia," *Journal of Modern African Studies* 9, no. 1 (May 1971): 31-47.

Kremlinologists may already be acquainted with "Soviet-Somalian statement," issued following a visit of President Mohammed Siad Barre of Somalia to Russia, November 16-22, 1971.[43]

The new labor code in Somalia is discussed briefly in the *International Labour Review* 102, no. 5 (November 1970): 507-508. See also the International Labour Office's "Report to the Government of the Republic of Somalia on Manpower Assessment and Planning," (1970), 192 p. (1LO/TAP/Somalia/R5). This study was sponsored in cooperation with the United Nations Development Program.

Fundamental to a study of economics in Somalia are the *Statistical Abstracts.* The seventh one, issued by the Ministry of Planning and Coordination Central Statistical Department in November 1971, contains fourteen main groups of tables devoted to population, education, development programs, foreign trade, public finance, banking and balance of payments, prices, transporation and communication, fuel and power, health, meteorology, industry and mining, and crime.

POLITICAL SCIENCE AND LAW

The following article speaks for itself: P. Contini, "The Evolution of Blood-money for Homicide in Somalia," *Journal of African Law* (London) 15, no. 1 (1971): 77-84.

Saadia Touval, *Somali Nationalism, International Politics and the Drive for Unity in the Horn of Africa* (Cambridge: Harvard University Press, 1963), 214 p., is quite readable.[44]

Chapter 6 of Christian P. Potholm, *Four African Political Systems* (Englewood Cliffs, N.J.: Prentice-Hall, 1970), deals with the Somali political system.

On constitutional law, there are the publications of Renato Angeloni (published in Milan by Giuffre): *Diritto costituzionale Somalo* (1964), 336 p., and *Codice penale Somalo commentato ed annotato in base ai lavori preparatori* [The Somali penal code with comments and annotations based on preliminary studies] (1967), 431 p.

The former United Nations legal adviser to the Somali government, 1960-1964, Paolo Contini has published: *The Somali Republic: An Experiment in Legal Integration* (London: Cass, 1969), 92 p.

The following author was with the Peace Corps as legal adviser from 1966 to 1969: Martin Ganzglass, *The Penal Code of the Somali Democratic Republic: With Cases, Commentary and Examples* (New Bruswick, N.J.: Rutgers University Press, 1971), 645 p.

Turning now to the contemporary political scene, the writings of the late Alfonso Arturo Castagno (who was director of the Boston University African Studies Center) dominate. Among his last articles on Somalia are two published in *Africa Report* (New York): "Somalia Goes Military: The Supreme Revolutionary Council Follows a Pragmatic Course and Seeks to End Corruption," 15, no. 2 (February 1970): 25-27, and " 'We Want to Restore Dignity and Confidence to the People': Somali's President Talks to A. A. Castagno," 16, no. 9 (December 1971): 23-25.

Other recent commentators have been: E. A. Bayne, "Somali Myths Are Tested," *American Universities Field Staffs, Field Staff Report: North East Africa Series* 16, no. 1 (1969): 19 p.; Keith Irvine, "Storm Clouds over the African Horn," *Current History* 58, no. 343 (March 1970): 142-147; and, finally, U.N. observer Edward Rice, "Somalia," *Vista* 6, no. 4 (1971): 34-40.

For miscellaneous subjects, including tourism, see: Leonard W. Doob and Ismael M. Hurreh, "Somali Proverbs and Poems as Acculturation Indices," *Public Opinion Quarterly* 34 (Winter 1970-71): 552-559; William Travis, *The Voice of the Turtle* (London: Allen and Unwin, 1967), 203 p.; and R. W. Hamelin, "Motoring through the Somali Republic," *Travel* 137 (February 1972), 34-39, an interesting, beautifully illustrated account.

BIBLIOGRAPHY

This is a skimpy area indeed. There is, of course, the excellent guide compiled by Helen Conover: *Official Publications of Somaliland, 1941-1959* (Washington, D.C.: U.S. Government Printing Office, 1960), 41 p., with 169 numbered references, many of them annotated. See also African Bibliographic Center, Washington, D.C., *Somalian Panoramas: A Select Bibliographical Survey, 1960-1966* (1967), 17 p. (Special Bibliographical Series 5, no. 3).

Two earlier Italian sources are: Mario Paliere, *Contributo alla bibliografia e cartografia della Somalia* (Rome: Instituto Coloniale Fascista, 1932), and Camera di Commercio Industria and Agricultura della Somalia, Sezione Fere e Mostre, Mogadiscio, *Bibliografia somala* (Mogadishu: Scuola Tipografica Missione Catolica, 1958), 135 p. The latter has more than two thousand items and an index.

Somewhat special is John W. Johnson, "A Bibliography of the Somali Language and Literature," *African Language Review* (Freetown Fourah Bay College, University of Sierra Leone) 8 (1969): 279-297.

A fine review article or, perhaps, bibliographical essay is: A. Castagno, "Social Science and the Horn of Africa," *Research Review* (University of Ghana, Institute of African Studies) 5, no. 3 (1969): 33-44. The emphasis is on post-independence British and American sources.

EAST AFRICA

This section, like the ones devoted to West Africa and the vast area between East and West, is concerned with tropical Africa. The stereotype of this area which still lingers in the minds of Americans, Europeans, and others is based largely on a mistaken notion of tropical Africa. Many areas of East and West Africa have a common British colonial heritage. There are, too, differences in the two regions—above all, the presence of the Rift Valley, with its high elevation, in much of East Africa. Whereas West Africa, at least its Anglophonic countries, never had a sizable number of European settlers, Kenya in East Africa has attracted many Europeans. Part of the reason for its appeal is its superb climate, at least in the highlands.

Works common to two or all three countries, Kenya, Uganda, and Tanzania of East Africa will be mentioned first; individual treatment of the countries will follow.

The anthropological literature of East Africa is large. (Many of the best bibliographies and actual works in anthropology and other fields will be found in Duignan's *Guide* in his chapter "East Africa.")

Favorably reviewed by Audrey Isabel Richards in *Africa* 42, no. 3 (July 1972): 244-245, is Philip H. Gulliver, ed., *Tradition and Transition in East Africa: Studies of the Tribal Element in the Modern Era* (London: Routledge and Kegan Paul; Berkeley, Los Angeles: University of California Press, 1969), 378 p. Dr. Richards has worked in Uganda and was one of the earliest directors of Makerere Institute of Social Research. She has recently published the following series of lectures: *The Multicultural States of East Africa* (London: McGill-Queens University Press, 1969), 123 p. (Keith Callard Lectures No. 3).

Kenya has recently joined Tanzania in designating Swahili as its official language. Much pertinent background can be acquired from William H. Whiteley, ed., *Language and Social Change: Problems of Multilingualism with Special Reference to East Africa* (London: Oxford University Press, for the International African Institute, 1971), 406 p. This is the report of the Ninth International African Seminar held in Tanzania in 1968. It was favorably reviewed by R.E.S. Tanner in the *Journal of Modern African Studies* 10, no. 1 (1972): 156-157.

For historical studies of East Africa, the situation has much improved during the last ten years. Two books published since 1963 are: Roland Oliver and Gervase Mathew, eds., *History of East Africa*, vol. 1 (Oxford: Clarendon Press, 1963), 500 p., and Vincent T. Harlow and E. M. Chilver, eds. *History of East Africa*, vol. 2 (1965), 766 p. This is not to imply that all historical accounts published prior to 1963 have been fully replaced by later publications. There is still much use for: Sir Reginald Coupland, *The Exploitation of East Africa, 1856-1890: The Slave Trade and the Scramble* (Evanston, Ill.: Northwestern University Press, 1968), 507 p. This is a reprint, with a new introduction, of a work first published in 1939. The other work by Sir Reginald is: *East Africa and Its Invaders, from the Earliest Times to the Death of Seyyid Said in 1865* (1938, reprint ed., New York: Russell and Russell, 1965), 584 p.

A volume on East Africa aimed primarily at the secondary school market is: Gideon S. Were and D. A. Wilson, *East Africa through a Thousand Years: A History of the Years A.D. 1000 to the Present Day* (London: Evans Brothers, 1968), 344 p. This is a beautifully illustrated volume, which includes many maps. There are revision notes geared toward the date-and-name type of examination. A one-page glossary lists "name used in book" with "common alternatives." There are neither footnotes nor bibliography to help teachers and more advanced students. Another well-illustrated volume aimed at pre-adult Americans is Lawrence Fellows, *East Africa* (New York: Macmillan, 1972), 138 p. It includes a suggested reading list.

Results of one historical process are still a matter of concern for persons in East Africa, Great Britain, and elsewhere: Asians in East Africa. When the British built the railway from Mombasa, Kenya, to Kampala, Uganda, much of the work was done by Indian laborers. The British imported a few thousand Indians in the late nineteenth and early twentieth centuries, most of whom remained in Africa; these people constitute another social class, particularly in the eastern and southeastern parts of Africa. A useful survey article is "Asians in Africa," *Times Literary Supplement* (September 1, 1972): 1029, which briefly reviews the following three titles: Robert G. Gregory, *India and East Africa: A History of Race Relations within the British Empire, 1890-1939* (Oxford: Clarendon Press, 1971), 555 p.; C. S. Nicholls, *The Swahili Coast* (London: Allen and Unwin, 1971), 419 p.; and Dharam P. Ghai and Yash P. Ghai, eds., *Portrait of a Minority*, rev. ed. (Nairobi: Oxford University Press, 1972), 230 p.

The remaining references that will be cited are mainly political and economic.

A good political overview is given in: Anthony J. Hughes, *East Africa; Kenya, Tanzania, Uganda*, rev. ed. (Harmondsworth: Penguin, 1969), 271 p. (Penguin African Library AP11).[45] Hughes is a former English journalist who has become a Kenyan citizen.

Turning now to quite specific and recent references, we cite: D.H.N. Johnson, "East Africa's Boundary Problems," *Geographical Journal* (London) 138 (March 1972): 68-69, and Ali A. Mazrui, *Cultural Engineering and Nation Building in East Africa* (Evanston, Ill.: Northwestern University Press, 1972), 301 p. (Studies in Political Culture and National Integration).

In November 1970, the Institute of Social Research at Makerere University in Uganda began publishing *Policy Abstracts, A Journal of Policy Communication*. It consists of three-hundred to five-hundred word abstracts arranged under broad subjects, to aid decision makers in East Africa.[46]

See also: David Segal, "On Making Customs Unions Fair: An East Africa Example," *Yale Economic Essays* 10, no. 2 (Fall 1970): 115-160; K. J. Davey, "Local Bureaucrats and Politicians in East Africa," *Journal of Administration Overseas* (London) 10, no. 4 (October 1971): 268-279; and Richard Vengroff, "Urban Government and Nation Building in East Africa," *Journal of Modern African Studies* 9, no. 4 (December 1971): 577-592.

The January 1972 issue of *African Review* was devoted to selected papers presented at the conference on comparative administration in East Africa which was held in Arusha, Tanzania, in 1971.

ECONOMICS

On economics, first are two monographs from the Ifo Institute in Munich, Germany, both in English: Peter Marlin, ed., *Financial Aspects of Development in East Africa* (1970), 396 p. (Afrika studien no. 53), and Paul Zajadacz, ed., *Studies in Production and Trade in East Africa* (1970), 441 p. (Afrika studien no. 51). Other recent publications are: D. Jackson, "Economic Development and Income Distribution in Eastern Africa," *Journal of Modern African Studies* 9, no. 4 (December 1971): 531-542; D. H. Pearson, *Industrial Development in East Africa* (London and Nairobi: Oxford University Press, 1970), 213 p. (Studies in African Economics, no. 2);[47] Carl Widstrand, *Cooperative and Rural Development in East Africa* (Uppsala: Scandinavian Institute of African Studies; New York: Africana Publishing Corp., 1970), 271 p.;[48] A. Meister, "Ambition and Risks of Cooperative Socialism in East Africa," *Journal of Asian-African Studies* (Toronto) 4, no. 4 (October 1969): 241-274; and E. S. Clayton, "Mechanisation and Employment in East African Agriculture," *International Labour Review* 105 (April 1972): 309-334.

BIBLIOGRAPHY

In 1966, the Library of Congress opened an office in Nairobi under the aegis of the U.S. embassy. Operating under the National Program for Acquisitions and Cataloging (NPAC) established under Title II-C of the Higher Education Act of 1965, this office acquires two copies of all publications thought to be of scholarly significance, does some preliminary cataloging, lists them in *Accessions List: Eastern Africa* (1967-) quarterly, and then ships them to the Library of Congress.[49]

In fiscal year 1972, a total of 33,273 pieces were acquired (25,316 in 1971 and 24,025 in 1970). Of these, 1,917 were monographs, 28,355 were periodicals and newspapers, and the remainder were maps, posters, and ephemera.[50] No doubt there were too few pieces of ephemera. Unfortunately, no other Title II office exists in Africa. (There is, however, a Public Law 480 office in Cairo that collects multiple copies of publications predominantly from the Arab Republic of Egypt on behalf of the Library of Congress and other United States libraries.)[51]

LIBRARIANSHIP

The university librarians of East Africa meet frequently or at least exchange communications; many are associated in SCAUL-E (Standing Conference of African University Librarians, Eastern Area Conference).

A useful volume on the common and diverse themes of librarianship in East Africa, particularly as it relates to adult education, is Anna-Britta Wallenius, ed., *Libraries in East Africa* (Uppsala: Scandinavian Institute of African Studies; New York: Africana Publishing Corp., 1971), 219 p.

"Interlibrary Cooperation in East Africa: Initial Strategy to Formal Cooperation" was the subject of a paper at the fourth conference of the East African Library Association by T. K. Lwanga, university librarian at Makerere. It is reported in *Focus on International and Comparative Librarianship* (London, Library Association) 2, no. 1 (January 1971): 5-11.

Guides helpful to a study of libraries and librarianship in East Africa are: M.E.C. Kibwika-Bagenda, et al., *Directory of East African Libraries*, 2d rev. ed. (Kampala: Makerere University College Library, 1969), 113 p. (Makerere Library Publication 4); E. E. Kaungamno, "The East African Library Movement and Its Problems," *East African Journal* (Nairobi) 6, no. 6 (June 1969): 36-39; and Robert Plant, "The East African School of Librarianship," *Library Review* 23, no. 1-2 (Spring-Summer 1971): 39-42. The student body of the library school functioning at Makerere since 1964 was estimated to total 95 in 1972-1973. The University of East Africa's division into three national universities is "proving a turning point for the school's better."[52]

Until the revised edition of the Library of Congress' *East Africa: Subject Guide to Official Publications of Kenya, Tanzania and Uganda* is published, SCOLMA's listing of periodicals will have to be relied on: "Periodicals Published in East African Community, Kenya, Tanzania, Uganda," Supplement to *Library Materials on Africa* 6, no 3 (March 1969) (Periodicals Published in Africa Pt. 8).

The computer-generated union list to East African periodicals produced at West Virginia University in Morgantown is discussed by its director in: Robert F. Munn, "The Use of Modern Technology in the Improvement of Information Resources and Services in Developing Countries," *International Library Review* 3, no. 1 (January 1971): 9-13.

EDUCATION

A comprehensive overview of education in East Africa is found in: William Ernest F. Ward and L. W. White, *East Africa: A Century of Change, 1870-1970* (London: Allen and Unwin, 1971), 282 p. The senior author is a well-known writer on education in Africa, particularly in Ghana.

Other works are: W. S. Kajubi, "New Directions in Teacher Education in East Africa," *International Review of Education* (The Hague, Netherlands) 17, no. 2 (1971): 197-210; and O.M.N. Mutibwa, *Education in East Africa 1970: A Selected Bibliography* (Kampala: Makerere University Library, 1971), 100 p.

Nancy Stowbridge, comp., *Education in East Africa, 1962-1968* (Kampala: Makerere University College Library for National Institute of Education, 1969), 35 p. (Makerere Library Publication no. 5), contains more than 450 entries pertaining to published and unpublished material. Stowbridge prepared a sixty-five page supplement that was issued in 1970.

Angela Molnos has prepared a number of bibliographies. Particularly noteworthy are her: *Cultural Source Material for Population Planning in East Africa* (Nairobi: East African Publishing House, 1972-73), 4 vols.; *Language Problems in Africa; A Bibliography* (1946-1967); *Summary of the Present Situation with Special Reference to Kenya, Tanzania and Uganda* (Nairobi: East African Research Information Centre, 1969), 62 p.; *Development in Africa: Planning and Implementation, A Bibliography* (1946-1969); *Outline with Some Emphasis on Kenya, Tanzania and Uganda* (Nairobi: East African Academy, Research Information Centre, 1970), 120 p.

The following bibliography is divided into twelve broad subject sections: Nelson Kasfir and Timothy M. Shaw, *Bibliography on Administration in East Africa* (Kampala: Makerere University College, Department of Political Science and Public Administration, 1968), 26 p.

Charles W. Barr, *Eastern Africa: References Related to Development Planning and Housing* (Monticello, Ill.: Mary Vance, ed., October 1972), 75 p. (Exchange bibliography 330), Council of Planning Librarians. The seven hundred items in this work were compiled by the associate director of the School of Urban Planning and Landscape Architecture of Michigan State University. The arrangement is by countries, preceded by nineteen biliographies. A useful packaging of references is found in: Brigitte Gass, "Literatur über Ostafrika aus den Beständen des Instituts für Auslandsbeziehungen," *Zeitschrift für Kulturaustausch* (Stuttgart, 1971): 73-83.

SCIENCE

First in importance is: *Science and Technology in East Africa: A Bibliography of about 200 Papers and over 500 Entries* (Nairobi: East African Academy, 1973).

The two volumes of V. Nadanasabapothy, *East African Medical Bibliography,* vol. 1, (1970); vol. 2, nos. 6-7 (June-July 1971) were complied by the medical librarian at Albert Cook Library, Makerere University, P. O. Box 7072.[53]

See also S. Cooney, "The East African Scientific Literature Service: A Report Prepared for the Director, East African Agriculture and Forestry Research Organisation" (November 1968), contains a summary of the largest archives.[54]

KENYA

Kenya, a country of 224,960 square miles, had an estimated population of 11.69 million in 1971. The northern three-fifths of the country, bisected by the equator, is arid; most economic activites thus take place in the south, much of it elevated three thousand to ten thousand feet. Kenya is bordered on the east by the Indian Ocean and Somalia, on the north by Ethiopia and the Sudan, on the west by Uganda, and on the south by Tanzania. The main cities are the capital, Nairobi, and the port of Mombasa.[55] Nairobi is also East Africa's major city and center of communication for air, road, rail and also of publishing (Africa's largest and most significant publisher, The East African Publishing House, is located there).[56]

For a succinct, up to date statement on the country, see the appropriate issue of *Background Notes.* This series, issued by the United States government, is available for nearly all countries of the world (the pamphlets are revised as necessary): U.S., Department of State, Bureau of Public Affairs, Office of Media Services, *Republic of Kenya,* rev. ed. (Washington, D.C.: U.S. Government Printing Office, 1972), 6 p. (Publication No. 8024). For a more rounded thumbnail sketch, note the article on "Kenya" contributed to the *Encyclopedia Britannica* (1971).

A fine scholarly analysis is John Ndegwa, *Printing and Publishing in Kenya: An Outline of Development* (London: SCOLMA, 1973), 28 p.

See also Edward W. Soja, *The Geography of Modernization in Kenya: A Spatial Analysis of Social, Economic and Political Change* (Syracuse: Syracuse University Press, 1968), 143 p.

TOURISM

Before proceeding to more detailed studies, mainly those by political scientists and economists, one must stress that much of Kenya, including the superbly located Nairobi, is a very attractive place for its residents, large numbers of expatriates from Britain, and tourists.[57] A good guidebook is Kenneth Bolton, *Harambee Country, A Guide to Kenya* (London: Bles, 1970), 233 p. Those bitten by the Leakey bug will already be aware of "The Leakey Tradition Lives On," *National Geographic* 143, no. 1 (January 1973): 143-144. Potential or past tourists may also enjoy: Peter Robson, *Mountains of Kenya* (East African Publishing House, 1969), 80 p., and Peter Matthiessen, "Reporter at Large: Tree Where Man Was Born," *New Yorker* 48 (September 16, 1972): 39-74; (September 23); 39-62; (September 30): 47-75.

POLITICS

A good work is likely to be: Carl Gustav Rosberg, *Kenya* (Ithaca: Cornell University Press), forthcoming (Africa in the Modern World).

Carl Rosberg and John Nottingham are the authors of the *Myth of Mau Mau: Nationalism in Kenya* (New York: Praeger for the Hoover Institution, 1966), 427 p., a significant study of pre-independence nationalism.

Good also is the work of Cherry Gertzel. Note *The Politics of Independent Kenya* (London: Heinemann Educational Books; Nairobi: East African Publishing House; Evanston, Ill.: Northwestern University Press, 1970), 180 p.,[58] and Cherry Gertzel, Maure Goldschmidt, and Donald Rothchild, *Government and Politics in Kenya* (Nairobi: East African Publishing House, 1969), 611 p. (A Nation Building Text). Among the works of a productive author, Colin Leys, is: "Politics in Kenya: The Development of Peasant Society," *British Journal of Political Science* 1, no. 3 (July 1971): 307-337.

KENYATTA

One of Africa's—and possibly the world's—greatest leaders is President Jomo Kenyatta. For a handy reference, see Colin Legum's contribution on him to the 1970 *Britannica Book of the Year.*

Of Kenyatta's own writings, *Facing Mount Kenya: The Tribal Life of the Gikuya,* first published in 1938 and frequently reprinted, is best known. Also note his *Suffering Without Bitterness: The Founding of the Kenya Nation* (Nairobi: East African Publishing House, 1968), 348 p.

For an understanding of the changes in attitude of Kenya's white residents toward President Kenyatta, see Peter Knauss, "From Devil to Father Figure: The Transformation of Jomo Kenyatta by Kenya Whites," *Journal of Modern African Studies* 9, no. 1 (May 1971): 131-137. Also note: "Kenyan President Challenge of Power," *Ebony* (Chicago) 27 (August 1972): 108; Donald Savage, "Kenyatta and the Development of African

Nationalism," *International Journal* (Toronto) 25, no. 3 (Summer 1970): 518-537; and Jeremy Murray-Brown, *Kenyatta* (London: Allen and Unwin, 1972), 381 p.[59]

Two other Kenyan leaders, the first regrettably assassinated a few years ago, have written books: Tom Mboya, *The Challenge of Nationhood* (London: André J. Deutsch; New York: Praeger, 1970), 288 p.; and Oginga Odinga, *Not Yet Uhuru* (New York: Hill and Wang, 1967). ("Uhuru" is the Swahili word for "freedom.") For recent works, see: A. M. Sharp and N.M. Jetha, "Central Government Grants to Local Authorities: A Case Study of Kenya," *African Studies Review* 13, no. 1 (April 1970): 45-56; J. Andersson, "Self-help and Independence: The Political Implications of a Continuing Tradition in African Education in Kenya," *African Affairs* 70 (June 1971): 9-22; Yash P. Ghai and J.P.W.B. McAuslan, *Public Law and Political Change in Kenya: A Study of the Legal Framework of Government from Colonial Times to the Present* (Nairobi: Oxford University Press, 1970), 536 p.; John W. Harbeson, "Land Reform and Politics in Kenya, 1954-1970," *Journal of Modern African Studies* 9, no. 2 (April 1971): 231-251; and D. Rothchild, "On Becoming Bwana in Kenya," *Trans-Action* 9 (January 1972): 23-29.

ECONOMICS

Economic development and the extent of foreign capital investment are described in: Kenya, Ministry of Finance and Planning, Statistical Division, *Statistical Abstract* (1971), 217 p., *Economic Survey* (1972) (June 1972), 199 p.; Susan P. Hansen, "Basic data on the economy of East Africa," U.S. Bureau of International Commerce, (June 1972), 52 p. (Overseas business report OBR 72-030) U.S.G.P.O. Two items of applied economics are: Peter Marris and Anthony Somerset, *The African Entrepreneur: A Study of Entrepreneurship and Development in Kenya* (New York: Africana Publishing Corp., 1972),[60] and Alice Hoffenberg Amaden, *International Firms and Labor in Kenya: 1945-1970* (London: Cass, 1971), 186 p.

Of a large literature pertaining to development in East Africa or just Kenya, only two examples will be cited: Arthur Dobrin, "The Role of Agrarian Cooperatives in the Development of Kenya," *Studies in Comparative International Development* (Beverly Hills, Calif.) 5, no. 6 (1969-1970), 107-133, and Centre of African Studies, University of Edinburgh, "Development Trends in Kenya: Proceedings of a Seminar Held at the Centre, April 28 and 29, 1972," 337 p. (mimeo.). This is an edited transcript of the papers and the discussion that followed.

ARCHAEOLOGY AND HISTORY

The first human remains were found in Kenya. A description of the area of these findings is given in: L. H. Robbins, "Archaeology in the Turkhane District of Kenya," *Science* 176 (April 28, 1972): 359-366; Kenneth King and Ahmed Salin, *Kenya Historical Biographies* (Published for the Department of History, University of Nairobi, East African Publishing House, 1971), 192 p. (Nairobi Historical Studies No. 2) contains nine biographical sketches.

Bethwell A. Ogot has edited, and the East African Publishing House in Nairobi has published speedily and well since 1967, *Hadith,* proceedings of the annual conference of the Historical Association of Kenya. Each volume contains between eight and fourteen papers, maps, illustrations, and an index. *Hadith* is a model for the efficient and speedy, scholarly, yet attractive, publication of the proceedings of a learned conference. Not all papers presented at the annual conference are included.

BIBLIOGRAPHY

Excellent is *A Study Guide for Kenya,* comp. Jay E. Hakes (Development Program, African Studies Center, Boston University, 1969), 76 p. The study guide consists of nine sections, each with its brief bibliographic essay, followed by formal bibliographic entries listed alphabetically, in one or more series.

Below, with one exception, will be listed only materials pertaining to bibliography and librarianship not found in the Duignan *Guide* or Hakes' *Study Guide for Kenya.* The one exception is:

Syracuse University, Maxwell Graduate School of Citizenship and Public Affairs, Program of Eastern African Studies, *A Bibliography of Kenya*, comp. John B. Webster, et al. (Syracuse, N.Y.: Syracuse University, 1967), 461 p. (Syracuse University, Eastern African Bibliographical Series, No. 2). According to Hakes, "the book has no organization, so that the user encounters difficulty separating the wheat from the chaff. The book contains numerous typographical errors and inaccuracies." This is overly severe. The more than seven thousand entries located by John Webster and his associates are certainly suggestive and helpful to many.

To update and correct Webster, some of the following entries may be useful, together with the *Eastern African Accession List* published in Nairobi by the Library of Congress, *The Accessions List of the National University in Nairobi*, and the Library of Congress' forthcoming *Subject Guide to Official Publications of Kenya, Tanzania and Uganda*. Note also: Marion E. Doro, "A Bibliographical Essay on Kenya Colony: Political Themes and Research Resources," *A Current Bibliography on African Affairs* 5, no. 5-6 (September-November 1972): 480-496; Robert G. Gregory, Robert M. Maxan, and Leon P. Spencer, *A Guide to the Kenya National Archives. To the Provincial and District Annual Reports, Record Books and Handing Over Reports; Miscellaneous Correspondence; and Intelligence Reports* (Syracuse: Program of Eastern African Studies, Syracuse University, Syracuse New York, 1968), 452 p. (Syracuse University Eastern African Bibliographical Series No. 3, Kenya); Kenya, Government Printer, *The 1972 Catalogue of Government Publications* (Nairobi, April 1972), 78 p.; J. L. Abukatsa, *Kenya Coffee: A Bibliographical Survey, 1900-1966* (London: Fellow of the Library Association (FLA) thesis 1968/1969; N. P. Dosaj, *Bibliography of the Geology of Kenya, 1859-1968* (Nairobi: Ministry of National Resources, Geological Survery of Kenya, 1970), 65 p.; L. A. Martin, *Education in Kenya Before Independence, An Annotated Bibliography* (London: Fellow of the Library Association [FLA] thesis 1967/1968).

In Anna-Britta Wallenius, *Libraries in East Africa* (Uppsala: Scandinavian Institute of African Studies, 1971), see particularly

John Ndegwa, "The University of Nairobi Library," p. 21-29, and F. O. Pala, "The Kenya National Libary Service," p. 31-41. The two short papers were written by the head librarians of the two chief institutions.

Those interested in the work of a librarian with the Voluntary Service Overseas should see: G. Burwood, "Librarianship with V.S.O.," *Assistant Librarian* (London) 64, no. 8 (August 1971); p. 122-123. It describes the work of volunteer librarian Sheila Alliez who was branch librarian of the Eastlands Library in Nairobi.

UGANDA

Uganda, with a population estimated in 1972 at 10.5 million, is about the size of Oregon, and in 1970 had a population of a mere 2.091 million.

Uganda, which for years had been a backwater within the British sphere, has in recent years received much publicity in the United States and elsewhere in the more or less popular press. See: Cyril Vaughn Hughes and Llewelyn Williams, *Rheng o ddau,* Ammanford (Carms) Lilyfrau'r Dryw, 1970, 128 p. This is an attractively illustrated travel book about East Africa written in Welsh and published in Wales. Donald Rothchild, *Uganda* (Ithaca: Cornell University Press, forthcoming); *Area Handbook of Uganda,* American University, Washington, D.C., Foreign Areas Studies Division, (Washington, D.C.: U.S. Government Printing Office, 1969), 456 p. (Pamphlet No. 550-74).

HISTORY

Uganda has a long and distinguished history that is only beginning to become written or at least more available. M.S.M. Semakula Kiwanuka, *A History of the Buganda from the Foundation of the Kingdom to 1900* (London: Longman, 1971), 332 p., goes back some five centuries, and is based on oral and published sources. Among the latter are the works of Sir Apolo Kaggwa, the former traditional ruler or Kabaka, of the kingdom of Buganda, that is, central Uganda. Kiwanuka, a member of the History

Department at Makerere University, includes in his volume valuable appendixes, illustrations, a genealogy of the Kiganda dynasty, and a bibliography. Note also Sir Apolo Kaggwa (1864?-1927), *The Kings of Buganda,* trans. and ed. M. Semakula M. Kiwanuka (Nairobi: East African Publishing House, 1970), 256 p. Recently, a history of the peoples to the east of the Buganda, the Busoga, has appeared: David William Cohen, *The Historical Tradition of the Busoga, Mukama and Kiutu* (Oxford: Clarendon Press, 1972), 218 p. (Oxford Studies in African Affairs). This is a particularly well-edited volume with informative maps, a bibliographical note, and a select bibliography. Cohen refers to two previous studies of the Busoga; the more significant one by far is Y. K. Lubogo, *A History of the Busoga* (Jinja, 1960). See also Cohen's *Selected Texts: Busoga Traditional History* (Baltimore, 1969), 147 p. The writings of Lloyd Fallers are significant. His latest on the Busoga is *Law without Precedent: Legal Ideas in Action in the Courts of Colonial Busoga* (Chicago: University of Chicago Press, 1969), 365 p. To be noted is John A. Rowe's dissertation: "Revolution in Buganda, 1856-1900: Part I, The Reign of Kabaka Mukabya Mutesa, 1856-1884" (Ph.D. dissertation, University of Wisconsin, 1966), 277 p. Note also his "Myth, Memoir and Moral Admonition: Luganda Historical Writings, 1893-1969," *Uganda Journal* (Kampala) 33 no. 1 (1969): 17-40; 2 (1969): 217-219.

POLITICS

Three good political studies are: David E. Apter, *The Political Kingdom of Uganda: A Study in Bureaucratic Nationalism,* 2d ed. (Princeton: Princeton University Press, 1967), 481 p.; Donald Anthony Low, *The Mind of Buganda: Documents of the Modern History of an African Kingdom* (Berkeley and Los Angeles: University of California Press, 1971), 234 p.; and Peter M. Gukiina, *Uganda, A Case Study in African Political Development* (Notre Dame, Ind.: University of Notre Dame Press, 1972), 190 p. Gukiina's work is more a tract than an academic study and should be welcomed all the more for it. The author provides notes and a bibliography but no index. See also Ali A. Mazrui, "Leadership in

Africa, Obote of Uganda," *International Journal* (Toronto) 25, no. 3 (Summer 1970): 538-564.

IDI AMIN

Few political coups in Africa—no doubt because of its consequent expulsion of Indians, and the nature of some of President Amin's statements—have given rise to such extensive coverage overseas as Idi Amin's. The following references are just a sampling of those available. The arrangement is largely chronological by date of publication: Norman N. Miller, "Military Coup in Uganda: The Rise of the Second Republic," *American Universities Field Staff Reports, East Africa Series* 10, no. 3, (April 1970); James H. Mittleman, "The Anatomy of a Coup: Uganda, 1971," *Africa Quarterly* (New Delhi) 11 (October 1971): 184-202; Michael Lofchie, "The Uganda Coup—Class Action by the Military," *Journal of Modern African Studies* 10, no. 1 (May 1972): 19-35; Colin Legum, "The Tragedy of Amin's Uganda," *Venture* (London) 24, no. 6 (June 1972): 16-18; Michael Twaddle, "The Amin Coup," *Journal of Commonwealth Political Studies* 10 (July 1972): 99-112; Christopher Munnin, "If Idi Amin of Uganda is a Madman, He's a Ruthless and Cunning One," *New York Times Magazine* (November 12, 1972): 33 ff.; S. Meisler, "From Dream to Brutality," *Nation* (New York) 215 (November 13, 1972): 463-466, and "Reports and Comment," *Atlantic* 230 (December 1972): 27-28; "Big Daddy Amin Rules a Country in Big Trouble," *Life* (December 29, 1972): 48-49; and Judith Listowel, *Amin* (Dublin: Irish University Press, 1973), 188 p.[61]

AGRICULTURE

Turning now to the applied arts and sciences, we start with agriculture. For retrospective titles we refer the reader to the large bibliographic section of the Jameson volume: J. D. Jameson, ed., *Agriculture in Uganda*, 2d ed. (Published for the Uganda Government, Ministry of Agriculture for the Uganda Government, Ministry of Agriculture and Forestry, Oxford University Press, 1971), 395 p.[62] Other works are: E. R. Kagambirwe, *Causes and Consequences of Land Shortage in Kigezi* (Kampala, Uganda: Makerere University, Department of Geography, 1972), 175 p. (Occasional Paper No. 23); and R. B. Pollnac and M. C. Robbins, "Gratification Patterns and Modernization in Rural Buganda," *Human Organization* 31, (Spring 1972): 63-72.

ECONOMIC DEVELOPMENT

Uganda, Ministry of Planning and Economic Development, Statistical Division, *Statistical Abstract 1971* (Entebbe: Government Printer, 1972), 118 p. "Uganda Economic Survey, 1972," *African Deveopment,* (London) June 1972, 60 p. section.

EDUCATION

David R. Evans, *Teachers as Agents of National Development: A Case Study of Uganda* (New York: Praeger, 1971), 245 p. (Praeger Special Studies in International Economics and Development),[63] deals with the attitudes of secondary school teachers as related to Uganda's development goals. Not surprisingly, there are differences in attitudes among teachers of different ethnic groups: S. G. Weeks, "Youth in Uganda: Some Theoretical Perspectives," *International Social Science Journal* (Paris) 24, no. 2 (1972): 354-365; C. A. Pratt, "Uganda Sets an Example: New Audio-Visual Aids Center at the National Institute of Education," *Audio-Visual Media* (London) 3 (Winter 1969): 44-48; A. Nsibambi, "Language Policy in Uganda: An Investigation into Costs and Politics," *African Affairs* (London) 70 (January 1971): 62-71.

BIBLIOGRAPHY

There is no single comprehensive retrospective bibliography of Uganda. The excellent *Uganda Journal,* which has been published since January 1934 and is available in reprint from Johnson Reprint in New York City, has carried much bibliographical material. Since 1963, Bryan W. Langlands has compiled the

"Annual Bibliography of Uganda" in *Uganda Journal*. Langlands no doubt has the raw material for a retrospective bibliography of Uganda. One can only hope that such a work, with the collaboration of professional bibliographers at Makerere University library, will be published.

There is a none-too-good article by Glenn L. Sitzman in *College and Research Libraries* 29, no. 3 (May 1968): 200-209. Sitzman remarks that the senior East African University library has been surpassed by younger institutions in Dar es Salaam and Nairobi. But the situation has changed since 1968. A Ugandan, not an expatriate, is now in charge (Tucker K. Lwanga),[64] and the library has regained its vigor. "A Uganda Bibliography" section appeared for the first time in Makerere University, *College Library Bulletin and Accessions List* no. 55 in the January-February 1965 issue. The bibliography includes material (including government publications) received on legal deposit and books about Uganda published outside the country.

In the case of Uganda, as is other countries of Africa and elsewhere where retrospective bibliographical work is scarce, use has to be made of library accession lists and similar publications aimed essentially for the use of the local clientele. Important manuscripts, typescripts, and the like found there appeared in the no. 6, May 1962 issue of the *Library Bulletin and Accessions List,* and was reproduced in the first issue of the first volume of *Library Materials on Africa* (London, 1962), p. 10.

Little is known about recent bibliographical matters in Uganda beyond a "Bibliographical Note" by Sanford Berman in the September 1972 issue of *American Libraries* (Chicago), p. 923.

Special material in the collection of Uganda's University Library can be found in: Makerere College Library, Kampala, Uganda, *Annotated list of theses submitted to the University of East Africa and held by Makerere University Library,* 1970, 52 p. (Makerere University library publication, no. 7), and the *Library Bulletin and Accession List.*

LIBRARIANSHIP

"UTIS: The Uganda Technical Information Service to Industry from the Uganda Technical College" is the subject of an F.L.A. thesis by G. A. Thompson, 1967/8.

The East African Library School is well described in the literature, most recently probably by a man who may still be its current director: S. S. Saith, "The East African School of Librarianship: Past, Present and Future," in Anna-Britta Wallenius, ed., *Libraries in East Africa* (1971), p. 171-187. One of its graduates, who for part of his diploma wrote a thesis on "Development of Public Libraries in Uganda," is I.M.N. Kigongo-Bukenya; he is the author of "The Public Libraries Board in Uganda," in Wallenius, p. 145-162.

TANZANIA

Tanzania, a country resulting from a merger of Tanganyika and Zanzibar in 1964, has an area of 363,708 square miles —about the size of Texas and Colorado combined. The population was estimated in 1973 at almost 14 million. Tanzania accepts some aid from other countries but is trying to develop principally through its own efforts. It has relatively poor resources. Swahili, the official language, is the first language of some 88 percent of the population on the mainland.

HISTORY

Tanzania Zamani, first issued in July 1967 by the Department of History of the University of Dar es Salaam, regularly reports on precolonial historical research.

A useful synthesis is Andrew Roberts, ed., *Tanzania before 1900* (Published for the Historical Association of Tanzania by the East African Publishing House, 1968), 162 p.

Probably the most interesting work on the precolonial history of Tanzania has been done by Isaria N. Kimambo, formerly chairman of the Department of History and now chief academic officer of the University of Dar es Salaam. His main works are: "The Political History of the Pare People to 1900," (Ph.D. dissertation, Northwestern University, 1967); and *A Political History of the Pare of Tanzania, 1500-1900* (Nairobi: East African Publishing House, 1969), 253 p. The Pare, or Asu, are a Bantu-speaking people, numbering about 150,000 in northeastern Tanzania. The language spoken in the area is Kipare or Cham.

Of less specialized interest are the well-edited conference papers by Dr. Kimambo and A. J. Temu: *A History of Tanzania* (Nairobi: East African Publishing House for the Historical Association of Tanzania, 1969), 276 p.: "The revised ten papers presented to the second Conference for history teachers [were] sponsored by the Ministry of National Education for the Institute of Education and the Historical Association of Tanzania in December 1967."[67]

A fine survey by Dr. Kimambo presented in 1968 as part of the Proceedings of the Twentieth Anniversary Conference of the Program of African Studies of Northwestern University is "Historical Research in Mainland Tanzania," in Gwendolen M. Carter and Ann Paden, eds., *Expanding Horizons in African Studies* (Evanston, Ill.: Northwestern University Press, 1969), 75-90. This paper is amply documented.

Even nonspecialists of history will be interested in the following discussion: Donald Denoon and Adam Kuper, "Nationalist Historians in Search of a Nation: The 'New Historiography' in Dar es Salaam," *African Affairs* 69, no. 277 (October 1970): 329-349. A rebuttal to this article by Terence Ranger, former chairman of the Department of History in Dar es Salaam, is "New Historiography," *African Affairs* 70 (January 1971): 50-61. Denoon and Kuper replied in *African Affairs* 70 (July 1971): 287-289.

An interesting essay on an early phase of colonial history, concerned with an island just off the Tanzanian coast, is Terry H. Elkiss, "Kilwa Kisiwani: The Rise of an East African City-State," *African Studies Review* 16, no. 1 (April 1973): 119-130.

From the German period (Tanganyika was for about thirty years before World War I a part of the German empire) only one work will be cited: Rainer Tetzlaff, *Koloniale Entwicklung und Ausbeutung: Wirtschafts und Sozialgeschichte Deutsch-Ostafrikas, 1885-1914* (Duncker und Humblot, 1970), 295 p. (Schriften zur Wirtschafts- und Sozialgeschichte, Band 17).[66] This work is based

216   A BIBLIOGRAPHY OF AFRICANA

on German archival resources. The main German archives are in Potsdam, near Berlin, in East Germany.

Two other samples of Tanzanian colonial history contributed by a distinguished political scientist and geographer, respectively, are: J. Gus Lievenow, *Colonial Rule and Political Development in Tanzania: The Case of the Makonde* (Evanston, Ill.: Northwestern University Press, 1971), 360 p. (the Makonde live along the Ruvuma River in southeastern Tanzania), and Peter Gould, "Tanzania 1920-1963: The Spacial Impress of the Modernization Process," *World Politics* 22 (1970): 149-170.

POLITICAL SCIENCE

A recent summary of Tanzania as seen by the United States Department of State is: *Background Notes,* Bureau of Public Affairs, Office of Media Services, *United Republic of Tanzania,* rev. ed. (Washington, D.C.: U.S. Government Printing Office, 1972), 8 p. (Publication 8097). See also: John Hatch, *Tanzania: A Profile* (London: Pall Mall Press; New York: Praeger, 1972), 214 p.;[67] Henry Bienen, *Tanzania: Party Transformation and Economic Development,* ed. (Princeton: Princeton University Press, 1970), 490 p.; Patrick McGowan and Partrick Bolland, *The Political and Social Elite of Tanzania: An Analysis of Social Background Factors* (Syracuse: Syracuse University, Program of Eastern African Studies, 1971), 140 p.; S. K. Sahu, "Foreign Policy of Tanzania, 1961-1970," *United Asia* 23 (July-August 1971): 256-260; C. Nieblock, "Tanzania Foreign Policy: An Analysis," *African Review* (Dar es Salaam) 1 (September 1971): 91-101; and Seth Singleton, "Tanzania since Arusha," *Africa Report* (New York) 16, no. 9 (December 1971): 10-14. The final three references above are just a few of the recent ones on Tanzania's foreign policy.

A former *Time* correspondent in East Africa has written about President Julius Nyerere: William Edgett Smith, *We Must Run While They Walk: A Portrait of Africa's Julius Nyerere* (New York: Random House, 1971), 296 p. Some collections of the president's speeches have been published. The best selection is probably still *Freedom and Socialism: A Selection from Writing and Speeches, 1965-*

1967 (Dar es Salaam: Oxford University Press, 1968), 422 p. A recent additional essay is : J. K. Nyerere, "Tanzania Ten Years After," *The African Review* (Dar es Salaam) 2, no. 1 (June 1972): 1-64 (originally published by the Ministry of Information and Broadcasting).

ZANZIBAR

The union of the island of Zanzibar and Tanganyika took place in 1964. One is still uncertain of the causes and effects of the union. To a brief visitor in 1967, leaving the mainland, landing in Zanzibar, and returning had all the aspects of traveling into another country and not of moving within one sovereign state.

Zanzibar's long and exciting history is documented in its extensive archives. For an overview, there is Samuel G. Ayanyi's *A History of Zanzibar* (Nairobi: East African Literature Bureau, 1970), 220 p.

The Zanzibar Papers, 1841-1898 (Shannon: Irish University Press, 1971), is an expensive, yet handy, repackaging of British parliamentary papers.

Colin Legum, "Zanzibar: Another Papa Doc?" *Venture* (London) 23 (June 1971): 21-25, examines the constitutional relationship between Zanzibar and the rest of Tanzania.

Marrine Howe, "Zanzibar, Where Africa and the Orient Meet," *Africa Report* 16, no. 9 (December 1971): 28, 30, contains one attractive photograph, but is too brief to tell us very much.

ECONOMIC DEVELOPMENT

In "Tanzania: Commitment to Self-Reliance," *Current History* 58 (March 1970): 160-164, William H. Lewis states that "Nyerere's basic commitment to self-reliance has been pursued with a consistency and tenacity which have lent order and stability to post-independence Tanzania."

M.J.H. Yaffey, *Balance of Payments Problems of a Developing Country: Tanzania* (Munich: Weltforum; New York: Humanities,

1970), 290 p. (Afrika studien No. 47), is a work produced under joint editorship of the University of Dar es Salaam Economic Research Unit and the Ifo Institut in Munich.[68]

William H. Friedland, *Vuta Kamba: The Development of Trade Unions in Tanganyika* (Stanford, Calif.: Hoover Institution Press, 1969), 280 p. (Hoover Institution Publication 84),[69] is a study of the National Union of Tanganyika Workers, largely prior to independence. Two somewhat specialized studies are: "Tanzania: Some Employment Aspects of the Second Five Year Plan," *International Labor Review* 103 (March 1971): 287-290, and G. T. Yu, "Working on the Railroad: China and the Tanzania-Zambia Railway," *Asian Survey* 11 (November 1971): 1101-1117. There are many other references to what was popularly known as the Tanzam railway.

For hard economics, see: *Tanzania: The Economic Survey 1971-72* (Dar es Salaam: Government Printer, 1972), 139 p., and "Tanzania: Uhuru + 10. Economic Survey," *African Development* (London) 57 (December 1971).

EDUCATION

Marjorie J. Mbilinyi, "The 'New Woman' and Traditional Norms in Tanzania," *Journal of Modern African Studies* 10, no. 1 (May 1972): 57-72, is a scholarly study. Ms. Mbilinyi is a lecturer in educational psychology at the University of Dar es Salaam. Another work is: K. Prewitt, et al., "School Experiences and Political Socialization: A Case Study of Tanzanian Secondary School Students," *Comparative Political Studies* 3, no. 2 (July 1970): 203-225.

Lyndon Harries, "Language Policy in Tanzania," *Africa* 39, no. 3 (July 1969): 275-280, is a nontechnical discussion by one of the leading scholars of Swahili. Finally, before turning to the bibliography of Tanzania: James L. Brain, "Kamusi ya maneno ya utaalamu wa mambo ya kibinadamu," [A short dictionary of social science terms for Swahili speakers] (Syracuse University, Program of Eastern African Studies, 1969), 70 p. (mimeo.) (Occasional Paper No. 51).

BIBLIOGRAPHY

Those who plan to seek references beyond those already cited should see the following two brief guides to the literature, both compiled by political scientists: Margaret L. Bates, *A Study Guide for Tanzania* (Boston: Development Program, African Studies Center, Boston University, 1969), 83 p., and Samuel Decalo, comp., *Tanzania: An Introductory Bibliography* (Kingston: University of Rhode Island, 1968), 56 leaves (Occasional Papers in Political Science No. 4).

There is as yet no published retrospective bibliography of Tanzania—or even of Tanganyika and Zanzibar. There are numerous bibliographical listings in *Tanzania Notes and Records* and elsewhere.

Bibliography Documentation Terminology 12, no. 2 (March 1972): 71-73, contains an entry for Tanzania reporting the situation as of 1970. These pages are hardly more up to date than the analysis and recommendations made by the former university librarian at Dar es Salaam at the 1967 Nairobi conference: Harold Holdsworth, "The Acquisition and Recording of Current Tanzanian Materials," in J. D. Pearson and Ruth Jones, eds., *The Bibliography of Africa* (1970): 45-56. The major change is that there now exists the Tanganyika Library Services Board's annual *Printed in Tanzania, 1969: A List of Publications Printed in Mainland Tanzania during 1969 . . . Together with Some Publications Published in Tanzania but Printed Elsewhere* (Dar es Salaam, 1970), 79 p.

The following special bibliographies should be noted: M. Sumar and E. McGee, comps., *National Policies in Tanzania: A Bibliography* (Dar es Salaam: Tanganyika Library Services, 1972), 66 p., which is arranged by broad subject headings (for example, "President Julius K. Nyerere, books, pamphlets, articles etc. by and about him"); and George A. Auger, *Tanzania Education since Uhuru: A Bibliography, 1961-1971* (Nairobi: East Africa Academy, 1973), 178 p. Auger's bibliography is the East African Academy's Information Circular no. 8. It is a scholarly bibliography arranged in a classified manner.

See also Dar es Salaam, University College, *A Bibliography of Economic and Social Material Concerning the Four Lake Regions (Mara, Mwanga, Shinyanga and West Lake), Prepared for the Evaluation Team of the UNESCO Sponsored Pilot Literacy Project* (Dar es Salaam, 1967), 12 p.

SWAHILI

Two important works are Alteito Mioni, "La bibliographie de la langue Swahili. Remarques et supplement à la *Swahili Bibliography* de M. van Spaandonck," *Cahiers d'études Africaines* 7 (1967), 485-532; and J.W.T. Allen, *The Swahili and Arabic Manuscripts and Tapes in the Library of University College, Dar-es-Salaam, a Catalogue* (Leiden: Brill, 1970), 116 p. Allen's catalog is divided between a first part on Swahili manuscripts, Arabic manuscripts, and tapes; and a second one on verse (for which no adequate description can yet be given) and prose.

In addition, see Elise Rasmussen, "Hvad laeser folk i Mwanga [What people read in Mwanga, Tanzania]" *Bogens Verden* (Copenhagen) 52, no. 2 (1970: 115-118 (the article notes that there is a great need for books in Kiswahili, Swahili in the vernacular); and Farouk Topan, "Swahili Literature Plays Major Social Role: 'Traditional' Poetry and Experimental Drama Express Tanzania's New National Consciousness," *Africa Report* 16, no. 2 (February 1971): 28-30.

LIBRARIANSHIP

A casual survey of libraries and librarians in Tanzania leads one to the impression that libraries matter to all Tanzanians, including persons in government and others in influential positions.

P. L. Mhaiki, director of the Institute of Adult Education at the University of Dar es Salaam, has written "Libraries Are Assets in National Development," in Anna-Britta Wallenius, *Libraries in East Africa*, p. 125-130. Note also: M.L.M. Baregu, "Rural Libraries in Functional Literacy Campaigns," *UNESCO Bulletin of Libraries* 26, no. 1 (January-February 1972): 18-24, and "Library Service for New Literates and Others in Rural Areas in

Tanzania," *Focus on International and Comparative Librarianship* (London) 2, no. 2 (August 1971): 21-28; F. K. Tawete, "Development of Libraries in Tanzania," in George Chandler, *International Librarianship* (London: The Library Association, 1972), p. 32-37; T. Nilsson, "The Library and Adult Education in Tanzania: A Discussion," in Wallenius, *Libraries in East Africa*, p. 53-82 (Nilsson is a trade unionist and adult educator within the Swedish labor movement); Nnaoke O. Arunsi, "The Library and Adult Education in Tanzania: A Survey," in Wallenius, *Libraries in East Africa*, p. 83-124 (Arunsi is a Nigerian who has been working as acquisitions librarian at the University of Dar es Salaam since 1969); E. Frost, "School-Library Development in Tanzania," in J. E. Lowrie, ed., *School Libraries: International* (Metuchen, N.J.: Scarecrow Press, 1972), p. 57-74; M. Wise, "The Library of the University of Dar es Salaam," in Wallenius, *Libraries in East Africa*, p. 43-51; and Nnaoke O. Arunsi, "Ten Years Growth of the University of Dar es Salaam Library, 1961-70," *UNESCO Bulletin for Libraries* 25, no. 5 (September-October 1971): 263-266.

ARCHIVES

J. R. Ede, chief archivist of the Public Record Office, has written *Tanganyika, Development of National Archives* (Paris: UNESCO, 1964), 14 p. (WS/1064.46-BMS).

See also Walter T. Brown, "German Records in the National Archives of Tanzania," *African Studies Bulletin* 12, no. 2 (September 1969): 147-149. The same issue in an article by Beverly Brown and Walter Brown lists the diaries and other papers of the "White Father Archives in Tanzania." The White Fathers, or Society of Missionaries of Africa, are a Roman Catholic international missionary society of priests and brothers.

ZAMBIA

For political rather than geographic reasons, Zambia along with Tanzania is considered almost a part of East Africa rather than Central or even Southern Africa, where it belongs geographically.

Zambia has an area of 290,586 square miles, which is about the size of Texas. In 1972, Zambia's population was estimated at 4.5 million, compared to Texas's 11.2 million.

GEOGRAPHY

D. Hywel Davies, ed., *Zambia in Maps* (New York: Africana Publishing Corp., 1971), 128 p., was intended for school use in Zambia but is also helpful to non-Zambians. A more sophisticated, yet intelligible and interesting text to the layman is: David J. Siddle, "Rural Development in Zambia: A Spatial Analysis," *Journal of Modern African Studies* 8, no. 2 (July 1970): 271-284.

In the area of political geography, no doubt the most interesting question currently is the length of common border between Namibia's (Southwest Africa's) Caprivi Strip and Zambia. This is the topic of: United States, Department of State, Bureau of Intelligence and Research, *South-West Africa (Namibia)—Zambia Boundary* (July 2, 1972), 6 p. [Bibliography and maps] (International Boundary Study No. 123).

The scholar should not fail to note: United States, Board on Geographic Names, *Zambia: Official Standard Names Approved by the United States Board on Geographic Names (March 1972)*, 585 p. It can be obtained free of charge from the Geographic Names Division of the U.S. Army Topographic Command in Washington, D.C. These volumes are available for most countries of the world. They are revised from time to time.

HISTORY

The following volume is written by a historian who is a senior fellow of the Hoover Institution on War, Revolution and Peace. Lewis Henry Gann is a sound historian who tends to be sympathetic to the colonizers rather than the colonized: Lewis Henry Gann, *Central Africa: The Former British States* (Englewood Cliffs, N.J.:

Prentice-Hall, 1971), 180 p. (The Modern Nations in Historical Perspective).

There is, unfortunately, no recent general history of Zambia that can be recommended since the following was published: Richard Hall, *Zambia* (New York: Praeger; London: Pall Mall, 1965), 357 p. This now somewhat dated volume has everything one could want except illustrations.

Somewhat specialized is: Eric Flint, "Trade and Politics in Barotseland during the Kololo Period," *Journal of African History* 11, no. 1 (1970): 71-86; this paper documents, with over one hundred footnotes, that the relationship of trade to politics has long been a central theme in African history. See also: P. Slinn, "Commercial Concessions and Politics during the Colonial Period: The Role of the British South Africa Company in Northern Rhodesia—1890-1964," *African Affairs* 70 (October 1971): 365-384. This scholarly article with sixty-seven footnotes often makes use of official British archives, the Public Records Office, and the sources of trading companies.

Henry S. Meebelo, *Reaction to Colonialism: A Prelude to the Politics of Independence in Northern Zambia, 1893-1939* (Manchester University Press, 1971), 304 p., contains a brief preface by the president of Zambia, Dr. Kenneth D. Kaunda. In addition to a rather long bibliography, there are numerous notes referring to sources at the end of each chapter. Finally, see James R. Hooker, "Zambia since Independence: Yesterday's Hopes," American Universities. *Field Staff Reports Service: Central and Southern Africa* 15, no. 12 (December 1972).

ANTHROPOLOGY AND SOCIOLOGY

Brian M. Fagan, now of the University of California at Santa Barbara, is the author of: *Iron Age Cultures in Zambia*, vol. 1: *Kalomo and Kangila*, vol. 2: *Dambwa, Ingombe Tlede and the Tongo* (London: Chatto and Windus, 1967-1969). These volumes provide the first major study of the Iron Age period of Zambian prehistory. The choice of sites for excavations were in southern Zambia where persons used to live in relative isolation from the rest of Africa. It was also an area of little interest to the colonialists. The first volume is entirely by Fagan who used to be at what was called the Livingston Museum, now the National Museum of Zambia. The second volume has three co-authors: Fagan, D. W. Phillipson, and Daniels. Phillipson, compiler of *An Annotated Bibliography of the Archaeology of Zambia* (Lusaka National Monuments Commission, 1968), 28 p., attempted to list all formally published works on the archaeology of Zambia that appeared through February 1967. The book contains 147 numbered items listed alphebetically, a period and subject index, and a site index.

Other works include Victor W. Turner, *The Drums of Afflication: A Study of Religious Processes among the Ndembu of Zambia* (Oxford: Clarendon Press and International African Institute, 1968), 326 p.,[70] and Victor W. Turner, *The Forest of Symbols: Aspects of Ndembu Ritual* (Ithaca, N.Y.: Cornell University Press, 1967), 405 p.[71]

In George Clement Bond, "Kinship and Conflict in a Yombe Village: A Genealogical Dispute," *Africa* 42, no. 4 (October 1972): 275-288, the author shows that myth among the Yombe does not dogmatically control their sòcial life. (The Yombe are a Bantu-speaking people in the northern province.)

Alan J. F. Simmance, *Urbanization in Zambia* (New York: The Ford Foundation, [1972]), 52 p.; is a working paper submitted as supportive material for an international survey of urbanization in developing countries.

Patrick O. Ohadike, "The Nature and Extent of Urbanization in Zambia," *Journal of Asian and African Studies* (Leiden, Netherlands) 4, no. 2 (April 1969): 107-121, and "Aspects of Domesticity and Family Relationship: A Survey Study of the Family," *Journal of Asian and African Studies* 6, no. 3-4 (1971): 191-204, were written by a former research fellow of the University of Zambia who then worked for the United Nations Economic Commission for Africa. Both articles are fully documented and contain statistics and maps.

Ronald Frankenberg, "The Indian Minority of Zambia, Rhodesia and Malawi: A Review Article by Floyd and L. O. Dotson of Same Title," *African Social Research* (Lusaka) 7 (June 1969): 555-558, is a lengthy and critical appraisal of the volume by the Dotsons. Yale University Press published it in 1968 (444 pages).

ECONOMIC DEVELOPMENT

The Economic development of Zambia is dependent on the mining of copper. Many of the following references deal with aspects of the copper industry. Robert H. Bates, "Input Structures, Output Functions and Systems Capacity: A Study of the Mineworkers' Union of Zambia," *Journal of Politics* 32, no. 4 (1970): 898-928, is a scholarly article by a political scientist on the faculty of the California Institute of Technology. The author acknowledges the support of the project by the Institute of Social Research of the University of Zambia and weighty United States bodies such as the Foreign Area Fellowship Program, the National Science Foundation, and the Center for International Studies of the Massachusetts Institute of Technology (MIT). The article contains fifty-three useful footnotes and seventeen tables.

Robert H. Bates, *Union Parties and Political Development: A Study of Mine Workers in Zambia* (New Haven: Yale University Press, 1971), 291 p., is an important addition to the slowly growing number of studies of African labor unions. It is fully documented, footnoted, containing seven charts and seventy-two tables. Bates has also written "Trade Union Membership in the Coppermines of Zambia. A Test of Some Hypotheses," *Economic Development and Cultural Change* (Chicago) 20, no. 2 (January 1972): 280-298; this study focuses on the patterns of membership in the mineworkers' union of Zambia. It refers to much of the best literature concerning voluntary associations in Africa and elsewhere.[72]

Another article is: R. C. Harkema, "Zambia's Changing Pattern of External Trade," *The Journal of Geography* 71 (January 1972): 19-27.

John Anthony Hellen, *Rural Economic Development in Zambia, 1890-1964* (Munich: Weltforum Verlag, 1968), 297 p. (Afrika-Studien no. 32), is based on a dissertation submitted to a German university by a former district officer in Northern Rhodesia (Zambia) who changed his career, becoming an academic at the

Department of Geography, University of Newcastle upon Tyne. This work of a geographer is supported by eleven maps, eleven tables, and a full bibliography.

W. Radmann, "Staatlich Beteiligungs-und Verstaatlichungs-vereinbarungen mit den ausländischen Kupferberg-baugesellschaften in Chile und Sambia" [Agreements on participation and on state nationalizations with the companies for the extraction of copper in Chile and Zambia], *Verfassung und Recht-Übersee* 4, no. 3 (1971): 301-317, is concerned with the nationalization of the copper industry of Chile, Peru, Zaïre, and finally that of Zambia, which followed the example of Chile. "The Control of Inflation in a Very Open Economy: Zambia 1964-9," *Eastern African Economic Review* 3 (June 1971): 41-64. Nairobi, Oxford University Press, written by Charles Harvey, a member of the faculty of the University of Zambia, argues a well-documented case.

"Zambia Economic Survey" is a forty-two page section following: *African Development* (London) 6; October 1972. This special supplement is a survey by *African Development.* It opens with a photograph of President Kaunda playing golf, captioned "gets away from it all—Businessman style." Within the section there are five separately signed articles and four anonymous ones. The Section is paged Z2-Z40.

1972 Zambian Industrial Directory (Ndola: Associated Reviews, 1972), 72 p., is a librarian/cataloguer's nightmare. This brief essay, by a professor of political science at the University of Colorado at Boulder and one of his students, contains seventy-one footnotes. Catalogers may have trouble with this pamphlet because it has too many elements of corporate entries. This little volume is full of advertising; it includes products made or assembled in Lusaka.

Frank C. Ballance, *Zambia and the East African Community* (Syracuse: Syracuse University, Maxwell School of Citizenship and Public Affairs, The Program of Eastern African Studies, 1971), 139 leaves (Eastern African Studies No. 1) traces Zambia's desire to become associated with the community. The stress is on Zambia's economic relationship with her neighbors to the north, east, and south.

POLITICAL SCIENCE

A recent work in political science is James R. Scarritt and John L. Hatter, "Racial and Ethnic Conflict in Zambia," *Studies in Race and Nations* (Denver) 2, no. 2 (1970-1971): 32 p.

William Tordoff, "Political Crisis in Zambia" [Events from 1967 to early 1970], *Africa Quarterly* 10 (October-December 1970): 225-236, is in the journal of the Indian Council for Africa and is published in New Delhi. It is a useful background article for an understanding of Zambian politics, at least as they were in March 1970.

Fola Soremekun, "The Challenge of Nation Building: Neo-Humanism and Politics in Zambia: 1967-1969," *Genève-Afrique* 9, no. 1 (1970): 3-41, is largely documented with local Zambian sources. It is written by a lecturer in history in the School of Humanities at the University of Zambia at Lusaka.

KAUNDA

Richard Hall, *The High Price of Principles: Kaunda and the White South,* rev. ed. (Harmonsworth, Middlesex: Penguin, 1973), 287 p., in the Penguin African Library (which is edited by Ronald Segal), is by an English journalist who spent many years in Zambia. It was originally published in a hard-cover edition in 1969. The revised Penguin volume is excellent.

"One Party Problems," *Economist* 245 (November 4, 1972): 61-62, a short note from the *Economist's* Lusaka correspondent, includes a photograph of President Kaunda conducting a police or army band labeled "Kaunda Calls the Tune."

John Hatch, "Kaunda's One-Party State," *New Statesman* 84 (December 29, 1972): 971-972, by one of the most knowledgeable journalists writing on Africa, presents a good portion of hard fact.

Robert Molteno, "Zambia and the One Party State," *East Africa Journal* 9 (February 1972): 6-18, is authored by a research fellow in political Science, Institute of Political Administration, University of Zambia. The journal publishing this article has ceased.

John Hatch, "Taming Zambia's Whites," *New Statesman* 82 (August 13, 1971): 197-198, starts by asking "What has happened to the wild men of Northern Rhodesia, now Zambia?"

Frank C. Ballance, *Zambia and the East African Community* (Syracuse: Syracuse University, Program of Eastern African Studies, 1971), 139 p. (Eastern African Studies no. 1), includes four pages of bibliography. It is by a lawyer who has had extensive experience in East Africa and Zambia. It is a scholarly and thorough study of Zambia and the East African community.

Finally, see "Security Council Meets on Closing of Zambian Border by Southern Rhodesia," *UN Monthly Chronicle* 10 no. 2 (February 1973): 13-29.

EDUCATION

Richard E. Hicks, "Two Zambian Studies," *Measurement and Evaluation in Guidance* 4 no. 3 (October 1971): 145-153, is an interesting, though somewhat technical, work by a psychologist.

S. Goldberg, "Infant Care and Growth in Urban Zambia," *Human Development* (formerly *Vita Humana*) 15, no. 2 (1972): 77-89, is based on the observation of thirty-eight infants in a high-density suburb of Zambia, from four to twelve months of age. The main focus is on the mother-infant relationship. The mother's practice of constantly carrying her infant on her back is discussed, and the effects of this practice on motor, cognitive, and social development are examined.

ART

Jan B. Deregowski, "Pictorial Art in Zambia," *African Arts* 4, no. 2 (Winter 1971): 36-37, 90, includes six good reproductions of Zambian paintings, a page of text, and twelve footnotes.

LIBRARIES AND ARCHIVES

The Zambia Library Association, consisting now of some eighty members, was founded in 1967. It publishes *Zambian Library Association Journal.*

Lovemore Z. Cheelo, "The Zambia Library Association: Past

History, Present and Future Development," *Journal of Library History* 7, no. 4 (October 1972): 316-328, is written by the city librarian of Lusaka and chairman of the Zambian Library Association. It is a clear statement and contains both footnotes and bibliography.

Zambia Library Service, *Directory of Library Centres,* 2d ed. (Lusaka: Ministry of Education, 1969), 61 p., is arranged alphabetically by region, within each region alphabetically by district, and within each district alphabetically by center. At the end of the directory, there is an alphabetical index of centers.

Elizabeth M. Brown, "Travels with a Kombi," *New Library World* 73, no. 858 (December 1971): 161-64. is an informative short article. It is written in the style of a travelogue by an expatriate librarian who had completed one three-year tour working for the Zambia Library Service and had begun a second tour when this article was published.

The Zambia Library Service has almost six hundred library centers, some operated by rural councils (*bomas*) and many on a voluntary basis.

Another recent article is L. E. Mukwato, "School Library Service in Zambia: Present Position and Future Plans and Work of the Zambia Library Service," *Focus on International and Cooperative Librarianship* 2, no. 3 (October 1971): 43-51.

I. M. Graham and B. C. Halwindi, *Guide to the Public Archives of Zambia,* vol. 1: *1895-1940* (Lusaka: National Archives of Zambia, 1971), 153 p., includes historical notes.[73] This professionally prepared guide to the National Archives of Zambia is arranged broadly on a geographical basis. The Minister of Home Affairs in his foreword writes: "Should this 'Guide' succeed in inspiring the Zambian public in general and research scholars in particular to come forward and explore this minefield of information, our efforts will have been rewarded."

WEST AFRICA

The jump from Zambia to West Africa is a long diagonal one of some three thousand miles. While there are many differences between most of the inhabitants of Zambia and those of a West African country, some of their colonial experiences were similar. Today, there are other common factors: being part of Africa, of the Third World, perhaps producers of a single primary cash crop for export, and similar environment and ecology.

West Africa, looking at that part of the continent that is closest in distance to the Americas and Europe, is, from a Eurocentric point of view, the "real" Africa, if only because it supplied a large proportion of the slaves for the New World. Before embarking on a discussion of books and bibliographies of individual countries of Anglophonic and Francophonic West Africa, titles covering most of Anglophonic West Africa will be cited.

For a casual overview of the area, one may recommend two works: Nancy L. Hoepli, ed., *West Africa Today* (New York: H. W. Wilson, 1971), 197 p. (The Reference Shelf 42, no. 6), which consists of reprints from newspapers; and "West Africa" in *Negro History Bulletin* 35, no. 4 (April 1972): 76-94. Two excellent brief volumes are: W. Arthur Lewis, *Politics in West Africa* (London: Allen and Unwin, 1965), (The Whidden Lectures for 1965); and Aristide Zolberg, *Creating Political Order: The Party-States of West Africa* (Chicago: Rand McNally, 1966), 168 p.[74]

HISTORY

J. F. Ade Ajayi and Michael Croder, eds., *History of West Africa,* vol. 1 (London: Longman; New York: Columbia University Press, 1972), 568 p., is an unusually authoritative volume.[75] Thirteen authorities on the history of West Africa contributed chapters that appear in the first volume. Each chapter has a good map.

Michael Crowder and Obaro Ikime, eds., *West African Chiefs: Their Changing Status under Colonial Rule and Independence* (New York: Africana Publishing Corp., 1970), 453 p., contains the proceedings of a seminar held at the Institute of African Studies, University of Ife, December 17-21, 1968.[76]

A theme that has been of much recent interest is explored in: Michael Crowder, ed., *West African Resistance: The Military Response to Colonial Occupation* (New York: Africana Publishing

Corp.; London: Hutchinson, 1971), 320 p. This volume makes a fair beginning of a complex field of study.[77]

Most useful are two volumes edited by Colin W. Newbury: *British Policy toward West Africa: Select Documents, 1786-1874* (Oxford: Clarendon Press, 1965), 656 p., and *1875-1914, with Statistical Appendices, 1800-1914* (Oxford: Clarendon Press, 1971), 636 p.[78] Newbury is an economic historian of the former empire.

Finally, see Daniel F. McCall, et al., *Western African History* (New York: Praeger for African Studies Center, Boston University, 1969), 258 p. (Boston University Paper on Africa No. 4).

Those readers who want additional references, an evaluation, or a guide should consult: J. D. Fage, "Continuity and Change in the Writing of West African History," *African Affairs* (London) 70, no. 280 (July 1971): 236-251.

Interesting and more specialized works are: Polly Hill, *Studies in Rural Capitalism in West Africa* (Cambridge University Press, 1970), 173 p.,[79] and Margaret Peil, "The Expulsion of West African Aliens," *Journal of Modern African Studies* 9, no. 2 (August 1971): 205-229. The Peil article, by a sociologist with many years of teaching and research experience in Ghana, is largely concerned with the aliens there.

Henry S. Wilson, ed., *Origins of West African Nationalism* (London: Macmillan, 1969), 391 p., is an anthology of early nationalist writings.[80] It is virtually impossible to obtain a copy of the original papers, even in a large research library.

Those interested in the increasing role of the military in African affairs should see: Claude E. Welch, *Soldier and State in Africa* (Evanston, Ill.: Northwestern University Press, 1970), 320 p., a comparative analysis of military intervention and political change. This volume contains six essays concerned with the general topic and the particular situation in Dahomey and Upper Volta, Zaïre, Ghana, and Algeria. There are two helpful appendixes—"Armed Strength and Defence Expenditure . . ." and "Violence and Military Involvement . . . independence through 1968"—and a bibliography.

Note also Welch's "Praetorianism in Commonwealth West Africa," *Journal of Modern African Studies* 10, no. 2 (July 1972):

203-221. Very good is a work edited by Anton Bebler, *Military Rule in Africa, Dahomey, Ghana, Sierra Leone and Mali* (New York: Praeger, 1973), 267 p.

ECONOMIC DEVELOPMENT

Works in this area of study include Davidson R. Gwatkin, "Policies Affecting Population in West Africa," *Studies in Family Planning* 3, no. 2 (September 1972): 214-221, and Robert H. T. Smith, "Spacial Structure and Process in Tropical West Africa," *Economic Geography* 48, no. 3 (July 1972): 229-344.

Henry Patrick White and M. B. Gleave, *An Economic Geography of West Africa* (London: Bell, 1971), 322 p. (Bell's Advanced Economic Geography), was written by two faculty members in geography from the University of Salford in Britain. Most chapters contain tables, maps, and diagrams. There are useful references at the end of chapters.

Claude Meillassoux, ed., *The Development of Indigenous Trade and Markets in West Africa* (London: Oxford University Press for International African Institute, 1971), 444 p.,[81] consists of twenty papers presented and discussed at the Tenth International African Seminar at Fourah Bay College, Freetown, Sierra Leone, in December 1969. These seminars, supported by grants from the Ford Foundation, were published for the International African Institute by Oxford University Press. The introduction by Meillassoux is in French, followed by an English translation. Other papers are in French or English with summaries in the other language. The twenty papers cover most aspects of indigenous trade and markets. The volume includes a good bibliography.

Akin L. Mabogunje, *Regional Mobility and Resource Development in West Africa* (Montreal: McGill-Queens University Press, 1972), 154 p. (Centre for Developing-Area Studies, McGill University, Keith Callard Lectures No. 4), contains four lectures given at McGill in March and April 1969.[82]

MISCELLANEOUS

Noteworthy among the many additional works are the annual

West African Journal of Archaeology, which began publication in 1971,[83] and Dinah Ameley Ayensu, *The Art of West African Cooking* (Garden City, N.Y.: Doubleday, 1972), 145 p.

BIBLIOGRAPHY

At least one old pamphlet deserves a listing as a model of a selective, annotated guide: H. A. Rydings, *The Bibliographies of West Africa* (Ibadan, Nigeria: Published on behalf of the West African Library Association by the Ibadan University Press, 1961), 36 p. This attractive pamphlet evaluates fifty bibliographies, some of which appeared to be parts of larger works. Others are: Malcolm A. McKee, "Recent British Publications on Commonwealth West Africa," London, *British Book News,* (London) (November 1971): 855-862. McKee is assistant librarian for African studies, School of Oriental and African Studies, University of London. His is a useful bibliographical essay.

Another recnt bibliography is Samir M. Zoghby, comp., "A Bibliography of Medieval West Africa," Part I of Daniel Matthews, ed., *Current Themes in African Historical Studies* (Westport, Conn.: Negro Universities Press, 1970), p. 9-139. The compiler, Dr. Zoghby, is the second-in-command of the African section of the Library of Congress. Daniel Matthews is the editor-in-chief of the African Bibliographic Center in Washington, D.C. According to Zoghby, this bibliography complements a bibliographic essay on medieval West Africa in the April and May 1969 issues of *A Current Bibliography on African Affairs,* vol. 2, no. 4 (new series), p. 5-16 and vol. 2, no. 5 (new series), p. 5-13. The period covered by Zoghby in the longer 1970 essay is from the eighth to the seventeenth centuries. Some more recent material on the medieval period is also included. The arrangement is alphabetical. There is a general index to part one of the bibliography.

Carl K. Eicher, *Research in Agricultural Development in Five English-speaking Countries in West Africa* (New York: The Agricultural Development Council, 1970), 152 p., is by a professor of agricultural economics and African Studies at

Michigan State University. The Agricultural Development Council is a nonprofit private organization mainly active in Asian studies. Eicher's work, after brief preliminary chapters, is a classified research inventory arranged by country and type of publication.

Sanford H. Bederman, "Urbanization in West Africa; A Selected Listing of Recently Published Literature (in English)," *Bulletin of the Special Libraries Association's Geography and Map Division* no. 84 (June 1971): 24-30, 39, is a short article consisting of one hundred and nine unannotated references, arranged alphabetically.

In Commonwealth Bureau of Agricultural Economics, Oxford, *The Marketing of Agricultural Produce in West African Countries with Special Reference to Ghana* (1971), 6 p., the arrangement is classified, by country.

Other works are: C. Tettey, *Medicine in British West Africa* (London: Fellowship of the Library Association, 1967-1968), and Adebisi Aladejana, comp., *The Marketing Board System* (Ibadan: Nigerian Institute of Social and Economic Research, 1970), 87 p. [Prepared for participants in the seminar on the marketing board system scheduled for March 1971]. The Adadejana bibliography is arranged in a classified manner by type of publication. A name index is included.

LIBRARIANSHIP

A.J.E. Dean, "Organization and Services of University Libraries in West Africa," in Miles M. Jackson, Jr., ed., *Comparative and International Librarianship* (Westport, Conn.: Greenwood Press, 1970), p. 113-137, is written by a librarian with extensive experience as the university librarian in Legon, Ghana, and as a professor of librarianship at the University of Ibadan.

Louise Silvey Spear, "Patterns of Librarianship in West Africa," in William Landram Williamson, *Assistance to Libriares in Developing Nations: Papers on Comparative Studies* (Proceedings of a conference held at the Wisconsin Center, Madison, Wisconsin, May 14, 1971, University of Wisconsin, Library School, 1971), p. 50-

56, was written by a master's candidate who had been studying in Ghana.

There has been some discussion recently in library circles about reviving the West African Library Association, one of the results of the UNESCO Seminar on the Development of Public Libraries in Africa held in Ibadan in 1953. What soon became known as *Wala News* was published two or more times a year from March 1954 to June 1962.

NIGERIA

This volume now enters a new phase of rigid selection among the many possible sources that could be cited. Nigeria is large in size and population—almost 70 million in 1972 according to the United Nations estimate.[84] In addition, it has long been the focus of interest of foreign scholars, who will soon be outnumbered by indigenous ones. Just as historians of the United States tend to be mostly Americans, historians of Africa will increasingly be Africans. This tendency also applies to other scholars, including librarians. As we shall see below, Nigerian librarians occupy almost all library positions in Nigeria, certainly the senior ones.

The fact that the references that follow will be mostly recent is not to be interpreted as a sign that older works have been re-placed by newer publications. By and large, works recorded in Duignan's *Guide* will not be presented here. Many of them, often with much of the same phrasing, can be found in Helen Con-over's 1963 publication, *Africa South of the Sahara,* a selected annotated list of writings.

HISTORY

Nigeria's first historian, now at Harvard University, is Dr. Kenneth Onwuka Dike, who, unfortunately, has been too preoccupied with administrative and diplomatic work to publish much since his *Trade and Politics in the Niger Delta, 1830-1885: An Introduction to the Economic and Political History of Nigeria*

(Oxford: Clarendon Press, 1956), 250 p. (Oxford Studies in African Affairs).

So as not to think that expatriates desist from writing Nigerian history, here are two examples. The first is by one of the governors of the Gold Coast (a work that first appeared in 1929): Alan Burns, *History of Nigeria,* 8th ed. (London: Allen and Unwin, 1972), 366 p.[85] Sir Alan first went to Nigeria sixty years ago. His history continues to be of significance.

The other expatriate is also not a professional historian but a journalist who writes good history: John Hatch, *Nigeria: A History* (London: Secker and Warburg, 1971), 288 p.[86]

Of the many works that have appeared by present or former members of the Ibadan Department of History, many published by Ibadan University Press, only one will be mentioned here: E. J. Alagoa, *History of the Niger Delta: An Historical Interpretation of Ijo Oral Tradition* (Ibadan: Ibadan University Press, 1972), 231 p. It contains a selected bibliography.

Turning to western Nigeria, note: J. Humphrey Fisher, "Review Article: Independency and Islam: The Nigerian Aladuras and Some Muslim Comparisons" *Journal of African History* 11, no. 2 (1970): 269-277.

Of particular interest to those interested in the north is: John N. Paden, *Religion and Political Culture in Kano* (Berkeley: University of California Press, 1973), 461 p., which compares religious and political sectors in Kano. It examines two aspects of each sector: orientation toward authority and orientation toward community.

See, too, Victor N. Low, *Three Nigerian Emirates: A Study in Oral History* (Evanston, Ill.: Northwestern University Press, 1972), 296 p.

THE CIVIL WAR

Sources on the Civil War, including those of the vanquished side, are being collected by the Cooperative Africana Microform Project (CAMP) at the Center for Research Libraries in Chicago.

The following works may be of interest, although none of them attempts to explain the direct and indirect role of those who tried to influence government policy—for example, the Vatican or concerned United States groups.

First are two anonymous (as was their custom) and important survey articles from the *Times Literary Supplement*: "The Literature of Civil War" (March 3, 1972): 247-248, and "Nigerian Fratricide Refighting the Civil War" (August 25, 1972): 981-983.

S. K. Panter-Brick, ed., *Nigerian Politics and Military Rule: Prelude to the Civil War* (London: Athlone Press for the Institute of Commonwealth Studies, 1970), 276 p., contains seminar discussions held at the Institute of Commonwealth Studies during the early part of the war.[87].

Note also: Anthony H. M. Kirk-Greene and Christopher C. Wrigley, "Biafra in Print: Two Views," *African Affairs* 69, no. 275 (April 1970): 180-184. The first view is by Kirk-Greene and is followed by Wrigley's, who tends to lean toward the former secessionists. Both list some of the many titles available by 1970.

George B. Affia, *Nigerian Crisis, 1966-1970: A Preliminary Bibliography* (Lagos: Yakubu Gowon Library, University of Lagos, 1970), 24 leaves, is by a librarian on the staff of the University of Lagos. The articles and monographs, including government documents, are presented in one alphabetical sequence.

Wilson O. Aiyepeku, *Geography, Wars and the Nigerian Situation:A Bibliographical Analysis* (Ibadan: University of Ibadan, Insitute of Librarianship, 1970), 26 p. (Occasional Paper No. 4), is by a member of the faculty of the Institute of Librarianship, University of Ibadan. His article, a small pamphlet, demonstrates the extent to which geographical literature in selected periodicals has reflected the events of two world wars and the Nigerian Civil War.

John Oyinbo, *Nigeria: Crisis and Beyond* (London: Charles Knight, 1971), 214 p., contains an introduction by John P. Mackintosh, who now has second thoughts about his *Nigerian Government and Politics* (London: Allen and Unwin, 1966), 651 p. Oyinbo's good presentation is essentially a historical one. A useful Appendix B enumerates the legislative lists.

Another article is: Steven Jervis, "From Nigeria to Biafra,"

Michigan Quarterly Review 10, no. 4 (Fall 1971): 275-286. Jervis has a Ph.D. in English from Stanford University, and taught at the University of Nigeria at Nsukka (now East Central State) until June 1967.

Zdenek Cervenka, a Czechoslovak international law and relations specialist with many years of service in Ghana and now in exile in Sweden, has written: *The Nigerian Civil War, 1967-1970: History of the War: Selected Bibliography and Documents* (Frankfurt: Bernard and Graefe, 1971), 459 p. The abbreviated version is *A History of the Nigerian War, 1967-1970* (Ibadan: Onibonoje Press, 1972), 160 p. A bibliography of some 1,500 cards, classified into thirteen categories, is held by Northwestern University Library and is available on microfilm from CAMP.

A. A. Ayida and H.M.A. Onitri, both economists, have edited *Reconstruction and Development in Nigeria* (Ibadan: Oxford University Press, 1972), 768 p., proceedings of a conference held at Ibadan, March 24-28, 1969.

Anthony H. M. Kirk-Greene, *Crisis and Conflict in Nigeria: A Documentary Sourcebook, 1966-1969* (London, New York: Oxford University Press, 1971), is a two-volume work. A large bibliography appears in volume 2.[88]

E. Wayne Nafziger, author of "The Economic Impact of the Nigerian Civil War," *Journal of Modern African Studies* 10, no. 2 (July 1972): 223-245, is an American academic economist.

Probably the best book on the civil war that has been written to date is: John D. de St. Jorre, *The Nigerian Civil War* (London: Hadder and Stoughton; Boston: Houghton Mifflin, 1972), 437 p.[89]

The following is edited by a Nigerian, who is a successful publisher and entrepreneur in the United States: Joseph Okpaku, ed., *Nigeria: Dilemma of Nationhood, An African Analysis of the Biafran Conflict* (New York: The Third Press, and Westport, Conn.: Greenwood Press, 1972), 426 p.[90] The ten chapters (introduction and conclusion by Okpaku) are by otherwise unknown and unintroduced contributors.

Suzanne Cronje, *The World and Nigeria: A Diplomatic History of the Biafran War, 1967-70* (London: Sidgwick and Jackson, 1972), 409 p. The author, a journalist working in London, once lived and worked as a journalist in Nigeria. This interestingly written volume is not a history of the Nigerian Civil War but rather an analysis of the role Britain, and, to a lesser degree, the United States and the Soviet Union, played.

Stanley Diamond, "The Ibo's Plight," letter to the editor, *The New York Review of Books* 18, no. 3 (February 24, 1972): 46, was written by an American anthropologist who was among the active supporters of the Biafran cause.

Ntieyong Akpan, author of *The Struggle for Secession, 1966-1970* (London: Cass; Portland, Ore.: Scholarly Book Service, 1972), 225 p., was a non-Ibo; he was chief secretary to the government and head of the civil service of easter Nigeria.[91]

Jean Herskovits, "One Nigeria," *Foreign Affairs* 51, no. 2 (January 1973): 392-407, is a good statement of the situation of Nigeria after the war, all but forgotten by the foreign press.

Some references on the effects of the war on libraries are: John D. Fage, "Rehabilitation of the Library of the University of Nigeria," *Library Materials on Africa* (London) 7, no. 3 (March 1970): 191-195; Cosmas E. Enu, "The Effects of the Nigerian Civil War on the Library Services in the Former Eastern Region," *Libri* 20. no. 3 (1970): 206-217; Joseph C. Anafulu, "An African Experience: The Role of a Specialized Library in a Wider Situation," *Special Libraries* 62, no. 1 (January 1971): 32-40; B. U. Nwafor, "Recorded Knowledge: A War Casualty," *Library Journal* 96, no. 1 (January 1971): 42-45; and N. Okpa-Iroha, "Reconstruction of Devastated Library Services in War Affected Areas of Nigeria," *Library Association Record* (London) 73, no. 6 (June 1971): 108-109. There are no doubt many more articles. A joint library meeting of the Nigerian Library Association, where librarians from all parts of the country meet, occurred in Jos in 1971, and was reported on in *Bulletin of the Nigerian Library Association* 7, no. 3 (December 1971).

ECONOMIC DEVELOPMENT

The literature in the area of economic development is largely repetitive and uneven. The following works, arranged chronologically by date of publication, are among the better ones: Pius N. C. Okigbo, *Nigerian Public Finance* (London: Longmans; Evanston, Ill.: Northwestern University Press, 1965), 245 p.

(African Studies Number 15);[92] Paul O. Proehl, *Foreign Enterprise in Nigeria: Laws and Politics* (Chapel Hill: University of North Carolina Press, 1965), 250 p.;[93] Alan Sokolski, *The Establishment of Manufacturing in Nigeria* (New York: Praeger, 1965), 373 p. (Praeger Special Studies in International Economics and Development); [94] Charles V. Brown, *The Nigerian Banking System* (London: Allen and Unwin; Evanston, Ill.: Northwestern University Press, 1966), 214 p.;[95] Wolfgang F. Stolper, *Planning Without Facts; Lessons in Research Allocation from Nigeria's Development, with an Input-Output Analysis of the Nigerian Economy, 1959-1960*, by Nicholas G. Carter (Cambridge: Harvard University Press, 1966), 348 p. (Center for International Affairs);[96] Ojetunji Aboyade, *Foundation of an African Economy: A Study of Investment and Growth in Nigeria* (New York: Praeger, 1966), 366 p. (Praeger Special Studies in International Economics and Development);[97] Peter Kilby, *Industrialization in an Open Economy: Nigeria 1945-1966* (Cambridge University Press, 1969), 399 p.;[98] David R. Smock, *Conflict and Control in an African Trade Union: A Study of the Nigerian Coal Mines Union* (Stanford: Hoover Institution Press, 1969), 170 p. (Hoover Institution Studies 23);[99] Adebayo Adedeji, *Nigerian Federal Finance: Its Development, Problems and Prospects* (London: Hutchinson Educational; New York: Africana Publishing Corp. 1969), 308 p.;[100] Sayre P. Schatz, *Economics, Politics and Administration in Government Lending: The Regional Loan Banks of Nigeria* (Ibadan: Oxford University Press, 1970), 146 p.;[101] Scott R. Pearson, *Petroleum and the Nigerian Economy* (Stanford: Stanford University Press, 1970), 235 p.;[102] "Agricultural Administration and Development in Nigeria: A Symposium," *Quarterly Journal of Adminstration* (University of Ife) 6, no. 1 (October 1971): 17-69; "The Nigerian Economy in the 1970's," *The Nigerian Journal of Economic and Social Studies* (Ibadan) 13, no. 1 (March 1971): 3-124 (the entire issue is devoted to the papers of the 1971 meeting of the Annual Conference of the Nigerian Economic Society); Audrey C. Smock, *Ibo Politics: The Role of the Ethnic Unions in Eastern Nigeria* (Cambridge: Harvard University Press, 1971), 274 p.; [103] R. O. Ekundare, "The Political Economy of Private Investment in Nigeria," *Journal of Modern African Studies* 10, no. 1 (May 1972): 37-56; and David R.

Smock and Audrey C. Smock, *Cultural and Political Aspects of Rural Transformation: A Case Study of Eastern Nigeria* (New York: Praeger, 1972), 387 p. (Praeger Special Studies).[104]

ANTHROPOLOGY AND REGIONAL LITERATURE

For the east, see Victor Chikezie Uchendu, *Ibgo of Southeast Nigeria* (New York: Holt, Rinehart and Winston, 1965), 111 p. (Case Studies in Cultural Anthropology), an early work by a distinguished anthropologist interested in some of the applied aspects of his profession, such as in agriculture and nutrition. See also: E. Okechukwu Odita, "Universal Cults and Intra-diffusion: Igbo Ikenga in Cultural Retrospection," *African Studies Review* (Lansing) 16, no. 1 (April 1973): 73-82; Richard N. Henderson, *The King in Every Man: Evolutionary Trends in Onitsha Ibo Society and Culture* (New Haven: Yale University Press, 1972), 576 p. This book is primarily a study of the changes that occurred in a West African society before its inclusion in a wider British colonial system. Nnamdi Azikiwe, *My Odyssey: An Autobiography* (London: C. Hurst; New York: Praeger, 1970), 452 p.,[105] is the autobiography of one of the great nationalist leaders of Nigeria and its first governor-general as an independent state. He carries his story from before his birth in 1904 to the early 1940s.

One work on the west is William Bascom, *The Yoruba of Southwestern Nigeria* (New York: Holt, Rinehart and Winston, 1969), 118 p. (Case Studies in Cultural Anthropology).[106]

For the north, see Polly Hill, *Rural Hausa, A Village and a Setting* (London: Cambridge University Press, 1972), 368 p.;[107] C. S. Whitaker, Jr., *The Politics of Tradition* (Princeton: Princeton University Press, 1970), 563 p.,[108] is a product of the best tradition in post-1960 American political science. The sections of this book are entitled "Path of Reform," "The Local System in Action," and "Dynamics of Regional Politics." It contains an unusually full bibliography.

Frank Edgar, *Hausa Tales and Traditions,* trans. Neil Skinner, (London: Cass, 1969), 440 p., is the first of three volumes; the second and third have not yet been published. It is an English translation of *Tatsunijoji Na Hausa,* or *Litafi Na Tatsuniyoyi Na Hausa,* compiled originally by Frank Edgar and published and edited by W. E. Mayne, 1911-1913. The first volume, translated and edited by Neil Skinner, includes a foreword by M. G. Smith, a translator's introduction, and glossary. It contains tales about animals and caricatures—"ethnic and other stereotypes," "moralizing," "Men and women, young men and maidens," "Dilemma Tales" and "Cases at Law."

Robert Sutherland Rattray, *Hausa Folklore Customs and Proverbs. . . .* (Oxford: Clarendon Press, 1969), 2 vols., was originally published by the Clarendon Press in Oxford, England, in 1913 and reprinted by them as well as the Negro Universities Press. Rattray is on the title page described as "of Exeter College, Oxford [;] Assistant District Commissioner, Ashanti, West Africa [;] author of 'Chinyanja Folk-Lore' [;] Qualified Interpreter in Hausa, Twi, Chinyanja, Mole." The stories are fascinating in English and no doubt also in Hausa.

A.J.N. Tremearne, *Hausa Superstition and Customs,* is an introduction to the folk-lore and the folk. This volume, originally published in 1913, contains a new introductory note by Mervyn Hiskett (London: Cass, 1970), 548 p.

Neil Skinner, *Hausa Readings* (Madison, Wis.: University of Wisconsin, 1968), 279 p., was published for the University of Wisconsin's Department of African Languages and Literature. The first part of the book is in Roman script, the second in Arabic and Roman script.

For a review by A.H.M. Kirk-Greene of the last four books named above see *Africa* 41, no. 1 (January 1971): 80-82.

In June 1972, a new journal, *Savanna,* began publication. A semi-annual, *Savanna* is a journal of environmental and social sciences published by Ahmadu Bello University in Zaria.

GENERAL

Robert Melson and Howard Wolpe, eds., *Nigeria: Modernization and the Politics of Communalism* (East Lansing: Michigan State University Press, 1971), 680 p., consists of twenty-five papers, of which eight are original contributions.[109]

ARCHAEOLOGY

See Thurstan Shaw, *Igbo-Ukwu: An Account of Archaeological Discoveries in Eastern Nigeria* (London: Faber for Institute of African Studies, University of Ibadan; Evanston, Ill.: Northwestern University Press, 1970), 2 vols.[110] This is a record of the work of a professional archeologist in what is now known as the East Central State of Nigeria. The two volumes are a detailed, lavishly illustrated, report of the "dig."

Frank Willett, "Nigeria," in Peter Louis Shinnie, *The African Iron Age* (Oxford: Clarendon Press, 1971), p. 1-35, is a scholarly yet readable essay. It is fully documented and contains two full-page maps.

Graham Connah, "Archaeology in Benin," *The Journal of African History* 13, no. 1 (1972): 25-38, a learned and well-illustrated article, is by an archaeologist from the University of New England, New South Wales, Australia.

Sylvia Leith-Ross, comp., *Nigerian Pottery: A Catalogue* (Ibadan: Ibadan University Press for the Department of Antiquities, Lagos, 1970), 220 p., is a beautiful volume containing an introduction by Michael Cardew, the master-potter. The pottery is well illustrated, frequently with details. The catalog is based on the pots at the Jos Museum. The last work includes a foreword by Thurston Shaw and an excellent essay on pottery techniques in Nigeria by Michael Cardew.[111]

GEOGRAPHY

Reuben Udo. *Geographical Regions of Nigeria* (Berkeley: University of California Press, 1970), 212 p., is based on lectures given to undergraduates at the University of Ibadan. It should be of use to senior high school as well as university students. The book contains eighty-four maps and diagrams and fifty-two plates. Part one deals with "The Coastlands of Guinea"; part two, "The Middle Belt"; and part three, with "The Nigerian Sudan and the Eastern Borderlands."

K. M. Barbour, "North-Eastern Nigeria—A Case Study of State Formation," *Journal of Modern African Studies* 9 no. 1 (May 1971):

49-71, is by the professor of geography at the University of Ibadan. He considers future economic prospects of the largest of Nigeria's twelve states. The article contains five excellent maps and three tables.

SCIENCES

One recent article is Claudia Zaslavsky, "Mathematics of the Yoruba People and Their Neighbors in Southern Nigeria," *Two Year College Mathematics Journal* (Boston) 1, no. 2 (1970): 76-99.[112]

Ralph Schram, *A History of the Nigerian Health Services* (Ibadan: Ibadan University Press, 1973), 480 p.,[113] is the work of a physician and historian who has found the time to write and document his account. It contains a twenty-one-page bibliography.

LITERATURE

A discussion of Nigerian literature deserves volumes, not just a few references. Quite a useful general introduction of the critical writings, largely by non-Nigerians, appears in Bruce King, ed., *Introduction to Nigerian Literature* (New York: Africana Publishing Corp., 1972), 216 p.

Nigeria's greatest author, and probably one of the giants of contemporary world literature, is Wole Soyinka, whose most important work is *The Interpreters* (New York: Africana Publishing Corp., 1972), 260 p. Other important works are *Madman and Specialists* (New York: Hill and Wang, 1972), 118 p., *A Shuttle in the Crypt* (New York: Hill and Wang, 1972), 89 p., and *The Man Died: Prison Notes of Wole Soyinka* (London: Rex Collings, 1972), 315 p. *The Man Died* is in the greatest tradition of prison or ex-prison literature, and as such will make it impossible for him to live in Nigeria in the foreseeable future. Soyinka chose as publisher a man who had been concerned about his welfare while in prison. For a biography, see Gerald Moore, *Wole Soyinka* (New York: Africana Publishing Corp., 1971), 253 p.[114]

Only one other Nigerian author will be mentioned: Chinua

Achebe, *Girls at War and Other Stories* (New York: Doubleday, 1973), 118 p.[115]

BIBLIOGRAPHY

Nduntuei O. Ita, *Bibliography of Nigeria: A Survey of Anthropological and Linguistic Writings from the Earliest Times to 1966* (London: Cass, 1971), 273 p., is by a Nigerian librarian. It is divided into two parts, with a total of 5,411 entries. There are indexes to authors, ethnic groups, and Islamic studies.[116]

A not-too-different but much more selective and annotated work is Christian Agnolu, *Nigeria, a Bibliography in the Humanities and Social Sciences, 1900-1971* (Boston: G. K. Hall, 1973), 620 p.

John Harris, the founding librarian of the University of Ibadan, has issued *Books about Nigeria: A Select Reading List,* 5th ed. (Ibadan: Ibadan University Press, 1969), 83 p. This is a useful classified bibliography with an index.

There is a need to produce an up to date study guide for Nigeria. Meanwhile, the following, while much too old, is still of some use: Howard Wolpe, *A Study Guide for Nigeria* (Development Program, African Studies Center, Boston University, 1966), 78 p. This guide is arranged in broad sections and subsections, such as "Nigeria History, Precolonial History." There are brief subsections, the last one being bibliography.

In many ways, the bibliography of Nigeria is largely the result of the work and original initiative of John Harris, although he rarely has taken time to describe the entire Nigerian bibliographical field. One such attempt was his "National Bibliography in Nigeria," in James D. Pearson and Ruth Jones, eds., *The Bibliography of Africa,* p. 34-44, 349-355. Particularly useful is the fourth appendix, "A Select List of Nigerian Bibliographies."

Another attempt at stock-taking in the realm of Nigerian bibliography is the periodic report to UNESCO's *Bibliography Documentation Terminology.* The most recent issue replaces earlier information. The three most recent entries appeared in the July 1970 (vol. 10, no. 4), March 1971 (vol. 11, no. 1), and

November 1972 (vol. 12, no. 6) issues. The last updates: Paul Avicienne, comp., *Bibliographical Services throughout the World, 1965-1969* (Paris: UNESCO,1972).

A multitude of general and special bibliographies has been published by Nigerian librarians working in Nigeria and elsewhere. In some instances, more so in former times, expatriate librarians worked in Nigeria, or other foreigners concerned themselves with listing publications on all or part of Nigeria. The medley that follows bears witness to the current and near current efforts. The really important fact is that all current Nigerian publications, regardless of language or form, are listed by the National Library and are made available and cumulated in Nigeria and beyond. As of July 1970, the National Library of Nigeria has been issuing the national bibliography.

Bernard Struck, "Linguistic Bibliography of Northern Nigeria," *Journal of the Royal African Society* 11 (1911-1912): 47-61, 213-230, is a rare example of old Nigeriana, rarely cited.

A recent example of the type of bibliography which, hopefully, will be increasing is: Stephen Goddard, "The Papers of a Colonial Administration, the Nigerian Colonial Service," *Library Materials on Africa* 10, no. 2 (October 1972): 98-103.

Harry A Green, *Urban Conditions in Nigeria: A Preliminary Bibliography* (Zaria: Institute of Administration, Ahmadu Bello University, 1972), 31 p., is a classified, unannotated bibliography with no author index.

Rather specialized are: Oyeniyi Osundina, *Bibliography of Nigerian Sculpture* (Lagos: University Library, 1968), 35 p., and Paula Ben-Amos, *Bibliography of Benin* (Greenwich, Conn.: New York Graphic Society, 1968), 17 p. (Primitive Art Bibliography No. 6).

On periodicals and the press, see: "Periodicals Published in Nigeria," *Supplement to Library Materials on Africa* 7, no. 3 (March 1970), 83; this, the tenth list compiled by Miriam Alman for the Standing Conference on Library Materials on Africa (SCOLMA), consists of periodicals published in Nigeria. The arrangement is geographical and alphabetical within the former regions.

Hans Zell's *New Periodicals for Nigeria* are reviewed in Bill Katz's "Magazines," *Library Journal* (July 1972): 2366. In Bill Katz's column "Magazines," Hans Zell gives subscription information and a lengthy annotation of eleven Nigerian periodicals.

Marcia A. Grant, "Nigerian Newspaper Types," *Journal of Commonwealth Political Studies* (Leicester University Press, Leicester, England) 11, no. 2 (July 1971): 95-114, is fully documented. The author, now at Oberlin College, did her fieldwork in Nigeria in 1963-1965.

This article is followed by (in the same journal) John D. Chick, "The Nigerian Press and National Integration," p. 115-133.

The following references refer to samples of the regional literature. For the West see:

S. K. Taiwo Williams, "Sources of Information on Improved Farming Practices in Some Selected Areas of Western Nigeria," *Bulletin of Rural Economics and Sociology* (Ibadan) 4, no. 11 (1969): 30-51. This author was at the University of the South Pacific at the time the article was printed. He supplies a suggestive but inconclusive analysis of the role of the Nigerian press.

John Harris, "A Preliminary List of Books about the Western Region of Nigeria" (Ibadan, 1956) (typescript);[117] F. Ogunsheye, *Nigerian Library Resources in Science and Technology* (Ibadan: Institute of Librarianship,University of Ibadan, 1970), 44 p. (Occasional Paper No. 2).

John Harris, *Ibadan University Library: Some Notes on Its Birth and Growth* (Ibadan University Press, 1968), 44 p., is a reprint of an article that originally appeared in *Ibadan,* no. 18 (February 1964). It includes a useful bibliography.

A. Olu Olafioye, *Lagos Past and Present, an Historical Bibliography,* 2d ed. (Lagos: National Library of Nigeria, 1970), 102 p. (National Library Publication 21), is a classified bibliography of 404 numbered items. There are separate author and title indexes and several pages of photographs.

For the North, see:

G. J. Williams, comp., "A Current Bibliography of the Savanna States of Nigeria (1970-1971)," *Savanna* (Zaria) 1, no. 1 (June 1972): 131-142. Each of the first two issues of this journal contains a classified bibliography concerning Nigeria's savanna regions, regardless of place of publication.

Dealing with the East are the following:

André Nitecki, *Onitsha Publications* (Bibliography of Market Literature in English) (Syracuse University, 1967), 24 p. (Program of Eastern African Studies, Occasional Paper No. 32), by a man who has worked in Nigeria for many years, is a guide to *Onitsha Publications* that Nitecki has deposited in the Rare Books Department of Syracuse University library. Onitsha literature is very tricky bibliographically. The booklets have been compared to chap books.

Mark W. Delancey, "The Igbo: A Biographical Essay," *Africana Library Journal* 3, no. 4 (Winter 1972): 3-30, is confined to pre-1970 material. An essay is followed by 691 numbered, alphabetically arranged entries.

A. N. Ekpiken, comp., *A Bilbiography of the Efik-Ibibio Speaking Peoples of the Old Calabar Province of Nigeria, 1668-1964* (Ibadan University Press, 1970), 138 p. (Ibadan University Library, Bibliographical Series no. 1), is a detailed bibliography with more than a thousand references arranged under twenty-three subject headings. Sources include manuscripts and other unpublished materials.

Jigekuma A. Ombu, comp., *Nigerian Delta Studies, 1627-1967: A Bibliography with a Note on Archival Material by E. J. Alagoa* (Ibadan: Ibadan University Press, 1970), 138 p. (Ibadan University Library, Bibliographical Series No. 2), is a compilation of 1,724 entries divided into subject areas. There is an author index.

EDUCATION

J. W. Lieber, *Human Ecology and Education: A Catalogue of Environmental Studies, 1957-1970* (Ibadan, 1970), 46 p. (University of Ibadan, Institute of Education, Occasional Paper No. 10), is a listing by type of study and by state. A total of 130 studies pertaining to Nigeria, including two of the Cameroon, are included. In former times much of this work would have been called anthropological.

Adedeji Adelabu, "Studies in Trends in Nigeria's Educational Development: An Essay on Sources and Resources," *West African Journal of Education* 15 no. 2 (June 1971): 84-91, also appeared in *African Studies Review* 14, no. 1 (April 1971): 101-112. Useful also is Mr. Adelabu's article: "Education in Nigeria: A Selected and Annotated Introductory Bibliographical Survey of Current Resources," *A Current Bibliography on African Affairs* (Washington, D.C.) 4, no. 1 (Series 2) (March 1971): 78-87.

N. R. Olu Oshin and H. A. Odetoyingo, *Education in Nigeria, A Bibliographical Guide* (Lagos: West African Examinations Council, 1972), 452 p., contains 2,302 references arranged by subject. There is an author and title index.

LIBRARIANSHIP

Nigerian librarians are now active in Nigeria and elsewhere. Initially, what was not learned on the job was acquired in Great Britain and, to a lesser extent, the United States. In more recent years, the Department of Library Studies, a part of the Faculty of Education at the University of Ibadan, and to a lesser degree, the Department of Librarianship of the Faculty of Education at Ahmadu Bello University in Zaria have supplied Nigeria's need for librarians at all levels.

In 1964, the Nigerian Library Association had a membership of 164. The figure for 1969 was 156.[118] It publishes a significant journal, *Nigerian Libraries,* three times a year.

F. A. Ogunsheye, head of the Department of Library Studies at the University of Ibadan, discussed library education in Nigeria at a meeting of SCOLMA, the Standing Conference on Library Materials on Africa, summarized in the journal: *Library Materials on Africa* 6, no. 2 (November 1968): 58-60. The Department of Library Studies issues an occasional paper series, some of which deal with general topics of librarianship. Others in the series are a bibliography by Wilson O. Aiyepeku (already referred to) and John Dean, ed., *Standards of Practice for West African Libraries* (1969), 116 p. (Occasional Paper No. 1). Somewhat earlier, a former faculty member, André Nitecki, compiled: *Personal*

Names and Place Names of Nigeria (Institute of Librarianship, University of Ibadan, 1966), 77 p., an alphabetical order table giving 18,657 names and Cutter numbers.

The librarian of the University of Ife has written several valuable papers, including: J. O. Dipeolu, "Administrative Problems in Academic Libraries with Particular Reference to Nigeria," *UNESCO Bulletin for Libraries* 24, no. 6 (December 1970): 294-301; and by Dipeolu, "The Structure of Library Services in National Development," *Nigerian Libraries* 7, no. 3 (December 1971): 113-124.

Noteworthy also is: Adedeji Adelabu, "Personnel Problems in Nigeria's University Libraries: In Search of a Realistic Solution," *International Library Review* 3, no. 4 (October 1971): 355-362;[119] Monica Greaves, "Training the Cataloger in Nigeria," *Journal of Librarianship* 3, no. 3 (July 1971): 169-179.

Rosly A Mould, "The Development of Libraries in Northern Nigeria," *Library Materials on Africa* 10, no. 3 (December 1972): 179-183, contains twelve references.

A survey of school libraries in the Federal Territory of Lagos is: L. E. Green, *Nigeria, Ministry of Education Library Service* (Paris: UNESCO, 1969), 81 (Serial No. 1371/BMS.RD/DBA).

Finally, from the National Library of Nigeria is Ibok Hogan Bassey, "Librarianship in Nigeria: National Library Decree and Library Development in Nigeria," *Leads* International Relations Round Table (IRRT), American Library Association 15, no. 3 (January 1973): p. 4.

GHANA

The Ghana scene is not unlike Nigeria's, although the country is, of course, much smaller. It's about the size of England with a population of over 9 million. It has a long history of scholarship and an extensive library system, which is not confined to universities and secondary schools. Ghana has an impressive system of public libraries.

For a general guide, see Irving Kaplan, et al., *Area Handbook of Ghana* (Washington, D.C.: Foreign Area Studies [FAS] of the

American University, 1971), 447 p. This is a revision of the 1962 volume, although the bibliography is merely somewhat updated through a supplement.

Kwame Yeboa Daaku, *Trade and Politics in the Gold Coast, 1600-1720* (Oxford: Clarendon Press, 1970), 219 p. (Oxford Studies in African Affairs).[120] The subtitle of this volume is "A Study of the African Reaction to European Trade." The author is on the history faculty at the University of Ghana. This scholarly study makes use of archives in Britain and Holland.

G. B. Kay, *The Political Economy of Colonialism in Ghana: A Collection of Documents and Statistics, 1900-1960* (Cambridge University Press, 1972), 431 p., [121] is a volume of documents edited and introduced by a lecturer in economics, City University, London. The arrangement is by broad subject, e.g., finance, agriculture; each subject or chapter has its own bibliography. The volume contains forty-seven tables and two maps.

David Ernest Apter, *Ghana in Transition,* 2d rev. ed. (Princeton: Princeton University Press, 1972), was first published as *Gold Coast in Transition* in 1955. It was a pioneering work of Weberian sociology applied to the political process of what in 1957 was to become the first of the new nations of Africa.

Francis Agbodeka, *Ghana in the Twentieth Century* (Accra: Ghana University Press, 1972), 152 p., is a good study suitable for senior high school as well as college students. Kwamina B. Dickson, *A Historical Geography of Ghana* (Cambridge University Press, 1969), 379 p., is the first major geography text of Ghana. Philip J. Foster and Aristide R. Zolberg, eds., *Ghana and the Ivory Coast: Perspectives in Modernization* (Chicago and London: University of Chicago Press, 1971), 303 p., compares the very different political environment of otherwise similar countries.

Robert Pinkney, *Ghana under Military Rule, 1966-1969* (London: Methuen, 1972), 182 p. (Studies in African History No. 6),[122] is a useful case study of the operation of a military government. The author is a political scientist who did his research in both Ghana and England. His references are helpful to those wanting to look further into either Ghana's history or that of military regimes.

KWAME NKRUMAH

T. Peter Omari, *Kwame Nkrumah: The Anatomy of an African Dictatorship* (Accra: Moxon; London: C. Hurst, 1970), 229 p., is dedicated to the memory of J. B. Danquah, the great Ghanaian nationalist leader. Omari traces the rise and fall of Kwame Nkrumah and the Convention People's party.

Jon Woronoff, "Nkrumah—The Prophet Risen," *World View* (New York) 16, no. 3 (March 1973): 32-36, is a perceptive, interesting article.

Other useful references pertaining to Nkrumahism are: Thomas A. Howell and Jeffrey P. Rajasooria, *Ghana and Nkrumah* (New York: Facts on File, 1972), 205 p.; and Henry L. Bretton, *The Rise and Fall of Kwame Nkrumah* (New York: Praeger, 1966), 232 p., a very critical account. For a more favorable statement by someone with inside knowledge see: Geoffrey Bing, *Reap the Whirlwind; An Account of Kwama Nkrumah's Ghana from 1950 to 1966* (London: MacGibbon and Kee, 1968), 519 p.

Basil Davidson, *Black Star: A Biography of Kwame Nkrumah* (London: Allen Lane, 1973), 225 p., by a distinguished journalist and historian, presents a balanced assessment of the late president. Basil Davidson knew him well. The volume has an index but lacks footnotes.

Useful for additional reference to the work of and about Dr. Nkrumah is: Oyeniyi Osundina, comp. *Nkrumah, Ghana and the World—A Bibliography of Writers by and about Him and of Writings on His Leadership in Ghana. Being a Select List to Support an Exhibition on the Life and Death of Nkrumah* (Ibadan: Ibadan University Library, 1972), 10 p.

Geneva Marais, *Kwame Nkrumah as I Knew Him* (Chichester, England: January Publications, 1972), 138 p.,[123] according to the author, "is an attempt to reveal Kwame Nkrumah, the man." The attempt is fairly successful. The book contains many photographs.

Related to the Nkrumah period are the following:

W. Scott Thompson, *Ghana's Foreign Policy, 1957-1966: Diplomacy, Ideology and the New State* (Princeton, N.J.: Princeton University Press, 1969), 462 p. This is a useful and probably a definitive study of Ghana's post-independence foreign policy.

Maxwell Owusu, *Uses and Abuses of Political Power: A Case Study of Continuity and Change in the Politics of Ghana* (Chicago and London: University of Chicago Press, 1970), 364 p. This is a study of Swedru in south central Ghana. The volume contains a significant preface by David Apter.

Herbert H. Werlin, "The Roots of Corruption—The Ghanaian Enquiry," *Journal of Modern African Studies* 10, no. 2 (July 1972): 247-266. This thoroughly documented article is in part supported by references to articles in Ghana's newspapers.

ANTHROPOLOGY

One of the few solid ethnological studies to appear on Ghana recently is: John Rankine Goody, *The Myth of the Bagre* (Oxford: Clarendon Press, 1972), 381 p.[124] The author has for more than twenty years been concerned with the Lo-Wiili people of northern Ghana. His interpretation is as close to that of the original myth and cosmologies as possible.

MODERN SOCIOECONOMIC STUDIES

Robert Chambers, ed., *The Volta Resettlement Experience* (London: Pall Mall, 1971), 286 p., is an anthology based on the Volta Resettlement Symposium that took place at the University of Science and Technology, Kumasi, in March 1965.

John D. Esseks, "Government and Private Enterprises in Ghana," *Journal of Modern African Studies* 9, no. 1 (May 1971): 11-29, is the work of a political scientist who did research in Ghana, focusing on the role of private enterprise.

Margaret Peil, *The Ghanaian Factory Worker: Industrial Man in Africa* (London: Cambridge University Press, 1972), 254 p. (African Studies Series No. 5), [125] is by a sociologist who taught for five years at the University of Ghana and now teaches at the Centre of West African Studies, University of Birmingham. Hers is a careful analysis of largely survey work in Ghana's factories. The text is peppered with many tables and five maps.

Peter C. Garlick, *African Traders and Economic Development in*

Ghana (London: Oxford University Press, 1971), 172 p.,[126] is the work of an economist with teaching and research experience in Ghana. Like the Peil volume it rests largely on interview that the author conducted with many traders.

In Naseem Ahmad, *Deficit Financing, Inflation and Capital Function: the Ghanaian Experience, 1960-1965* (Munich: Weltform, Verlag, 1970), 164 p.,[127] Department of Economics, University of Ghana, Legon, and IFO Institut für Wirtschaftforschung, Munich (Afrika-Studien no. 57), the main object was "an evaluation of the experience of Ghana with money creations as a method of financing economic development." This brief work contains thirty-two tables.

BIBLIOGRAPHY

Ghana is fortunate in the quality of its retrospective and current bibliographies. The place of honor belongs to Allan W. Cardinall's *A Bibliography of the Gold Coast* (Accra: Government Printer, 1932), 384 p., a classified bibliography of 5,168 entries. It was reprinted by Negro Universities Press, Westport, Connecticut, in 1970. This work has been updated by: Albert F. Johnson, *A Bibliography of Ghana, 1930-1961* (London: Longmans; Evanston, Ill.: Northwestern University Press for Ghana Library Board, 1964), 210 p.; it has 2,608 classified entries.

David Brokensha and S.I.A. Kotei, "A Bibliography of Ghana: 1958-1964," *African Studies Bulletin* 10, no. 2 (September 1967): 35-79, is the third part of Ghana's retrospective bibliography in the official journal of the African Studies Association, now known as the *African Studies Review*. The Ghana Library Board issues the current annual national bibliography, *Ghana National Bibliography*.[128]

Also of note is the Atlas Bookshop, Accra, *Ghana in Print: A Half-Yearly Catalogue of Ghana Books, Periodicals, Reports and Other Printed and Pictorial Matter in English, Currently Available* (Accra: Moxon Paperbacks, October 1970-March 1971), 15 p.

Andrew N. deHeer, "A Note on the Ghana Bibliography," *Current Bibliography on African Affairs* 2, no. 9 (September 1969),

5-9, is by the director of the Research Library on African Affairs, Ghana Library Board, in Accra. His short article dicusses retrospective as well as current national bibliographies of Ghana.

G. M. Pitcher, *Bibliography of Ghana, 1957-1960, Kumasi*, 2d ed. (The Library, Kwame Nkrumah University of Science and Technology, 1962), 111 p., is arranged according to an alphabetcial list of subjects. There is an author and title index of periodicals from which articles are included.

E. Y. Amedekey, *The Culture of Ghana, a Bibliography* (Accra: Published for the University of Ghana Universities Press, 1970), 215 p., is divided into nine broad subject areas and then by tribal clusters. There are 1,670 entries, many of them annotated.

Christian Aguola, *Ghana: A Bibliography in the Humanities and Social Sciences, 1900-1971* (Metuchen, N.J.: Scarecrow Press, 1973): 469 p.,[129] is "comprehensively selective" and supplements the other retrospective ones. The compiler includes references to unpublished works such as master's theses, doctoral dissertations, conference papers, and research reports. The arrangement is a classified one of the over 4,000 numbered items. Many entries are annotated. There is an author index.

Julian W. Witherell and Sharon B. Lockwood, *Ghana, A Guide to Official Publications, 1872-1968* (Library of Congress, General Reference and Bibliography Divison, Reference Department, 1969), 110 p., contains 1,283 entries. It includes a selection of documents issued by the Gold Coast (1872-1957) and Ghana (1957-1968), and relevant British, League of Nations, and United Nations documents relevant to British Togoland, which became a part of Ghana.[130]

See also David Opare Bampoe, "A Guide to the Despatches from and to the Gold Coast of the British Administration, 1850-1902," 2 vols., 1967. Thesis, Fellowship of the Library Association. Microfilm of typescript, (High Wycombe, England: University Microfilms, 1969?), 1 reel.

Joseph Kofi T. Kafe, *Ghana: An Annotated Bibliography of Academic Theses, 1920-1970, in the Commonwealth, the Republic of Ireland and the United States of America* (Boston: G. K. Hall, 1973), 251 p.,[131] according to the Preface, "lists dissertations and theses on Ghana accepted for higher degrees by universities and other institutions of high learning in the Commonwealth, the Republic of Ireland and the United States of America." The bulk of the volume, its first part, consists of classified entries for 522 theses and dissertations. The second part is arranged by country and institution awarding the degree. There is an author index.

Richard R. Brand, *A Selected Bibliography on Accra, Ghana, a West African Colonial City (1887 to 1960)* (Monticello, Ill.: Council on Planning Libraries, 1971), 27 p. (Exchange Bibliography No. 242), is by a professor of geography at the University of Rhode Island. The aim of this bibliography is to facilitate base-line research on African urban systems. The arrangement is according to type of publication.

Sampson Andrews Afre, *Ashanti and Brong-Ahafo: An Annotated Bibliography* (High Wycombe, England: University Microfilms, 1969), 539 leaves, is a bibliography classified by subject. Included in the work are author and subject indexes to 1,836 numbered items. The bibliography attempts to list all books, pamphlets, periodical articles, theses, maps, atlases, and plans relating to Ashanti and Brong-Ahafo, published or available through 1965.

T. W. Cochrane, comp., "Bibliography of the Volta River Project and Related Matters" (Accra: Volta River Authority, August 1971), 83 p. (mimeo.), *Supplement* (May 1972), 6 p. (mimeo.), was compiled by the librarian of the Volta River Authority. The entries cover history and the natural and social sciences. The arrangement of the entries is classified. There are no indexes but the table of contents is helpful.

Judith R. Thoyer, "The Use of Ghana Statutory Materials, Including a Bibliography on Ghanaian Law," *University of Ghana Law Journal* 1, no. 2 (1964): 125-135, discusses the sources for primary and subsidiary legislation, followed by "Bibliography of Ghanaian Legal Materials held by the University of Ghana Law Library." The author is the law librarian of the University of Ghana.

Ghana, Bureau of Ghana Languages, *Bibliography of Works in Ghana Languages* (Accra: The Bureau, 1967), 161 p., is arranged by language. There are subject indexes for each language included in this volume. It is likely to be difficult to obtain a copy of the publications cited, even in Ghana.

Akan Literature of Ghana: A Bibliography, comp. Dennis M. Warren, ed. Alan R. Taylor (An occasional bibliography by the Literature Committee of the African Studies Association. Published in cooperation with the Research Liaison Committee of the A.S.A. 1972), 46 p., contains 492 references arranged by type of publication. This pamphlet is an extract from a bibliography of the Akan (Twi-Fanti) languages of Ghana to be published by Indiana University's Research Center for the Language Sciences.

Margaret D. Patten, comp., *Ghanaian Imaginative Writing in English, 1950-1969* (Legon: Department of Library Studies, University of Ghana, 1971), 60 p., is divided into four sections by genres. These are: anthology, poetry, fiction, and drama. There are separate author and title indexes. The works of ninety-two Ghanaian authors are included in this bibliography.

Ime Ikiddeh, "Popular Fiction in Ghana: An Introductory Study," *Okyeame, Ghana's Literary Magazine* 4, no. 2 (January 1969): 93-103, is an article "adapted from the text of a paper 'Woman Is Poison: The Character of Popular Fiction in Ghana.' " The author cites the number of copies sold for some popular books: 40,000 each for two titles.

Sources on education include: J. K. A. Villars, "Education in Ghana: An Annotated Bibliography of Education and Social Change 1925-1957," *Fellowship of the Library Association* (1968-1969); (High Wycombe, England: University Microfilms [1968] microfilm of typescript. One reel of film, reproduction of 239 leaves).

K.A.B. Jones-Quartey, "The Gold Coast Press: 1822-1930, and the Anglo-African Press, 1825-1930, the Chronologies," *University of Ghana, Institute of African Studies Research Review* 4, no. 2 (1968): 30-46, cites first and last dates of newspaper titles that are arranged chronologically. An appendix lists nineteenth-century newspapers published in Ghana according to their name, frequency, town, dates and founder, proprietors, edition or other.

Andrew N. deHeer, comp., *A List of Ghanaian Newspapers and Periodicals* (Accra: Research Library on African Affairs, 1970), 16

p. (Special Subject Bibliography No. 6), supplements Professor K.A.B. Jones-Quartey's "The Gold Coast Press." DeHeer's listing of titles is alphabetical; for most titles, place of publication, publisher, dates, and frequency are indicated.

LIBRARIANSHIP

Eve Evans built up a public library network, starting in pre-independence times. The work was first described for a wide audience in her *The Development of Public Library Services in the Gold Coast* (London: The Library Association, 1956), 31 p. (Library Association Pamphlet No. 14), and in much more detail in *A Tropical Library Service: The Story of Ghana Libraries* (London: André Deutsch, 1964), 174 p.

S.I.A. Kotei, now senior lecturer in librarianship at the Department of Library Studies, University of Ghana, has described the main university library in: "Development of Balme Library, University of Ghana, Legon," *Library Materials on Africa* 7, no. 3 (March 1971): 177-190, and "The Social Determinants of Library Development in Ghana with Reference to the Influence of British Tradition" (M. Phil. dissertation undertaken at University College, University of London).

Additional sources for Ghana's libraries include the *Ghana Library Journal*, which has been issued irregularly three times a year since October 1963, and *The Department of Library Studies Newsletter*, which has been issued three times a year since October 1971.

SIERRA LEONE

Sierra Leone has 28,000 square miles—somewhat the same as South Carolina—and an estimated (1972) population of 2.6 million. Among the better studies on it are: John I. Clarke, ed., *Sierra Leone in Maps*, 2d ed. (London: University of London Press, 1969), 120 p.; John Barry Riddell, *The Spatial Dynamics of Modernization in Sierra Leone: Structure, Diffusion and Response* (Evanston, Ill.: Northwestern University Press, 1970), 142 p.

This is a scholarly analysis by a geographer who was in Sierra Leone in 1967. He also examined archival sources in London. The volume includes seventeen tables and thirty-four figures.

Gershon Collier, *Sierra Leone: Experiment in Democracy in an African Nation* (New York: New York University Press, 1970), 143 p. This volume is by a Sierra Leonian barrister, ambassador, minister, chief justice, who spent nearly two years at the Center for International Studies, New York University. The book contains an index and notes at the end of chapters.

John R. Cartwright, *Politics in Sierra Leone, 1947-1967* (Toronto: University of Toronto Press, 1970), 296 p.,[132] is the work of a political scientist who held a three-year appointment, between 1963 and 1966, at Fourah Bay College, the University College of Sierra Leone. He approaches his subject chronologically.

Jean M. Due and Gerald L. Karr, "Strategics and Increasing Rice Production in Sierra Leone," *African Studies Review* 16, no. 1 (April 1973): 23-71, summarizes research in the economics of rice production in Sierra Leone and then discusses four strategies for increasing rice production. "Self-sufficiency in rice production has become the central focus of the national agricultural policy as established by the government of Sierra Leone." (p. 23.) A reference in the realm of applied pastorology that may be of interest is: Darrell L. Reeck, "Transformation of Missionary Christianity in Rural Sierra Leone," *Genève-Afrique* 11, no. 2 (1972): 45-61.

BIBLIOGRAPHY

Sierra Leone is relatively well off, bibliographically. There are general retrospective bibliographies, some current bibliographies, and specialized bibliographies.

We'll start with retropective general bibliographies. (First, a minor historical note: Harry Charles Lukach and Harry Charles Luke are the same person. Anti-German feeling in Great Britain during World War I may have accounted for the change of name.)

Henry Charles Lukach, *A Bibliography of Sierra Leone with an Introductory Essay on the Origin, Character and People of the Colony* (Oxford: Clarendon Press, 1910), 144 p., is similar in arrangement to the first edition; it contains 1,103 entries. This second edition has been reprinted by Negro Universities Press. Lukach's work was continued by Geoffrey Williams, formerly at the Department of Geography of Fourah Bay College and now at Ahmadu Bello University in Zaria. See his *A Bibliography of Sierra Leone, 1925-1967* (New York: Africana Publishing Corp., 1971), 209 p.[133] Williams' work is impressive indeed; 3,047 items are arranged according to the Universal Decimal Classification. Author and geographical indexes are provided. See also his "A Note on 'A Bibliography of Sierra Leone, -1967,' " *Africana Research Bulletin* (Fourah Bay) 1, no. 4 (June 1971): 49-50

Julia Thompson, "Library Development in Sierra Leone," *Library Materials on Africa* 6, no. 3 (March 1969): 91-94, reports that Fourah Bay College had compiled a national bibliography but that it had not yet been published.

In "A Note on 'A Bibliography of Sierra Leone,' " mentioned above, Williams pleads for as full a listing of annual publications on Sierra Leone as possible. To a considerable degree this has been accomplished in an annual report prepared since 1962 by the Sierra Leone government. The most recent one on hand is *Sierra Leone Publications 1969-1971: A List of Books and Pamphlets in English Received by the Sierra Leone Library Board under the Publications (Amendment) Act 1962.* The list of fifteen pages consists of a section of "official" and "semi-official and other" publications. It is unfortunate that the law restricts deposit to publications in English. Of the three mandatory copies deposited, one goes to the national library, another to Fourah Bay College, and the third to the British Museum.

One fairly recent bibliography is: John P. Switzer, *A Bibliography of Sierra Leone, 1968-1970* (Freetown: Nyala University College Library, 1971), 49 p.[134]

Useful is Geoffrey Williams' "Current Bibliography of Sierra Leone," *Sierra Leone Geographical Journal* no. 13 (1969): 58-62, hopefully continued in later issues of that journal.

The following are a few special bibliographies pertaining to

Sierra Leone: T.L.F. Devis, "A Bibliography of Population Studies in Sierra Leone," *Africana Research Bulletin* (Fourah Bay College) 1, no. 3 (April 1971): 38-46; Greta Avery, "Bibliography of Literature in Sierra Leone," *Africana Research Bulletin* 1, no. 1 (October 1970): 46-55; Kenneth C. Wyle, "A Provisional Bibliography of Temne History with Some Comments on Methodology on the Study of a Pre-literate Culture," *Africana Research Bulletin* 1, no. 2 (January 1971): 13-26; Michael D. Jackson, "A Short Bibliography of Published Material on the Kuranko," *Africana Research Bulletin* 1, no. 4 (June 1971): 45-48.

THE GAMBIA

The Gambia is the classic example of a sovereign state resulting from the effects of colonial division, yet institutionalizing these divisions in the modern state. Gambia has an area of 4,005 square miles, somewhere in size between the states of Delaware and Connecticut, and an estimated population of 380,000 for 1972.

Percy David Gambel is the author of many linguistic works. The following important bibliography on the Gambia was compiled by him in 1959 and again in 1967: *Bibliography of the Gambia* (Bathurst: Government Printer, 1967), 153 p. This is a fine bibliography, more or less arranged according to the Dewey Decimal Classification. One important item Gamble has published since the appearance of his bibliography is "Published Charts, Maps and Town Plans of the Gambia," *Sierra Leone Studies* 23 (July 1968): 66-70.

A recent note is an undated dispatch from Bathurst by Thomas A. Johnson, "Gambia Wrestles with Problems of Underdevelopment," *New York Times* (March 4, 1973): 22.

A mini-state such as the Gambia, a member of the United Nations and the Organization of African Unity (OAU), gains from being represented in all global books of reference on Africa, such as "Gambia," in Donald George Morrison, et al., *Black Africa: A Comparative Handbook* (1972): 246-250, and "Gambia," in Colin Legum, ed., *Africa Contemporary Record* 4 (1972): B545-B551.

Florence Mahoney, a professional historian from Bathurst (now called Banjul), is at work on a history of the Gambia, which will be published by Oxford University Press in London.

LIBERIA

Liberia, another of the smaller states of West Africa, has an area of 43,000 square miles and a population estimate for 1971 of 1.5 million.

Liberia and Ethiopia are the only independent states of Africa that predate the 1960s. Liberia was in practical, though never in legal terms, a United States colony and/or protectorate.

The best studies are those by J. Gus Liebenow, a political scientist at Indiana University. See his *Liberia: The Evolution of Privilege* (Ithaca: Cornell University Press, 1969), 247 p. (Africa in the Modern World). It is an elaboration of his chapter in Gwendolen M. Carter, *African-One-Party States* (Ithaca: Cornell University Press, 1969), 325-394. Note also his chapter in: James S. Coleman and Carl G. Rosberg, eds., *Political Parties and National Integration in Tropical Africa* (Los Angeles: University of California Press, 1964), p. 448-481.

The work of another political scientist is: Thomas P. Wrubel, "Liberia: The Dynamics of Continuity," *Journal of Modern African Studies* 9, no. 2 (August 1971): 189-204.

Alfonso K. Dormu, *The Constitution of Liberia and Declaration of Independence* (New York: Exposition Press, 1970), 119 p., also lists the incumbents of principal offices of the state.

The following is a sample of detailed historical study that has only recently begun to become available: Penelope Campbell, *Maryland in Africa: The Maryland State Colonization Society, 1831-1857* (Urbana, Ill.: University of Illinois Press, 1971), 264 p.

An instance of the praise literature on the late President Tubman is: A. Doris Banks Henries, *A Biography of President William V. S. Tubman* (London: Macmillan, 1967), 180 p. The book, addressed principally to young readers, contains numerous photographs of Tubman with various heads of state. Somewhat better is: Charles Morrow Wilson, *Liberia: Black Africa in*

Microcosm (New York: Harper Row, 1971), 249 p. It contains a bibliography and an introduction by J. William Fulbright.

The *Liberian Studies Journal,* edited by Svend E. Holsoe and now published at Newark, Delaware, by the Department of Anthropology of the University of Delaware, began publication in 1968. It is the best source of information for serious scholars.

Noteworthy also are: Mary Louise Clifford, *The Land and People of Liberia* (Philadelphia: Lippincott, 1971), and Stefan von Gnielinski, ed., *Liberia in Maps* (London: University of London Press, 1972).

BIBLIOGRAPHY

Liberiana used to be rarely cited or, once cited, hard to locate in any library. The situation has improved somewhat largely as a result of Svend E. Holsoe. He has prepared: *A Study Guide for Liberia* (Development Program, African Studies Center, Boston University, October 1967), 32 p.; "A Bibliography of Liberian Government Documents," *African Studies Bulletin* 11, no. 1 (April 1968): 39-63; no. 2 (September 1968): 149-194; and *A Bibliography on Liberia* (Newark, Del.: Department of Anthropology, 1971), pt. I, Books, 123 p., pt. II, Publications Concerning Organizations, 63 p.

In part I of "Liberian Studies Research Working Paper No. 1," there are 1,078 entries arranged alphabetically. There is a subject index that also includes additional names. Part II, "Working Paper No. 3," consists of 444 entries arranged in three sections: works published by the American Colonization Society, general published material on African colonization, and colonization materials with reference to specific states. Again there is an index.

In need of a better edition is: Marvin D. Solomon and Warren L. d'Azevedo, comps., *A General Bibliography of the Republic of Liberia* (Evanston, Ill.: Northwestern University 1962), 68 p. (Northwestern University Working Papers in Social Science No. 1).

An excellent short bibliography, but dating only from 1966, is not as specialized as sponsorship might lead one to believe. John Gilissen, *Bibliographical Introduction to Legal History and Ethnology*

(Brussels: Institut de Sociologie, 1966), 19 p., is a classified bibliography of seventy-six items. Most other states of Africa have been the subject of a contribution to this looseleaf five-volume set.

LIBRARIANSHIP

There are librarians in Liberia, but many accept positions in the United States.

Liberia has probably been excessively surveyed by foreigners. One of the better works in librarianship is: Harold Lancour, *The University of Liberia Library: Report of a Survey* (Urbana, Ill., 1960), 17 p. It is a pity that the unified library system for which Lancour pleaded in this survey has not become a reality.

FRANCOPHONIC AFRICA

There are basic differences between the bibliographies and libraries of English and French-speaking Africa. One may generalize that, bibliographically, material pertaining to Francophonic Africa is not easily available anywhere. Bibliographies from or on French-speaking Africa are perhaps more scholarly than those from English-speaking Africa. The situation pertaining to school and public libraries tends to be better in predominantly English-speaking areas.

Francophonic Africa has more than its fair share of very poor, often semi- or largely desert states. The same is true of Africa's interior countries with no outlet to an ocean. A great deal of land in Africa—at one time under the French, less when under Belgian rule—remains among the world's poorest.

Nineteen political units, sovereign states at least nominally, that are members of the United Nations and the Organization of African Unity (OAU) will now be described at least sketchily. The order is largely geographical, although it is somewhat modified so that the richer and usually coastal states precede the land-locked ones. Before turning to individual countries, there are a few references that pertain to all or some parts of Francophonic West Africa. Two are: Virginia Thompson, *West Africa's Council of the*

Entente[135] (Ithaca and London: Cornell University Press, 1972), 313 p. (Africa and the Modern World), and Ronald Bornstein, "The Organization of Senegal River States," *The Journal of Modern African Studies* 10, no. 2 (July 1972): 267-283.

For a bibliography of French-speaking West Africa, see Julian Wood Witherell, comp., *French-speaking West Africa: A Guide to Official Publications* (Washington, D.C.: Library of Congress, 1967), 201 p. It lists 2,431 items. "Included are publications of the federation of French West Africa, its eight component colonies, French mandated Togo and documents of the autonomous and national government of each state. Selected documents on Togo issued by the League and the U.N. are also included . . . as is some French government material relating to the area, also material issued by the French Union, the French Community and the Organisation Commune Africaine et Malgache."

See also: Margarita Dobert, "Women in French Speaking West Africa: A Selected Guide to Civic and Political Participation in Guinea, Dahomey and Mauritania," *A Current Bibliography on African Affairs*, n.s. 3, no. 9 (September 1970): 5-21, and T. H. Bowyer, "Dahomey, Guinea, Ivory Coast, Mali, Niger, Senegal, Togo and Upper Volta," in Valerie Bloomfield, comp., *SCOLMA Conference on the Acquisition of Material from Africa* (1969) 48-52.

SENEGAL

Senegal has an area of 75,750 square miles, about that of South Dakota, with a population estimated of 4.02 million in 1971 (that of South Dakota, according to the 1970 census, was 666,247). It is situated on the West African bulge, the part of Africa that is closest to the United States. There is, in fact, nonstop air service between New York and Dakar, Senegal's capital, in just under eight hours of flying time.

Senegal has a poor resource base consisting of little beyond a surplus of peanuts. Its most important resources are its location on the African continent, with its relatively short distance to Europe and America, and perhaps its special relationship with France, which its president since independence, Leopold Sedar Senghor, has exploited to the fullest.

Leopold Sedar Senghor

Leopold Sedar Senghor has been the subject of at least three full-length biographical studies in English while still in office. The most significant is the first: Jacques Louis Hymans, *Leopold Sedar Senghor, an Intellectual Biography* (Edinburgh: University Press, 1971), 312 p.[136] Hymans is an American historian who has for some years been teaching at San Francisco State College. The two others are: Irving Leonard Markovitz, *Leopold Sedar Senghor and Politics of Negritude* (New York: Atheneum, 1969), 300 p., and Barend v.D. Van Niekerk, *The African Image (Negritude) in the Work of Leopold Sedar Senghor* (Cape Town: Balkema, 1970), 140 p.

There is, unfortunately, no bibliography or bibliographical articles of the works by and about Senghor. His main works, all published in Paris by Editions de Seuil, are *Chants d'ombre* (1945), *Hosties noires* (1948), *Ethiopiques* (1956), and *Nocturnes* (1961). *Nocturnes* is available in a translation by: John Reed and Clive Wake, *Nocturnes* (London: Heinemann Educational Books, 1969), 60 p. (African Writers Series No. 71).

Some readers may find it helpful to consult: J. Rial, "Glossaire pour servir à la lecture de L. S. Senghor," *Bulletin Trimestrel du Centre d'Etude des Problèmes Sociaux/Indigènes* (CEPSI) (Lubumbashi) no. 69 (June 1965): 27-70.

Other recent scholarly studies of Senegal are: G. Wesley Johnson, Jr., *The Emergence of Black Politics in Senegal: The Struggle for Power in the Four Communes 1900-1920* (Stanford University Press for Hoover Institution; London: Oxford University Press, 1972), and his "The Senegalaise Elite, 1900-1945," in Philip Curtin, ed., *Africa and the West* (Madison, 1972), p. 139-187.

Donal Cruise O'Brien, "Mouride Studies" (review article), *Africa* 40, no. 3 (July 1970): 257-260, discusses the Mouride brotherhood, a Sufi *tariqa* which draws its following from the Wolof of northwestern Senegal.[137]

Lucy Behrman's scholarly study, *Muslim Brotherhoods and Politics in Senegal* (Cambridge: Harvard University Press, 1970), 224 p., tackles the complex relationship between religion and politics. Rita Cruise O'Brien, *White Society in Black Africa: The French of Senegal* (London: Faber; Evanston, Ill.: Northwestern University Press, 1972), 320 p., the work of an English sociologist, analyzes the all important role of the French in Senegal. There are few studies of the expatriate communities in Africa. Walter A. E. Skurnik, *The Foreign Policy of Senegal* (Evanston, Ill.: Northwestern University Press, 1972), 308 p., is one of the few studies of the expatriate community in Africa. Skurnik, a political scientist, analyzes the factors, especially President Senghor, that have influenced Senegal's foreign policy.

Another work is Guy Pfefferman, *Industrial Labor in the Republic of Senegal* (New York: Praeger, 1968), 325 p. (Praeger Special Studies in International Economics and Development).[138]

BIBLIOGRAPHY AND LIBRARIANSHIP

The bibliographical situation for Senegal is not as poor as one would suspect from a glance at entries found in Duignan's *Guide*. Additional titles are found in: Paule Brasseur-Marion and J. F. Maurel, *Les sources bibliographiques de l'Afrique de l'Ouest et de l'Afrique Equatoriale d'Expression francaise* (Dakar: Bibliothèque de l'Université 1970), p. 70-77. This eighty-eight page publication should be on the desk of anyone concerned in any depth with Francophonic Africa.

Less recently have appeared: Rosemary Abi-Saab, "Le Senegal des Origines à l'independence, élements de bibliographie," *Genève-Afrique* 3, no. 2 (1964): 288-297; Laurence Porges, *Bibliographie des régions du Senegal* (Dakar: Ministère du Plan et du Developpement, 1967), 705 p., which includes about 3,150 items;[139] and Irving L. Markovitz, "A Bibliographical Essay on the Study of Ideology, Political Thought, Development and Politics in Senegal," *A Current Bibliography on African Affairs*, n.s. 3, no. 3 (March 1970): 5-29; 3, no. 4 (April 1970): 5-35.

Dakar has Francophonic Africa's only library school. This institution has been much described and discussed:

S. Willemin, *Senegal développement des bibliothèques* (Paris: UNESCO, 1966), 11 p. (AT/AFRICAC 4); this brief report, which only exists in French, was concerned with the development of public libraries in Senegal from 1964 to 1966. Particular attention was given to the need for library education.

T. H. Bowyer, "The University of Dakar School of Librarianship," *Library Materials on Africa* 7, no. 3 (March 1970): 62-72, was written when Bowyer was deputy librarian at the University of Birmingham and editor of *Library Materials in Africa*. He relies heavily on the *UNESCO Bulletin for Libraries*. In the present article he analyzes the curriculum of the Dakar library school in depth.

Another source is Amadou Bousso, "University of Dakar School for Librarians, Archivists and Documentalists," *UNESCO Bulletin for Libraries* 27, no. 2 (March-April 1973): 72-77, 107. Bousso is director of the school. The abstract of his article reads: "The School . . . was set up in 1967 to replace the regional centre for the training of librarians that operated in Dakar from 1963 to 1967. At present, the school provides a two-year training course in two sections: training for librarians and training for archivists. . . . Fifty-four students attended the school in 1971-72." (p. 72.)

IVORY COAST

The Ivory Coast has an area of 127,520 square miles, roughly the same as New Mexico, with a population estimate for 1971 of 4.42 million (versus 1.016 million for New Mexico). It has been much less the focus of foreign study than Senegal.

A useful overview will be found in: Victor DuBois, *Ivory Coast* (Ithaca: Cornell University Press, forthcoming), one of the series edited by G. M. Carter.

Aristide Zolberg, *One-Party Government in the Ivory Coast*, rev. ed. (Princeton: Princeton University Press, 1969), 400 p., first appeared in 1964. A more recent work is: Mireille Laporte, *La pensée sociale de Felix Houphet-Boigny* (Bordeaux: Centre d'études Afrique noire, 1970), 103 p., and Jon Woronoff, *West African Wager: Houphouet versus Nkrumah* (Metuchen, N.J.: Scarecrow Press, 1972), 357 p. (Bibliography p. 330-343). On April 6, 1957, the leader of the Ivory Coast, Felix Houphouet Boigny, made a wager with Kwame Nkrumah to see whose country would develop further over the next ten years. Woronoff hedges his answer as to who won the wager. He leans in many aspects more in the direction of Houphet as the winner.

ECONOMIC DEVELOPMENT

Suzanne Laurent, "Formation, information et developpement en Côte d'Ivoire," *Cahiers d'études Africaines* (Paris) 10, no. 3 (1970): 422-468, includes references to Ivorian newspapers and journals and their circulation. See also Albert Ley, *Le régime dominial et foncier et le développement de la Côte d'Ivoire* (Paris: Librairie générale de droit et de jurisprudence, 1972), 746 p. (Bibliothéque africaine et malgache 18).

BIBLIOGRAPHY AND LIBRARIANSHIP

None of the retrospective bibliographies is very satisfactory. Organisation de Cooperation et de Développement Economiques, Centre de Développement, *Essai d'une bibliographie de la Côte d'Ivoire* (Paris, 1964), 122 p., contains references to 254 monographs and 407 journal articles.

Philippe Bonnefond, *Esquisse bibliographique du département du Centre de le Côte-d'Ivoire* (Bouké, 1968), 49 p., is a classified bibliography in the social sciences, including particularly agriculture. There is no author index.

A current national bibliography, issued quarterly since 1969, is Côte d'Ivoire, Ministère de l'Education Nationale, *Bibliographie de la Côte d'Ivoire* (Abidjan: Bibliothequè nationale B.P. 398, 1969-). The issue for 1969 appeared in a larger format than the following two for 1970 and 1971.

Suzanne Delrieu, "La bibliothèque de l'Université d'Abidjan," *SCAUL Newsletter* no. 6 (July 1971): 9-12, is a brief, factual statement of the condition of the University of Abidjan library system as it was in 1969.

Work on a retrospective bibliography of works published in and about the Ivory Coast is in progress at the university library.[140]

MISCELLANEOUS

Christian Forlacroix, "La photographie au service de l'histoire de l'Afrique," *Cahiers d'études Africaines* 10, no. 1 (1970): 125-143, describes a collection of photographs taken by Marcel Monnier on a journey in the Ivory Coast with L. G. Binger in 1892. The collection is kept in the library of the University of Abidjan; a second collection belongs to M. Monnier's son.[141]

ARCHIVES

Note the following reports commissioned by UNESCO: J. d'Orleans, *Réorganisation et développement des archives* (Paris: UNESCO, 1971), 19 p. (2609/Rmo. RD/DBA). The expert spent February to December 1971 in the Ivory Coast. His work was continued between January and July 1972 by B. Delmas, *Archives nationales réorganisation et développement* (Paris: UNESCO, 1972), 15 p. (2750/RMO.RD/DBA).

GUINEA

Guinea has an area of 94,925 square miles, about the size of Oregon, with a population estimated at 4.1 million in 1972.[142]

The important fact differentiating Guinea from other Francophonic countries is that it was the only African country in 1958 that chose to cut all administrative ties to France.

A good general source will be: L. Gray Cowan and Victor DuBois, *Guinea* (Ithaca, N.Y.: Cornell University Press, forthcoming). Meanwhile, for French readers there is: Jean Suret-Canale, *La république de Guinea* (Paris: Editions Sociales, 1970), 423 p.[143] The bibliography of some 400 items is arranged alphabetically by author within seven broad sections.

BIBLIOGRAPHY

Two retrospective bibliographies are: Organisation de Cooperation et de Développement Economique, Centre de

Développement. *Bibliographie de la Guinée* (Paris, 1965), 46 p., and, B. Kake, *Bibliographie critique des sources imprimées d'histoire de la Guinée, publiées avant 1914* (Dakar: Université. Faculté des lettres et Sciences humaines, 1962) (Diplome d'études supérieures).[144]

The archives are rich in volume of material deposited, and at least some ten years ago held 166 cubic meters of organized documents and a further 60 cubic meters not yet organized.[145] There is at least one published guide: Damien d'Almeida, *Premier répertoire des archives nationales de Guinée serie A á Serie N, 1720-1935* (Conakry: 1962), 224 p. (République de Guinée, Memoires de l'Institut national de recherches et de documentation No. 1), Serie A: *Actes officiels,* 1720-1935; Serie B: *Correspondence générale,* 1890-1935; Serie D: *Administration générale,* 1907-1932; Serie E: *Affaires politiques,* 1896-1936; Serie N: *Affaires militaires,* 1907-1919.[146]

TOGO

Togo has an area of 21,850 square miles, about the size of West Virginia, with a population estimated at almost 2 million in 1972. The Republic of Togo is about half the size of the German colony of Togoland; the other half joined Ghana in 1960. It is a long, thin country running north-south from the Atlantic Ocean. It has a coastline of some fifty miles and stretches to the border with Upper Volta, about 330 miles to the north. A good general history of Togo is Robert Cornevin, *Histoire du Togo, 3d ed.* (Paris: Berger-Levrault, 1969), 555 p.

D. Noel and M. Santraille, "Contribution à la bibliographie du Togo" (Lomé: Direction des Etudes du Plan, Republique de Togo, 1971), 139 p. (mimeo.), contains 1,549 numbered items arranged alphabetically. There is a subject index. Locations are indicated by symbols, which are explained in Appendix 1. Appendix 3 lists the key to acronyms. See also: Raymond Guillaneuf, *La presse au Togo, 1911-1966* (Dakar: Faculté des lettres et sciences humaines, 1968), 526 p.

DAHOMEY

Dahomey, to the east of Togo, is about the same shape as Togo. It contains 43,483 square miles, much the same size as Tennessee, with a population estimated at 2.8 million in 1972. A general source is Robert Cornevin, *Le Dahomey,* 2d rev. ed. (Paris: Presses Universitaires de France, 1970), 128 p. (Collection Que sais-je? no. 1176).

Martin Staniland, "The Three Party System in Dahomey, I, 1946-1956," *Journal of African History* 14, no. 2 (1973): 291-312 is the first of two articles describing Dahomeyan political parties. Formal political parties started in 1945. The article contains almost one hundred footnotes and three tables. One of the analyses in depth is the voting for the national assembly elections in 1951. "The purpose of this and a subsequent article is to examine the creation of regionally based political parties in Dahomey and the ways in which they accommodate their tactics to a rapid expansion of the electorate from 1951 onwards."

Guillaume Da Silva, "Contribution à la bibliographie du Dahomey,"*Etudes dahoméennes* 12, tome II and III (June 1968 and January 1969) includes 4,286 items.[117] This is an alphabetical listing of over four thousand items. It also contains a broad subject index.

Institut de Recherches Appliquées de Dahomey (IRAD) *Dictionnnaire bio-bibliographique du Dahomey* (Porto-Novo: 1, 1969), 183 p., is basically a biographical dictionary of Dahomey. The entries, individually signed, include a small photograph and full bibliographical information on the publications of the subject of the biography. The remainder of the volume contains various subject arrangements.

Ernst Kohl, "Bibliographie der Zeitschriften aus Dahomey," *Afrika Archiv, Beilage zur Zeitschrift Afrika Heute* 1 (January 15, 1970): 3 p., is a checklist covering ninety-three newspapers magazines, and periodicals, including those now defunct, published in Dahomey from 1890 through 1966.[148]

Margaret Marshall, "Libraries in Dahomey," *Library World* 72, no. 847 (January 1971): 208-212.

UPPER VOLTA

Upper Volta has a land area of 105,869 square miles, similar to that of Colorado; the population for 1972 was estimated at 5.6 million.

Elliott P. Skinner, *The Mossi of Upper Volta: The Political Development of a Sudanese People* (Stanford: Stanford University Press, 1965), is written by a professor of anthropology at Columbia University, who also served as United States ambassador in Ouagadougou, the capital of Upper Volta.

Albert Salfo Balima, *Genèse de Haute-Volta* (Ougadougou: Presses Africaines, 1970), 253 p.,[149] an attractive handbook, is the work by one of Upper Volta's distinguished citizens, who has spent many years in France and the United States. It is generously illustrated with photographs.

François Djoby Bassolet, *Evolution de Haute-Volta de 1898 au 3 Janvier, 1966* (Ougadougou: Imprimerie Nationale, 1968), 135 p., is by a journalist, who was formerly director of the Information Service in Upper Volta. The book is a useful general introduction, although it is becoming a little dated.

Tiémoko Marc Garango, *Le redressement financier de la République de Haute-Volta* (Ougadougou: Presses Africaines, 1971), 98 p., is a political pamphlet by an army officer and lawyer of Upper Volta. He is mainly concerned with his government's financial administration between 1966 and 1970.

Bienvenu en Haute-Volta (Boulogne, Paris: Editions Delroisse, 1972), 128 p., was published on behalf of the Upper Volta presidency. It is beautifully illustrated with virtually no text.

Michel Izard, "Introduction a l'histoire des royaumes Mossi," *Rechercehs Voltaiques* 12, no. 3 (1970): 2 vols.[150] Izard's two volumes constitute a scholarly history of Mossi kingdoms from the fifteenth and sixteenth centuries until 1896. The author is an anthropologist who has many years of experience in Upper Volta.

Paul Ladouceur, "Voltaic Political Life," *African Studies Review* 15, no. 3 (December 1972): 521-527, is a review essay of four titles of works in Upper Volta that were published in Ougadougou.

BIBLIOGRAPHY

Françoise Izard with the collaboration of Philippe Bonnefond, *Bibliographie de la Haute Volta, 1956-1965* (Paris-Ougadougou: CNRA-CVRS, 1967), 300 p. (Recherches voltaiques No. 7), is a scholarly, classified bibliography with over fifteen hundred entries. There are separate indexes for authors, subjects, ethnic groups, languages, places, and journals cited.

Michel Cartry and Françoise Izard, "Note sur la situation de la documentation en Haute-Volta," *Notes and documents voltaiques* 1, no. 2 (January-March 1968): 9-14, clearly discusses the five documentation centers in Upper Volta. These are;

1. Department of Documentation, Centre Voltaïque de la Recherche Scientifique (CVRS);
2. The library of the Centre de Documentation et de Perfectionnement Pédagogique (CDPP);
3. The library of the Ecole Nationale d'Administration (ENA);
4. The library of the Centre Cultural Franco-Voltaîque;
5. The library of Centre Culturel Américain.

African Bibliographic Center, "French-speaking West Africa: Upper Volta Today, 1960-1967. A Selected and Introductory Bibliographical Guide" (Westport, Conn.: Negro Universities Press, 1969), 37 p. (*Special Bibliographic Series* 6, 1), is useful classified bibliography with unnumbered entries. A list of bookdealers with addresses and an author index are included.

Marcel Poussi, "Upper Volta," *Bibliography Documentation Terminology* 11, no. 6 (November 1971): 266-267, is the usually brief report published in UNESCO's bibliographical journal. This particular report was supplied by Marcel Poussi, director of the Centre Voltaîque de la Recherche Scientifique (CVRS) in 1969. Ambitious plans are announced pertaining to retrospective or current national bibliographies, though little progress is evident. Poussi sketches the low level of current development bibliographically and in Upper Volta's libraries. Yet plans are announced for subsequent volumes of retrospective bibliographies: a second volume for 1936 to 1955, a third volume from the earliest to 1935, and also a current national bibliography for 1966 and later years.

MAURITANIA

The area of Mauritania, which is largely desert or semi-desert, consists of 419,231 square miles (the size of Texas, Colorado, and Nevada combined), with a population estimated at 1.2 million for 1972.

Ursula Wolff, "Mauritania's Nomadic Society Preserves Its Lifestyle," *Africa Report* (New York) 17, no. 8 (September-October 1972): 11-16, is an entertaining, well-illustrated article, including a helpful map, "Mauritania Separates the Traveler from the Tourist," p. 40-42. Potential visitors to Mauritania will find the author's hints and addresses helpful.

The theme of Richard Westebbe, *The Economy of Mauritania* (New York: Praeger, 1971), 200 p.,[151] is the prospect and problems of development under conditions of economic dualism. The author became chief of the International Bank for Reconstruction and Development's (IBRD) technical assistance mission in 1967. The book is above all a critical examination of Mauritania's development.

Adam Heymowski, *Mauritanie, organisation de la bibliothèque nationale de Mauritanie* (Nouakchott, Paris: UNESCO, 1965), 15 p. (WS/0866.47-CLT), is followed by *Rapport concernant la bibliographie de la Mauritanie*, 5 p.

Bernard Van Maele, with the collaboration of Adam Heymowski, *Bibliographie Mauritanie*, Tome I: *Histoire, religion, géographie, sciences sociales* (Nouakchott: Ministère de l'Information et de la Culture, Ministère de la Planification et de la Recherche, République Islamique de Mauritanie, November 1971), 108 p., is a useful bibliography presented in a classified arrangement. There is no author index. Most of the references are to journal articles and reports.

MALI

Mali has a total of 464,000 square miles. It is a little larger than Mauritania, with a much larger population (estimated at 5.3 million in 1972).

Francis G. Snyder, "1. An Era Ends in Mali," *Africa Report* 14, no. 3 and 4 (March-April 1969): 16-22 (the title on top of the first page is: "The Keita Decade,") is by a graduate of Yale and Harvard Law School. He writes well about the salient features that caused the overthrow of President Keita by a military coup in 1968.

William I. Jones, "2. Economics of the Coup," *Africa Report* 14, no. 3 and 4 (March-April 1969): 23-26, 51-53, is by a specialist in Malian economics, who studied in Mali, Senegal, and at the University of Geneva. He also wrote "The Mise and Demise of Socialist Institutions in Rural Mali," *Genève-Afrique* 11, no. 2 (1972): 19-44. At the time this article was written the author was with the Economic Development Institute of the World Bank in Washington, D.C. The article contains tables and footnotes.

Nicholas S. Hopkins, *Popular Government in an African Town, Kita, Mali* (Chicago and London: University of Chicago Press, 1972), 246 p., is about Kita, a Malian town on the railroad some one hundred miles east of the capital of Bamako.[152] The author is an anthropologist who taught English in Mali in the early 1960's and did fieldwork on a National Institute of Mental Health grant during 1964-1965.

BIBLIOGRAPHY AND LIBRARIANSHIP

Paule Brasseur-Marion, *Bibliographie générale du Mali (Ancien Soudan français et Haut-Senegal-Niger)* (Dakar: IFAN, 1964), 462 p. (Catalogues et documents, 16), is a classified bibliography of 4,902 references through 1960. Many of the entries are annotated briefly. A continuation for publications from the years 1961 to 1970 is in preparation. Also note: Mme. Brasseur's "Les difficultés recontrées dans l'établissement d'une bibliographie de type national: l'example du Mali," Pearson and Jones, eds., *The Bibliography of Africa*, p. 103-112.

Harold Lancour, *Report of a Survey Mission to Mali.* 1963), 29 p., 6 p. unpublished, is a survey carried out by the former dean of the University of Pittsburgh library shcool. It deals with the possiblities of setting up a pedagogical institute which would include a strong professional education library.

I. Bekeny, *Mali, reorganisation des archives* (Paris: UNESCO, 1970), 17 (2231/BMS.RD/DBA), written by a UNESCO expert, is based on a two months' stay in Bamako near the end of 1969. The author recommends that an expert be dispatched to Bamako for two or three years, that the archives building be enlarged, and that the restoration of documents begin at once.

NIGER

Niger's area is 489,189 square miles, twice that of Texas. The population was estimated at 4.13 million in 1971.

Note Virginia Thompson, "Niger," in Gwendolen M. Carter, ed., *National Unity and Regionalism in Eight African States,* (Ithaca: Cornell University Press 1969), p. 151-230. The author starts her chapter with the statement: "Niger is the least well-known nation in former French West Africa because it lies off the beaten track of travel and has few recognized attractions." The Thompson chapter is a broad survey of Niger of the past and of recent times—at least what it was a decade ago. It is footnoted and contains a bibliography.

Pierre Donaint and François Lancrenon, *Le Niger* (Paris: Presses Universitaires de France, 1972), 128 p. (Que-sais-je? no. 1461), is in a pocket-size format. It attempts to cover all influences on contemporary leaders in Niger, especially socioeconomic questions. The short bibliography merely cites some of the sources, all of them written in French.

Finn Fuglestad, "Djibo Bakary, the French and the Referendum of 1958 in Niger," *Journal of African History* 14 no. 2 (1973): 313-330, is a study of the reasons why Djibo Bakary voted "No," as Sekou Touré did in 1958, and the causes of Bakary's failure.

Leo F. Van Hoey, "The Coercive Process of Urbanization: The Case of Niger," in Scott A . Greer, et al., *The New Urbanization* (New York: St. Martin's Press, 1968), p. 15-32, is concerned with the social process that results in the concentration of masses of people in one place. The study of Niger is used to evaluate theories of urbanization. For greater detail see Van Hoey's dissertation: "Emergent Urbanization: Implications of the Theory of social scale verified in Niger, West Africa" (Northwestern University, 1966), 218 leaves.

Centre nigérien de recherches en sciences humaines, *Bibliographie sommaire de la republique du Niger* (Niamey, 1970), 50 leaves, is in one alphabetical sequence. It includes references to monographs and articles in learned journals. All entries, except for the reference to Thompson's chapter, are in French.

The next five states are in what was once known as French Equatorial Africa.

CHAD

The area of Chad is 495,753 square miles. In 1971, its population was estimated at 3.8 million.

Harold D. Nelson, et al., *Area Handbook for Chad* (Washington, D.C.: U. S. Government Printing Office, 1972), 261 p., is one of a series of handbooks "designed to be useful to military and other personnel who need a convenient compilation of basic facts about the social, economic, political, and military institutions and practices of various countries." (Foreword, p. iii.) As these books tend to be revised periodically, they fulfilled their aim. This book is certainly the best start, in English, for someone who wants to learn about Chad.

Tchad: Une Néo-Colonie (Paris: Editions Git-le-Coeur, 28 Rue Geoffrey Saint-Hilaire, 152, Paris V, 1972), 176 p., is written from the point of view of the Chad National Liberation Front which has been fighting the Chad government for many years. The author is anonymous.

Georges Diguimbaye and Robert Langue, *L'essor du Tchad* (Paris: Presses Universitaires de France, 1969), 440 p., is by the minister for Chad's development plan and one of his associates. It is a broadly conceived socioeconomic study in historical perspective. The book includes a full bibliography, a key to abbreviations, numerous photographs, tables, and plans.

Philippe Decraene, "Chad at World's End," *Africa Report* 13, no. 1 (January 1968): 54-58, is the translation of an article that originally appeared in *Le Monde.* It is by the newspaper's sub-Saharan correspondent. It gives basic information that one should also find in a good encyclopaedia.

Jacqueline Moreau and Danielle Stordeur, *Bibliographie du Tchad* (sciences humaines, Etudes et documents tchadiens, Series A, no. 5), 2d ed. (Fort-Lamy: Institut National Tchadien pour les Sciences Humaines, 1970), 353 p., contains more than 2,400 numbered items arranged alphabetically. The sources are indicated, and separate lists of maps, phonograph records, and films are included. The final section is a subject index.

"Chad," *Bibliography Documentation Terminology* 12, no. 6 (Novermber 1972): 284-285, is based on information, supplied in 1970, by Jean-Paul Lebeuf, director of the Institut National Tchadien pour les Sciences Humaines. He lists fourteen publications on Chad, including one bibliography and an atlas.

See also "Présentation du fichier éthnique du C.A.R.D.A.N. et du projet de publication de l'inventaire provisoire des populations du Tchad," 'Notes and News,' *Africa* 38, no. 2 (April 1968): 204-208.

ARCHIVES

Institut national tchadien pour les sciences humaines (INTSC), *Documents d'archives (Tchad, Nigeria, Niger)* (Fort-Lamy: UN-ESCO, 1968), 180 p. (Etudes et documents tchadiens, series B, no. 1), was compiled by Jean Chapelle. It has not been seen by the present writer.

CENTRAL AFRICAN REPUBLIC (CAR)

The area of CAR is about 238,000 square miles. The population estimate for 1972 was between 1.5 million and 2 million.

As may be expected, sources about the CAR are scarce. Much of the data and descriptions are embedded in a discussion of several related countries. In colonial times, CAR was known as Ubangi-Shari (spelled "Oubangi" in French).

R. De Bayle des Hermens, "Quelques aspects de la préhistoire en République Centrafricaine," *Journal of African History* 12, no. 4 (1971): 579-597, is a thoroughly documented account.

Pierre Kalck, *Central African Republic: A Failure in Decolonisation* (London: Pall Mall, 1971), 206 p. (Praeger Library of African Affairs),[153] claims that CAR lies in the least known region in the world. His book is a broad useful account to which are appended notes and references and a bibliography.

Richard West, "Bokassa the Tyrant," *New Statesman* 84, no. 2160 (August 11, 1972), 182, is hardly an attractive portrait.

BIBLIOGRAPHY AND LIBRARIANSHIP

Publications from the CAR continue to be listed in the *Bibliographie de la France.*[154] See Edouard Reitman, *Republique centrafricaine, organisation de bibliothèques* (Paris: UNESCO, 1967) 42 p. (WSO367.97-CLT).

CAMEROON

Cameroon's area is about 183,581 square miles. The population estimate for 1973 was 6 million.

"Kamerun" was a German colony which was divided between the British and the French after World War I. The northern part of British Cameroons joined Nigeria and the southern became part of the Federation of Cameroon.

Willard R. Johnson, *The Cameroon Federation: Political Integration in a Fragmentary Society* (Princeton: Princeton University Press, 1970), 426 p.,[155] an excellent in-depth study, is by a political scientist on the faculty of the Massachusetts Institute of Technology. He is concerned with the question of political integration in the theoretical as well as real world. The bibliography is an exceptionally full one in spite of the fact that it does not include all documents cited in the footnotes.

Victor T. LeVine, *The Cameroon Federal Republic* (Ithaca and London: Cornell University Press, 1971), 205 p. (Africa in the Modern World), includes the subtitle "From Mandate to Independence." The book's main focus is on the French colonial experience of Cameroun from 1916 to 1960. The author is a political scientist who has adopted an essentially historical approach.

Neville Rubin, *Cameroun, an African Federation* (London: Pall Mall, 1971), 259 p. (Library of African Affairs),[156] is the work of a law school professor. He attempts (1) to trace the process which led to the formation of the Federal Republic of Cameroon; and (2) to outline the institutions and policies that have been created in its first ten years of independence.

Robert Brain, *Bangwa Kinship and Marriage* (Cambridge University Press, 1972), 195 p.,[157] is by an anthropologist who makes a solid contribution to Bamilike studies. (The Bangwa are a people who live in the western part of Cameroun not far from Douala.

BIBLIOGRAPHY

Martin Njikam, "Quelques sources bibliographiques de Cameroun," in Pearson and Jones *The Bibliography of Africa* (New York: African Publishing Corp., 1970), p.113-119.

Victor T. LeVine, "Introduction to the Study of Cameroon: A Bibliographic Essay," *Journal of Cameroon Affairs* (Yaoundé) 1, no. 2 (March-June 1972): 4-10, is in the journal of the Cameroon Students Association of Arts and Sciences. The editor of the journal may still be a student at Juniata College, Hungtingdon, Pa. 16652.

Max F. Dippold, *Une bibliographie du Cameroun, les écrits en langue allemade* (Yaoundé; Editions Clé, 1972), 343 p., presents 6,266 references arranged in a classified manner. They cover the period 1624 to 1968, but the concentration is on the colonial period. There is an author and subject index.

GABON

Gabon's area is 102,089 square miles (about the size of Colorado). Its population estimate for 1970 was 500,000.

Gabon is associated in the eyes of many, particularly non-Africans, with the work of the late Albert Schweitzer (1875-1965), the Alsation philosopher, theologian and mission doctor, who worked in Lambaréné on the River Ogooue.

Brian G. Weinstein, *Gabon: Nation-building on the Ogoou* (Cambridge, Mass.: MIT Press, 1966), 287 p., is an excellent book with an unusually full bibliography.[158]

Charles F. and Alice B. Darlington, *African Betrayal* (New York: David McKay, 1968), 359 p., describes neocolonialism in Gabon as seen by the former United States ambassador to that country.

Another source is Jacqueline Bouquerel, *Le Gabon* (Paris: Presses Universitaires, 1970), 127 p. (Que-sais-je? 633).

BIBLIOGRAPHY

Claude Perrot, "Le Gabon: Repertoire relatif aux sciences humaines" (Paris: Bureau pour le développement de le production agricole (BDPA) 1962), 40 p. (mimeo.), is a classified bibliography of 333 numbered items with an author index.

Françoise Perrois, *Le Gabon: Répertoire bibliographique des études de sciences humaines, 1960-1967* (Libreville: L'Office de la recherche scientifique et technique, Outre-Mer, 1969), 58 p., contains 229 numbered items, some annotated. They are arranged in a classified manner, with the classification presented and used as an index. There is also an author index.

Zoe Draquet, *Gabon: Repertoire bibliographique des études de sciences humaines (1967-1970)* (Libreville: ORSTOM, 1971), 33 p., has 167 numbered items arranged alphabetically; a few are annotated, and there is an author index. The CARDAN classification is indicated as in the earlier volume by Perrois, cited above.

CONGO (BRAZZAVILLE)

The People's Republic of Congo is the former French Congo that lies to the northwest of Zaïre. The area is 132,046 square miles, comparable in size to Montana. The Congo had a population as estimated by the United Nations for 1971, of 960,000 (compared to Montana's population of 694,409 in 1970).

Sources include Gordon C. McDonald, et al., *Area Handbook for the People's Republic of the Congo* (Congo Brazzaville) (Washington, D.C.: Foriegn Area Studies, American University, 1971), 255 p. (Pamphlet No. 550-91); and Georges Balandier, *The Sociology of Black Africa: Social Dynamics in Central Africa*, trans. Douglas Garman (London: André Deutsch; New York: Praeger, 1970), 540 p.

René Gauze, *The Politics of Congo-Brazzaville* was translated, edited, and supplemented by Virginia Thompson and Richard Adloff (Stanford, Calif.: Stanford University, Hoover Institution Press, 1973), 283 p. The original manuscript from which the major part of this book was translated comprised 739 pages. All the sections not dealing with Congo-Brazzaville were eliminated. Gauze has worked throughout the former French colonial empire, and was in Congo-Brazzaville until mid-1961. He finished his manuscript in 1963. The translators have added a hundred-page supplement covering the 1962 to 1972 decade.

See also Christian Comeliau, *Conditions de la planification du développement: L'example du Congo* (The Hague: Mouton, 1970), 369 p. (Récherches africaines no. 7).

BIBLIOGRAPHY, LIBRARIANSHIP, AND ARCHIVES

U. Perrot and H. Sauvalie, *Republique de Congo-Brazzaville Repertoire bibliographiques* (Paris: BDPA, 1965), 112 p., contains 867 entries arranged by subject; there is an author index. The work is based on sources in Paris. The book is flawed by many omissions.

André Jacquot, "Catalogue de publication et rapports du service des sciences humaines, (1948-1967)" (Brazzaville: ORSTOM, September 1968), 91 p. (mimeo.), contains only forty-seven entries. The bibliography is strong on method of collection and classification of the rather small amount of material discovered.

Susan Lauffer, *Bibliography on Party Politics in Congo-Brazzaville, 1950-1962* (Evanston, Ill.: Northwestern University, International Comparative Political Parties Project, 1968), 13 p. (ICPP Bibliography Series No. 7. 1), is a computer generated by-product of the comparative political parties project conducted by Kenneth Janda. Most of the references refer to works not restricted to Congo-Brazzaville, let alone political parties therein.

Roger Abel Samba, "Libraries in the People's Republic of the Congo," *UNESCO Bulletin for Libraries* 25, no. 4 (July-August 1971): 212-216, 220, describes the poor library situation that now exists (and is likely to continue) in the Congo.

J. Valette, *République populaire du Congo: La mise sur pied d'un service national d'archives* (Paris: UNESCO, 1972), 29 p. (2718/RMO.RD/DBA), is another source available.

ZAIRE

The Democratic Republic of Congo changed its name to Zaïre on October 27, 1971. Its area is 905,328 square miles (comparable to Alaska, Texas, and Colorado), and according to a United Nations estimate for 1972, the population totals 22.9 million.

As Peter Duignan's *Guide* provides ample references to Zaïre and its colonial predecessors, this section will be restricted to more recent contributions.

Robert Cornevin, *Histoire du Congo, Leopoldville-Kinshasa des origines préhistoriques à la République démocratique du Congo*, 3d ed. (Paris: Berger-Levrault, 1970), 391 p. (Collection monde d'outre mer, Ser. Histoire) includes an eighteen-page bibliography (p. 353 to p. 370). See also the author's *Le Zaïre* (Paris, Presses Universitaire de France, 1972), 128 p. (Que sais-je? No. 1489) and "Chronique de l'histoire d'outre mer. Le Congo-Kinshasa." (République démocratique du Congo), *Revue française de l'histoire d'outre mer* 56, no. 203 (1969): 164-183.

Benoit Verhaegen, *Rébellions au Congo*, Brussels: Centre de Récherche et d'information Socio-Politiques (CRISP) vol. 1, 1966, 568 p., vol. 2, 1969, 830 p. CRISP is a Belgian/Zairean research organization that has published a large volume of primary documentation, including analysis of data. The volumes are for those who desire a thorough understanding of the Congo, as it was called in the 1960s.

PATRICE LUMUMBA

Jean Van Lierde, *Lumumba Speaks: The Speeches and Writings of Patrice Lumumba,* trans., Helen Lane, with an introduction by Jean-Paul Sartre (Boston: Little Brown 1972), 433 p.,[159] is perhaps the most important compilation of Patrice Lumumba's speeches and writing covering the December 1958 to November 1960 period.

Thomas Kanza, *Conflict in the Congo: The Rise and Fall of Lumumba,* trans. from the French (Harmondsworth, Middlesex, Baltimore, Md.: Penguin Books, 1972), 436 p. (Penguin African Library),[160] traces the history of Lumumba's part in the liberation of the Congo, now Zaïre, and the struggle to create a viable government which was undermined by imperialist forces. Kanza was a close friend of Lumumba and a minister in his government.

Robert Govender, *The Martyrdom of Patrice Lumumba* (London: Neillgs, 1972), 265 p.,[161] is another recent work on Lumumba. It has not been possible to obtain a copy of it, however. The publisher's address is not generally known.

Wyatt MacGaffey, *Custom and Government in the Lower Congo* (Berkeley and London: University of California Press, 1970), 321 p.,[162] is the work of an anthropologist who studied a village well known by outsiders in the nineteenth century: Mbanza Manteke, near Kinshasa. MacGaffey described the social organization of the village and also *la coutûme,* the received idea of traditional government.

Finally, see John J. Putnam, photographs by the late Eliot Elisofon, "Yesterday's Congo, Today's Zaïre," *National Geographic* 143, no. 3 (March 1973): 398-432.

BIBLIOGRAPHY AND LIBRARIANSHIP

Bibliographies include: Edouard Bustin, *A Study Guide for Congo-Kinshasa* (Boston: Development Program, African Studies Center, Boston University, 1970), 167 p., and his *Congo-Kinshasa:*

Guide Bibliographique (Brussels: Centre d'études et documentation africaine, 1971), 2 vols. (Cahier du CEDAF 3, 4). "Zaïre," *Bibliography Documentation Terminology*, 12, no. 6 (November 1972): 318-319.

The following appears three times a year: *Bibliographie nationale des publications congolaises ou relatives a le RDC acquises par le Bibliothéque Nationale Kinshasa Kaline, Ministère de la culture et des arts, Direction des archives et bibliothèques.*

Max Liniger-Gaumaz, *Préhistoire et protohistoire de la Règublique democratique du Congo: Bibliographie* (Geneva: Editions du Temps, 1969), 64 p., presents 329 items alphabetically, and contains numerous indexes. See also the compiler's *Villes et Problèmes Urbains de la Republique Democratique du Congo, Bibliographie* (Geneva: Editions du Temps, 1968), 86 p.; this work is presented in a classified arrangement by form.

Another source is Marcel Boogaerts, *Bibliographien zu Erziehung Politik and Geschichte im Kongo-Kinshasa* (Bielefeld: Bertelsmann, 1969), 169 p. (Materialien des Arnold-Bergstraesser Instituts fur kulturwissenschaftliche Forschung, 25). The table of contents is given in three languages: German, English, and French.

For an attempt to penetrate the voluminous archival resources of Zaïre available through a combination of entrepreneurial factors found in Belgium and the Netherlands (only the office is in Switzerland), see: "The Congo Kinshasa Microfiche Project," *Africa* (London) 41, no. 3 (July 1971): p. 249, and "Centre d'études et de la documentation africaines (CEDAF), Brussels," *Africa* 40, no. 4 (October 1970): p. 374. Under the editorship of Benoit Verhaegen, the Inter-Documentation Company (IDC) of Zug, Switzerland, according to a 1970 sales catalog, can provide: Monographs (twenty of them), newspapers (also on microfiche), government publications, specific documentation, and bibliographies, including: Frederick Starr, *Bibliography of Congo Languages,* (Chicago, 1908), 9 p.; Alphonse-Jules Wauters, *Bibliographie du Congo, 1880-1895* (1895), 356 p.; and Theodore Heyse, *Documentation générale sur le Congo et le Ruanda-Urundi, 1953-1955* (Brussels, 1956), 56 p. All the IDC Africa items, and much more, are available on loan from CAMP in Chicago and from other institutions.

RWAKDA

The area of Rwanda is 10,166 square miles (a size between Vermont and Maryland). According to the United Nations estimate for 1972, its population was 3.83 million, which was just about the 1970 population of Maryland.

The country is not easily visible on most of the poor and frequently too old maps of Africa. Rwanda lies between Zaïre and Uganda, north of Burundi. First a reference to the two countries: René Lemarchand, *Rwanda and Burundi* (London: Pall Mall, 1970), 562 p.[163]

American University, Washington, D.C., *Area Handbook for Rwanda* (Foreign Area Studies Division, American University, 1969), 212 p., describes the socioeconomic and political aspects of Rwanda, based on a thorough examination of the literature. The senior of the six co-authors of this volume is Richard F. Nyrop. Research and writing were completed in April 1969 and the book was published in November of the same year.

Baudouin Paternostre de la Mirien, *Le Rwanda, son effort de développement; Antécédents historiques et conquètes de la révolution rwandaise* (Brussels: Editions A. de Boeck; Kigali: Editions Rwandaises, 1972), 413 p., is an attractive volume with numerous fine photographs and is documented with footnotes.

Augustin Gatera, "Les sources de l'histoire africaine: example du Rwanda," *Présence Africaine* no. 80 (4th quarter 1971): 73-90, is an essay helpful for those wanting to explore Rwanda's history.

Université nationale du Rwanda, "Fichier topographique de la collection rwandaise à la bibliothèque nationale du Rwanda," 1 (June 1969), 202 p., 2 (October 1969): 49 p. (mimeographed on one side of the page only), has entries arranged according to the Dewey Decimal Classification. As there are four entries per page, each measuring 3 by 5″, more than eight hundred entries comprise this bibliography's first issue, and almost two hundred are in the second issue.

BURUNDI

Burundi's area is 10,747 square miles—a little larger than Rwanda's—and the population estimate for 1972 was 3.42 million, somewhat less than Rwanda's. The country lies south of Rwanda to the west of Tanzania, along Lake Tanganyika. The capital is Bujumbura.

Gordon C. McDonald, et al., *Area Handbook for Burundi* (Washington, D.C.: U.S. Government Printing Office, 1969), 203 p., follows the standard format for area handbooks, making it a good base-line study for 1969. McDonald had four co-authors for this project.

Of general interest is Terence Nsanze, *L'édification de la République de Burundi au carrefour de l'Afrique* (Brussels: Editions Remarques Africaines, 1970), 156 p. (Collection Etudes Africaines no. 15).

The following bibliography was submitted by its compiler to obtain his library diploma in Geneva: Simon Nahayo, *Contribution à la bibliographie des ouvrages relatifs au Burundi (Afrique centrale)* (Geneva, 1971), 68 p. (Travail presenté à l'Institut d'études sociales de Genève, Ecole des bibliothecaires, en vue de l'obtention du diplome), "Contribution à la bibliographie des ouvrages relatifs au Burundi (Afrique Centrale)" *Genève-Afrique* 10, no. 1 (1971): 92-99; 10, no. 2 (1971): 100-111; 11, no. 1 (1972): 94-104. The arrangement is a classified one without an author index. The piece submitted for the diploma contained annotations. The three articles in *Genève-Afrique* have the same entries in the same arrangement, without annotation.

H. Mununi, "Bibliothèque centrale de l'Université officielle de Bujumbura (Burundi)," *SCAUL Newsletter* no. 6 (1971): 15-19, represents a basic introduction to this small university library, which in 1971 contained only 29,000 volumes and 400 periodical titles.

Occasionally *The New York Times* carries a dispatch of Agence France Presse from Bujumbura, such as the one accusing neighboring Rwanda of exterminating part of its Tutsi population.[164]

MADAGASCAR (MALAGASY REPUBLIC)

The area of Madagascar is 228,000 square miles (smaller than Texas but larger than California), and the United Nations population estimate for 1972 was 7.7 million. The Malagasy Republic is the world's fourth largest island. Its inclusion for discussion in a volume on Africa can be justified on political and ethnic grounds.

Hubert Deschamps, *Histoire de Madagascar* (Paris: Berger-Levrault, 4th ed. 1972), 358 p., is the standard scholarly history of Madagascar, complete with photographs and bibliography.

Charles Cadoux, *La république Malgache* (Paris: Berger-Levrault, 1969), 125 p., is a socioeconomic, legal, and political study. Some documents are reproduced.

Nigel Hesseltine, *Madagascar* (London: Pall Mall; New York: Praeger, 1971), 334 p. (Library of African Affairs), is a good study by an agronomist and economist who has lived in Madagascar for more than ten years. He has written about Malagasy history, politics, and the economy, including prospects for development.

Raymond K. Kent, *Early Kingdoms in Madagascar, 1500-1700* (New York: Holt, Rinehart and Winston, 1970), 336 p.,[165] attempts to trace early Malagasy history using both printed sources, manuscripts, and oral informants.

Raymond Decary, "Chronique de l'histoire d'outre-mer. Madagascar (1961-1966)," *Revue française de l'histoire d'outre-mer* 55 (1968): 106-133, is a scholarly article containing numerous footnotes.

See also Michel Massiot, *L'Administration publique à Madagascar, Evolution de l'Organisation administrative Territoriale de Madagascar de 1896 a la Proclamation de la République Malgache* (Paris: Pichin et Durand-Auzias, 1971), 472 p.

BIBLIOGRAPHY AND LIBRARIANSHIP

Jean Valette, "Basic Bibliography on Madagascar," *Journal of Modern African Studies* 7, no. 2 (July 1969): 337-342, provides a useful basic list of sources for the student of Madagascar. Valette is with the Service des Archives et de la documentation de la République Malgache, Tananarive. This is a classified list with annotation. Books "at present" unobtainable were omitted from the list.

M. S. deNucé, "La bibliographie nationale à Madagascar," in Pearson and Jones, *Bibliography of Africa* (1970), p. 120-125, discusses questions pertaining to the compilation of the annual Malagasy bibliography. The article is based only on the volume for 1964 which, like succeeding volumes, lists all types of publications from, as well as on, Madagascar.

Jean Fontvieille, comp., *Bibliographie nationale de Madagascar, 1956-1963* (Tananarive, 1971), 511 p., is by the former university librarian of Madagascar. This work updates the Grandidier Madagascar Bibliography. The Grandidiers, Guillaume and Alfred (father and son) prepared the monumental *Bibliographie de Madagascar, 1905-1955*, 3 vols.

A current annual bibliography available from 1964 on is: *Bibliographie Annuelle de Madagascar* (Tananarive: Bibliothèque Universitaire et Bibliothèque Nationale). All of these bibliographies present numbered entries in a classified manner, with author indexes.

Bibliothèque nationale, Paris, *Catalogue des periodiques par langues et pays,* Tome I: *Périodiques malgaches de la Bibliothèque Nationale* par Jean-Claude Poitelon, Germaine Razafintsalama and Rasoahanta Randrianarivels (Paris: La Bibliothéque, 1970), 200 p.

Finally, see M. S. deNucé, "Les nouvelles installations de la bibliotheque Universitaire de Madagascar," *Bulletin des bibliothéques de France* 14, no. 12 (December 1969): 503-512.

MAURITIUS

Mauritius's area is 720 square miles (about half the size of Rhode Island); its population was estimated at 840,000 in 1972. The island, a sovereign state since March 1968, lies 550 miles east of Madagascar.

Little can be added to the good treatment the crowded island received in Duignan's *Guide*, except: Auguste Toussaint, *Histoire de l'Ile Maurice* (Paris: Presses Universitaires, 1971), 128 p. (Que sais-je? no. 1449) The author is the long-time archivist, librarian, and writer on Mauritius. This small volume gives a good survey of the island's past history.

H. Hannam, "Mauritius and Seychelles," in Valerie Bloomfield, *SCOLMA Conference on the Acquisition of Material from Africa* (1969), p. 118-119. There is an exchange agreement between the Foreign and Commonwealth Office and Mauritius for equivalent values of publication. The output of Mauritius publishers is recorded in the quarterly "Memorandum of Books Printed in Mauritius and Registered in the Archives Office" which appears in the *Mauritius Gazette.*

REPUBLIC OF SOUTH AFRICA

The Republic of South Africa has 472,359 square miles, slightly less than Niger or Mali, with a population estimated by the United Nations in 1972 to be almost 23 million. The population can be broken down into five groups: African (Zulu, Khosa, Sotho, and others), 16.25 million; Afrikaans, 2.5 million; colored people of mixed ancestry, 2.0 million; English-speaking, 1.5 million; and Asians, mainly Indian, 0.66 million.[166]

Writing about South Africa is perhaps more difficult than about other parts of the continent. First of all, there is an abundance of publications, even bibliographies that offer access to a vast amount of literature. More importantly, it is difficult to discuss dispassionately what is to varying degrees a wicked colonial situation.

Once again, the references cited will merely supplement and update those found in Duignan's *Guide.* For South Africa, Duignan rested heavily on the work of Reuben Musiker, who has recently been appointed university librarian at the University of Witwatersrand in Johannesburg. Musiker has written widely on South African bibliography. Particularly noteworthy are *Guide to South African Reference Books,* 5th ed. (Cape Town: Balkema,

1971), 138 p., and *South African Bibliography* (London: Crosby Lockwood; Hamden, Conn.: Anchor Books, 1970), 105 p. As is well known, much of the literature pertaining to South Africa is either unavailable in South Africa, or is otherwise restricted. Note particularly: Betty Lunn. "From Whitest Africa—A Dark Tale of Censorship," *Library Journal* 95, no. 2 (January 15, 1970): 131-133.

An interesting document is: South Africa, *Commission of Enquiry in Regard to Undesirable Publications* (Pretoria: The Government Printer, 1957), 285 p.[167] This may be a negative approach to the study of writings about South Africa. Censorship is so important in the Republic of South Africa, however, that it has to be mentioned at the outset and not merely treated as a residual matter.

HISTORY

While not everything of a historical nature about South Africa pertains to race, a great deal of it does.

A good introduction is: Leopold Marquard, *The People and Policies of South Africa*, 4th ed. (London: Oxford University Press, 1969), 266 p. Another book by the same author is *A Federation of Southern Africa* (London: Oxford University Press, 1971), 142 p. These are the views of an enlightened Afrikaner.[168]

The following works, a motley array, are only partially the work of professional historians, such as the first: Monica Wilson and Leonard Thompson, eds., *The Oxford History of South Africa* (Oxford: Clarendon Press, 1969, 1971), Vol 2.[169] This is the standard history of South Africa. Volume 1 covers the period up to 1870 and volume 2 from 1870 to 1966. There are individual authors for each chapter. When this work was first published, Leo Kuper's essay in volume two, "African Nationalism in South Africa," was omitted from copies destined for South Africa. More recently the complete volume has been admitted. One should perhaps note that the senior editor is professor of anthropology at the School of African Studies, University of Cape Town. The other editor is a historian from South Africa now teaching at Yale.

Shula Marks, "Khoisan Resistance to the Dutch in the

Seventeenth and Eighteenth Centuries," *Journal of African History* 13, no. 1 (1972): 55-80, is by a historian at the School of Oriental and African Studies and the Institute of Commonwealth Studies, both of the University of London. Dr. Marks is also an editor of the *Journal of African History*. His excellent article documents the stereotype of the Bushman and Hottentot as willing to accept the colonizing Dutch as incorrect. Like other colonized people the Khoisan people fought their oppressors.

Another work is: David Welsh, *The Roots of Segregation: Native Policy in Colonial Natal, 1845-1910* (Cape Town: Oxford University Press, 1971), 381 p.[170] The closing words of Monica Wilson's foreword to the Welsh volume are: "The width of the author's interests makes this book worth careful attention. It throws light on current issues in government, law, economic policy, and education in Africa generally."

Ronald Hyam, *The Failure of South African Expansion, 1908-1948* (London: MacMillan; New York: Africana Publishing Corp., 1972), 219 p., is an interim report by a professional historian. A final report cannot come for many more years. The interim report is well written and documented with references, maps, and photographs.

Edgar Harry Brookes, *Apartheid, A Documentary Study of Modern South Africa* (London: Routledge and Kegan Paul, 1968), 228 p. This work is a carefully documented explanation of the doctrine of apartheid. Parts I, II, and III deal with the meaning of apartheid for all of South Africa; IV, V, and VI concentrate on its implication for education and the churches; and Parts VII, VIII, and IX demonstrate the social consequences of apartheid doctrine.

Margaret Ballinger, *From Union to Apartheid: A Trek to Isolation* (New York: Praeger, 1969), 499 p., is a discussion of African representation in the South African Parliament for twenty-three years, until 1960. After all African representation was abolished in 1960, the author spent a year at Nuffield College, Oxford University, writing about her experience. Her references are largely to government documents, particularly issues of *Hansard*.

The aim of Alexander Hepple, *South Africa, A Political and*

Economic History (New York: Praeger, 1966), 282 p., according to its preface, was "to set out a simple account of the historical background of South African society, as a guide to current events in that country." The author succeeded admirably in his purpose.

D. Hobart Houghton and Jennifer Dagut, *Source Material on the Southern African Economy, 1860-1970* (Cape Town: Oxford University Press, 1972), 3 vols.,[171] is arranged by broad subject and then geographically and chronologically. The senior editor of these volumes was the professor of economics at Rhodes University. The documents were well selected. The originals are practically unavailable outside South Africa.

Thomas Karis and Gwendolen Carter, eds., *From Protest to Challenge: A Documentary History of African Politics in South Africa, 1882-1964* (Stanford: Hoover Institution Press, 1972), 378 p., are the first two volumes of the long-awaited three, or possibly four, volumes of the history of South African African nationalism and related phenomena. A wide variety of publications are presented, usually in extract form. As these volumes show, African nationalism in South Africa goes back almost a hundred years.[172]

Two political scientists of a historical persuasion are: Donovan Williams, "African Nationalism in South Africa: Origins and Problems," *Journal of African History* 11, no. 3 (1970): 371-383, and Peter Walshe, *The Rise of African Nationalsim in South Africa, 1917-1952* (Berkeley: University of California Press, 1971), 480 p.[173]

The excellent volumes of the Penguin African series edited by Ronald Segal deserve very special mention. Regrettably, they are not permitted to be imported into South Africa. Those pertaining to South Africa follow. Govan Mbeki, author of *South Africa, The Peasants' Revolt* (1964), 156 p., is serving a life sentence on Robben Island, off Cape Town. Brian Bunting, author of *The Rise of the South African Reich,* rev. ed. (1969), 552 p., was a South African journalist; he had to leave his native country and now works in London.

Mary Benson, *South Africa: The Struggle for a Birthright* (1966), 314 p., was first published as *The African Patriots* in 1963. See also H. Jack Simon and Ray Simon, *Class and Colour in South Africa, 1850-1950* (1969), 702 p.

Also of value is: Cosmos Desmond, *The Discarded People: An Account of African Resettlement in South Africa,* 3d ed. (Braamfontein, Transvaal: Christian Institute of South Africa, 1970), 268 p., and the Penguin edition (1971).

LABOR

Sheila T. Van der Horst, *Native Labour in South Africa* (London: Frank Cass, 1971), 340 p., was first published by Oxford University Press in 1942.[174] Because the situation it depicts has not basically changed, the book well deserves being reprinted and read.

In *Labour in the South African Gold Mines, 1911-1969* (Cambridge University Press, 1972), 218 p. (African Studies Series No. 6), Francis Wilson, an economic historian, demonstrates that African real wages may be lower now than they were in 1911.[175]

Francis Wilson, *Migrant Labour in South Africa* (Johannesburg: The South African Council of Churches and SPRO-CAS, 1972), 281 p., is an economic, historical exploration of the nature and causes of migrant labor, with emphasis on its effects on laborers in mining, agricultural, and industrial centers. The author is concerned with internal as well as foreign migrants. He musters effective evidence against the system.

See also Muriel Horrell, *African Reserves of South Africa* (Johannesburg: South African Institute of Race Relations, 1969), 142 p.; Harold Wolpe, "Capitalism and Cheap Labour Power in South Africa: From Segregation to Apartheid," *Economy and Society* (London) 1, no. 4 (November 1972): 425-456; Colin Bundy, "Vorster's Restless Slaves," *New Statesman* (London) 85, no. 2187 (February 16, 1973): 228; and Adrian Guelke, and Stanley Siebert, "South Africa's Starving Work Force" *New Statesman* 85, no. 2192 (March 23, 1973): 407-409.

RACE RELATIONS, APARTHEID, AND GENERAL BACKGROUND

The preface of Irving Kaplan, et al., *Area Handbook for the*

Republic of South Africa (Washington, D.C.: U.S. Government Printing Office, 1971), 844 p., notes: "This book, based on a wide sampling of the many published sources, attempts to provide in compact, convenient, and balanced form an exposition and analysis of the dominant social, political, and economic features of South African society." This aim has been largely achieved.

Bridglal Pachai, *The International Aspects of the South African Indian Question 1860-1971* (Cape Town: C. Struik, 1971), 318 p., is based on a dissertation at the University of Natal, done under the supervision of Professor Edgar Brookes. It was published while the author was teaching at the University of Malawi. The text is clear. It is supported by ample documentation and an excellent bibliography. The dedication reads: "To my parents, and the humble village of Umbulwana on the outskirts of Lodgsmith which is my South African birthplace and home."

Gwendolen Carter, M. Thomas Karis, and Newell M. Stultz, *South Africa's Transkei: The Politics of Domestic Colonialism* (Evanston, Ill.: Northwestern University Press, 1967), 200 p. (Northwestern University African Studies No. 19), is a significant study by three political scientists who have specialized in Southern Africa. Their work is based on published documents and fieldwork. Note also Gwendolen M. Carter, *Southern Africa, Prospects for Change,* New York: Foreign Policy Association, 1974, 63 p. (Headline Series no. 219) and her *Black Initiatives for Change in Southern Africa* (University of Edinburgh, Centre of African Studies, 1973), 18 p. (Eleventh Melville J. Herskovits Memorial Lecture).

SABRA study group at Fort Hare, "The Ciskei, a Bantu Homeland, A General Survey" (Fort Hare University Press, 1971), 215 p. (mimeo.), is based on a series of nine public lectures given by different persons at the Fort Hare-Alice Sabra Study Group. SABRA is the South African Bureau of Racial Affairs. These lectures were published as a *Festschrift* on the occasion of the University College of Fort Hare's attainment of university status. The reader is offered a bird's-eye view of one of South Africa's oldest *Bantustans:* the Ciskei.

Brian M. Du Toit, "Afrikaners, Nationalists and Apartheid,"

Journal of Modern African Studies 8, no. 4 (December 1970): 531-551, expresses the hope that the Afrikaners are becoming more flexible in their approach to apartheid. This, as the writer remarks, is due to the basic strength of the Afrikaners who have won their place in the sun.

Edward Feit, "Urban Revolt in South Africa: A Case Study," *Journal of Modern African Studies* 8, no. 1 (April 1970): 55-72, is concerned mainly with events in Port Elizabeth and East London. These places were studied because they are typical for revolts that are occurring in other parts of South Africa.

Edward Feit, *Urban Revolt in South Africa, 1960-1964: A Case Study* (Evanston, Ill.: Northwestern University Press, 1971), 365 p., is a case study of attempted urban insurgency written by a political scientist. The book concentrates on the ordinary men rather than the leaders. The main sources are the court records of fifteen trials, including the notorious Rivonia trial.

South African Studies, *Guerrilla Warfare* (London: African National Congress, 1970), 96 p., *The South African Trade Union Movement* (London: African National Congress, 1971), 63 p., and *The Road Is Via the Congress* (London: African National Congress, 1971), 95 p., may be defined as the first three numbers of a periodical with articles from different contributors. While many of the articles in the first issue are anonymous, some names are given. Numerous documents are reproduced in these three numbers.

Peter B. Orlik, "Divided Against Itself: South Africa's White Polity," *Journal of Modern African Studies* 8, no. 2 (July 1970): 199-212, stresses the differences between the United or predominantly British party and the Nationalist or Afrikaner party. Considerable attention is given to the role of the press.

M.R. Kettle and R.P. Moss, eds., *Southern African Studies: Report of a Symposium Held at the School of Oriental and African Studies in the University of London on 24th September 1969 by the African Studies Association of the United Kingdom (Centre of African Studies, University of Birmingham)* (African Studies Association of the U.K., 1970), 128 p., are essentially the papers of British, and a small number of South African scholars, which were distributed before the conference to facilitate discussion. Almost all the papers fall within the social sciences.

George F. Kennan, "Hazardous Courses in Southern Africa," *Foreign Affairs* 49, (January 1971): 218-236, is concerned with race relations, decolonization, and South Africa's role in the Rhodesian situation. This is an important article by a former senior officer of the Foreign Service of the United States Department of State. He states that "The United States government and to some extent the other Western governments have wisely recognized the danger and sterility of the movements that purport to solve the problems of South Africa by military violence." (p. 236)

Nathan M. Shamuyarira, ed., *Essays on the Liberation of Southern Africa* (Dar es Salaam: Tanzania Publishing House, 1971), 95 p. (University of Dar es Salaam, Studies in Political Science No. 3), in addition to the editor's introduction, contains four significant essays: Yoweri T. Museveni, "Fanon's Theory of Violence Its Verification in Liberated Mozambique"; Emmanuel M. Dute, "Relations Between Liberation Movements and O.A.U."; Joseph E. M. Mtuma, "Collective Decolonization in Southern Africa"; and Frank E. Minga, "The Refugee Problem in Tanzania".

Franz Johann Tennyson Lee, *Der Einfluss des Marxismus auf die Nationalen Befreiungsbewegungen in Südafrika (mit besonderer Berücksichtigung des Trotskismus und des Stalinismus)* (Frankfurt: Published by the author, 1971), 243 p., has four parts. The first part is historical, the second consists of Trotski versus Stalin in South Africa, the third deals with the land and national question, and the fourth with the organizational and revolutionary question in South Africa. The title in translation reads: The Influence of Marxism on the National Liberation Movements in South Africa, with particular attention being given to Trotskiism and Stalinism.

In Christian Potholm and Richard Dale, eds., *Southern Africa in Perspective, Essays in Regional Politics* (London: Collier-Macmillian; New York: The Free Press, 1972), 418 p., the introductory bibliographical essay by Richard Dale, "Southern Africa: Research Frontiers in Political Science," is particularly helpful.[176]

Herbert Adam, ed., *South Africa: Sociological Perspectives*

(Oxford University Press, 1971), 340 p., consists of much previously published materials, although thirteen of the fifteen papers are billed as original contributions.[177] Included in the volume is: Gwendolen M. Carter, "African Concepts of Nationalism in South Africa." Another work by Herbert Adam is: *Modernizing Racial Domination: The Dynamics of South African Politics* (Berkeley: University of California Press, 1971), 203 p.

Anthony S. Mathews, *Law and Order and Liberty in South Africa* (Cape Town: Juta, 1971; Berkeley: University of California Press, 1972), 318 p. (Perspectives on Southern Africa, 7), examines current South African security legislation.

Merle Lipton, "Independent Bantustans?" *International Affairs* (London) 48, no. 1, (January 1972): 1-19, is an excellent article by the research specialist on Southern Africa at Chatham House in London. The article is fully documented with footnotes, almost fifty of them, a map, and a table.

See also Charles Mohr, "South Africa's Course in Racism Less Certain," *The New York Times* (May 29, 1973) 1, 8.

RACE RELATIONS—BIBLIOGRAPHICAL LITERATURE

The literature on race relations in South and Southern Africa is very large. Some of the references to substantial contributions as well as trivia will be found in the following:

Francis A. Kornegay, Jr., "A Bibliographical Essay on Comparative Guerrilla Warfare and Social Change in South Africa," *A Current Bibliography on African Affairs*, n.s. 3, no. 2 (February 1970): 5-20, and his "Southern Africa and the Emerging Constituency for Africa in the United States: A Selected Survey of Political Literature," *A Current Bibliography on African Affairs*, n.s. 5, no. 1 (January 1972): 29-40.

Laverne Branden, "Booker T. Washington and D.D.T. Jabavu: Interaction Between an Afro-American and a Black South African," *A Current Bibliography on African Affairs*, n.s. 5, no. 5-6: 509-515.

Daniel Britz, comp., *Union List of Selected Newspapers, Serial Publications, Ephemera and Unpublished Material on Southern Africa Available in the U.S. (Includes Microfilmed Material Available in*

South Africa) (Evanston, Ill.: Program of African Studies, Northwestern University, June 1972), 46 p., is based on data, much of it on 3 by 5 inch cards, submitted by institutions and individuals strong on Southern Africana. It is a working document on which further work, supported by a grant from the Ford Foundation, is in progress.

United Nations Educational, Scientific and Cultural Organization (UNESCO), *Apartheid: Its Effects on Education, Science, Culture and Information,* 2d ed. (Paris, 1972), 256 p.

United Nations, Dag Hammarskjold Library, *Apartheid: A Selective Bibliography on the Racial Policies of the Government of the Republic of South Africa* (New York: United Nations, 1968), 52 p. (ST/LIB/22).

LITERATURE

Since this is a vast field in itself, only a few items will be mentioned here.

Racilia Jilian Nell, *Nadine Gordimer, Novelist and Short Stories Writer; A Bibliography of Her Works and Selected Literary Criticism* (Johannesburg: University of Witwatersrand, Department of Bibliography, Librarianship and Typography, 1964), 33 p., is a thorough work of Gordimer's writings through 1963. Among her recent works, particularly important are her *A Guest of Honour* (New York: Viking, London: Jonathan Cape, 1970), 504 p., and *Livingstone's Companions, Stories* (New York: Viking; London: Jonathan Cape, 1971), 248 p. While Gordimer is white, she should nevertheless be thought as an African or South African writer. She was born in South Africa and still lives there, and, more importantly, she writes about things African as an African.

Nelson Mandela, *No Easy Walk to Freedom* (London: Heinemann Educational Books, 1972), 192 p., is a collection of Nelson Mandela's most important writings that were initally published in 1965.

The *Seven South African Poets,* in *Poems of Exile,* collected and selected by Cosmo Pieterse (London: Heinemann Educational Books, 1971), 132 p. (African Writers Series No. 64), are Dollar Brand, Dennis Brutus, I. Choonara, C. J. Driver, Timothy Holmes, Keorapetse Kgositsile, and Arthur Nortje.

Alan Paton, "White South Africa's Only Hope for Survival," *New York Times Magazine* (May 13, 1973), 18-20 ff., is based on a lecture given at Yale in March 1973.

U.S. AND EUROPEAN POLICY TOWARD SOUTH AFRICA

"Black and White Students Struggle for Freedom in South Africa and the United States," *Africa Today* (Denver) 17, no. 3 (May-June 1970): 1-32, This is an excellent issue of *Africa Today*, which for some years has been published by the Center of International Race Relations, University of Denver. The particular number cited includes the following articles: Mary McAnally, "The Plight of Student Exiles in the United States," Gail Morlan, "The Student Revolt Against Racism in South Africa," Ragaei El Mallakh and Tapan Mukerjee, "The Education Dimension of U.S. Aid to Africa," and Richard P. Stevens, "Forum: South Africa's 'New Look', South Africa and Independent Black Africa."

Barnett F. Baron, "Southern African Student Exiles in the United States," *Journal of Modern African Studies* 10, no. 1 (May 1972): 73-91, discusses the effect study in the United States has on refugees from Southern Africa. He concludes that study in the United States may divert the exiles from what initially was their prime task of overthrowing the white regimes in Southern Africa.

Walter Darnell Jacobs, *South Africa Looks Outward* (New York: American-African Affairs Association, 1969), 13 p., is by a professor of government and politics at the University of Maryland. The author feels that South Africa has virtually unlimited economic opportunities in working with other countries in Africa.

William J. Pomeroy, *Apartheid Axis: The United States and South Africa* (New York: International Publishers, 1971), 95 p., gives a sinister interpretation for which data are available.

Katherine M. Roberts, "Sanctions in Southern Africa: United States Policy Dilemma," *Genève-Afrique* 9, no. 1 (1970):

67-87, points out the importance of finding a solution to South Africa's race questions, not merely for the sake of peace and justice in South Africa, but for resolving racial conflict all over the world.

Daisy Collins, "American Companies in South Africa and Human Rights," *Howard Law Journal* 15 (Summer 1969): 625-670, lists American firms having subsidiaries or affiliates in the Republic of South Africa, based on a U.S. Department of Commerce, Bureau of International Commerce source of 1968. The Collins article contains 288 footnotes, some of them referring to United Nations and U.S. House of Representatives documents and to articles in *Africa Today.*

Ruth First, Jonathan Steele, and Christabel Guerney, *The South African Connection* (London: Temple Smith 1972), 352 p. represents political pamphleteering on a high level of competence and persuasiveness.[178] While it is geared more to British connections, it is also highly recommended to Americans.

The best means of keeping up to date with happenings in South Africa is probably to read the publications of the Africa Bureau, London. *Africa Digest* has appeared monthly for the last twenty-one years. Its focus is increasingly on South Africa. *X-Ray, Current Affairs in Southern Africa* is also a monthly publication; it started in 1970. With it comes *Africa Bureau Fact Sheet,* a double-page publication. *X-Ray* and the *Fact Sheet* are sent free in the United Kingdom. Very good too is the work of the International Defence and Aid Fund for Southern Africa in London. Its *Southern Africa Information Service Manual* is a looseleaf manual divided into the following sections: the fund, social and political, economic, special reports, and index.

LIBRARIES

For the white population, South Africa has an almost adequate system of university, public, and special libraries. This is not the situation for the African, colored, and Asian majorities.

The white library world is described in a large literature, which includes three library journals with a national and international distribution. *South African Libraries,* 1933- (issued five times a year) is the official organ of the South African Library Association, from which Africans are excluded. *Quarterly Bulletin of the South African Library,* 1946-, is published by a quasi-national library comparable to the New York Public Library.

The other main public library is in Johannasburg, which publishes actively. The following items are noteworthy examples: Elizabeth Ann Newenham, *A Bibliography of Printed Catalogues of the Libraries of Southern Africa, 1820-1920* (Johannesburg Public Library, 1967), 165 p.,[179] and Anita Clifton, *African Serial Publications Currently Received* (Johannesburg Public Library, 1967).[180]

Another South African library journal, unlike the other two mentioned (largely in Afrikaans), is: *Mousaion Boek en biblioteekwese* [Books and libraries] 1955-, including no. 100: Paul Seth Manaka, *Non-White Library Services in the Transvaal* (Pretoria, 1972), 234 p. This is a scrupulously fair presentation, in historical perspective of the library situation for blacks, both as readers and librarians, in the Transvaal.

BIBLIOGRAPHY AND LIBRARIANSHIP

South Africa has a plentiful supply—at least for whites—of bibliographies and library services. The most important retrospective bibliography is: Sidney Mendelssohn, *South African Bibliography* (1910; reprint ed., London; Holland Press, 1957), 2 vols. For many years work has been in progress at the South African Library at Cape Town to record the many items missed by Mendelssohn.

The current national bibliography is: *South African National Bibliography,* 1959-. It is a quarterly that is then cumulated annually. A ten-year cumulation has been published.

The South African Unicat, arranged by International Standard Book Numbers, is available on microfiche starting with 1972.

Petrus Johannes Nienaber, *Bibliografie van Afrikaanse boeke* (Johannesburg, 1943-1970), 7 vols., is the official Afrikaans bibliography. Volume seven covers the period 1967 through 1970. The volume includes alphabetical lists by author and title as well as a subject index.

Reuben Musiker's main volumes were mentioned above; see also his "Bibliographical Achievement in South Africa," in Pearson and Jones, eds., *Bibliography of Africa* (1970), p. 83-87. (Because of his South African citizenship, Musiker was unable to participate in the conference.)

"South African Bibliography, Summary of the Scolma Seminar Held on March 21, 1972," *Library Materials on Africa* 10, no. 1 (July 1972): 17-19, and "Bibliographical Progress in South Africa, January 1971," *Africana Library Journal* 2, no. 1 (Spring 1971): 10-11, give the names of recently completed bibliographies by students at the Universities of Cape Town and Witwatersrand. For those in progress there is only a title. See also "Bibliographical Control in South Africa," *International Library Review* 4, (1972): 149-156.

Other broad surveys are: Conrad Reitz, *South African Bibliography* (Urbana, Ill.: University of Illinios Graduate School of Library Science, 1967), 15 p. (No. 96), and Dougles H. Varley, "Trends Abroad: South Africa," *Library Trends 19, no. 1 (July 1970): 139-151.*

GUIDES

Eric Rosentahl, comp. and ed., *Encyclopedia of Southern Africa,* 6th ed. (London and New York: Warne, 1973), 662 p., is a handy volume. Six editions have appeared over a twelve-year span. It consists of major, signed articles by South African experts on the natural habitat as well as man-made matters.

Hans Fransen, *Guide to the Museums of Southern Africa* (Cape Town: South African Museum Association, 1969), 147 p., is a handy volume recommended for those who do not have access to: German Africa Society, *Museums in Africa, A Directory* (Munich, 1970), 594 p. The entries in the Fransen guide are fuller than those in the German directory. They are also attractively illustrated.

The preface of Leonard Thompson, Richard Elphick, and Inez Jarrick, *Southern African History before 1900: A Select Bibliography of Articles* (Stanford: The Hoover Institution Press, 1971), 102 p. (Hoover Institution Bibliographical Series No. 49),[181] states: "This

is a select bibliography, designed by historians for historians."
The articles indexed are grouped into twenty-six sections some
with subsections. It contains an author index and more than one
thousand entries.

Johannes Christiaan Coetzee, *Annotated Bibliography of Research
in Education* (Pretoria: Human Sciences Research Council, 1970),
182 p., presents seventy-five doctoral and master's theses
chronologically. Annotations are lengthy. There is an author
index.

See also Marius F. Valkhoff, "Descriptive Bibliography of
Linguistics of Afrikaans: A Survey of Major Works and Authors,"
in T. A. Sebeok, ed., *Current Trends in Linguistics* (The Hague) 7
(1971): 455-500.

Richard Priebe, *Letters and Manuscripts from Southern Africa, A
Source of the Holdings of the Humanities Research Center* (The University of Texas at Austin, African and Afro-American Research
Centre, 1972), 24 p. (Occasional Publication No. 6), is a collection
of the letters and manuscripts of twelve South African authors,
some writing in English, others in Afrikaans. There is also a
Rhodesian writer to be added to this select group.

NAMIBIA (SOUTH WEST AFRICA)

Namibia has an area of 318,261 square miles, twice that of
California, with a population, estimated by the United Nations in
1972, of 770,000 (96,000 of them white). The United Nations has
not yet succeeded in persuading South Africa to grant the area its
independence.

In *History of South West Africa from the Beginning of the Nineteenth
Century* (Cape Town: Juta, 1971), 273 p., the author, Israel
Goldblatt, wanted initially to end his history in the mid-1950s but
he occasionally goes beyond this. He relies on the archives of
Windhoek, Namibia's capital, and other mission records. He did
not do his research in Germany.

Helmut Bley, ed. and trans. by Hugh Ridley, *South West Africa
Under German Rule, 1894-1914* (London: Heineman; Evanston,
Ill.: Northwestern University Press, 1971), 303 p.,[182] is important
for an understanding not just of colonial South-West Africa but

of German policies and even today's Namibia as well. The translation is a very good one.

Ruth First, *South West Africa* (Harmondsworth, Middlesex: Penguin Books, 1963), 269 p., an eleven-year old pocket book which has not been revised, is nevertheless still worth reading as nothing has taken its place. First was still a South African resident when she collected the data, but became a prohibited person even before the book was published.As is characteristic of the Penguin African Library (edited by Ronald Segal in London), the documentation in the first volume is slender.

Richard Hall, ed., *South-West Africa (Namibia): Proposals for Action* (London: The Africa Bureau, 1970), 45 p.,[183] is a distinguished pamphlet with contributions by Randolph Vigne, Jennifer Bray, Richard Plender, and Michael Scott.

Anthony Lejeune, comp., *The Case for South West Africa* (London: Tom Stacey, 1971), 245 p., unlike the Hall pamphlet mentioned above, argues from the South African point of view. It reprints the complete text of the dissenting opinion to the World Court's judgments.

See also Marcelle Kooy, "The Contract Labour System and the Ovambo Crisis of 1971 in South West Africa," *African Studies Review* (East Lansing, Michigan 16, no. 1 (April 1973): 83-105.

BIBLIOGRAPHY

Samuel Decalo, *South West Africa, 1960-1968: An Introductory Bibliography* (Kingston: University of Rhode Island, 1968), 20 leaves (Occasional Papers in Political Science No. 5), is an occasional paper that has now gone into a second printing. It begins with a quote from Sidney J. Webb: "I stoutly maintain that every orderly bibliography, however incomplete will be of use to somebody." Except for two pages of "bibliography," the remaining entries are presented alphabetically.

Richard F. Logan, *Bibliography of South West Africa; Geography and Related Fields: 2000 Titles (closed 1966)* (Windhoek: Committee of the S.W.A. Scientific Society, 1969), 152 p. (Scientific Research in South West Africa, 8th ser), begins with a subject index but is largely an alphabetical list of entries that refers by number back to the "subjects." The compiler has annotated about half the entries.

South West Africa Scientific Society, *Vorlaüfiges Verzeichnis der in der Bibliothek der S.W.A. Wissenschaftlichen Gesellschaft enthaltenden Literatur über Süd und Südwest Afrika* (Windhoek, 1969), 71 p. (mimeo.), a preliminary edition, consists of an alphabetical list of works found in the library of the South West Africa Scientific Institute in Windhoek. Location is given by Dewey decimal or box number.

Carl Schlettwein, "Bibliographie. Südwestafrika. (Namibia) 1971," *Mitteilungen der Basler Afrikabibliographien* 2/3 (1972): 17-24, is an alphabetical author catalog.

George Edward Stanley, "The Indigenous Languages of South West Africa," *Anthropological Linguistics* (Indiana University) 10, no. 3 (March 1968): 5-18, contains 108 references to monographs, and 43 to periodicals. It is based on standard bibliographies except for the C.J.C. Lemmer estate.

K. L. Baucom, "More on the Indigenous Languages of South West Africa," *Anthropological Linguistics* 12, no. 9 (December 1970): 343-348, is a bibliography on the Khoisan or Kosan languages.

THE FORMER HIGH COMMISSION TERRITORIES

Some common sources on Botswana, Lesotho, and Swaziland are: Jack Halpern, *South Africa's Hostages: Basutoland, Bechuanaland and Swaziland* (Harmondsworth, Middlesex, England: Penguin Books, 1965), 496 p.,[184] and P. M. Landell-Mills, "The 1969 Southern African Customs Union Agreement," *Journal of Modern African Studies* 9, no. 2 (August 1971): 263-281.

BIBLIOGRAPHY

Mildred Balima, comp., *Botswana, Lesotho and Swaziland, a Guide to Official Publications, 1868-1968* (Library of Congress, 1971), 84 p., was prepared by a former member of LC's African Section.[185]

Shelagh M. Willet, comp., *A Checklist of Recent Reference Books on Botswana, Lesotho and Swaziland* (Grahamstown: Rhodes University, Department of Librarianship, 1971), 6 p. (Bibliographical Series No. 1), is the work of the deputy librarian of the University of Botswana, Lesotho, and Swaziland. The arrangement of the entries is first by country and then by broad subject.

BOTSWANA (FORMERLY BECHAUANALAND)

Formerly known as Bechuanaland, Botswana has an area of 219,815 square miles, slightly larger than that of Texas; the United Nations estimated its population in 1972 at 650,000. It borders the Republic of South Africa, Namibia, Rhodesia, and Zambia.

Zdenek Cervenka, *Republic of Botswana: A Brief Outline of Its Geographical Setting, History, Economy and Politics* (Uppsala, Sweden: Scandinavian Institute of African Studies, 1970), is a useful publication for a generalist or a social scientist who wants to learn more about Botswana. A more formal edition was issued in Germany.

Seretse Khama, *Botswana—A Developing Democracy in Southern Africa* (Uppsala: Scandinavian Institute of African Studies, 1970), 17 p., is an address given by Sir Seretse Khama, Botswana's President, at a seminar arranged by the Dag Hammarskjöld Foundation and the Scandinavian Institute of African Studies in Uppsala, Sweden, November 1970.

Richard Dale, *Botswana and Its Southern Neighbor: The Patterns of Linkage and the Options in Statecraft* (Athens: Ohio University Center for International Studies, 1970), 22 p., is an example of thoroughly documented research. The pages contain more than fifty footnotes.

Philippus Smit, *Botswana: Resources and Development* (Pretoria: African Institute of South Africa, 1970) 256 p.,[186] is by the geographer of the Africa Institute of South Africa in Pretoria. The first section is entitled "The Land and Divison of Land," the second "The Population," the third "Economic Activities," and the fourth "Problems and Potential."

BIBLIOGRAPHY

Paulus Mohome and John B. Webster, comps., *A Bibliography of Bechuanaland* (Syracuse: Syracuse University, Program of Eastern African Studies, 1966) (Occasional Bibliography No. 5), is a classified bibliography divided into seventeen chapters without an author index.

John B. Webster, et al., comps., *Supplement to a Bibliography on Bechuanaland* (Syracuse: Syracuse University, Program of Eastern African Studies, 1968) (Occasional Bibliography No. 12) is divided into fourteen chapters. It includes an author index to the 325 numbered entries as well as a subject and key word index.

The Botswana National Library Service publishes *The National Bibliography of Botswana* twice a year, 1969. It strives to include all publications of Botswana. Entries are according to the Anglo-American code, arranged based on Dewey's seventeenth edition. There is an alphabetical index.

Q. N. Parsons, "University Theses and Dissertations on Botswana in the Humanities and Social Sciences: Checklist 1," *Botswana Notes and Records* 3 (1971): 277-280, is a useful classified list of theses and dissertations prepared in most parts of the world. Volume four of the same journal includes: Bridget Winstanley, "A List of Reports on Botswana in the Library of the Ministry of Finance and Development Planning" (p. 292-302). The works are arranged according to the Dewey Decimal Classification.

Doris Cruger Dale, "National Libraries in Developing Countries: The Case of Botswana," *Journal of Library History* 6, no. 3 (July 1971): 195-214, discusses the Botswana National Library within a broad perspective.

LESOTHO (FORMERLY BASUTOLAND)

The former Basutoland has an area of 11,716 square miles (about the size of Maryland) and a population of over 1 million as estimated by the United Nations in 1972. Lesotho is entirely

surrounded by the Republic of South Africa, being situated in-
land west of Durban. The capital of Lesotho is Maseru.
The main function of B. M. Khaketla, *Lesotho 1970* (London: C.
Hurst; Berkeley and Los Angeles: University of California Press,
1972), 350 p., is to serve as a polemic against Prime Minister Chief
Jonathan; nevertheless, it does provide much information on
Lesotho.[187]

Michael Ward, "Economic Independence for Lesotho?" *Journal of Modern African Studies* 5, no. 3 (1967); 355-368, documents
how South Africa has vested political and economic interests to
keep on good terms with Lesotho. When this article was
published, the author was at the Department of Applied
Economics at the University of Cambridge. In 1965-1966 he was
seconded to the Bureau of Statistics, Maseru, Lesotho.

BIBLIOGRAPHY

Bibliographies of Lesotho include: John B. Webster and Paulus
Mohome, comps., *A Bibliography of Lesotho* (Syracuse: Syracuse
University Program of Eastern African Studies, 1968), 59 leaves
(Occasional Bibliography No. 9); Dianne Lynn Shaskolsky,
"Basutoland to 1946, a Bibliography" (University of Cape Town,
1969), 20 leaves p.; and Loraine Gordon, comp., "Lesotho; a
Bibliography" (Bachelor's thesis, University of Witwatersrand,
1970), 47 p.

SWAZILAND

Swaziland's area is 6,704 square miles (Hawaii is slightly
smaller), with a population of 450,000 as estimated by the United
Nations in 1972. Swaziland is virtually surrounded by the
Republic of South Africa except for a small stretch of common
border with Mozambique.

There is little recent literature pertaining exclusively to Swaziland other than Christian P. Potholm, *Swaziland, the Dynamics of
Political Modernization* (Berkeley: University of California Press,

1972), 183 p. The best work is that by Hilda Kuper, in part in anthropological journals, but also available as fine literature. See her *Bite of Hunger: A Novel of Africa* (New York: Harcourt Brace and World, 1965), 210 p., and *A Witch in My Heart: A Play Set in Swaziland in the 1930's* (London: Oxford University Press, 1970), 70 p.

BIBLIOGRAPHY

John B. Webster and Paulus Mohome, *A Bibliography of Swaziland* (Syracuse: Syracuse University, Program of Eastern African Studies, 1968), 32 leaves (Occasional Bibliography No. 10), lists the compilers' major sources. The almost two hundred numbered entries are classified according to nineteen subjects, each of which is covered in a separate chapter. Included in the volume are author, subject, and key word indexes.

RHODESIA (ZIMBABWE)

Rhodesia, or Southern Rhodesia, is a British colony that delared itself independent in November 1965. It could have been considered above with the few remaining British possessions, but since Great Britain has failed to control the area for many years, one may justifiably consider it as a part of Southern Africa.

Rhodesia's area is 150,333 square miles and its population, in accordance with a government estimate in 1972, was 5.79 million. In 1966, the official total estimate was 4.46 million, of which 94.5 percent were African and 5.5 percent European (and a few Asians and coloreds).

Lewis H. Gann, *Central Africa, the Former British States* (Englewood, N.J.: Prentice-Hall, 1971), 180 p. (The Modern Nations in Historical Perspective) is sympathetic to white Rhodesians and their problems. It succeeds in compressing much data into a readable book.

Theodore Bull, *Rhodesia: Crisis of Color* (Chicago: Quadrangle Books, 1967), 184 p., is the work of the publisher and former editor of the *Central African Examiner,* who strove to present a fair picture of and to all races.[188] This book has the following title for its English edition: *Rhodesian Perspective.*

Terence O. Ranger, *The African Voice in Southern Rhodesia, 1898-1930* (London: Heinemann Educational Books; Nairobi: East African Publishing House; Evanston, Ill.: Northwestern University Press, 1970), 252 p.,[189] is by the former professor of history at the University College, Dar es Salaam, who used to teach in Salisbury. He discusses ten episodes about Africans in Rhodesia or Zimbabwe, and shows the relationships among to-day's leaders of Zimbabwe, most of whom are either in jail, at home, or in exile all over the world.

John Day "Southern Rhodesian African Nationalists and the 1961 Constitution," *Journal of Modern African Studies* 7, no. 2 (July 1969): 221-247, a review essay, deals entirely with the Sithole volume: John Day, "Sithole and African Nationalism, a Review Article," *African Social Research* (Lusaka) 9 (June 1970): 690-700.

Ndabaningi Sithole, *African Nationalism,* 2d ed. (London: Oxford University Press, 1968), 169 p.,[190] is a thorough revision of the 1957 edition. It was written while its distinguished author was serving (as he still is) an indefinite term of detention for being an African nationalist leader.

Ralph Zacklin, *Challenge of Rhodesia: Toward an International Public Policy* (New York: Carnegie Endowment for International Peace, 1970), 72 p., tests the validity of international law. Its main sources are United Nations documents, all of which are fully cited.

Frank Clements, *Rhodesia, the Course to Collision* (London: Pall Mall, 1969), 286 p.,[191] is good example of popular historical writing. The author clearly shows how the present illegal regime in Salisbury has reversed most gains that were made toward multi-racialism before Ian Smith came to power.

John Parker, *Rhodesia: Little White Island* (London: Pitman, 1972), 166 p., is an account of criticism of the white regime by a journalist who for some years was a part of it. Sir Roy in his foreword expresses his disagreement with the author but stresses the right of a dissident to be read.

Eshmael Mlambo, *Rhodesia: The Struggle for a Birthright*

(London: C. Hurst, 1972), 333 p.,[192] by a Zimbabwe author gives us a look at the history of the country through the eyes of a native. Mlambo's account goes from 1890 through 1971 and is well documented.

Great Britain, Parliament, *Papers by Command, Rhodesia, Proposals for a Settlement* (Cmmd 4835, 1971), 40 p., a brief official document, presents the constitutional position as it was in 1971. There are references to earlier relevant documents, several of which are reproduced. The crucial five points which Great Britain regards as preconditions to a granting of independence are stated.

Rhodesia, *Report on the Commission on Rhodesian Opinion. Under the Chairmanship of the Right Honourable the Lord Pearce.* Cmmd 4964 (London, 1972), 207 p., logically follows the preceding Command paper. The first half of the volume describes the work of the Commission; the second half goes into greater detail, including biographical notes on Commissioners and Appendix H, "Extracts from Commissioners' Reports and Other Material Relating to Intimidation."

Kees Maxey, *From Rhodesia to Zimbabwe* (London: Fabian Society, 1972), 40 p. (Fabian Research Series 301),[193] a pamphlet, is likely to have a noticeable impact even on a minority labor government in Great Britain. Particulaly useful is the map on page 39 that shows the location of the proposed bridge (where there is now only a feiry) between Botswana and Zambia, across the Zambezi River.

Robert McKinnell, "Sanctions and the Rhodesian Economy," *Journal of Modern African Studies* 7, no. 4 (December 1969): 559-581, work of an economist, documents with statistical tables the effects of sanctions on Rhodesia. He concludes that in 1967 Rhodesia had a choice between economic stagnation or South African dominance.

Leonard T. Kapungu, *The United Nations and Economic Sanction against Rhodesia* (Lexington, Mass.: Heath, 1973), 155 p. (Lexington Books), is a good study of the problem of Rhodesia, with emphasis on the roles of Great Britain and the United Nations.

George Kay, *Rhodesia: A Human Geography* (London: University of London Press, 1970), 192 p., is a good textbook written by a professor of geography at University College, Rhodesia. Note also the same author's *Distribution and Density of African Population in Rhodesia* (University of Hull, Department of Geography, 1972), 28 p. (Miscellaneous Series No. 12). This work consists mainly of maps and tables.

BIBLIOGRAPHY AND LIBRARIANSHIP

Surprisingly, there are no adequate retrospective bibliographies of Rhodesia. There is, however, a good current national bibliography: Rhodesia, National Archives, *Rhodesian National Bibliography: List of Publications Deposited in the Library of the National Archives, 1967* (Salisbury, 1968), annual. This has been evaluated by D. H. Varley, "The Rhodesian National Bibliography," *Library Materials on Africa* 7, no. 3 (March 1970): 85-86.

C. Coggin, "Rhodesian in Bibliography: A Survey," *Rhodesian Librarian* 2, no. 4 (October 1970): 81-89, is concerned with sketching broadly what is available and what might be undertaken. Note also Geoffrey Dellar, "The Pattern of Rhodesian Publishing," *The Rhodesian Librarian* 1, no. 3 (July 1969): 71-76.

Craig C. Smith and H. E. van der Heyde, *Rhodesian Geology: A Bibliography and Brief Index to 1968* (Salisbury: Causeway, National Museum of Rhodesia, 1971), p. 325-575 (Occasional Paper No. 31B), contains over 2,100 entries arranged alphabetically. There is an index to minerals and mines.

Rhodesia Research Index is an annual volume which first appeared in 1971 (for 1970) It is compiled by the Scientific Liaison Office of the Department of the Prime Minister and the Reference Department of the University Library, both in Salisbury. The index for 1972, the third volume, contains 991 entries arranged according to the Universal Decimal Classification. The entries include researcher name, sponsoring department, a brief abstract of the project, and resulting publications. Alphabetical indexes to subjects and research workers are included.

D. G. Clarke, "Economic Development in Rhodesia: A Selected

Bibliography," *Rhodesian Journal of Economics* (Salisbury) 4, no. 4 (December 1970): 46-59, and his "Economic Development in Rhodesia; A Revision of a Selected Bibliography," 5 no. 4 (December 1971): 37-42, both have a classified arrangement that facilitates access to the sources needed by students of the Rhodesian economy. Almost all government publications have been excluded insofar as they are available from the government List.

T. W. Baxter, ed., *Guide to the Public Archives of Rhodesia vol. 1, 1890-1923* (Salisbury: National Archives of Rhodesia, 1969), 262 p., is an amplified and revised edition of *A Guide to the Public Records of Southern Rhodesia under the Regime of the British South Africa Company* (1956). The 1969 volume has a useful historical introduction citing parts of key documents. This is followed by a listing of documents deposited by the various governmental agencies.

T. W. Baxter and E. E. Burke, *Guide to the Historical Manuscripts in the National Archives of Rhodesia* (Salisbury: National Archives of Rhodesia, 1970), 527 p., is a condensation of the Descriptive Catalogue of Historical Manuscripts, in six looseleaf volumes kept at the National Archives in Salisbury. The Index to Groups is an alphabetical listing to the personal names, organizations, clubs, and the like, represented in the Archives.

Norman W. Wilding, *Catalogue of the Paliamentary Papers of Southern Rhodesia and Rhodesia, 1954-1970, and the Federation of Rhodesia and Nyasaland, 1954-1963* (Salisbury: University College of Rhodesia, Department of Political Science, 1970), 161 p. (The Source Books in Political Science No. 6), is restricted to papers laid before Parliament.

The Rhodesian Librarian began in January 1969 as a quarterly. Of particular interest in the journal are: Albert Harrison, "Academic and Professional Education in Librarianship: A Consideration of Rhodesian Requirements," *Rhodesian Librarian* 2, no. 4 (October 1970): 99, 101, 103; and 3, no. 1 (January 1971): 1-4, 6-8, 10-12, 14-16, 18-21.

See also: C. Coggin, "Rhodesian Bibliography: A Survey," 2, no. 4 (October 1970): 81-98 (some advertising pages in between); "Rhodesian Bibliography: Recent Contributions," 3, no. 3 (July

1971): 70-72; "The Future of Rhodesian Bibliography in the Light of Recent Developments," 4, no. 3 (July 1972): 52-57; and "Rhodesian Bibliography: Part 3," 4, no. 4 (October 1972): 74-80.

MALAWI

Authorities differ on the size of Malawi, primarily because its size depends on the degee to which lake surface, mainly Lake Malawi, is included in the area; about 45,000 square miles (about the size of Pennsylvania) may be accurate. The United Nations population estimate for 1972 was 4.7 million, a heavy population density for an almost totally rural country.

Peter Randall, *Guide to Malawi* (Johannesburg: Winchester Press, 1971), 251 p., is a basic guidebook with many illustrations and much advertising matter.

Swanzie Agnew and Michael Stubbs, *Malawi in Maps* (University of London Press, 1972), 143 p., almost takes the place of a national atlas. Various experts supplied the data (socioeconomic, physical, etc.) for the maps. The scale of the maps is about 1 inch to 50 miles. The book includes a classified bibliography.

Bridglal Pachai, ed., *The Early History of Malawi* (London: Longman, 1972), 454 p.,[194] a wide-ranging collection of papers, is based on a conference held at the University of Malawi in July 1970.

Alifeyo Chilivumbo, "Social Research in Malawi, A Review of Some Methodogical Problems Encountered in the Field," *East African Journal of Rural Development* (Kampala) 3, no. 2 (1970): 81-95, is the work of the senior lecturer in sociology at Chancellor College, University of Malawi, in 1970. The author urges against the hasty application of foreign well-developed models in an African situation; models, he states, will have to be especially designed for the African situation.

Malawi—Dialogue and Development (London: African Publications Trust, 1973), 24 p., an anonymous pamphlet, is based largely on one author's two-year residence in Malawi. Others contributed to this documented account.

BIBLIOGRAPHY

Edward E. Brown, Carol A. Fisher, and John B. Webster, comps., *A Bibliography of Malawi* (Syracuse: Syracuse University Press, 1965), 161 p. (Syracuse University, Eastern Africa Bibliographical Series No. 1), "covers items down to the end of 1964 but excludes official publications. 3,000 titles including many periodical articles are classified under 24 headings. There is an author index and a title index for items without author."

Other bibliographies are: John B. Webster, and Paulus Mohome, *A Supplement to a Bibliography of Malawi* (Syracuse: Syracuse University, Program of Eastern African Studies, 1969), 62 p. (Occasional Bibliography No. 13); Malawi, National Archives, *List of Publications Deposited in the National Archives, 1965* (Zomba, 1967), annual; and Roger K. Tangri, "Political Change in Colonial Malawi: A Bibliographical Essay," *African Studies Bulletin* 11, no. 3 (December 1968): 269-285.

Jonathan M. Daube, "Education in Malawi: A Bibliography," 3d ed. (The Education Department, Soche Hill College, University of Malawi, Limbe, Malawi, 1970), 15 p., contains 212 items arranged alphabetically: journal articles, reports, government reports, and publications in typescript.

Malawi University, *An Interim Bibliography of Development in Malawi* (Limbe: Chancellor College Library, 1972), 26 p., lists items in the main University Library of the University of Malawi. Not all aspects of Malawian development are covered; for example, political development is excluded. The arrangement is a classified one. Some entires have brief annotations.

Wilfred J. Plumbe, "The University of Malawi Library," *Rhodesian Librarian* 2, no. 3 (July 1970): 55-63, is by the former university librarian who has had extensive experience also in Nigeria and Malawi.

A. F. Johnson, "The Malawi National Library Service: The First Two Years, 1968-70," *Rhodesian Librarian* 2, no. 3 (July 1970): 64-66, is a rather dry account of a pioneering situation.

See also Malawi National Library Service, *Books about Malawi, A Select Reading List* (Blantyre, 1969), 23 p.

Notes

[1]This is neither the practice in Duignan's *Guide* nor of the African Section of the Library of Congress (nor most of its publications). The last publication of the Section to include references to publications of countries that are the concern of the Orientalia Division was: Helen Conover, comp., *Serials for African Studies* (Washington, D.C.: Library of Congress, 1961): 164 p.

[2]*Times Literary Supplement* (October 13, 1972): 1222.

[3]Note Donald F. Jay's letter pointing out the existence of *Accessions List: Middle East,* which has been published by LC's Cairo office since 1962, and Michael J. Brigg's letter pointing out typographic errors in the Aman article. *College and Research Libraries* 31, no. 6 (November 1970): 411-412.

[4]"Nationalism in the Maghreb," *Times Literary Supplement* (September 29, 1972): 1172.

[5]See review article by Michael Brett, "Problems in the Interpretation of the History of the Maghreb in the Light of Some Recent Publications," *Journal of African History* 13, no. 3 (1972): 489-506.

[6]Favorably reviewed in 4 above (September 29, 1972): 1172, and Michael Brett, *Journal of African History* 13, no. 3 (1972): 489-506. Adversely reviewed by Gifford B. Doxsee, *African Studies Review* 15, no. 2 (September 1972): 343-346.

[7]Favorably reviewed by Robert A. Mortimer, *African Studies Review* 15, no. 2 (September 1972): 346-347.

[8]Author also of *Women of Algeria, An Essay on Change* (Cambridge, Mass.: Harvard University Press, 1968).

[9]Note the useful bibliography by Barbara Abrash, "Frantz Fanon," *Africana Library Journal* 2, no. 3 (Autumn, 1971); 9-12. For a biography, see Irene L. Gendzier, *Frantz Fanon, A Critical Study* (New York: Pantheon, 1973), 330 p., reviewed by Thomas Lask, "Blueprint for Liberation," *The New York Times* (January 13, 1973). Finally, see B. Marie Perinbam, "Fanon and the Revolutionary Peasantry—The Algerian Case," *Journal of Modern African Studies* 11, no. 3 (September 1973): 427-444.

[10]Favorably reviewed in the *Times Literary Supplement* (September 1, 1972): 1021.

[11]Reprinted by Negro Universities Press (New York, 1968).

[12]Reviewed in *Library Materials on Africa* 1, no. 3 (1963): 23.

[13]*Choice* 3, no. 7 (September 1966): 550.

[14]See "The Politics of Compromise: Habib Bourguiba of Tunisia," in

Ronald Segal, *African Profiles*, rev. ed. (Harmondsworth, Middlesex: Penguin, 1963), 358-371.

[15]Note, however, that President Harry S. Truman in the customary interview to the new minister, noting the meager economic base of Libya, suggested: "Perhaps there were minerals, maybe petroleum."

[16]Helen F. Conover, comp., *Introduction to Africa, A Selective Guide to Background Reading* (Washington, D.C.: The University Press of Washington, 1952), 190 p. This is the first of Helen Conover's general bibliographies of Africa.

[17]Reviewed in *Library Materials on Africa* 3, no. 3 (March 1966): 11.

[18]*Bibliography Documentation Terminology* 8, no. 5 (September 1968): 197-198.

[19]Note his *The Egyptian Army in Politics: Pattern for New Nations* (Bloomington, Ind.: University Press, 1961), 300 p.

[20]Originally published in French as *Egypte: société militaire* (Paris: Editions du Seuil, 1962).

[21]All material collected was deposited at the University of Michigan, Center for Near Eastern and North African Studies, a practice that other scholars should follow.

[22]*The Times* (London), August 26, 1882, contains the text of an interesting letter of the prince offering his services to the British army and the curt reply.

[23]This difference is ignored by Besterman in his *A World Bibliography of Bibliographies*, 4th ed. (1965-1966).

[24]The author refers for further details on Mahdist documents to his "The Archives of Mahdia," *Sudan Notes and Records* 36, no. 1 (1955); 71-80, and "The Mahdist Archives and Related Documents," *Archives* 5, no. 28 (1962): 193-200. Favorably reviewed by John Voll in *International Journal of African Historical Studies* 5, no. 2 (1972): 306-307.

[25]Review of first edition (1958) 1. Cunnison, *Africa* (London) 29, no. 3.: 319-320.

[26]Reviewed by Jean Buxton in *Africa* 41, no. 1 (January 1971): 68-69.

[27]Abstracted in *International Political Science Abstracts* 22, no. 2 (1972): 571, 1785.

[28]Renate Kleinschmid, trans., *African Abstracts* 18, no. 2 (April 1967): 62, 306.

[29]Favorably reviewed in *Times Literary Supplement* (January 19, 1973): 72.

[30]Favorably reviewed by P. S. Gilkes, *Journal of African History* 12, no. 3 (1971): 501-503.

[31]Reviewed by Peter Garretson, *Journal of African History* 12, no. 3 (1971): 503-504.

[32]Fine review by William A. Shack, *Africa* 36, no. 3 (July 1966): 333-334.

[33]Reviewed (in German) by W. Schild, *Africa* 11, no. 1 (January 1938): 118-119.

[34]Reviewed (in Italian) by Ernesta Cerulli, *Africa* (London) 30, no. 4 (October 1960: 412-413.

[35]A knowledgeable reviewer is adversely critical in *Times Literary Supplement* (July 21, 1972): 848.

[36]*International Political Science Abstracts* 22, no. 2 (1972): 870.

[37]Indifferently reviewed in *Choice* 9, no. 7 (September 1972): 846.

[38]Reviewed favorably and rather fully in "The Rise of Ras Tafari," *Times Literary Supplement,* 3, 717 (June 1, 1973): 609.

[39]Briefly reviewed anonymously in *Library Materials on Africa* 1, no. 1 (1962): 12-13.

[40]*Bibliography Documentation Terminology* 12, no. 3 (May 1972): 112.

[41]A most constructive review sketching recommended priorities for future research is by Enrico Cerulli, *Journal of African History* 8, no. 3 (1966): 530-532. Favorably and more conventionally reviewed by P.T.W. Baxter *Africa* 37, no. 4 (October 1967): 491-492.

[42]The excessive reliance on these official sources is the main criticism in one of the reviews. Leone Iraci, University of Rome, *Journal of Modern African Studies* 6, no. 2 (August 1968): 284-296. Much more gentle was I. M. Lewis *Journal of African History* 8, no. 3 (1967): 553-554.

[43]*Current Digest of the Soviet Press* 23, no. 10 (December 21, 1971).

[44]Favorably reviewed by Hassan A. Mirreh, of what was the Istituto Universitario, Mogadishu (now an independent university), *Journal of Modern African Studies* 2, no. 1 (March 1964): 130-132.

[45]The first edition was entitled *East Africa: The Search for Unity, Kenya, Tanganika, Uganda and Zanzibar.*

[46]Noted in a whole column in *Africana Library Journal* (New York) 2, no. 2 (Summer 1971): 2.

[47]Favorably reviewed by Okoro Okereke, *Journal of Modern African Studies* 10, no. 1 (May 1972): 159-161. Less favorably reviewed in *Choice* 8, no. 8 (October 1971): 1065.

[48]Favorably reviewed by Philip J. Thiuri in *Africana Library Journal* 2, no. 3 (Autumn 1971): 15-16. In the same review by Okereke, n. 47 above, *Choice* 8, no. 7 (September 1971): 869.

[49]For slightly earlier years, note Melchior Baregu and M. Wise, comps.,

"Bibliography-East Africana Published Between January 1963 and April 1964," *Tanganyika Notes and Records* 63 (1964): 249-253.

[50]The Library of Congress, National Program for Acquisitions and Cataloging Progress Report no. 13, January 1972, p. 2.

[51]The Nairobi office of the Library of Congress is described with a light touch by its first field director, Jerry R. James, in "A Personal Reminiscence: The Establishment of an Overseas Acquisitions Center," *The Quarterly Journal of the Library of Congress* 27, no. 3 (July 1970): 206-212, and more prosaically by another director, Alvin Moore, Jr., "A Review of the Library of Congress' Program in Eastern Africa," in Valerie Bloomfield ed., *Conference on the Acquisition of Material from Africa*, p. 1-6. Jerry R. James, "The Library of Congress Program in Eastern Africa," in James D. Pearson and Ruth Jones, eds., *The Bibliography of Africa*, p. 75-82.

[52]Library Information Science Abstracts (LISA) 71/1293. See also S. S. Saith, "The East African School of Librarianship," in Wallenius, *Libraries in East Africa*, p. 171-187.

[53]*Africana Library Journal* 2, no. 3 (Autumn 1971): 3.

[54]Valerie Bloomfield, *Conference on the Acquisition of Material from Africa*, p. 148.

[55]Harm J. De Blij, *Mombasa, an African City* (Evanston, Ill.: Northwestern University Press, 1968), 162 p.

[56]For a fine piece of muckraking, see Dan Schechter, et al., "The C.I.A. as an Equal Employer," *Ramparts* 7, no. 13 (June 1969): 25-33. John Ndegwa, *Printing and Publishing in Kenya: An Outline of Development* (London: SCOLMA, 1973), 28 p.

[57]M.P.K. Sorrenson, *Origin of European Settlement in Kenya* (Oxford: British Institute of History and Archaeology in East Africa, Memoir no. 2, 1968), 320 p. Bibliography, p. 302-307. See also: Simeon H. Ominde, *Land and Population Movements in Kenya* (Evanston, Ill.: Northwestern University Press; London: Heinemann, 1968), 204 p.

[58]Favorably reviewed by Kenneth King, *Journal of African History* 12, no. 3 (1970): 504-506.

[59]Very favorably reviewed in *Times Literary Supplement* (December 15, 1972): 1522.

[60]Previously published as *African Businessman* for the Institute of Community Studies (London: Routledge and Kegan Paul 1971). Favorably reviewed by Robert L. Curry, Jr., *Journal of Modern African Studies* 10, no. 3 (October 1972): 492-494, and *Choice* 9, no. 4 (June 1972), 546.

[61]Favorably reviewed in *Times Literary Supplement* (January 26, 1973): 83.

[62]Favorably reviewed by John Middleton in *Africa* 42, no. 3 (July 1972): 258-259.

[63]*Choice* 8, no. 11 (January 1972): 1484.

[64]See his "The Library at Makerere University," in Anna-Britta Wallenius, ed. *Libraries in East Africa* (Uppsala: Scandinavian Institute of African Studies, 1971), p. 131-143.

[65]*Africa,* 41, no. 1 (January 1971): 82.

[66]Reviewed by John Iliffe, *The Journal of African History* 12, no. 4 (1971): 659-660.

[67]Favorably reviewed by John Lonsdale, *Third World* (London) 1, no. 1 (September 1972): 30-31; *Choice* 9, no. 10 (December 1972); 1335; critically reviewed in *Times Literary Supplement* (January 26, 1973): 92.

[68]*Choice* 8, no. 1 (March 1971): 120.

[69]*Choice* 7, no. 8 (October 1970): 1097.

[70]Criticized by T. O. Beidelman, *Africa* 39, no. 1 (January 1969): 91-93, as not contributing anything new for those familiar with Turner's work, and F. Fraut, *Homme* 10, no. 1 (January-March 1970): 100-101.

[71]Also reviewed in *Africa* 38, no. 4 (October 1968): 483-484.

[72]See also Helmuth Heisler, "A Class of Target Proletarians," *Journal of Asian and African Studies* 5, no. 3 (1970).

[73]"Notes and News" in *Africa* 41, no. 1 (January 1971): 61; *UNESCO Bulletin for Libraries* 26, no. 1 (January-February 1972): 44.

[74]The two are reviewed favorably by William J. Foltz from Yale's Department of Political Science in *Journal of Modern African Studies* 5, no. 2 (September 1967): 281-283.

[75]Favorably reviewed in *Choice* 9, no. 7 (September 1972): 863. Very important is the review article by John D. Fage, "The History of West Africa," *Journal of African History,* 14, no. 1 (1973): 129-138.

[76]Review article by A. E. Afigbo, *Odu* n.s. 5 (April 1971): 99-110.

[77]See a none too favorable review by John Miles in *Journal of African History* 13, no. 1 (1972): 161-163.

[78]Rather adversely reviewed by John D. Hargreaves in *Journal of African History* 13, no. 1 (1972): 163-165.

[79]Favorably reviewed by Alifeyo Chilinimbo, *Journal of Modern African Studies* 10, no. 2 (July 1972): 324-326.

[80]D. H. Jones reviews the book briefly, yet favorably, in *Journal of African History* 12, no. 1 (1971): 168-169.

[81]Favorably reviewed by P. C. Lloyd in *Africa* 42, no. 3 (July 1972): 254-255.

[82]The anonymous reviewer of *Choice* liked the volume: 9, no. 5-6 (July-August 1972): 686.

[83]Frank Willett liked it. See his review in *Journal of African History* 12, no. 4 (1971): 675-679.

[84]See in particular: S. A. Aluko, "How Many Nigerians? An Analysis of Nigeria's Census Problems, 1901-1963," *Journal of Modern African Studies* 3, no. 3 (October 1965): 371-392.

[85]A most interesting review entitled "Europe's Nigeria," *Times Literary Supplement* (January 26, 1973): 82.

[86]Favorably reviewed in *Times Literary Supplement* (March 10, 1972): 268. Also in *Choice* 8, no. 2 (April 1971): 276.

[87]Reviewed by Lucy Mair in *Africa* 41, no. 2 (April 1971): 167-169.

[88]Reviewed by Edmund O. Egbok of the Department of History/Archaeology, University of Nigeria, Nsukka, in *Journal of Modern African Studies* 10, no. 4 (December 1972): 650-652.

[89]Favorably reviewed in *Times Literary Supplement* (August 25, 1972): 981-983. Most favorably reviewed by Hollis R. Lynch, *New York Times Book Review* (January 7, 1973): 30-31.

[90]Unfavorably reviewed in *Times Literary Supplement* (August 25, 1972): 981-983. Reviewed by Hollis R. Lynch, *The New York Review of Books* (January 7, 1973): 30-31.

[91]Favorably reviewed in *Times Literary Supplement* (August 25, 1972): 981-983. Also favorably reviewed in *Choice* 9, no. 8 (October 1972): 1024.

[92]Reviewed together with two other works in *Journal of Modern African Studies* 4, no. 2 (October 1966): 263-265 by M. S. Levitt.

[93]*Choice* 3, no. 2 (April 1966): 151.

[94]*Choice* 2, no. 10 (December 1965): 719.

[95]*Choice* 4, no. 3 (May 1967): 320. *Journal of Modern African Studies* 5, no. 1 (May 1967): 156.

[96]*Choice* 4, no. 5 (July-August 1967): 559.

[97]*Choice* 3, no. 9 (November 1966): 823.

[98]Reviewed with one other work by A. E. Ewing in *Journal of Modern African Studies* 9, no. 1 (May 1971): 150-153. *Choice* 7, no. 8 (October 1970): 1104.

[99]*Choice* 6, no. 11 (January 1970): 1633.

[100]S. A. Aluko of the Department of Economics, University of Ife, reviews in *Journal of Modern African Studies* 8, no. 2 (July 1970): 323-326; *Choice* 7, no. 8 (October 1970): 1100.

[101]Favorably reviewed by E. Wyane Nafziger, *Journal of Modern African Studies* 10, no. 1 (May 1972): 162-163.

[102]*Choice* 8, no. 9 (November 1971): 1222-1223.

[103]Well reviewed by Simon Ottenberg, *International Journal of African*

History (New York) 5, no. 2 (1971): 337-340, and *Choice* 8, no. 5-6 (July-August 1971): 707.

[104]*Choice* 9, no. 7 (September 1972): 848.

[105]Favorable reviews by: Donald Rothchield, *International Journal of African History* 5, no. 2 (1972): 352-354; Naomi Mitchison, *Journal of Modern African Studies* 10, no. 2 (July 1972): 323-324.

[106]Reviewed by Kola Folayan, University of Ife, *Journal of African History* 12, no. 3 (1971): 499-501; Eva Gillies, *Africa* 41, no.1 (January 1971): 66-67.

[107]Very favorably reviewed by: Josephy P. Smaldone, *African Studies Review* 16, no. 1 (April 1973): 150-154 and in the *Times Literary Supplement* (June 23, 1972): 715.

[108]Very favorably reviewed by A.H.M. Kirk-Greene, *Journal of African History* 12, no. 4 (1971): 663-665.

[109]Reviewed by A.H.M. Kirk-Greene, *Africa* 42, no. 4 (October 1972): 356.

[110]Enthusiastically reviewed by Frank Willett in *Journal of African History* 13, no. 3 (1972): 514-516.

[111]Reviewed by G. I. Jones, *Africa* 42, no. 4 (October 1972): 357-358.

[112]Reference from *International African Bibliography* 1, no. 4 (October 1971): 76.

[113]Reviewed briefly and favorably in *Times Literary Supplement* (March 16, 1973): 305.

[114]For a review of Soyinka's books, see *Choice* 9, no. 11 (January 1973): 1453-1454.

[115]Anatole Brogard, "Of Totems and Technology—Books of the Times," *The New York Times* (March 14, 1973): 35.

[116]This work has received numerous reviews to date, all but the one in *Choice* favorable: Robert Koester, *Library Journal Book Review* (1972): 16-17; Onuma Ezera, *Africana Library Journal* 3, no. 2 (Summer 1972): 25; *West Africa* 2858 (March 24, 1972): 354; "Nigeria Up to 1966," *Times Literary Supplement* (June 16, 1972): 696; and *Choice* 9, no. 8 (October 1972): 953.

[117]This is referred to in *Library Materials on Africa* 2, no. 3 (January 1965): 15, and cited (as well as other typescripts) by John Harris in his appendixes to "National Bibliography in Nigeria," in Pearson and Jones, *The Bibliography of Africa,* p. 354.

[118]*Nigerian Libraries* 7, no. 3 (December 1971): 154.

[119]LISA 71/2410. Library Information Science Abstracts.

[120]Favorably reviewed by A. Adu Boahen in *Transactions of the Historical Society of Ghana* 12 (1971): 105-107.

[121]*Choice* 9, no. 7 (September 1972): 846.

[122]Favorably reviewed by Robert W. Steel, *Africa* 41, no. 1 (July 1972): 78.

[123]*Times Literary Supplement* (September 15, 1972): 1046.

[124]Favorably reviewed in ibid. (July 21, 1972): 848.

[125]*Choice* 9, no. 5-6 (July-August 1972): 691.

[126]Favorably reviewed by Keith Hart, *Africa* 42, no. 3 (July 1972): 248-250.

[127]Favorably reviewed by Jon Kraus, *Journal of Modern African Studies* 10, no. 1 (May 1972): 157-159.

[128]Reviewed by T. H. Boyer, "The Ghana National Bibliography," *Library Materials on Africa* 6, no. 2 (November 1968): 62-65.

[129]"Notes and News," *Africa* 42, no. 1 (January 1972): 61.

[130]Referred to in a review by J.M.D. Crossey in *Africana Library Journal* 1, no. 3 (Fall 1970): 23.

[131]*Africa* 42, no. 2 (April 1972): 150.

[132]Robert E. Johnston favorably reviews both Riddell's and Cartwright's work in *Journal of Modern African Studies* 9, no. 3 (August 1971): 329-331.

[133]For reviews of Williams' bibliography, all favorable ones, see: Christopher Fyfe, *Journal of African History* 13, no. 1 (1972): 173-174, and C. F. Scott, *Library Materials on Africa* 9, no. 2 (November 1971): 120-121.

[134]Cited in *A Current Bibliography on African Affairs* n.s. 5, no. 2 (March 1972): 275, item 1254.

[135]The following countries are part of the Entente: the Ivory Coast, Upper Volta, Niger, Dahomey, and Togo. Members of the "Organisation des états riverains de Senegal" are Senegal, Guinea, Mauritania, and Mali.

[136]"Assimilation or Association," *Times Literary Supplement* (November 3, 1972): 1313, reviews favorably the works (discussed below) by Hymans, G. Wesley Johnson, and Rita Cruise O'Brien.

[137]This and the following book are reviewed favorably by P-Kiven Tunteng of the Université du Cameroun, Yoaundé, in *Journal of Modern African Studies* 11, no. 3 (September 1973): 492-496. The first is reviewed more cirtically by Margaret Peil, *Journal of African History* 14, no. 1 (1973): 164-165.

[138]Reviewed favorably in *Choice* 6, no. 1 (March 1969).

[139]Reviewed by T. H. Bowyer, *Library Materials on Africa* 7, no. 3 (March 1970): 87-88.

[140]See also the brief entry on the Ivory Coast in *Bibliography, Documentation Terminology* 11, no. 5 (September 1971): 207-208.

[141]*Library Materials on Africa* 8, no. 11 (July 1970: 80.

[142]This United Nations figure may be an overestimate. See Donald G. Morrison and others, *Black Africa* (1972), p. 259.

[143]Reviewed by C. Rivienes in *Cultures et développement* (Paris) 3, no. 2 (1971): 310-312.

[144]Brasseur and Morel, *Les sources bibliographiques,* 58. In the annotation it is stressed that no copy was deposited with the University Library in Dakar, or with the department.

[145]E. W. Dadzie and J. T. Strickland, *Directory of Archives, Libraries and Schools of Librarianship* (Paris: UNESCO, 1965), p. 18.

[146]*Library Materials on Africa* 1, no. 2 (1963): 14.

[147]Reviewed by T. H. Bowyer, *Library Materials on Africa* 7, no. 3 (March 1970): 88-89.

[148]*Africana Library Journal* 1, no. 2 (Summer 1970): 8.

[149]These and some other titles are referred to in a review article: Paul Ladouceur, "Voltaic Political Life," *African Studies Review* 15, no. 3 (December 1972): 521-527.

[150]Reviewed favorably by Nehima Levtzion, *Journal of African History* 12, no. 3 (1971): 496-498.

[151]Reviewed by Marvin Miracle, *African Studies Review* 15, no. 1 (April 1972): 152-154.

[152]Reviewed in *West Africa* 2877 (August 11, 1972): 1044.

[153]Reviewed favorably in *West Africa* (February 11, 1972): 152-153; critically reviewed in *Choice* 9, no. 10 (December 1972): 1335.

[154]Paul Avicienne, comp., *Bibliographical Services throughout the World, 1965-1969* (Paris: UNESCO, 1972), p. 87.

[155]This volume and the following two are reviewed favorably by W. Norman Haupt, *Journal of Modern African Studies* 11, no. 2 (June 1973): 326-329.

[156]Favorably reviewed by Philip M. Allen, *Africa Report* 17, no. 6 (June 1972): 35-38.

[157]Favorably reviewed in *Times Literary Supplement* (July 28, 1972): 874.

[158]Reviewed favorably in French by Hubert Deschamps, *Africa* 38, no. 1 (January 1968): 88.

[159]Favorably reviewed by Catherine Hoskins, "Martyr by Choice," *New York Review of Books* 20, no. 5 (April 5, 1973): 8-10.

[160]Reviewed appreciatively in *Choice,* 9, no. 8 (October 1972): 1024-1025.

[161]Reviewed in *Times Literary Supplement* (September 15,1972: 1046. As one can assume from the title, this work is written from a strongly pro-Lumumba point of view.

[162]Reviewed by Adam Kuper as a complex and significant book, *Africa* 42, no. 1 (January 1972): 82.

[163]Reviewed quite favorably by Lucy Mair in *Africa* 41, no. 2 (April 1971): 167-169.

[164]Attached to a dispatch from Dar es Salaam, "Rwanda Tribal Tensions Raise Fear of Fighting," *The New York Times* (March 4, 1973): 23, "Witnesses Tell of Horror in New Burundi Slaughter," ibid., (June 17, 1973): 1, 14.

[165]Appreciatively reviewed by Hubert Deschamps in French in *Journal of African History* 13, no. 1 (1972): 151-152.

[166]Estimate by Alan Paton, *New York Times Magazine* (May 13, 1973): 24.

[167]Note also D. L. Ehlers, "Die Bibliotekaris 'n Sensuur 'n teoretiese. Siening" [The librarian and censorship, a theoretical view], *South African Libraries* 38, no. 4 (January 1971): 218-223.

[168]Favorably reviewed by Klaas Woldring, *Journal of Modern African Studies* 10, no. 2 (July 1972): 330-332.

[169]Note the helpful review article by Martin Legassick, *Journal of African History* 13, no. 1 (1972): 145-150.

[170]Reviewed by M. D. D. Newitt, *Journal of African History* 14, no. 1 (1973): 151-153.

[171]Recommended in *Choice* 10, no. 1 (March 1973): 61.

[172]See the favorable review in *Times Literary Supplement* (February 1, 1974): 99.

[173]Favorably reviewed by Shula Marks, *Journal of African History* 13, no. 4 (1972): 699-700, and John Sheridan, *International Journal of African Historical Studies* (New York) 5, no. 2 (1972): 350-352.

[174]See *Choice* 8, no. 12 (February 1972): 1622.

[175]Highly recommended: *Choice* 9, no. 10 (December 1971): 1328; Alan Baldwin, *Africa Digest* (London) 20, no. 2 (April 1973): 45-46.

[176]Reviewed favorably by Richard Bengnoff, *Journal of Modern African Studies* 11, no. 1 (March 1973): 170-172.

[177]Not too favorably received: Martin Legassick, *Journal of African History* 13, no. 1 (1972): 145-150. Richard Vengroff, *Journal of Modern African Studies 11, no. 1 (March 1973): 170-172.*

[178]Favorably reviewed in *Times Literary Supplement* (December 1, 1972): 1451.

[179]*Library Materials on Africa* 5, no. 3 (March 1968): 87.

[180]Ibid. (November 1967): 67.

[181]Shula Marks reviewed this briefly and favorably in *Journal of African History* 13, no. 2 (1972): 528.

[182]Favorably reviewed by Ibrahim A. Gambari, *Journal of Modern African Studies* 9, no. 3 (October 1971): 484-486.

[183]Ibid.

[184]Reviewed by E. L. Muth, *Journal of Modern African Studies* 4, no. 1 (May 1966): 119.

[185]Reviewed by J.M.D. Crossey, *Africana Library Journal* 3, no. 2 (Summer 1972): 24.

[186]Khama, Dale, and Smit are reviewed by Willie Henderson, *Journal of Modern African Studies* 11, no. 1 (March 1973): 172-175.

[187]Favorably noted briefly in *Times Literary Supplement* (January 26, 1973): 82. Reviewed by Richard F. Weisfelder, *African Studies Review* 15, no. 3 (December 1972): 520-521.

[188]Reviewed favorably by Barry M. Schutz, *Journal of Modern African Studies* 8, no. 1 (April 1970): 164-167.

[189]Favorably reviewed by Donald Denoon, *Journal of Modern African Studies* 9, no. 2 (August 1971): 321-324.

[190]The first edition (1959) was reviewed favorably by Thomas Hodgkin, *Journal of African History* 1, no. 2 (1960): 328-329.

[191]See note 188 for review.

[192]Favorably reviewed by Alan Baldwin, *Africa Digest* (London) 19, no. 3 (June 1972): 70.

[193]Ibid.

[194]Favorably reviewed by Terence Ranger, *Journal of African History* 13, no. 3 (1972): 511-513.

PART SIX

On Collecting and
Disseminating Africana

PUBLISHING AND BOOK TRADE IN AFRICA

It is hard to make generalizations about Africa's publications. They range from Onitsha-type chapbooks to formal, high-grade scholarly books. Publishing houses may be wholly or partially African owned. They may be European subsidiaries with varying relations to the company's head office, usually located in the former metropole. It seems likely that the state of publishing in Africa will continue very fluid. The rate of title and frequency change of serial publications seems to be a very high one, for example.

Little has been published or even written about publishing and the book trade in Africa. The following is a chronological listing of relatively recent references: P. K. Kalmakov, "The Emergence of Printing and the Periodic Press in African Countries," *Azii i Afrki* (Moscow) 4 (1969): 177-190. *Book Developments in Africa: Problems and Perspectives* (Paris: UNESCO, 1969), 37 p. (Reports and Papers on Mass Communications, 56). Robert Plant Armstrong, "Developments in African Publishing: Book Publishers in Sub-Saharan Africa," in John N. Paden and Edward W. Soja, eds. *The African Experience* (Evanston Ill.: Northwestern University Press, 1970), 3B, *Guide to Resources,* 17-31. Rex Collings, "Publishing in Africa: An Industry Emerges," *Africa Report* 15, no. 8 (November 1970): 31-33. "Government Printers in Africa (Part I, English Speaking Nations)," *Africana Library Journal* 1, no. 1 (Spring 1970): 16. "Publishers in Africa: A Select Directory," *Africana Library Journal* 1, no. 2 (Summer 1970): 11-16. "Publishers in Africa: A Select Directory and Supplement I," *Africana Library Journal* 1, no. 4 (Winter 1970): 33-34. Stephen H. Grant, "Published for the Many," *Africa Report* 17, no. 1 (January 1972): 26-27, is a discussion of Asare Konadu and the Anowuo Educational Services in Accra.

In the report on UNESCO's information and documentation program for 1971-1972, we hear that "surveys will be undertaken in Africa on problems of co-publication and the establishment of co-operative book production and distribution services."[1] Not much has been released to date. The following article is related to this topic: Kalu K. Oyeoku, "Publishing in Developing Countries: A Programme of Research Based on the Nigerian Situation," *UNESCO Bulletin for Libraries* 26, no. 3 (May-June 1972): 150-156. The author, an acquisitions librarian at the University of Nigeria, Nsukka, is planning to take a hard look at publishing industries and the state of the book in Nigeria.

Finally, a contribution which appeared in the *Bowker Annual 1973* is Moore Crossey, "Book Trade Developments, Publishing in Africa South of the Sahara," p. 255-262. The bibliography cites some articles and reports not found in the section above.

BOOK DEALERS

There are at least two directories to book dealers in Africa. The first is Sigfred Taubert, *African Book Trade Directory, 1971* (Munich: Verlag Dukumentation, 1971), 319 p.,[2] a very ambitious volume indeed. Too many publishers and book dealers are listed, however, without any indication of their effectiveness.

Much more serviceable is: Economic Commission for Africa, *Directory of Government Printers and Prominent Bookshops in the African Region* (Addis Ababa: UNECA, 1970), 48 p. (E/CN. 14/Lib/Ser. D/1). Hopefully, this pamphlet will be revised periodically though it will be impossible to keep up with the constantly changing scene.

One dealer in the United States deserves special mention: Walter Goldwater, University Place Book Shop, 821 Broadway, New York City. A rather different establishment in England is: Ronald and Anita C. Gray, Hammersmith Books, Barnes High Street, London, S.W. 13.

REPRINTERS

Many books on Africa have been reprinted or otherwise reproduced in the past. Not all of them have merited reprinting, of course. There have even been instances of reprints being offered when copies of the original edition were still available. A typical reprint is the following: Kofi A. Busia, *The Position of the Chief in the Modern Political System of Ashanti* (London: Oxford University Press, 1951). It was reprinted in 1968 by Frank Cass, one of the best reprinters of Africana, but is now selling at three times the 1951 price. (See Cass's complete catalog, *African and Caribbean Studies.*)

John Ralph Willis, one of Cass's editorial advisors, has written "Windfalls for African Studies, Some Forthcoming Reprints," *Africana Studies Bulletin* 8, no. 2 (September 1965): 54-62, and a very similar article with the same title in *Africana Newsletter* (Hoover Institution) 2, no. 2 (1964): 32-36. Also see Joan Ells's various publications: "Reprints of Books and Journals on Africa," *African Studies Bulletin* 11, no. 3 (December 1968): 329-362; "Books and Documents on Africa in Microform," *African Studies Bulletin* 12, no. 1 (April 1969): 91-110; "Books and Documents on Africa in Microform," *African Studies Bulletin* 12, no. 2 (September 1969): 177-192; and "Newspapers and Periodicals on Africa in Microform," *African Studies Bulletin* 12, no. 2 (September 1969): 193-209. For more recent information on reprints, whether in microform or not, one must consult the general guides to publications.

Reprints of Africana are evaluated in two useful journal articles and one thesis: Alan R. Taylor, "Arm Chair Travels and Researches in Darkest Africa," *Victorian Studies* (Bloomington, Ind.) 13, no. 4 (June 1970): 385-392; A.H.M. Kirk-Greene, "The Scramble for Africana, A Review Article," *African Affairs* 70, no. 278 (January 1971): 77-83; and Kathryn Kadane Crane, "An Evaluation of Revisions since 1961 of Books on Africa" (Master's thesis, Catholic University of America, 1966), 56 p. Of thirty-five books listed in the *Cumulative Book Index* on Africa as revised between 1961 and 1965, fifteen were located in the Washington area at the time of the study. Few of the fifteen books were found to have meaningful or substantial revisions. Only one of the books revised was reviewed in the usual review media available to librarians.

There are few frank reviews of reprints. Useful indeed is the brief note by David Birmingham on Filippo Pigafetta's *A Report on the Kingdom of Congo and the Surrounding Countries* (London: Cass reprint, 1970), 174 p. This work contains a preface by Margaret Hutchinson written in 1881 which had been rightfully displaced by Wily Bal's masterful translation of 1963.[3] Birmingham points out that copying the original text would cost £1.60 against the £4 charged for the reprint.

ON AFRICAN COLLECTIONS

We cannot expand here on the African collections housed in Africa or elsewhere. The only worthy criterion is effective service, which sometimes can be better at a smaller than at a larger collection. No library can ever be complete for even significant publications. All one can hope to have, besides the hypothetical basic collection, is sufficient bibliographcial information to expedite loans or advise scholars as to the institutions holding what he needs.

One of the most encouraging ways to help solve the needs of scholars and students has been not merely the use of microform but the cooperative nonprofit holding of master negatives and loan positives. Of course, microform reproductions of texts should be widely held, but in some cases one loan copy may suffice.

The Cooperative Africana Microform Project (CAMP) is an example of such cooperation. It was established by Peter Duignan of the Hoover Institution, Conrad Reining, at the time in charge of the African Section of the Library of Congress, and Gordon Williams, director of the Center for Research Libraries, during a conference on the acquisition of Africana called by the Association of Research Libraries in 1963.[4]

For publications on CAMP, see: Robert Gordon Collier, "The Cooperative Africana Microform Project," *Africana Library Journal* 2, no. 3 (Autumn 1971): 12-14; "Cooperative Africana Microform Project," *UNESCO Bulletin for Libraries* 24, no. 5 (September-October 1970): 284-285; and J.M.D. Crossey, "Cooperative Africana Microform Project," *Library Material on Africa* 10, no. 1 (July 1972): 65-68. In the same issue, Crossey reviews the *CAMP Book Catalog* issued by the Research Liaison Committee of the African Studies Association in 1972.

The broad canvass of microform acquisition and handling is covered in Robert C. Sullivan, "Microform Developments Related to Acquisitions," *College and Research Libraries* 34, no. 1 (January 1973): 16-28; Hans E. Panofsky, "The Role of Microform in the Acquisition and Bibliographical Control of Africans," in James Pearson and Ruth Jones, eds., *The Bibliography of Africa* 286-300; and Charles E. Bryant, "International Aspects of Area Studies Librarianship: Some Comments on Papers by Alan R. Taylor and Robert Gordon Collier," *Leads* (American Library Association, International Relations Round Table) 15, no. 3 (January 1973): 5-7. The best means of keeping up with the complex picture of microform is regular consultation of *Microform Review,* a quarterly journal published in Weston, Connecticut. Note: Moore Crossey, "A Survey of Africana in Microform," *Microform Review,* 3, no. 2 (April 1974): 96-105.

Specialized lists of microform compilations will continue to appear. A most useful recent example is: Malcolm D. McKee, comp., "African Newspapers on Microfilm" (London: Standing Conference on Library Materials on Africa, 1973), unpaged (mimeo.). It contains information available as of mid-1972 on holdings in fourteen institutions in Great Britain, the United States, France, and South Africa. A new edition is planned for 1974.

LIBRARY COOPERATION

Cooperation is (or at least ought to be) inherent in librarianship. Yet it is also a costly process that may not be agreed to by those best able to enter cooperative ventures. One of the means of fostering cooperation is through the holding of meetings, such as the First International Conference on African Bibliography held in Nairobi in 1967.[5]

The Standing Conference on African University Libraries (SCAUL) resulted from a conference of librarians at University College, Salisbury, in 1964 with the support of the Leverhulme

Foundation. The conference papers have been circulated widely, and reports appeared in *Libri*, in March 1965 and in the March-April 1965 issue of the *UNESCO Bulletin for Libraries*.

The next landmark was the 1967 Nairobi conference referred to above. The publication of the full papers, even three years later, was well worth it. Next came the 1969 Lusaka meeting: *Conference of Libraries from the Commonwealth Universities in Africa, Lusaka, August 1969* (London: The Commonwealth Foundation, 1970), 70 p. (Occasional Paper No. 8). There it was decided to set up regional groups: SCAUL-East and SCAUL-West.

SCAUL-East met in Zambia in Lusaka at the time of the conference funded by the Commonwealth Foundation. In 1971, it met in Addis Ababa: Rita Pankhurst and Joan Proudman, eds., *Standing Conference of African University Librarians, Eastern Area Conference. Proceedings, Addis Ababa*, 1971, 112 p. In April 1973 SCAUL-East met in Mauritius with the support of the Canadian International Development Research Centre, the Commonwealth Foundation, and the Agency for Cultural and Technical Co-operation (Paris). The SCAUL-West group has thus far only met twice—in Lagos in April 1972," and again in Dakar in 1974.

Progress is slow, but would be even slower without these exchanges of information. Resolutions voted on at these meetings may influence the policy of African governments with regard to such matters as the passage and enforcement of copyright legislation, better provision of aid for libraries, and training of librarians. Yet there are still governments in this world that consider libraries not as an arm for development but as luxuries they cannot afford.

CATALOGING OF AFRICANA

The cataloging of Africana is not too different from that of material pertaining to any other continent. Most of the material is printed in a roman script. Transliteration and translation present no unusual difficulties. Arabic has its own script as does Amharic.

Both have standard transliterations developed or at least accepted by the Library of Congress.

Reference has already been made to the high mortality rate of serials and frequent changes of name, be it corporate or individual.

Relatively little has been published to date on questions that concern librarians who are catalogers. No doubt African library schools, particularly the one in Ibadan, will release publications (including seminar papers) which will be helpful to librarians in and out of Africa. The following references, arranged chronologically, pertain to the cataloging of Africana: Mary Darrah Herrick, with Adelaide Cromwell Hill, "Problems of Bibliographical Control for an Area Research Program," *College and Research Libraries* 16 (1955): 291-295. Mary Darrah Herrick, "African Government Documents," *College and Research Libraries* 18 (1957): 206-209. Leslie Brierly, "The Indexing and Classification of African Tribal Names," *Library Materials on Africa* 5, no. 3 (March 1968): 76-78. Jean Fontvieille, "Le nom des ecrivains d'Afrique noire, essai de catalographie," in Pearson and Jones, *The Bibliography of Africa,* p. 155-192, and his "Le patronyme des auteurs negro-africains et malgaches d'expression francaise et la catalographie," *Bulletin des bibliographies de France* (Paris) 13, no. 11 (November 1968): 489-507. Sanford Berman, *Prejudices and Antipathies: A Tract on LC Subject Heads Concerning People* (Metuchen, N.J.: Scarecrow Press, 1971), 249 p.[7] An application of what Berman would like the subject heading to be is found in his "Subject Headings Employed at the Makerere Institute for Social Research, a Select List" (February 1972), 56 p. (Berman is now working in Minneapolis; copies of the list are probably still available by writing the Institute at Kampal, Uganda.)

Nwozo Amankwe, "Africa in the Standard Classification Scheme," *Library Resources and Technical Services* (Chicago) 16, no. 2 (Spring 1972): 178-194, is a thorough exploration, but it is not too helpful as a guide to future policy.

On March 15, 1973, a conference took place at McGill University on the acquisition and control of African publications and manuscripts. Three of the papers in particular merit publication:

J.M.D. Crossey, "Acquisition of Current African Imprints: Some Problems and Possible Solutions"; Walter Goldwater, "African Acquisitions: Past, Present and Future"; and David Michener, "Cataloging Africana." David Michener, the only full-time cataloger of original Africana (at least in the United States) is planning to publish his very useful paper soon.

What is the future? The future is essentially the one that the countries of Africa will carry out for themselves or in concert with one another. Each African country is increasingly preserving its own publications and making its national bibliography available internally as well as abroad; this is the work of African Africanists. What about the non-African ones (and this includes people of the diaspora)? They still have a role to fill as subject or specialist bibliographers. It is their duty to ensure that copies of dissertations and other publications are deposited in the African countries to which the work pertains or where the work was done. Librarians working in non-African institutions frequently have the books and other publications that the African universities lack and need. These may be publications issued by colonial governments, or the writings of early nationalists. As far as possible, much of the ephemera should be preserved and disseminated in microform through the Cooperative Africana Microform Project administered by the Center for Research Libraries in Chicago.

The newly developed techniques (such as placing the South African Union Catalogue onto microfiche arranged by International Standard Book Numbers) should be examined widely and, if found advantageous, adapted or adopted elsewhere.

Far from being a luxury that only rich countries can afford, libraries are an essential means of development. They are a means of attaining and sustaining literacy and of helping to educate the whole person.

Notes

[1] *UNESCO Bulletin for Libraries* 25, no. 3 (May-June 1971): 131.

[2] Reviewed by the present writer in *Africana Library Journal* 2, no. 2 (Summer 1971): 13.

[3]*Journal of African History* 12, no. 3 (1971): 508-509.

[4]The result was a statement drafted by Gordon Williams and others, "A Proposal for Increasing the Availability of Africana to U.S. Libraries" (1962), 4 sheets.

[5]The proceedings and papers were edited by James D. Pearson and Ruth Jones in *Bibliography of Africana* (London: Cass; New York: Africana Publishing Corp., 1970), 362 p.

[6]Louis B. Frewer, "Standing Conference of African University Librarians (SCAUL), Western Area Conference, April 4-7, 1972, at the University of Lagos, Nigeria," *Library Materials on Africa* 10, no. 1 (July 1972): 20-25.

[7]Noted briefly in *LC Information Bulletin* 30, no. 52 (December 30, 1971): 750, and reviewed at length (on the whole favorably) by Joseph Z. Nitecki, *The Library Quarterly* 42, no. 3 (July 1972): 355-357.

Index

343